CLASSROOM LITERACY ASSESSMENT

SOLVING PROBLEMS IN THE TEACHING OF LITERACY
Cathy Collins Block, Series Editor

RECENT VOLUMES

Conceptual Foundations of Teaching Reading
Mark Sadoski

The Literacy Coach's Handbook: A Guide to Research-Based Practice
Sharon Walpole and Michael C. McKenna

Comprehension Process Instruction: Creating Reading Success in Grades K–3
Cathy Collins Block, Lori L. Rodgers, and Rebecca B. Johnson

Adolescent Literacy Research and Practice
Edited by Tamara L. Jetton and Janice A. Dole

Tutoring Adolescent Literacy Learners: A Guide for Volunteers
Kelly Chandler-Olcott and Kathleen A. Hinchman

Success with Struggling Readers: The Benchmark School Approach
Irene West Gaskins

Making Sense of Phonics: The Hows and Whys
Isabel L. Beck

Reading Instruction That Works, Third Edition: The Case for Balanced Teaching
Michael Pressley

Narrowing the Literacy Gap: What Works in High-Poverty Schools
Diane M. Barone

Reading Assessment and Instruction for All Learners
Edited by Jeanne Shay Schumm

Word Sorts and More: Sound, Pattern, and Meaning Explorations K–3
Kathy Ganske

Reading the Web: Strategies for Internet Inquiry
Maya B. Eagleton and Elizabeth Dobler

Designing Professional Development in Literacy: A Framework
for Effective Instruction
Catherine A. Rosemary, Kathleen A. Roskos, and Leslie K. Landreth

Best Practices in Writing Instruction
Edited by Steve Graham, Charles A. MacArthur, and Jill Fitzgerald

Classroom Literacy Assessment: Making Sense of What Students Know and Do
Edited by Jeanne R. Paratore and Rachel L. McCormack

Classroom Literacy Assessment

MAKING SENSE OF WHAT STUDENTS KNOW AND DO

Edited by

Jeanne R. Paratore
Rachel L. McCormack

THE GUILFORD PRESS
New York   London

© 2007 The Guilford Press
A Division of Guilford Publications, Inc.
72 Spring Street, New York, NY 10012
www.guilford.com

Printed in the United States of America

This book is printed on acid-free paper.

Last digit is print number: 9 8 7 6 5 4 3 2 1

Library of Congress Cataloging-in-Publication Data is available from the Publisher.

ISBN-13: 978-1-59385-438-6 (pbk. : alk. paper)
ISBN-10: 1-59385-438-2 (pbk. : alk. paper)
ISBN-13: 978-1-59385-439-3 (hardcover : alk. paper)
ISBN-10: 1-59385-439-0 (hardcover : alk. paper)

About the Editors

Jeanne R. Paratore, EdD, is Associate Professor of Education at Boston University, where she teaches courses in literacy, language, and cultural studies. From 1989 to 1997 she was an integral member of the Boston University/Chelsea, Massachusetts, Public School Partnership, a comprehensive urban school reform effort, in which she focused her efforts on improving classroom literacy instruction and building strong home–school partnerships. She was a core advisor to Teaching Reading K–2: A Video Library of Effective Classroom Practices, a project funded by the Annenberg Foundation and produced by WGBH television. At present, Dr. Paratore works with school-based literacy leaders in Lowell, Massachusetts, to support effective instruction in classrooms throughout the city. She has written articles and book chapters about family literacy, classroom grouping practices, and classroom assessment.

Rachel L. McCormack, EdD, is Associate Professor of Literacy Education at Roger Williams University in Bristol, Rhode Island. Her research interests include effective strategies for teaching comprehension using flexible grouping. Recent investigations have focused on finding ways to prepare preservice teachers to teach in diverse urban settings. A frequent presenter at national conferences, Dr. McCormack has coauthored and coedited several publications with Jeanne Paratore.

Contributors

Peter Afflerbach, PhD, Department of Curriculum and Instruction, College of Education, University of Maryland at College Park, College Park, Maryland

Kathryn Au, PhD, Standards Network of Hawaii, Honolulu, Hawaii

Ann Bates, EdD, National College of Education, National-Louis University, Chicago, Illinois

Donald R. Bear, PhD, Center for Learning and Literacy, Department of Educational Specialties, University of Nevada, Reno, Nevada

Camille L. Z. Blachowicz, PhD, National College of Education, National-Louis University, Chicago, Illinois

M. Joyce Brigman, MEd, doctoral student in Curriculum and Instruction, Department of Middle, Secondary, and K–12 Education, College of Education, University of North Carolina at Charlotte, Charlotte, North Carolina; Charlotte Mecklenburg Schools, North Carolina

Karen Bromley, PhD, School of Education, Binghamton University, Binghamton, New York

Roberta Buhle, EdD, National College of Education, National-Louis University, Chicago, Illinois

David Chard, PhD, Special Education Area, College of Education, University of Oregon, Eugene, Oregon

Mark W. Conley, PhD, Department of Teacher Education, Michigan State University, East Lansing, Michigan

Brenda Drye, MEd, doctoral student in Curriculum and Instruction, Department of Middle, Secondary, and K–12 Education, College of Education, University of North Carolina at Charlotte, Charlotte, North Carolina; Union County Schools, North Carolina

Douglas Fisher, PhD, School of Teacher Education, San Diego State University, San Diego, California

James Flood, PhD, School of Teacher Education, San Diego State University, San Diego, California

Nancy Frey, PhD, School of Teacher Education, San Diego State University, San Diego, California

Sharon Frost, EdD, National College of Education, National-Louis University, Chicago, Illinois

Charles Fuhrken, MA, Department of Curriculum and Instruction, College of Education, University of Texas, Austin, Texas

Linda B. Gambrell, PhD, Eugene T. Moore School of Education, Clemson University, Clemson, South Carolina

Victoria Ridgeway Gillis, PhD, Eugene T. Moore School of Education, Clemson University, Clemson, South Carolina

Kathryn Glasswell, PhD, Literacy, Language, and Culture Program, Department of Curriculum and Instruction, University of Illinois at Chicago, Chicago, Illinois

Susan Mandel Glazer, EdD, Department of Graduate Education, Counseling, and Leadership, Rider University, Lawrenceville, New Jersey

Michelle Gress, BA, Kirby Middle School, San Antonio, Texas

Kristine Gritter, PhD candidate, Department of Teacher Education, Michigan State University, East Lansing, Michigan

Janis M. Harmon, PhD, Department of Interdisciplinary Learning and Teaching, University of Texas at San Antonio, San Antonio, Texas

Wanda B. Hedrick, PhD, Department of Childhood Education, University of North Florida, Jacksonville, Florida

Melanie R. Kuhn, PhD, Department of Learning and Teaching, Graduate School of Education, Rutgers University, New Brunswick, New Jersey

Diane Lapp, EdD, School of Teacher Education, San Diego State University, San Diego, California

Sangeun Lee, MS, Special Education Area, College of Education, University of Oregon, Eugene, Oregon

Sandra Madura, PhD, Washoe County School District, Reno, Nevada

Rachel L. McCormack, EdD, Department of Literacy Education, School of Education, Roger Williams University, Bristol, Rhode Island

Sarah McDonagh, PhD, School of Teacher Education, Charles Sturt University, Bathurst, Australia

Lea M. McGee, EdD, College of Education and Human Ecology, The Ohio State University, Columbus, Ohio

Kelly Moore, PhD, San Diego City Schools, San Diego, California

Lesley Mandel Morrow, PhD, Department of Learning and Teaching, Graduate School of Education, Rutgers University, New Brunswick, New Jersey

Jeanne R. Paratore, EdD, Department of Literacy and Language, Counseling and Development, School of Education, Boston University, Boston, Massachusetts

P. David Pearson, PhD, Graduate School of Education, University of California, Berkeley, Berkeley, California

Taffy Raphael, PhD, College of Education, University of Illinois at Chicago, Chicago, Illinois

Virginia Reece, PhD, Blumberg Center, College of Education, Indiana State University, Terre Haute, Indiana

Heather Reutschlin, MEd, Department of Curriculum and Instruction, College of Education, University of Maryland at College Park, College Park, Maryland

D. Ray Reutzel, PhD, Emma Eccles Jones Early Childhood Center, Utah State University, Logan, Utah

Nancy L. Roser, EdD, Department of Curriculum and Instruction, College of Education, University of Texas, Austin, Texas

Sharon Russell, PhD, School of Education, University of Michigan, Ann Arbor, Michigan

Peggy Semingson, MA, Department of Curriculum and Instruction, College of Education, University of Texas, Austin, Texas

Lina Soares, MS, doctoral student in Curriculum and Instruction, Department of Middle, Secondary, and K–12 Education, College of Education, University of North Carolina at Charlotte, Charlotte, North Carolina

D. Bruce Taylor, PhD, College of Education, University of North Carolina at Charlotte, Charlotte, North Carolina

William H. Teale, EdD, Literacy, Language, and Culture Program, Department of Curriculum and Instruction, University of Illinois at Chicago, Chicago, Illinois

Shane Templeton, PhD, Center for Learning and Literacy, Department of Educational Specialties, University of Nevada, Reno, Reno, Nevada

Sheila W. Valencia, PhD, Department of Curriculum and Instruction, College of Education, University of Washington, Seattle, Washington

Karen D. Wood, PhD, College of Education, University of North Carolina at Charlotte, Charlotte, North Carolina

Introduction

Jeanne R. Paratore

At the outset, our goal in preparing this book was to develop a comprehensive volume on research and practice in classroom-based literacy assessment. We were particularly motivated by our concern—shared by so many researchers and teachers of literacy—that in a climate in which teachers and students are held increasingly accountable to high-stakes tests, the types of assessments that can make a difference in planning effective instruction are being set aside. Our purpose, then, was to develop a book that made a strong case for why classroom and curriculum-based assessment is an essential element of good instruction and to provide teachers with clear and straightforward strategies for implementing such assessment.

As we selected and invited the authors we hoped would contribute to this book, we explained to each the purpose of the text, and we emphasized that we wanted the information to be accessible and useful for classroom teachers. Not only did the authors meet our expectations, they went beyond what we expected. As we read and reviewed each chapter, we found ourselves seriously pondering our own thinking about the assessment issues that are critical in making decisions about sound instruction. We are confident that you will find, as we did, the cases and issues presented to be important, current, and relevant.

Although chapters differ in the particular grade level, literacy domain, and scope (i.e., individual classroom, across classrooms, school) that each addresses, they are united in four fundamental underlying premises: that trustworthy assessment (1) is situated in an authentic learning context and uses classroom-based reading and writing materials and purposes; (2) is based on multiple episodes or images of students' performance; (3) examines learning processes as well as learning products; and (4) examines children's uses of literacy across varied learning contexts.

We have divided the chapters into four sections: Foundations for Trustworthy Classroom Assessment of Children's Literacy Knowledge, Assessing Word Knowledge and Reading Fluency; Assessing Comprehension and Composition, and Broadening the Context: Looking across Assessments, Classrooms, and Schools.

Part I begins with the work of Sheila W. Valencia, who grounds her chapter, and by so doing all those that follow, in the fundamental premise that in the enterprise of teaching and testing, first and foremost, the teacher makes the difference. In Valencia's words: "I turn to teachers, themselves, as the best assessment tools—to the knowledge and disposition teachers need to bring disciplined inquiry to assessment and their interactions with students" (p. 3). Toward this end, she provides a brief review of the tensions between external and internal assessments that have become the mainstays of the standards movement and recent educational policies; she argues that internal assessments are being misused in many instances and, as a result, are not meeting their potential to provide valid and trustworthy information about students' instructional strengths and needs; and she outlines an inquiry approach that teachers can bring to all assessments that should strengthen the links among assessment, instruction, and learning.

In the next chapter, Mark W. Conley and Kristine Gritter maintain Valencia's theme that good assessment requires us, as teachers, to assume an inquisitive stance, but they suggest another way to do so. Rather than suggesting that teachers consider alternative forms of assessment for the purposes of instructional decision making, they encourage teachers to step back and take a more critical and detailed look at precisely what the mandated, large-scale assessments are asking of students. They acknowledge the influence such assessments have on teachers' curricular decision making, and they note their concern that in many schools, teachers' attempts to connect standards and assessments lead to "long lists of concepts, tasks, and skills, which, when multiplied by grade level and subject area, become expansive scope and sequence charts" (p. 22). They suggest "backward mapping" as a way to analyze testing tasks with respect to goals and expected student performance, and they provide several detailed examples of how to implement this approach to guide teaching and learning.

In Chapter 3, D. Ray Reutzel and Lesley Mandel Morrow remind us that as teachers we are obligated to attend not only to the types of assessments we give, but also to the context in which children experience learning. As such, they argue, we must examine not only how well children learn but also the extent to which we have created a context in which children have optimal opportunities to learn. They describe research-based characteristics of classroom environments that support literacy learning and provide explicit guidelines for orchestrating such environments. Then they describe particular assessments that help teachers and administrators evaluate and monitor the quality and appropriateness of classroom learning contexts.

In Chapter 4, Linda B. Gambrell and Victoria Ridgeway Gillis turn our attention to evidence that to understand students' achievement in reading and writing, we must also understand their motivation to read and write. They help us unpack complex theories of motivation and engagement and provide clear and straightforward explication of the many factors that influence students' motivation and engagement in reading and writing as they progress in age and in grade. Then they relate these ideas to the process of assessment, and through clear and accessible examples and test item samples, they illustrate how to apply our understanding of motivation and engagement to assessing our students' disposition toward reading and writing.

Although Part II primarily is intended to explore the processes of assessing word knowledge and reading fluency, most involved in the teaching of reading and writing acknowledge that truly isolating word knowledge from other literacy domains is difficult to do. This difficulty occurs because students bring to the task of reading and writing word knowledge beyond the surface structure of words, and this knowledge influences their ability to read and write words. As a result, most of the chapters in this section have more to offer than *just* guidance in the assessment of word knowledge and reading fluency. Perhaps this added element is most evident in Chapter 5, in which Lea M. McGee examines language and literacy assessment of preschool-age youngsters. At the outset, McGee explains her intent to share a "comprehensive assessment model" that guides teachers in the examination of what children know and of the extent to which classroom activities are supporting children's growth in literacy. In doing so, McGee addresses the full array of literacy and language domains that are important as preschool-age youngsters acquire a foundation for eventual success in reading and writing. Throughout this chapter, McGee reminds us in gentle but explicit terms that teaching actions have learning consequences, and that effective teachers pay attention to the data they collect and use it to inform instruction of both individuals and groups of children in meaningful ways.

In Chapter 6, David Chard, Sara McDonagh, Sangeun Lee, and Virginia Reece highlight the complexity of word reading abilities and remind us that although word reading seems to come easily to many, for those who struggle, their inability to read words can have wide-reaching and long-term learning consequences. Thus the stakes are high for accurate and reliable assessment of word knowledge, and Chard and his colleagues provide a clear and manageable framework for word reading assessment that includes screening, diagnosis, progress monitoring, and outcomes. Within each of the areas of focus, they present assessments that can be embedded easily within the context of classroom literacy routines.

Although reading fluency has long been recognized as a characteristic of effective reading (Allington, 1983; Samuels, 2002), it has recently been the focus of renewed interest. In Chapter 7, Melanie R. Kuhn defines what it means to be a fluent reader, reviews teaching practices that promote fluency, and provides detailed guidelines for assessment. Kuhn has a knack for giving the reader a window into her thinking, and as a consequence, the reader understands with clarity not only what to do but also why particular strategies or practices are more or less effective.

This section closes with a chapter by Shane Templeton, Donald R. Bear, and Sandra Madura, who describe the nature of the English spelling system and summarize the significant research underlying a developmental model of spelling knowledge and its relationship to writing and reading. They present case studies of students in grades 1, 3, and 5 in which they detail the ways they used assessment to guide instruction. We believe most teachers will see in these profiles many similarities to the children in their own classrooms.

Part III shifts our attention from the ways in which students read and write words to the processes of comprehension and composition. Janis M. Harmon, Wanda B. Hedrick, Lina Soares, and Michelle Gress (Chapter 9) open the section with a discussion of the characteristics of effective vocabulary instruction and related vocabulary assessment principles. They then provide four examples of ways teachers might plan instructional activities that serve, at once, to advance and assess middle school students' vocabulary knowledge.

In Chapter 10, Nancy L. Roser, with Charles Fuhrken and Peggy Semingson, addresses ways to assess what they refer to simply as children's "sense making." As they begin the chapter, they note: "More than ever before, teachers should be both convinced and convincing that each child's emerging sense of story, each child's growing literary understandings, and each child's way of approaching and constructing meanings are of great significance to his or her literate lives" (p. 155). We think that it is highly unlikely that readers will come away from this chapter without having been convinced, and further, we believe that they will also come away armed with the knowledge they need to be convincing as they talk with others. Roser and her colleagues make the case not only with clear and credible evidence, but also with elegant and engaging writing. You will find that these authors do not provide "tools." Rather, they state that their intent is "to help teachers listen and look carefully at children's book talk (and responsive writing/drawing) so as to make decisions about how children are approaching literature, and what their responses reveal about their literary experiences and understandings" (p. 156). Like others in this volume, they believe that the knowledgeable and attentive teacher is likely the most valuable "assessment tool" available to children.

In Chapter 11 Peter Afflerbach, Heather Ruetschlin, and Sharon Russell extend our understanding of comprehension to include the process of strategic reading. They explain that strategic readers (1) make critical and evaluative judgments about texts, authors, and their purposes; (2) determine the accuracy and trustworthiness of texts; and (3) uncover and understand the biases and agendas that influence how texts are created and read. The authors ground these claims in a thorough and thoughtful review of relevant research and theory, and they help teachers to understand how to assess these abilities by providing exquisitely detailed examples of what expert teachers say and do to discover students' ability to read strategically.

In Chapter 12, Karen D. Wood, D. Bruce Taylor, Brenda Drye, and M. Joyce Brigman focus on assessment of students' comprehension of informational texts. Following a research-based description of methods for assessing students' understanding, they take us into three classrooms to illustrate their application across subject areas typical of the intermediate and middle school curriculum. They share actual teacher-developed assessment practices along with representative samples of student performance.

The final chapter in this section addresses the assessment of writing. Like the authors in each of the other chapters, Karen Bromley's work emerges from her belief that classroom-based assessment makes a difference in myriad ways. In her words: "Writing assessment and evaluation not only promote learning; they demonstrate progress and achievement, drive good instruction, facilitate grading, and provide accountability for students, parents, and administrators" (p. 211). Bromley emphasizes that good assessment is a process of co-investigation by teachers and students as they engage in practices that lead them to co-construct an understanding of students' writing strengths and needs. She frames her discussion with the types of questions teachers frequently ask, and she answers these using examples of instructional materials, charts, and rubrics that have grown out of her work with teachers and students.

In Part IV, we broaden the context and bring together chapters in which the authors look at the "bigger picture"—that is, beyond the particular literacy domain or beyond the individual classroom or school. This section begins with a chapter by Susan Mandel Glazer on portfolio assessment. Glazer describes a system that she describes as both "a means for managing learning" and "a vehicle of inquiry." Consistent with the views stated by authors throughout this book, Glazer perceives assessment as an inquiry-driven process in which teachers and children together seek information about each child's learning needs, and through which teachers search for evidence of the instructional practices that are likely to be most beneficial in meeting identified needs. In assembling a complete profile of the needs of struggling readers and writers, Glazer and her colleagues put into practice many of the good ideas described and recommended in previous chapters. As you read Glazer's words and the transcripts of the teachers and children with whom she works, we believe you will sense, as we did, the implied sense of urgency—the idea that these are not simply good or useful ideas but, rather, fundamental to making a difference for students who struggle.

In Chapter 15 Camille L. Z. Blachowicz, Roberta Buhle, Sharon Frost, and Ann Bates turn the lens from a focus on assessment practices in the context of an individual classroom to a focus on assessment practices across schools. Professional development is central in this effort to influence the ways in which schools and districts use assessment to inform teaching. Across the cases they share, the authors rely on teachers' voices to convey how teachers come to understand and use large-scale, mandated assessments in ways that have the potential to advance young children's literacy learning. Evident throughout this chapter is what we would characterize as a disposition toward reflective practice on the part of the teachers who were responsible for teaching and assessing, on the part of the teacher leaders who were responsible for professional development, and on the part of the researchers, themselves, who were responsible to the professional community.

In the next chapter Kathryn Glasswell and William H. Teale largely address the same need—evaluating schools and districts. But unlike Blachowicz and her colleagues, who focus on ways to make sense of large-scale assessment, Glasswell and Teale examine ways in which teachers can develop a common approach to assessing what they describe as authentic student work. The chapter details implementation and evaluation of the In2Books Program (a classroom-based program of authentic literacy activity for teachers and children), a year-long series of professional development sessions focused on effective literacy practices, the use of high-quality assessment practices to support teaching and learning, and the development of support materials for use by teachers and school-based literacy leaders. They provide compelling evidence that their focus on authentic and challenging work, their insistence on holding to rigorous high standards for all our children, and their reliance on authentic assessment paid off in uncommon ways for children who too often underachieve.

In Chapter 17 Douglas Fisher, Diane Lapp, Nancy Frey, James Flood, and Kelly Moore also situate their work within the context of professional development. They begin their chapter with the evidence-based claim that many school settings fail to provide adequate opportunities for teachers to engage in structured conversations with their peers about teaching and learning issues that may affect student achievement. They suggest that school contexts must change if effective supports for student growth are to become common practice in classrooms across a school or a district. They describe a system intended to create a context for shared dialogue as a potential solution to issues of teacher isolation and student underperformance. Integral to the system is the development of a standards-based curriculum, systems for reviewing student performance, and a focus on quality instruction. They provide examples of how such a system of collaboration works in one school district.

Chapter 18 is a bit of a departure from the others in this text in that its particular focus is on children who are identified as having special learning needs and on the efforts of teachers and other educators to assess and support those needs. Rachel L. McCormack, P. David Pearson, and Jeanne R. Paratore explain that as they began this work, their intent was to describe the ways in which teachers and other learning specialists use formal and informal assessments to develop an understanding of children's learning needs and an instructional plan to address them. Along the way, however, they discovered that the study itself was a catalyst for changes in the case review process. To tell the story, they rely on the words of teachers, parents, and administrators, and through them, they raise some important questions that challenge us to consider the ways that we position and privilege different forms of assessment as we make educational decisions that are consequential for children.

In the final chapter, Kathryn Au and Taffy Raphael take us back, in a sense, to where we began with Sheila Valencia: to a focus on the teacher him- or herself, and the critical role of teacher-developed assessments in improving students' literacy achievement. Like others in this text, they argue that if teachers are to be effective evaluators, they "must construct their own understandings of standards-based education while working within schools as professional learning communities" (p. 307). To exemplify this point, they present examples from schools in two projects: Standards Network of Hawaii (SNOH) and the Chicago-based partnership READ (Reading Essentials and Assessment Development). They describe these as "sister" projects that have the purpose of improving students' literacy achievement, especially in high-poverty schools, by providing teachers with professional development that enables them to create a coherent literacy curriculum that revolves around classroom assessment.

As you read this text, we predict that you will often find yourself nodding in agreement about a particular context, teacher, or child and see a place or a person that "rings true"—places or persons very much like those you encounter day in and day out. We hope that as you read and reflect on your reading, your understanding of classroom literacy assessment will deepen, along with your will to work with others to put into place assessment practices that make a difference for teachers and their students in all of the settings in which we meet them.

REFERENCES

Allington, R. L. (1983). Fluency: The neglected reading goal. *The Reading Teacher, 36,* 556–561.

Samuels, S. J. (2002). Reading fluency: Its development and assessment. In A. E. Farstrup & S. J. Samuels (Eds.), *What research has to say about reading instruction* (3rd ed., pp. 166–183). Newark, DE: International Reading Association.

Contents

Part I. Foundations for Trustworthy Classroom Assessment of Children's Literacy Knowledge

1. Inquiry-Oriented Assessment　　　　　　　　　　　　　　3
Sheila W. Valencia

2. A Pathway for Connecting Standards with Assessment:　21
Backward Mapping of Assessment Tasks
Mark W. Conley and Kristine Gritter

3. Promoting and Assessing Effective Literacy Learning　33
Classroom Environments
D. Ray Reutzel and Lesley Mandel Morrow

4. Assessing Children's Motivation for Reading and Writing　50
Linda B. Gambrell and Victoria Ridgeway Gillis

Part II. Assessing Word Knowledge and Reading Fluency

5. Language and Literacy Assessment in Preschool　　　65
Lea M. McGee

6. Assessing Word Recognition　　　　　　　　　　　85
David Chard, Sarah McDonagh, Sangeun Lee, and Virginia Reece

7. Effective Oral Reading Assessment　　　　　　　101
(or Why Round Robin Reading Doesn't Cut It)
Melanie R. Kuhn

8. Assessing Students' Spelling Knowledge:　　　　113
Relationships to Reading and Writing
Shane Templeton, Donald R. Bear, and Sandra Madura

Part III. Assessing Comprehension and Composition

 9. Assessing Vocabulary: Examining Knowledge about Words 135
    and about Word Learning
    Janis M. Harmon, Wanda B. Hedrick, Lina Soares, and Michelle Gress

10. Assessing Literary Understandings through Book Talk 154
    Nancy L. Roser with Charles Fuhrken and Peggy Semingson

11. Assessing Strategic Reading 177
    Peter Afflerbach, Heather Ruetschlin, and Sharon Russell

12. Assessing Students' Understanding of Informational Text 195
    in Intermediate- and Middle-Level Classrooms
    Karen D. Wood, D. Bruce Taylor, Brenda Drye, and M. Joyce Brigman

13. Assessing Student Writing 210
    Karen Bromley

Part IV. Broadening the Context:
Looking across Assessments, Classrooms, and Schools

14. A Classroom Portfolio System: Assessment *Is* Instruction 227
    Susan Mandel Glazer

15. Formative Uses of Assessment: Cases from the Primary Grades 246
    Camille L. Z. Blachowicz, Roberta Buhle, Sharon Frost, and Ann Bates

16. Authentic Assessment of Authentic Student Work in Urban Classrooms 262
    Kathryn Glasswell and William H. Teale

17. Putting the CIA System to Work: Linking Curriculum, Instruction, 280
    and Assessment to Improve Student Achievement
    Douglas Fisher, Diane Lapp, Nancy Frey, James Flood, and Kelly Moore

18. Developing an Individualized Education Plan: 294
    What Counts as Evidence?
    Rachel L. McCormack, P. David Pearson, and Jeanne R. Paratore

19. Classroom Assessment and Standards-Based Change 306
    Kathryn Au and Taffy Raphael

Index 323

CLASSROOM LITERACY ASSESSMENT

PART I

Foundations for Trustworthy
Classroom Assessment
of Children's Literacy Knowledge

CHAPTER 1

Inquiry-Oriented Assessment

Sheila W. Valencia

The value of classroom assessment is not in question. Even at the very start of the standards-based reform movement, most educators and policy makers acknowledged that assessment serves multiple purposes, and that the instruments designed to serve one purpose do not necessarily serve another. Classroom assessments, many argued, were uniquely able to provide timely, specific information that could inform classroom instruction and ultimately improve student learning. After all, it's not the assessments themselves—whether large-scale, high-stakes or classroom-based—that improve student achievement. It is how they are used to inform teaching and learning.

Ironically, classroom assessment is now at risk of losing the unique potential it once had. The drive for more accountability spurred by No Child Left Behind (NCLB) and the push from Reading First to implement progress monitoring assessments may threaten the vitality of classroom assessment. It is being marginalized by more and more high-stakes tests and more and more requirements for teachers to monitor student progress and to report results based on a narrow set of approved classroom assessments.

The purpose of this chapter is to breathe new life into the classroom assessment process, not by suggesting specific classroom assessments or calling for additional professional development and support for teachers. To be sure, both are needed. However, they are not sufficient. Instead, I turn to teachers, themselves, as the best assessment tools—to the knowledge and disposition teachers need in order to bring disciplined inquiry to assessment and their interactions with students. I begin with a review of external and internal assessments, which have become the mainstays of the standards movement and recent educational policies, and I describe the tensions between them. I point out how, in my view, the power of internal assessments to inform teaching and learning is being eroded. Then I outline an inquiry approach that teachers can bring to all assessments that should strengthen the links among assessment, instruction, and learning.

EXTERNAL AND INTERNAL ASSESSMENTS

We are all familiar with the large-scale assessments typically given by states or school districts. These are often referred to as "external assessments"—assessments that are initiated, developed, and reported for audiences outside the classroom (Shepard, 2001; Wixson, Valencia, & Lipson, 1994). For example, state assessments associated with accountability and NCLB, district-mandated standardized tests, and tests used to qualify students for special education services are external assessments. They are generally given once a year, administered in group settings, and focus on broad areas such as reading comprehension, word identification, and vocabulary, and aspects of writing such as conventions, organization, and ideas. Although external assessments don't necessarily have high stakes attached to the results, they often do.

In contrast, "internal assessments," or classroom assessments, are intended to be used inside the classroom to inform instruction. Both formal and informal assessments can serve this purpose. For instance, teachers might administer informal reading inventories or published tests such as Concepts about Print (Clay, 1993), or they may hold conferences, observe students at work, and collect classroom work samples (Valencia, 1998). Student self-assessment is also viewed as an integral part of internal assessment because it brings students directly into the assessment process. In general, internal assessment has been conceptualized as a broad toolkit of strategies and tasks initiated and guided by teachers. These assessments are (1) tied to the curricular content and instructional strategies of the classroom; (2) more fine-grained than external assessments so that they help teachers plan specific lessons; (3) focused on both the process and products of learning; (4) timed to provide teachers and students with immediate feedback; and (5) designed to provide opportunities for teachers to interact with students and adapt assessment to their individual needs.

Although both internal and external assessments have been advocated as part of a complete assessment system (National Council on Education Standards and Testing, 1992; Sirotnik, 2002), and standards-based reform has helped to align their content and focus (Shepard, 2001; Wixson et al., 1994), it is easy to imagine the tensions that emerge between the two. Traditionally, much of the tension is brought about by the power differential—the high stakes associated with most external assessments and the corresponding low stakes of most internal, classroom assessments (Shepard, 2000; Stiggins, 2004; Wixson et al., 1994). The effect of this tension can cause classroom assessments to have low status as well as low stakes, sending the message that they are not as valuable or trustworthy as external assessments. As a result, the school curriculum is narrowed and students spend classroom time practicing on "miniature" state tests and engaging in activities that may be counterproductive in producing real gains in student achievement (Linn, 2000). Furthermore, time devoted to this type of test preparation reduces the time available for high-quality instruction and classroom assessment (Guthrie, 2002). Constituents other than policy makers come to trust external assessments more than internal assessments and the teachers who work with children every day. Teachers, in turn, are deprofessionalized (Darling-Hammond, 1988; McNeil, 1988). As Black and Wiliam (1998) note, in the high-stakes environment of external assessments, the commitment to classroom assessment becomes marginalized.

A more insidious problem has been gaining momentum in recent years. That is, a shift in the purpose, format, and control of classroom assessment. In an effort to address the ongoing "progress monitoring" and "data-driven decision-making" requirements associated with Reading First, and, some would suggest, to exert more control over classroom instruction and assessment, many school districts are now requiring teachers to administer, score, and report the results of classroom assessments that have been selected and mandated by the state or the district. According to Sharp (2004), this practice has led to more teachers using the same assessments in their classrooms than ever before. She reports that of the 45 Reading First plans available on the Internet, 39 include Dynamic Indicators of Basic Early Literacy Skills (DIBELS), 11 include Texas Primary Reading Inventory (TPRI), and 5 include Phonological Awareness Literacy Survey (PALS) either as a requirement or as one of several options to be given several times a year in Reading First schools. Furthermore, in an effort to test all five reading domains identified by the National Reading Panel across the four kinds of assessment identified by Reading First, the number of required classroom-administered tests has skyrocketed (Sharp, 2004). Many non-Reading First schools have followed suit, identifying these or other assessments to be given to all students several times a year. The appeal of these mandated classroom assessments is fourfold: (1) they are intended to provide teachers with information they can use to adjust instruction; (2) they provide a way for administrators to monitor student progress; (3) they may have substantial correlations with high-stakes external assessments and therefore serve as a bellwether of coming performance (Fuchs, Fuchs, Hosp, & Jenkins, 2001; Invernizzi, Landrum, Howell, & Warley, 2005); and (4) some argue that they control for the unreliability of teachers' assessments (Invernazzi et al., 2005).

The problems with this new strain of mandated classroom assessment are not a result of collecting ongoing information about student learning or even using "common tools" (Valencia, 1998) to systematically assess students; in fact, we know that both are critical to informing instruction (Black & Wiliam, 1998; Shepard, 2001). The problems reside in the effects, both intended and unintended, of using such mandated assessments—what Messick (1994) called *consequential validity*. Three consequences seem most important to note.

1. The first consequence is an unexpected change in the purpose of classroom assessment. By all accounts, the purpose of these mandated classroom assessments is to monitor general progress in reading, a purpose typically reserved for external assessments. By their very nature, many of these classroom tests cannot provide the level of specificity, breadth of coverage, flexibility, timely feedback, or student engagement that are essential to the purpose of classroom assessment and the goal of informed instruction (Black & Wiliam, 1998). They are selected by people outside the classroom to be used with all students, administered according to a fixed timetable, and reported to central school district administrators. In addition, although some may be individually administered, most of these assessments are selected without consideration of the particular curriculum in the classroom or specific needs of individual children. Although they may help teachers monitor students' general reading progress, the uniform nature and infrequency of these types of internal assessments mean that they will "rarely ask the right questions at the right time to be an effective part of the ongoing learning process" (Shepard, 2001, p. 1080). What we have, then, is a form of external assessment masquerading as classroom assessment.

2. A second consequence of these mandated classroom assessments is the influence they have on instruction. Because they have been "officially" sanctioned by policy

makers and often have high stakes attached, teachers are inclined to teach to these assessments in the same way as they have been driven to teach to the external assessments that spawned them, thereby replicating the array of problems discussed above. The high stakes and accountability issues also result in a focus on the statistical reliability of these measures—the ability to yield consistent results. As a consequence, many of these tests focus on specific skills and easily quantifiable scores, ignoring a good deal of what is taught or what students need to learn.

3. Perhaps the most problematic consequence of this confounding of external and internal assessments is the stifling effect it has on other forms of classroom assessment and on teachers' dispositions toward classroom assessment. The content and format of these externally imposed classroom assessments send a message to teachers about what and how classroom assessment should take place, especially because they have high stakes. So not only does assessment influence instruction, it influences other forms of assessment. Most obvious is that classroom assessment becomes synonymous with a formal event. Instead of conceptualizing classroom assessment as an informal, ongoing process that is joined with other more formal classroom assessment events, classroom assessment is equated with a test given two or three times a year, and it is viewed as separate from instruction (Black & Wiliam, 1998; Bliem & Davinroy, 1997). The message is that if teachers are administering and scoring these externally mandated classroom tests, they are engaged in classroom assessment. There is little time or need to do more. Ironically, in some places, the burden of administering and scoring these tests is so great that SWAT teams—schoolwide assessment teams—are conducting the assessments and handing the scores to teachers. Teachers are not encouraged to critically evaluate assessments and assessment evidence or to invoke assessment as needed to inform daily instruction. Moreover, the model of "good" classroom assessment conveyed by these tests is one of narrowly focused learning targets (particularly product-oriented rather than process-oriented), objectivity that produces scores, externally established reliability, and students as objects of assessment rather than participants and collaborators in assessment.

Good teacher-guided classroom assessment is challenging (Pearson, Vyas, Sensale, & Kim, 2001; Shepard et al., 1996; Valencia & Au, 1997). Shepard (2001) found that even when teachers who were involved in a long-term professional development project to enhance classroom assessment deepened their thinking about instructional practices, their conceptions of classroom assessment remained fairly traditional and in line with externally imposed assessments. For example, teachers felt more comfortable using separate measures to assess oral reading and comprehension rather than, for example, asking students to retell a story read as part of a running record. They were also less likely to conduct individualized assessment for students who were performing below grade level, and were drawn to quantitative scores in an effort to demonstrate objectivity and reliability. Shepard argued that such inclinations have a long history in teaching and assessment and are particularly difficult to change, given the pressure from external assessments and limited professional development. Ironically, the infiltration of externally mandated assessments under the name of classroom assessment may increase the challenge of making classroom assessment a natural part of classroom practice. Lost are teacher prerogative and responsibility to engage in assessment and to engage students in their own assessment process. Lost, too, is the disposition to bring thoughtful, disciplined inquiry to every act of assessment and every piece of evidence of student learning and to use that evidence to inform instruction.

Two examples may illuminate the problems. The first example is based on evidence from several school districts across the country that require teachers to administer 1-minute timed readings to their students several times each year. Teachers are given sets of grade-level reading passages, instructed to administer them, count the number of words read correctly in 1 minute, and then report student scores to the district office once each quarter. In many instances there has been little professional development around the assessment, and when there was, the focus often was more on procedures for scoring (to emphasize reliability) than on what such an assessment can and can't reveal about students' reading. Unfortunately, this practice has translated into a classroom focus on reading faster and weekly measures of words read correctly per minute without regard to comprehension or efforts to understand students' strengths and difficulties.

A second example comes from efforts in several states and school districts to implement variations of informal reading inventories. Again, the focus has been on reporting the scores to the district or state. So, instead of helping teachers interpret this rich data source and use the information to plan for instruction, the professional development has been focused on accurately counting errors (omissions, substitutions, insertions), scoring comprehension questions, judging retellings, and recording scores. Recently, I learned of a school district that required every teacher to administer such assessments after just one 3-hour in-service training. They were given a testing kit, told to administer whatever passage they thought best, and report the scores. The kits were used twice a year but never in between. The process of listening diagnostically to students' reading was linked only to the assessment, not to classroom instruction or ongoing assessment.

In my view, both of these examples demonstrate how classroom assessments can become corrupted and their potential lost. This situation needs attention. We need to rethink the purpose and definition of classroom assessment to assure that it can serve its primary purpose: to inform and precipitate improvement in teaching and learning. We need to reaffirm teachers' and students' prerogative and responsibility to conduct inquiry into learning and instructional practice.

In the next section I present an elaborated definition of teacher-guided classroom assessment that places ownership with teachers and students and that prioritizes an inquiry-oriented approach to assessment. Then I briefly outline the dispositions needed to enact this approach. Finally, I provide examples of how teachers can bring these dispositions to bear as they review student test scores from external assessments, work with mandated classroom assessments, and ultimately implement their own assessment tools and strategies.

RECLAIMING ASSESSMENT

It is helpful to recall the concepts that originally framed classroom assessment and to use the dilemmas outlined above to sharpen the focus and reclaim it on behalf of students and teachers. Drawing on the work of Airasian (2000); Black, Harrison, Lee, Marshall, and Wiliam (2004); Black and Wiliam (1998); Johnston (1997); International Reading Association and National Council of Teachers of English (1994); Shepard (2001); Taylor and Nolen (2005); and Valencia (1998), I highlight the critical attributes of teacher-guided classroom assessment.

The goal of classroom assessment is to promote student learning, not simply document or measure it. This goal can be accomplished only if assessment provides information that teachers and students can use to assess themselves and one another in order to adjust the teaching and learning activities in which they are engaged. Thus it requires collaboration among teachers and students to (1) identify important learnings, (2) gather multiple pieces of evidence about the process and products of learning, (3) interpret the evidence in light of the instruction that was provided as well as the characteristics and abilities of the students, and (4) communicate about and use that information to guide teaching and learning. Because teachers and students hold the ultimate power to improve learning, and because decisions about what and how to enhance learning occur on a moment-to-moment basis (Shavelson & Stern, 1981; Stiggins, 2004), classroom assessment must be defined as both a set of available tools under the control of teachers and students as well as an inquiry-oriented disposition toward evidence.

An inquiry-oriented approach to assessment directs us to think about and understand evidence of both teaching and learning. It is a disposition, a habit of mind, that provides a stark contrast to the technology of administering, scoring, and reporting results. Inquiry-oriented assessment has three key elements: (1) inquiry, (2) discipline, and (3) interaction and action.

Inquiry

In the context of assessment, inquiry is the process of asking questions, looking beneath and beyond the surface of scores and evidence of all types, and interrogating the student, the instruction, and oneself as a teacher and learner. Its essence is curiosity and openness to possibilities as well as the ability to be deliberate in searching for understanding. Dewey (1985) captured this disposition well in his description of the "double movement of reflection" (1985, p. 242). He argued that evidence is the raw material that "perplexes and stimulates." This inductive move leads to forming hypotheses that must then be tested deductively against more and more evidence. Dewey cautioned against jumping too quickly to conclusions, to "readily accepting any suggestion that seems plausible" simply because it is easier and more satisfying than the unrest of not knowing. It is this inclination to jump to conclusions and find solutions that has short-changed classroom assessment for teachers and students. A recent review of the literature on classroom assessment confirms that recording grades was given higher priority than analyzing student work (Black & Wiliam, 1998).

Of course, an essential component of inquiry is question raising that goes beyond trying to understand an obvious problem or unanticipated result to the next step of questioning what we *think* we understand. It also goes beyond asking questions about the student and his or her work to consider the particulars of the task, the context, and the interaction among all three in considering student performance and needs (Lipson & Wixson, 2003). For example, an inquiry-oriented approach to assessment would find the low standardized test scores of a student who is known to be reading several years below grade level as problematic as the high test scores of a student who is not performing well in class. As teachers work with classroom assessments—designing, selecting, and interpreting them—they ask questions such as:

- How might the student's comprehension change if he or she were given an easier passage; read a different genre; had more or less prior knowledge about the topic?
- What might have been the effect of time, response mode (oral/written), and the specific directions for the task?
- What do I know about this student's language skills or motivation that might have influenced his or her performance?
- What evidence from other work samples or observations can help me understand the student's strengths and needs?

Discipline

Discipline is also essential in an inquiry approach to assessment. Here I refer to both disciplinary knowledge (e.g., knowledge of the reading process, reading instruction, the reader) as well as a disciplined, systematic approach to gathering and examining evidence. Obviously, without knowledge it is difficult to implement responsive, inquiry-oriented classroom assessments and to use those opportunities to inform instruction and student learning. Take, for example, a scene from a recent documentary on the challenges facing first-year teachers, featuring a teacher who had gone through an alternative certification program that included minimal preparation in teaching reading ("The First Year," *www.pbs.org/firstyear/*). As this earnest and caring young man listens to a first-grade child read, he coaches him to sound out the word *two*. Clearly and slowly, the teacher articulates /t/ /t/ /t/, /w/ /w/ /w/, /oo/ /oo/ /oo/—*two*. Although a competent reader himself, the teacher did not have the necessary subject matter knowledge (knowledge of sound–symbol correspondences and sight words) or the pedagogical content knowledge (in this case, how to teach reading) to assess the student's needs or to provide appropriate intervention. What makes being a knowledgeable teacher even more complicated is the need to consider issues of reading processes and strategies, students, texts, and context, as well as the interaction among them, to gain a full understanding of students' abilities. Although it is obvious that this disposition is essential to classroom assessment, I demonstrate below (Inquiry-Oriented Assessment in Practice) that it is also essential to responsible interpretation of external assessments.

The second aspect of discipline refers to a planful and systematic approach to collecting and interpreting evidence. Sometimes this aspect may involve using a common set of assessments for a group of students in order to assess progress on specific learning outcomes over time (Valencia, 1998), and other times it may involve using different assessments and modes of assessment (interviews, observations, works samples) for different students. Each of these decisions is guided by conscious decisions about what and how to assess; assessments are not random events. Moreover, sometimes being disciplined means keeping a keen and focused eye on all interactions with students, bringing the best knowledge to bear on hypotheses and emerging evidence, and making decisions based on information. It is this kind of disciplined approach combined with multiple indicators of student learning that Shepard (2001) sees as an antidote to concerns about the "reliability" of classroom assessments. Because teachers are not relying on a single indicator and "because erroneous decisions can be corrected in the classroom context," a knowledgeable, focused approach to classroom assessment can provide accurate and fair information about students' learning (Shepard, 2001, p. 1095).

Interaction and Action

The third element of inquiry-oriented assessment contains the real strength and value of teacher-guided classroom assessment. Teachers actively engage with students to achieve the dual goals of gathering information and bringing students into the assessment process. The most productive interactions are characterized by two features. First, the teacher uses a combination of patient listening and thoughtful questions to enter into a dialogue with students in an effort to understand their learning processes (Johnston, 1997). The questions prompt thinking rather than simple answers, and they follow up naturally on students' responses. In addition, teachers allow sufficient wait time for students to respond and, when needed, provide specific feedback (Black et al., 2004). For example, teachers help students understand what they already know and can do as well as what they need to do to improve. In assessment conversations, students are as likely to ask for feedback and clarification as the teacher is to give it because the expectation is that students will use the feedback to learn something new or to accomplish an important task. And, of course, the value of genuine questions and honest exchanges is that they provide teachers with the needed information to modify instruction.

The second feature of these interactions between teachers and students is the adaptation of assessments and feedback to unique student needs. Assessment can take place in a student's zone of proximal development (Vygotsky, 1978), and teachers can scaffold students through assessment tasks (Wood, Bruner, & Ross, 1976). For example, teachers explore student performance by manipulating variables such as text difficulty or mode of response, and they prompt students during the assessment in an effort to understand what students are able to do and how they learn. They search for patterns of student performance over several assessments rather than relying on a single interaction. Such an approach is similar to concepts such as diagnostic teaching (Lipson & Wixson, 2003) and dynamic assessment (Campione, 1989; Lidz, 1987), both of which have demonstrated that when teachers assess students in the act of learning, watching as they try to complete a task and providing small scaffolds or prompts to see how they learn, that assessment is a better predictor of future learning than a static, non-interactive assessment. Ultimately, teachers and students use the insights gained during these interactions to chart the course for the next steps in learning.

An example of such interaction and action was apparent in a first-grade classroom when students were asked to use their magnetic letters to create five words that started with the consonant blends they had been studying. Noticing that one youngster hadn't generated any words, the teacher asked the little girl about the task. Although she clearly understood what was expected, she reported that she didn't know any words that started with the blends. Instead of assuming that the girl didn't know the sounds of the blends or providing her with the sounds, the teacher asked her to assemble a word she *did* know. Without hesitation, the girl generated three words and from there the teacher was able to determine that she knew the sounds of many single letters (including those that made up the blends), but that she appeared to have some difficulty with onset and rime and initial consonant substitution. As a result, the teacher provided a series of prompts that led the child to generate several words with the consonant blends.

INQUIRY-ORIENTED ASSESSMENT IN PRACTICE

An inquiry-oriented approach to assessment can be brought to all types of teacher-guided classroom assessment—samples of student work, classroom observations, interviews, conferences, and everyday interactions. But it can, and should, be brought to other assessments as well, including high-stakes external assessments and mandated classroom assessments. Of course, the more formal, more standardized the assessment, the less flexibility teachers and students have to inquire into it and to engage in diagnostic teaching and assessment. Nevertheless, the point of an inquiry-oriented approach is to view all assessment as a *springboard* to understand student learning, rather than a stable platform of fact. Below, I present examples of how this disposition toward assessment can help teachers understand student performance regardless of whether the evidence comes from external assessments, mandated classroom assessments, or teacher-guided assessments.

Bringing Inquiry to External Assessments

External, high-stakes test results are least likely to be subjected to inquiry, in part due to the nature of the tests themselves: Their content and format are less directly connected to classroom curriculum and authentic demonstrations of learning; the results are not provided in a timely fashion; and the items are often secure, so it is impossible to get specifics about student performance. Nevertheless, if the results are not simply assumed to be definitive indicators of students' abilities—if they are interrogated—we might not only learn from the evidence but we might also be able to raise cautionary concerns about misinterpretations.

School teams can bring inquiry to the results of external assessment by studying the test itself as well as the results, and then generating a set of questions the answers to which will reveal more about students, their needs, and current instruction. For example, at a school level, questions might include:

- What could we learn if we disaggregated the data according to time in school (e.g., new enrollees, absences), current and former ESL instructional support, etc.?
- What is the nature of the reading instruction currently provided to struggling readers in our school?
- How are school resources being used to support struggling readers?
- How well do various resources cohere or align to provide services?
- What literacy-related professional development opportunities have been provided over the past 2 years? How have they been received? What follow-up has been done? What do teachers want/need?

Using this approach, one school discovered that students who had been enrolled for 3 or more years performed significantly better than those who had been in the school fewer than 3 years. They decided to pilot an "intake" classroom for new students and to put into place strategies for providing more intensive support during their first year in the school. In another school, students who had been enrolled in ESL support for 4 or more years and then exited, performed significantly below students who had exited earlier. This finding suggested that although these students had passed a test to be exited, they needed additional support during their transition into mainstream classes. A third school discovered that they didn't have a systematic plan for coordinating services provided by their Title I Learning Assistance Program (LAP), literacy coaches, and extended day program—all of which were supposed to focus on literacy support for underachieving students. The teachers in these programs did not have a way to communicate about instruction or assessment, even when they were serving the same children, nor did they have time to communicate with the children's teachers.

A next level of inquiry into external assessments moves closer to the classroom, where teachers can add their knowledge about reading and their students. As a starting point, teachers would study the test content and format (sometimes this includes released items from secure tests). Using a process that Conley and Gritter describe as "backward mapping" (in Chapter 2 of this volume), teachers are encouraged to ask questions such as:

- What would students have to know and be able to do to score well on this test?
- Using information from my own classroom assessments, which students would I have predicted would have done well/poorly/etc.? How did they do? What may have contributed to their performance?
- What additional information do I need to help me plan appropriate instruction?

A recent study of students who failed a typical fourth-grade state reading test is an example of initial efforts to bring inquiry to external high-stakes tests (Riddle Buly & Valencia, 2002; Valencia & Riddle Buly, 2004). We were concerned that schools and districts were relying on the scores to mandate particular interventions and policies—specifically, some were calling for an intensive phonics program for all failing students. Instead of relying just on the test score, we used the state test as a sort of filter to identify students who were exhibiting difficulty. Asking "What would students have to know and be able to do to score well on this test?", we conducted a series of individual assessments aimed at providing more in-depth analyses of students' abilities in decoding, comprehension, vocabulary, and fluency. We found that students who failed to meet the state standard had distinctly different reading profiles that would point to different foci for instruction. Some students, for instance, had excellent decoding skills but struggled with comprehension (18%), whereas others had adequate decoding and comprehension but were slow and dysfluent (24%). Some students experienced difficulties with decoding and fluency but were surprisingly able to comprehend (17%). Similarly, some students were reading at first- or second-grade level whereas others were reading closer to grade level, yet still failed the test. Profiles such as these, constructed from existing classroom information, teacher knowledge, or supplemental testing (as we did), provide a good starting place to inquire beyond external assessments. Although our inquiry was not sufficient to provide targeted instruction for each student (that must be informed by more ongoing, classroom assessment), this type of interrogation of test results may guard against misuse and misunderstanding of scores, and it provides a closer layer of information upon which to base instruction.

Bringing Inquiry to Mandated Classroom Assessment

Mandated classroom assessments can target a variety of learning outcomes and take a variety of forms (e.g., district-developed comprehension tests; word lists; decoding tests; published tests of skills and strategies). Although these mandated classroom assessments are often administered and scored according to strict guidelines, the fact that they are in teachers' hands and that the results are immediately available makes inquiry even more possible and productive. For this example, I turn to our recent research on fluency assessment (Valencia et al., 2004).

Currently, one of the most popular mandated classroom assessments is the oral "1-minute read" in which students' scores are calculated and reported as the number of words they read correctly in 1 minute (wcpm). In some instances, states and districts have selected a short passage (or a published test with short passages) to be administered at each grade level; in other cases, teachers use longer reading selections from existing assessments (i.e., informal reading inventories, leveled reading passages) or from classroom material. Although questions have been raised about the construct and consequential validity of such measures (Valencia et al., 2004), teachers can bring inquiry to these types of assessments. It is useful, for instance, to look beneath and beyond wcpm to gain more diagnostic information about students' strengths and weaknesses in four essential aspects of fluency: accuracy, rate, expression, and comprehension. If the mandated assessment includes passages that are quite short, teachers can pull apart wcpm into two separate components (accuracy and rate) and add additional classroom information; if the passages are longer and have more substantial content, teachers can add the two additional measures of understanding (expression and comprehension).

Table 1.1 presents disaggregated information from four fourth-grade students who read orally from a fourth-grade fluency assessment as part of our study. Students A–C had scores (wcpm) that placed them in the 75%ile, according to Hasbrouck and Tindal guidelines (Hasbrouck & Tindal, 2005; wcpm ≥ 139), and at "low risk" according to DIBELS guidelines (*www.dibels.uoregon.edu/benchmarkgoals.pdf*; wcpm ≥ 105) for mid-

TABLE 1.1. Information from Four Fourth-Grade Students Who Read Orally from a Fourth-Grade Fluency Assessment

Student	wcpm	Accuracy (%)	Rate (wpm)	Expression (1–4)	Comprehension (%)
A	146	99	147	2	20
B	149	98	152	3	80
C	150	89	169	2	50
D	90	87	102	1	40
Retest	114	95	120	3	80

year fourth grade; Student D's score placed him in the 25%ile, according to Hasbrouck and Tindal (wcpm ≤ 87) and at "some risk" according to DIBELS (wcpm = 83–104). Using this information, we can demonstrate three levels of inquiry a teacher might explore to look beyond a score of wcpm and gain information to guide instruction.

At a first level of inquiry, teachers could raise questions about the relative contribution of rate and accuracy to the wcpm score and consider additional information gathered during the required assessment process. Using this simple inquiry, Table 1.1 reveals that these students have different needs. Among the three students scoring above the 75%ile, Students A and B have nearly perfect decoding and are reading at a reasonably fast rate. In contrast, Student C appears to be experiencing considerable difficulty with word identification (frustration level) yet is reading very quickly. Furthermore, because this is an individually administered assessment, the teacher could inquire about students' reading processes, considering issues such as the nature of the errors or how each student tackled the reading (e.g., self-corrections, strategies for decoding difficult words). For example, we found that Student C skipped or misread a good number of articles and minor words (e.g., *the, a, of*), most likely due to her fast pace of reading, which lowered her accuracy score. If the decoding errors had been more substantial, the teacher may have wanted to supplement the assessment by asking the student to read from an easier passage. In fact, that is what we did with Student D. We discovered that both rate and accuracy improved when he read third-grade text, suggesting a different instructional path than the one that might have been suggested from the fourth-grade results.

At the next level, the teacher could inquire about the comprehension abilities of Students A, B, and C because many mandated fluency assessments do not include direct measures of expression or comprehension. One way teachers can address this area is to use other classroom evidence to supplement the assessment. The teacher might ask, "What evidence do I have about this student's ability to comprehend at both literal and inferential levels? How does the student's performance on rate and accuracy fit with what I have observed during instruction and conferences?" Based on the results of the fluency assessment and additional classroom information, the teacher might decide to administer several running records and retellings during his or her reading conferences over the next few months to follow up on accuracy, rate, and comprehension and to be sure that his or her students are aware that reading fast is not the goal of good reading. Another option for inquiring into comprehension can be used if the mandated assessment is sufficiently long and substantive to make assessment of comprehension and expression meaningful. In this case, the teacher inquires about comprehension of the passages that students have read as part of the assessment. For this assessment we recommend that students read for at least 3 minutes. Table 1.1 shows the results of using this approach. We assessed expression using the rubric developed by the National Assessment of Educational Progress (NAEP) (Pinnell et al., 1995) and comprehension using a set of five questions (inferential and literal) and a retelling. By adding these two additional pieces to the assessment, we found a number of false negatives (i.e., students whose wcpm scores did not identify them as experiencing difficulties but who had significant comprehension problems).

A third level of inquiry for an individually administered mandated assessment such as this one involves engaging the student in self-evaluation and thinking aloud about the strategies he or she used before, during, and after reading. With questions such as "What was difficult for you in reading this passage?"; "I noticed that you stopped and reread this line; tell me more about what you did here?"; and "How is the way you read on this test similar or different from the way you read during silent reading?", the teacher can follow up on his or her observations during the assessment.

Bringing Inquiry to Teacher-Guided Classroom Assessment

The final set of examples takes advantage of teacher-guided classroom assessment during which teachers can design, adapt, and adjust assessment to align with their instruction and with student needs. For the first example, I draw on a videotape of a reading conference with a first grader whose teacher is taking a running record (New Standards, nd). Chelsea begins reading from *A Hole in Harry's Pocket* (Bloksberg, 1995) as her teacher takes the running record, but after just a few seconds she runs into difficulty:

> CHELSEA: Harry lik . . . liked to walk to the store. He liked to hop on the *ker, cr, crub, crub, kir, crib, crub* . . . (*22 seconds of working on the word*). See, my mom is teaching me the sound of the letters but and there's are all kinds of sounds for the *u*.
>
> TEACHER: And I can hear that you are trying out some different sounds for it.
>
> CHELSEA: (*spontaneously trying to sound out the word, 7 seconds*) Cube, kirb, crub, cr . . .
>
> TEACHER: I'll tell you the word. It's *curb*.
>
> CHELSEA: *Curb*. Well, I would expect a *i* or *r* or a *er* there because we have a chart in our classroom that has the /er/ sound and we don't have . . . we have the *ur* but I didn't expect it to be *ur*.
>
> TEACHER: I agree it is unusual, Chelsea.

This is where the videotape stops. From this brief assessment, the teacher can learn some helpful points about Chelsea's reading and she could inquire even further. For example, Chelsea clearly knows several *r*-controlled vowel patterns and is amazingly metacognitive about them as she reads, trying to make links to what she has learned in school and at home. And, she is persistent (29 seconds worth)! The assessment process could stop here, and the teacher might target *ur* words in the next lesson. But doing so would miss important information gained through inquiry. For example, the teacher might wonder if Chelsea has developed other strategies for tackling unknown words while reading, such as using picture clues or reading ahead for context and meaning or decoding by analogy. She persists at trying to decode the word, using the same strategies over and over, even though she isn't succeeding. The teacher might inquire to see if Chelsea is familiar with other strategies and might have her read a bit further to see if, with a bit of encouragement, she can use a combination of strategies. If she is not successful, the teacher might model and then have Chelsea practice on the next couple of sentences in the text. The teacher might also introduce the *ur* sound through words such as *turn*, *burn*, and *hurt*, encouraging Chelsea to see the similarities and differences with other *ur* patterns she knows. Because Chelsea is so metacognitively aware, the teacher would want to capitalize on her ability to think aloud and to encourage more problem solving while she is reading. Such an interactive assessment would reveal what Chelsea already knows and how easily she is able to learn new strategies.

The last example comes from a more formal classroom assessment developed by teachers to assess their district's comprehension content standard. The teachers worked together to identify grade-level passages, prompts, and scoring rubrics for retellings. They field-tested the passages and assessment process, and when they were satisfied, they decided to implemented the assessments three times a year as part of their portfolios (Valencia, 1998). After a good deal of instruction and practice with retelling narratives, the teachers administered this assessment to their classes. Because they had the option to match students with appropriate-level texts, the teachers actually used four different reading passages for the range of students in their classes.

The sample in Figure 1.1 is from a student whose teacher estimated that he was reading at fourth-grade level. After the student had read for a while, the teacher noticed that he seemed confused and frustrated. Stopping by his desk, she noticed that he apparently misunderstood the directions about prediction, even though they had been working on this area in class. More disturbing was that he hadn't written any-thing in the space for the retelling. Her initial reaction was that he hadn't done the read-ing or that she had misjudged the level of text for him. However, first she decided to talk with him about the assessment. They talked about his confusion with the predic-tion task, and then she decided to ask him to retell the story verbally. Figure 1.1 shows the information he dictated to her—a fairly complete retelling. Rather than assuming that the text was too difficult or that the student could not meet the grade-level reading standard, the teacher considered other factors that might have contributed to his poor performance on the assessment. Not only did he misunderstand the directions, he had a great deal of difficulty expressing his retelling in writing. As this teacher thought about her instruction and about the assessment, she decided that perhaps a full written retelling might involve too much writing for some of her students, and it certainly was a different task from the ones they had been working on in class. Insights such as these led the district teachers to rethink both their instruction and their assessments, and it helped them look beyond the assessment scores to learn more about their students' abilities.

CONCLUSION

Effective assessment will help us close the gap between where students are currently performing and where they could be. But it is not the simple act of giving an assess-ment or examining the results that will accomplish this goal. The only sure way is through inquiry-oriented assessment that is used to inform teaching and learning. As we are faced with more and more external assessment demands, we need to reaffirm our commitment to teacher-guided classroom assessment and to the inquiry, discipline, interaction, and action that mark both good teaching and assessment. Although we don't have control over all assessments we administer, we do have control over how we understand and use them.

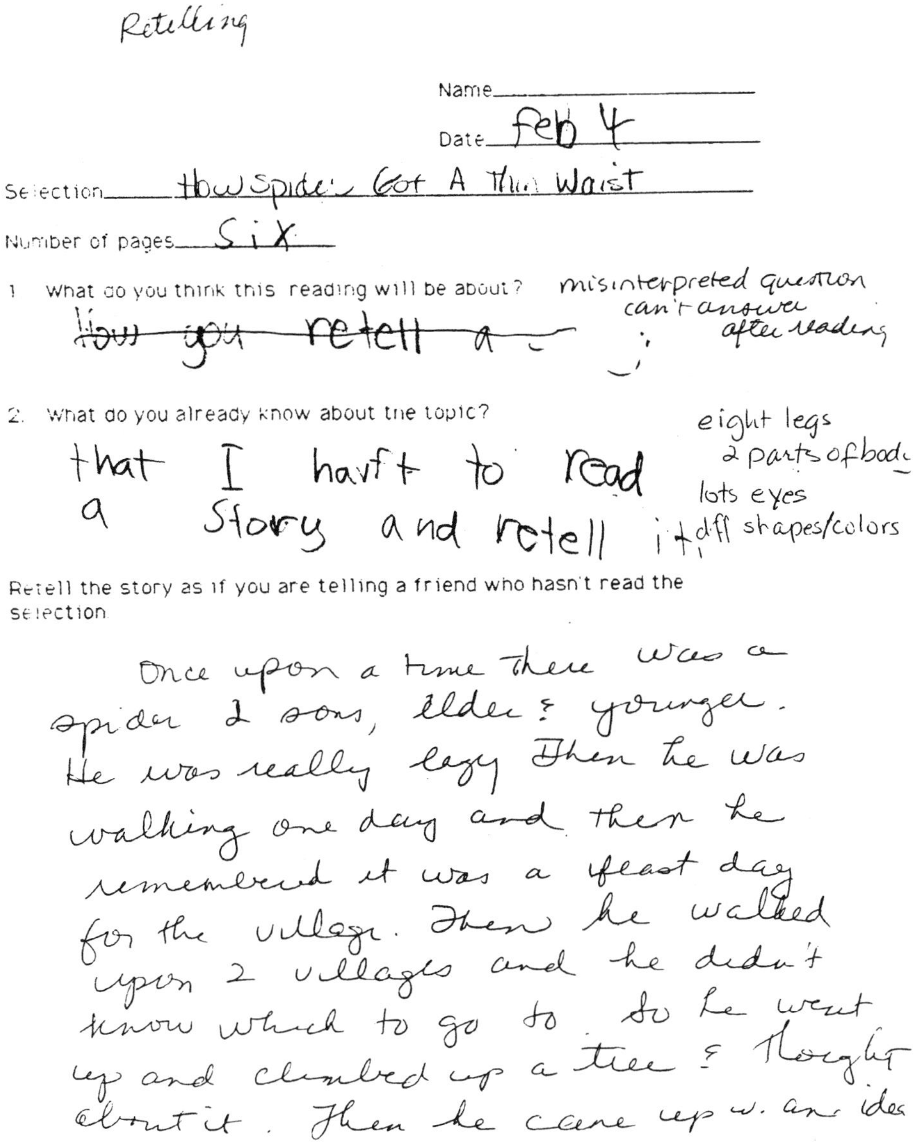

Retelling

Name_____

Date _feb 4_____

Selection____How Spider Got A Thin Waist_____

Number of pages____Six____

1 What do you think this reading will be about?   *misinterpreted question*
                                                    can't answer
   ~~How you~~ retell a ___ ;   *after reading*

2. What do you already know about the topic?   *eight legs*
                                                   2 parts of body
   that I havft to read   *lots eyes*
      a   Story and retell it; *dff shapes/colors*

Retell the story as if you are telling a friend who hasn't read the
selection

   Once upon a time there was a
spider & sons, elder & younger.
He was really lazy Then he was
walking one day and then he
remembered it was a feast day
for the village. Then he walked
upon 2 villages and he didn't
know which to go to. So he went
up and climbed up a tree & thought
about it. Then he came up w. an idea

FIGURE 1.1. Retelling assessment.

And he decided to go to one who opened first. So asked elder son to take one end of rope and take it to east villa & when that villages opened, pull rope hard. He asked younger son to take end of rope to east villages. and pull rope hard when opens. Then awhile later the ~~both~~ elder & younger son pulled at same time Then ~~the it sque~~ he didn't know which one to go to. The 2 sons didn't know why father was not coming. So they pulled harde and rope got so tight that it made the spider's waist really skinny. up until today, he was skin

1. How accurate was your prediction about the story?

Forgot - went up tree twice to think
danced after each time.

2. What surprised you in the story?

I thought when pulled rope. It wouldn't get stiff it would just sit there.

3. Who else do you think would enjoy reading this selection?

Somebody who likes celebration like reading about surprises and parties.
Or people who like insects.

FIGURE 1.1. (continued)

REFERENCES

Airasian, P. W. (2000). *Assessment in the classroom* (2nd ed.). Boston: McGraw-Hill.

Black, P., Harrison, C., Lee, C., Marshall, B., & Wiliam, D. (2004). Working inside the black box: Assessment for learning in the classroom. *Phi Delta Kappan, 86*(1), 8–21.

Black, P., & Wiliam, D. (1998). Inside the black box: Raising standards through classroom assessment. *Phi Delta Kappan, 80*(2), 139–148.

Bliem, C. L., & Davinroy, K. H. (1997). *Teachers' beliefs about assessment and instruction in literacy.* Unpublished manuscript, University of Colorado, Boulder.

Bloksberg, R. (1995). *There's a hole in Harry's pocket.* New York: Hyperion.

Campione, J. (1989). Assisted assessment: A taxonomy of approaches and an outline of strengths and weaknesses. *Journal of Learning Disabilities, 22*(3), 151–165.

Clay, M. M. (1993). *An observation survey of early literacy achievement.* Portsmouth, NH: Heinemann.

Darling-Hammond, L. (1988). Accountability and teacher professionalism. *American Educator, 12,* 8–13.

Dewey, J. (1985). *How we think.* Carbondale, IL: Southern Illinois University.

Dynamic Indicators of Basic Early Literacy Skills (DIBELS). Available at *www.dibels.uoregon.edu/benchmarkgoals.pdf.*

Fuchs, L. S., Fuchs, D., Hosp, M. K., & Jenkins, J. R. (2001). Oral reading fluency as an indicator of reading competence: A theoretical, empirical, and historical analysis. *Scientific Studies of Reading, 5*(3), 239–256.

Guthrie, J. T. (2002). Preparing students for high-stakes test taking in reading. In A. E. Farstrup & S. J. Samuels (Eds.), *What research has to say about reading instruction* (pp. 370–391). Newark, DE: International Reading Association.

Hasbrouck, J., & Tindal, G. (2005). *Oral reading fluency: 90 years of measurement* (Tech. Rep. No. 33). Eugene, OR: University of Oregon, College of Education, Behavioral Research and Teaching.

International Reading Association and National Council of Teachers of English. (1994). *Standards for the assessment of reading and writing.* Newark, DE: International Reading Association.

Invernizzi, M. A., Landrum, T. J., Howell, J. L., & Warley, H. P. (2005). Toward the peaceful coexistence of test developers, policymakers, and teachers in an era of accountability. *The Reading Teacher, 58*(7), 610–618.

Johnston, P. H. (1997). *Knowing literacy: Constructive literacy assessment.* York, ME: Stenhouse.

Lidz, C. S. (Ed.). (1987). *Dynamic assessment: An interactional approach to evaluating learning potential.* New York: Guilford Press.

Linn, R. L. (2000). Assessments and accountability. *Educational Researcher, 29*(2), 4–16.

Lipson, M. Y., & Wixson, K. K. (2003). *Assessment and instruction of reading and writing difficulty: An interactive approach* (3rd ed.). Boston: Allyn & Bacon.

McNeil, L. M. (1988). *Contradictions of control: School structure and school knowledge.* New York: Routledge.

Messick, S. (1994). The interplay of evidence and consequences in the validation of performance assessments. *Educational Researcher, 23*(2), 13–23.

National Council on Education Standards and Testing. (1992). *Raising standards for American Education.* Washington, DC: U.S. Government Printing Office.

National Reading Panel. (2000). *Teaching children to read: An evidence-based assessment of the scientific research literature on reading and its implications for reading instruction. Reports of the subgroups* (NIH Publication No. 00-4754). Washington, DC: U.S. Government Printing Office.

New Standards. (n.d.). *Reading and writing grade by grade.* Available at *www.ncee.org/store/products/.*

Pearson, P. D., Vyas, S., Sensale, L. M., & Kim, Y. (2001). Making our way through the assessment and accountability maze: Where do we go now? *The Clearing House, 74*(4), 175–182.

Pinnell, G. S., Pikulski, J. J., Wixson, K. K., Campbell, J. R., Gough, P. B., & Beatty, A. S. (1995). *Listening to children read aloud.* Washington, DC: U.S. Department of Education.

Riddle Buly, M., & Valencia, S.W. (2002). Below the bar: Profiles of students who fail state reading tests. *Educational Evaluation and Policy Analysis, 24*, 219–239.

Sharp, D. (2004). *Supporting teachers' data-driven instructional conversations: An environmental scan of Reading First and STEP literacy assessments, data visualizations, and assumptions about conversations that matter: Report to the Information Infrastructure System Project.* Chicago: John D. and Catherine T. MacArthur Foundation.

Shavelson, R. J., & Stern, P. (1981). Research on teachers' pedagogical thought, judgments, decisions and behavior. *Review of Educational Research, 41*(4), 455–498.

Shepard, L. (2000). The role of assessment in a learning culture. *Educational Researcher, 29*(7), 4–14.

Shepard, L. (2001). The role of classroom assessment in teaching and learning. In V. K. Richardson (Ed.), *Handbook of research on teaching* (4th ed., pp. 1066–1101). Washington, DC: American Educational Research Association.

Shepard, L., Flexer, R. J., Hiebert, E. H., Marion, S. F., Mayfield, V., & Weston, T. J. (1996). Effects of introducing classroom performance assessments on student learning. *Educational Measurement: Issues and Practice, 15*(3), 7–18.

Sirotnik, K. A. (2002). Promoting responsible accountability in schools and education. *Phi Delta Kappan, 83*(9), 662–673.

Stiggins, R. (2004). New assessment beliefs for a new school mission. *Phi Delta Kappan, 86*(1), 22–27.

Taylor, C. S., & Nolen, S. B. (2005). *Classroom assessment: Supporting teaching and learning in real classrooms.* Upper Saddle River, NJ: Pearson.

The first year. Available at *www.pbs.org/firstyear/*.

Valencia, S. W. (1998). *Literacy portfolios in action.* Ft. Worth, TX: Hartcourt, Brace.

Valencia, S. W., & Au, K. H. (1997). Portfolios across educational contexts: Issues of evaluation, professional development, and system validity. *Educational Assessment, 4*(1), 1–35.

Valencia, S. W., & Riddle Buly, M. (2004). What struggling readers REALLY need. *The Reading Teacher, 57*, 520–533.

Valencia, S. W., Smith, A., Reece, A., Newman, H., Wixson, K. K., & Li, M. (2004, December). *The rush for oral reading fluency: Issues of assessment and implications for instruction.* Paper presented at the National Reading Conference, San Antonio, TX.

Vygotsky, L. (1978). *Mind in society: The development of higher psychological process.* Cambridge, MA: Harvard University Press.

Wixson, K. K., Valencia, S. W., & Lipson, M. Y. (1994). Issues in literacy assessment: Facing the realities of internal and external assessment. *Journal of Reading Behavior, 26*(3), 315–337.

Wood, D. J., Bruner, J. S., & Ross, G. (1976). The role of tutoring in problem solving. *Journal of Child Psychology and Psychiatry, 17*, 89–100.

CHAPTER 2

A Pathway for Connecting Standards with Assessment

BACKWARD MAPPING OF ASSESSMENT TASKS

Mark W. Conley
Kristine Gritter

No one would dispute that testing is now center stage in the push for accountability. Testing is certainly at the heart of legislation inspired by No Child Left Behind. Test performance is the catalyst for worries and recommendations in the Third International Mathematics and Science Study (Martin, Mullis, & Chrostowski, 2004). And tests are the primary focus of concerns about whether or not students are well prepared for the future demands of society and the workplace (Achieve Inc., 2004).

There are several problems with such an emphasis (some would say *overemphasis*) on testing. First, tests do not guarantee that students are educated to higher standards. Tests can represent obsolete standards (Achieve Inc., 2005; Gates, 2005). If tests consist of content and skills that are not very worthwhile, then giving more tests or administering them more often will not increase academic rigor or student performance. A second problem concerns the ways in which the testing movement is disconnected from the push for higher academic standards. Throughout the 1990s and into the early new millennium, many tests and standards were created by entirely separate committees and groups under entirely different circumstances (Conley, 2005). State tests were designed in response to public pressure for greater school accountability, spurred by teacher unionization and rising costs. Curriculum standards emerged out of concerns for "standardizing" curricula. The need to create a system whereby teachers could respond to the same targets or goals underlies the modern standards movement. After all, how could accountability be assured if teachers were teaching to such diverse and idiosyncratic goals?

Unfortunately, though the testing and standards movements both address the issue of accountability, they do not necessarily point to the same goals or practices. Evidence of this disconnection comes from a phenomenon that we have observed repeatedly over the years: school staffs pouring over tests and standards documents, trying to make sense of the goals, content, skills, and strategies that are implied. Most often teachers work in grade-level and/or subject matter groups. The results are usually long lists of concepts, tasks, and skills, which, when multiplied by grade level and subject area, become expansive scope and sequence charts. It is no wonder that, more than ever, teachers feel pressure over demands to cover a much-elaborated curriculum.

Some states have begun to address this problem by actually revising curriculum standards and then revising tests to more directly reflect the standards. However, this approach can still lead to more, rather than less, complexity. The problem of grade-level and subject matter differences persists, accompanied by discrete bits of content, testing tasks, and skills. We have plenty of evidence that teaching and learning are not very effective when the curriculum is full of disconnected concepts and skills. How can teachers develop connections for themselves, and most importantly, for their students?

Backward mapping is an approach to curriculum design whereby goals or standards and evidence for learning are identified before planning instruction (Wiggins & McTighe, 1998). Backward mapping, considered revolutionary when it was first introduced, is a way to focus specifically on curriculum goals and expected student performance in order to guide teaching and learning. In the past, the process was applied to published standards. However, this approach is also useful for identifying standards and expected student performance with assessment tasks.

The purpose of this chapter is to explain backward mapping as a way to analyze testing tasks with respect to goals and expected student performance. The following section illustrates how backward mapping can be used to examine three common testing tasks found on many state assessments. Next we demonstrate how using this approach can provide productive ways for connecting standards and assessments.

BACKWARD MAPPING:
WHAT'S REALLY COVERED ON THE TESTS?

The multitude of ways in which content and tasks are represented on state and national tests contributes to the confusion over what tests cover or truly represent. The work of psychometricians has produced an entirely new assessment vocabulary. Three dominant question types are commonly used: (1) *selected response items*, or what we used to call multiple choice; (2) *constructed response items*, or questions that invite anywhere from a single word or number up to a sentence or paragraph response; and (3) *extended items* that require essay-length responses. But the complexity of the tests does not stop here. Item specifications, or what we like to call the *recipe* for the test items, consist of yet more lists of content knowledge and testing tasks.

Tests cover a vast amount of knowledge and skill from many disciplines. Consider this list taken from a perusal of item specifications from tests given across the United States. Many reading tests focus on fluency (including phonemic awareness and phonics), vocabulary, and comprehension (sometimes divided into intersentence interpretations and beyond text or thematic applications). Science tests require quantitative and qualitative observations, investigations of thoughtful questions, logical predictions, designing and conducting experiments, collecting and organizing data, offering reasonable explanations, exploring possible conclusions, and communicating data-based decisions. Math tests cover number sense and concepts, number operations, and natural numbers. And social studies tests require students to explain the causes and consequences of war, principles of government and economics, and the impact of climate and geography. Obviously, these specifications represent a complex mixture of targets and tasks that are not easily integrated across the grades or the curriculum.

But there are problems that extend well beyond this complex picture. The skills published in the item specifications—the same ones publicized by state departments of education and the ones used to provide staff development to teachers and instruction to students—may not actually be the only skills that are represented in the items (Conley, 2005). That's where backward mapping of assessment tasks becomes useful. To use backward mapping to find out what is really going on with an assessment task, we follow these steps:

1. *Read the question.* Figure out what kind of question it is and what it is asking. Determine the number of parts to the question. For multiple-choice questions, this may be very straightforward—a question and a fixed number of choices. But constructed meaning and extended response questions frequently have several parts that require many different kinds of responses. Note the parts of the question and what is being asked.

2. *Answer the question.* Provide a response to each part of the question. Consider what the question is asking and respond, taking note of the steps you are taking inside your head to generate answers.

3. *Map or record the steps you took to read and answer the question.* Do a think-aloud reflection, recapping what you did to answer the question. Write down the steps. Consider how these steps compare with item specification information about the purpose of the item.

We illustrate this process with an example from a mathematics test (Figure 2.1). The item specifications tell us that the item tests number sense and numeration, particularly number relationships and numerical comparisons. As an adult consumer, you may recognize the item as a comparison of unit costs. Now, let's use backward mapping to take a look at what it takes to actually complete the item.

First, there is the test question. What are the important parts? It is about the Spanish Club selling candy bars to raise money. Two companies are the possible sources of the candy bars. The tables depict a sliding scale of prices for each company that depend on the number of boxes a customer orders. The table for Company A reveals a straightforward pattern where each box costs $10 regardless of the quantity. The table for Company B reveals a different pattern wherein the candy gets cheaper the more a customer orders. Finally, we get to the point of the test question: We need to figure out which company the Spanish Club should use, depending on how much they want to buy. And, as with many questions like this one, we need to explain our decision.

We gain a great deal of information by analyzing questions this way. In fact, in our example, we probably have enough information to consider the number patterns and answer the question without actually working out the problem. Knowing something

MATH PROBLEM

The Spanish Club sells candy bars at lunch to raise money. They can buy boxes of candy bars from Company A or B, which charge different rates based on the number of boxes bought. The same kind of candy and number of bars per box are available from both companies. The tables show the number of boxes purchased and the cost per order for the two companies.

Company A

Number of Boxes	Cost (Dollars)
1	10.00
5	50.00
10	100.00
20	200.00

Company B

Number of Boxes	Cost (Dollars)
1	15.00
3	40.00
9	85.00
12	110.00

a. Which company plan is more economical if the Spanish Club purchases 1 or 2 boxes? Explain your answer.

b. Which company plan is more economical if the Spanish Club usually purchases 10–15 boxes? Explain your answer.

FIGURE 2.1. Backward mapping for a mathematics test item.

about the content—number sense and patterns—is, of course, essential. Yet it is also possible to possess the content knowledge and still not be able to apply it to the question. Consider students who miss the comparison between the companies, who overrely on one table and completely miss the other. Although this item is intended as an assessment of mathematics knowledge, the "hidden curriculum" on state and national tests requires skills such as reading and analyzing questions carefully. Many students are unsuccessful on these tests because they are unfamiliar with particular literacy skills demanded by the task—in this case, the ability to analyze questions and respond appropriately.

Let's use backward mapping with another example, this time from a reading test. Figure 2.2 depicts a typical reading test item. The item specifications call for a response to a set of reading selections in which students compare the characteristics of different texts, demonstrating their understanding of complex, enduring issues—recurring human problems and themes within and across texts. This kind of item has become more popular in recent years. Variations include scenario questions, as on this item, or the use of a quote, referred to as a "critical lens" for interpreting multiple passages. Using backward mapping, we can determine what the item requires beyond a close reading of the texts.

Let's start by unraveling the question into its components. There is a scenario and a question. The scenario directs attention to the theme of the question—how people follow their dreams and accomplish their goals regardless of what other people think. This step seems pretty clear-cut. However, it requires students to translate the theme into their own words and/or experiences. Students who rush forward without translating the scenario, or in other cases, without applying a critical lens, risk making faulty assumptions about how to respond to the item. For example, students could ignore the idea that sometimes people's goals are not popular or are uncommon—an idea that could be very prevalent in the reading selections upon which the students' answers must be based.

The scenario question provides three crucial details about appropriate responses to the item. Successful responses (1) *must* address the theme of the question—the value of people pursuing their dreams and goals, (2) *may* include students' own ideas and experiences, and (3) *must* refer to information and examples from both of the reading selections on the test. Implicit in these criteria, but explicit in rubrics used to evaluate responses to this kind of item, is the requirement to take a position and defend it. For

RESPONSE TO THE READING SELECTIONS

DIRECTIONS: Write a response to the scenario question that is stated in the box below. You may look back at both of the reading selections to help you answer the question at the end of the following scenario.

Scenario

Many successful people, both famous and unknown, have taken action to follow their dreams and accomplish their goals, regardless of what other people said or did. You have been asked to contribute an essay for a brochure that your school guidance department plans to publish about choosing a career.

Scenario Question

What would you have to say about the value of people pursuing their personal dreams and goals? Your own ideas may be used in your response, but you *must* refer to information and/or examples from both of the reading selections of this test to be considered for full credit. You must show a connection across the two selections.

FIGURE 2.2. Backward mapping for a reading test item.

instance, with this item, students must decide if it is a good idea, or not, for people to pursue their dreams regardless of what others think. Then they must support their decision with information from their own experiences and the reading selections.

There are many ways that students can misconstrue this type of test item. Some students might misunderstand the theme, focusing on what people *do* rather than on *what people dream*. Others might report some connected or disconnected experience from their lives without mentioning the reading selections. Still others could take a position and restate it over and over again without ever mounting any kind of informed defense. Consequently, analyzing the question is only the starting point. Students must also consider, practice, and reflect on the kinds of answers that make up a successful response.

So far, backward mapping has yielded insights about the importance of analyzing questions, taking a position, and defending responses within test questions. We can add yet another view of the curriculum implied by the tests by examining the following item taken from a social studies test (Figure 2.3). The specifications for this item focus on using knowledge about American government and politics to make thoughtful decisions about public policy issues and to act constructively to further the public good. Now we will use backward mapping to discover what it takes to answer the item successfully.

Analyzing the question, we can see some similarities with the response to reading test item (Figure 2.2). The social studies item asks students to take a stand and support it. However, the nature of the required support is far more complex. There are three

TAKING A STAND

You will now take a stand on the following public policy issue: **Should the United States Congress pass a law that requires political candidates to release a list of all organizations that contribute over $100?** You may either support or oppose a law requiring political candidates to release a list of these contributors. Write a letter to your congressional representative.

You will be graded on the following criteria. Your letter must include:

- A clear and supported statement of your position;
- Supporting information using a Core Democratic Value of American constitutional democracy;
- Supporting knowledge from history, geography, civics (other than the Core Democratic Values), or economics (it is not enough to state only your opinion);
- Supporting information from the data section; and
- A credible argument someone with the opposite point of view could use and an explanation that reveals the flaw in his or her argument.

Remember to: Use complete sentences.
                    Explain your reasons in detail.
                    Explain how the Core Democratic Value you use connects to your position.
                    Write or print neatly on the lines provided in your booklet.

FIGURE 2.3. Backward mapping for a social studies test item.

kinds of acceptable support: (1) a state document entitled Core Democratic Values, (2) knowledge about history, geography, civics, or economics, and (3) data provided earlier to answer several related test questions. For this item, it is not only important to understand that you must support your position; you must also know the difference between various kinds of support.

Teachers and students who encounter this complexity often throw up their hands in frustration. After all, it is difficult enough to understand the notion of supporting a position or statement. Many students, not knowing how to support a position, respond with restatements, or "Because my dad (or mom) says so . . . " or "Just because" when pressed to explain themselves. How will students ever rise to the level of offering multiple kinds of support when they do not yet understand what it means to take a position and defend it, even in very basic ways? As this test item illustrates, the kinds of questions—their parts, what they call for—and the ways in which students consider and reflect upon their answer and evidence—matter a great deal. These are the skills that are rarely, if ever, mentioned in the item specifications, but they are essential for successful test performance.

USING BACKWARD MAPPING
TO CONNECT TESTING TO STANDARDS

Curriculum standards are expressions of what we want students to know and be able to do. The most far-reaching standards are those that suggest goals for students as future citizens. Ideally, well-conceived standards guide students in finding a unique place for themselves in society and in life. The popularity of the standards movement in the 1990s and beyond is testament to the influence of standards in guiding teachers toward creating rich and relevant experiences for their students. Since the onset of the testing movement and its intensification, inspired by No Child Left Behind, many have questioned whether the standards movement, as originally conceived, would survive (Conley, 2005).

The test-taking skills identified through backward mapping provide one way to connect standards with those skills. Take, for example, the skill of analyzing a question. Consider the varied ways that standards promote the ability to analyze and respond to different kinds of tasks. As Figure 2.4 illustrates, students are encouraged to write for different technical purposes, including describing complex processes for varied audiences; investigating problems via complex questions and statistical study; analyzing earth systems with regard to their scientific and historical significance; communicating in age-appropriate ways within and across cultures; and evaluating world events and actions from opposing national and political perspectives. Clearly, understanding complex tasks and how to respond to them are major components of rigorous curriculum standards.

Consider also ways in which standards invoke the practices of taking a stand and providing support with reasoning and varied kinds of evidence. It is not enough merely to describe, investigate, analyze, communicate, and evaluate. Students are also required to examine why their position is better than another, why one person's approach to a task is more effective than another, why someone else's idea is not as promising as one in which they are invested. The social studies task in Figure 2.3 pro-

English

A student shall write in the English language for a variety of technical purposes, situations, and audiences by writing original technical compositions including a set of procedures or directions, a report or proposal, and informational correspondence that describe a complex process, procedure, or device for a particular audience

Mathematics

A student shall investigate a problem of significance by formulating a complex question, designing a statistical study, collecting data, representing data appropriately, using appropriate statistics to summarize data, determining whether additional data and analysis are necessary, drawing conclusions based on data, and communicating the results appropriately for the intended audience

Science

A student shall demonstrate understanding of earth and space systems by investigating and analyzing earth systems through the interaction of forces and energy, geochemical processes and cycles, theories of the origin and evolution of the universe, energy in the earth system, and the historical significance of major scientific advances

World Languages

A student shall demonstrate the ability to communicate in another language on age-appropriate topics including knowledge of cultural activities, products, and practices; and an understanding of features of the language and culture necessary for communication

Social Studies

A student shall evaluate events and actions from diverse United States and world perspectives

FIGURE 2.4. Curriculum standards. Data from Minnesota Content Standards (available at *education.state.mn.us/*).

motes this kind of intellectual rigor. If we believe in the vision represented by higher standards, students must learn to be adept at point and counterpoint, evidence and counter evidence.

And why would we doubt such standards? Consider for a moment the times in your experience—events in your career, your family history, and in your life—when you had to seriously examine a task so that you could respond appropriately. Recall the occasions when you had to take a stand and support it. The intersection of testing skills and curriculum standards represents the problem space that many adults experience every day. The important question is: How can we prepare students for their future, where analyzing and responding to varied tasks by mounting and defending arguments are stepping-stones to thriving as successful adults?

TEACHING STUDENTS ABOUT BACKWARD MAPPING

One short-term application of backward mapping for assessment is to prepare students for state and national tests. Many teachers and administrators are understandably anxious about teaching to the test, and that is not what we are recommending here. Popham (2001) makes a useful distinction between *item teaching*—using released items to teach specifically to a test—and *curriculum teaching*—teaching directed at valued content and skills, usually assessed by some form of testing. We are advocating the teaching of valued content and skills that are identified through backward mapping, such as analyzing tasks or taking a stand and defending positions with various kinds of evidence. It is not teaching to the test as much as it is developing content knowledge and skills found in the tests that is important.

Teaching students about backward mapping is one way to help them learn how to analyze tasks. We need to change the current emphasis in many classrooms from *doing and answering questions* to *analyzing* various kinds of tasks and *understanding* how to think about and respond to them. Here are some ways to start.

Think Aloud about Questions and Tasks

Whenever you assign a task to students—questions, a project, an assignment—take some time to think out loud about what skills are required to be successful. This practice is consistent with research on best practices for assessment (Stiggins, 2005). Involve students in considering questions such as:

What is the purpose of the task (question, project, assignment)?
What are the most important parts of the task (question, project, assignment)?
What does the task (questions, project, assignment) mean?
What kinds of performance (responses, answers, decisions) is the task asking for?

Avoid the Rush to the Answers

When you are teaching students to reflect on questions and other kinds of tasks, resist the urge to rush right to the answers or responses. Instead, take the time to help students reflect on the task at hand—what it says and what it means. After all, patience, reflection, and persistence are essential qualities in the classroom and in the testing room. An effective way for students to learn these behaviors is to observe teachers as they model how to think about a task.

Focus on Answers, Reasons, and Explanations

Only after spending a good deal of time working with your students on understanding questions and other kinds of tasks, consider answers, reasons, and explanations. A useful concept here is the idea of quality work. Many students view classroom tasks as something to get done and handed in without any further thought. Few may consider the kinds of work necessary to do a good job—one in which learning can take place and a good grade can be earned. Whenever you give students a task to perform, engage them in discussion of what it will take to do the task well. Many teachers use this conversation as an opportunity to develop an assessment rubric; that is, as you and your students list the qualities of an effective response, the list becomes the tool for evaluating student performances. An advantage of this approach is that students gain the opportunity to understand not only how they are going to be assessed but also what the assessment *means.* This fuller understanding puts students in a powerful position.

Another important part of working with answers consists of seeking reasons and explanations. Engage students in discussion about possible answers and why one answer may be better than another. These discussions are the context for considering what it means to take a position and defend it, what counts as evidence, as well as distinguishing between different kinds of evidence. Help students learn that just because they discover an answer to a question does not mean that that is necessarily the best answer. They also need to weigh reason and evidence.

Use Discussion, Modeling, and Guided Practice

Teachers need to show students how to become strategic in their mapping of various kinds of tasks and their responses and explanations through discussion, modeling, and guided practice. *Showing how* means labeling the strategy—*backward mapping*—discussing when it is useful—*unpacking and understanding various kinds of tasks*—and modeling how to employ the strategy to analyze and respond to various kinds of tasks. After students are given opportunities to learn about backward mapping, they need plenty of guided practice in working with the strategy.

AN EXAMPLE OF BACKWARD MAPPING

Consider this example from a middle school English class. The teacher wanted to teach her students about persuasive writing questions or prompts and how to respond to them. First, the teacher explained how the class would read and map out a question to analyze it thoroughly and consider different ways to respond—that is, the process called *backward mapping.* She also explained that this was a good approach for figuring out many different kinds of questions, even those on the state tests.

The teacher introduced a persuasive writing question that typically appears on the state writing test:

> The principal at your school has begun random locker and backpack/book bag searches to check for drugs and weapons. Anyone caught with these items will be immediately suspended and turned over to the police. The principal argues that the random searches will not only guard against illegal drugs and weapons at school but will also help students feel safer. What is your position on this issue? Write a letter to the editor of your local newspaper stating your position and supporting it with convincing reasons.

To start the backward mapping process, the teacher and her students discussed what it means to *persuade* someone rather than simply *describe* something. The prompt provided an opportunity to talk about when one should describe what the principal did versus when one should argue about whether or not the principal's actions were right.

The class then focused on the language of the question—*"the principal argues"*—*"what is your position"*—*"stating your position and supporting it with convincing reasons."* This focus led to a discussion about what it means to argue and hold a position. The students were curious about how individuals resolve differences of opinion, especially if opinions on opposing sides are very strongly held. The teacher pointed out how the question demonstrates the strength of the principal's views—that he is willing to suspend students and toss them in jail for their offenses. But the question leaves open the possibility of students suggesting an opposing opinion—disagreeing in their letter to the editor. The class discussed the need to consider their audience—the editor of the newspaper and the newspaper readers—in crafting their response. As one student suggested, "We can't just come off like little kids throwing a tantrum—we have to have good reasons!"

Next the class explored possible answers. They considered a directly opposing view: that the principal has no right whatsoever to search their property. They also considered a more moderate view: that the principal needs to be able to search, if he feels the school is in danger, but he should not be able to search without good reason. Again, the idea of audience arose. What would newspaper readers—their parents and others—think about each position? What reasons and evidence would they find acceptable? How might they disagree?

After an in-depth discussion of the essay prompt and possible answers, the class was ready to write. Because students were relatively inexperienced with persuasive writing, the teacher chose to write a whole-class essay. That way, she could model for the class good decisions about taking a position and supporting it with evidence. As she wrote the essay on an overhead projector, she was able to help students brainstorm different ways to answer and provide evidence, as well as help them learn to evaluate their responses. All along the way, the teacher reminded students what they had said about the prompt, different possible positions, evidence, and audience.

Finally, the teacher was ready for her students to practice with their individual writing. Students received a new set of prompts with a similar structure. With partners, they did think-alouds about the questions and considered possible answers before they wrote. The teacher circulated, offering feedback and advice. The teacher was pleased that her students spent a good amount of time deliberating—backward mapping the prompts—before setting out and writing. As students prepared to hand their papers in, the teacher held a class debriefing about the experience of backward mapping for persuasive writing questions.

CONCLUSIONS

Through backward mapping of assessment tasks on state and national tests, we have shown how many content area tests contain a hidden curriculum requiring students to deeply analyze and respond to varied tasks, take and defend positions, and defend a stand effectively with appropriate evidence. These are powerful life skills. Though the modern testing frenzy threatens to push aside much of the good work that has been accomplished with regard to curriculum standards, backward mapping allows us to see connections between the standards and the tests. At the core of both standards and assessment lies the need for students to learn how to prepare for, and respond to, challenging tasks, think for themselves, and communicate effectively both now and in their future. We believe that backward mapping provides the academic groundwork for this to happen.

REFERENCES

Achieve Inc. (2004). *Do graduation tests measure up?: A closer look at high school exit exams.* Washington, DC: Achieve, Inc.

Achieve Inc. (2005). *Rising to the challenge: Are high school graduates prepared for college and work?* Washington, DC: Achieve, Inc.

Conley, M. (2005). *Connecting standards and assessment though literacy.* New York: Allyn & Bacon.

Gates, W. (2005, February). [*Prepared remarks at the National Education Summit on High Schools*], Washington, DC.

Martin, M., Mullis, I., & Chrostowski, S. (2004). *Timms 2003 technical report.* Chestnut Hill, MA: TIMMS & PIRLS International Study Center, Boston College.

Popham, W. (2001). Teaching to the test? *Educational Leadership, 58*(6), 16–20.

Stiggins, R. (2005). *Student-centered classroom assessment for learning.* Englewood Cliffs, NJ: Prentice-Hall.

Wiggins, G., & McTighe, J. (1998). *Understanding by design.* Alexandria, VA: Association for Supervision and Curriculum Development.

CHAPTER 3

Promoting and Assessing Effective Literacy Learning Classroom Environments

D. Ray Reutzel
Lesley Mandel Morrow

Plato once wisely observed, "What is honored in a country will be cultivated there." And so it is in classrooms where teachers honor the development of reading and writing not only through teaching the curriculum but also through creating print-rich environments in which literacy-learning activities are an integral part of every school day.

The physical design of a classroom has been found to affect the choices children make among various learning activities (Reutzel & Cooter, 2004; Morrow & Weinstein; 1986). Classrooms that nourish literacy provide a print-rich environment, an interdisciplinary approach to promoting literacy growth, recognition of individual student differences, and a thorough understanding of the levels of literacy development. In this chapter we describe (1) the characteristics of classroom environments that support literacy learning; (2) how effective teachers create and orchestrate such environments; and (3) the types of assessments that help teachers and administrators evaluate and monitor the quality and appropriateness of classroom learning environments.

As a backdrop and as a way to create a context for the discussion that follows, we begin with a brief description of a print-rich classroom in which children participate in functional literacy activities, using materials and space that are deliberately arranged to stimulate young children's literacy development.

PORTRAIT OF A PRINT-RICH CLASSROOM

The children in Mrs. Fazzi's second grade are learning about community workers. While discussing an important news item, the children decided, in consultation with their teacher, that they wanted to have a news office in their classroom where they could be reporters, news writers, editors, and publishers of their own newspaper. Their teacher helped them create a news office where they placed writing paper, old type-writers, pencils, pens, telephones, phone directories, and computers with simple word processing software. Mrs. Fazzi supplied pamphlets, maps, and other appropriate reading materials to support various sections of the newspaper, such as sports, travel, weather, and general daily news.

After a week's effort, Mrs. Fazzi's second-grade class published its first edition of the newspaper. Damien was in charge of delivering the first week's edition to each of his classmates. Mrs. Fazzi provided a newspaper delivery bag, and each newspaper had the name of a student on it. As the delivery person, Damien had to read the names of his classmates and put the papers in the appropriate student cubby. Later, when the second-grade class read their newspapers, they shared them with great enthusiasm because each child had contributed something to the newspaper.

THEORY AND RESEARCH
CONCERNING LITERACY-RICH CLASSROOM ENVIRONMENTS

Historically, theorists and philosophers who studied child development emphasized the importance of the physical environment in learning and literacy development. Pestalozzi (Silber, 1973), Rusk and Scotland (1979), and Froebel (1974) described real-life environments in which children's learning could flourish. Both described the preparation of manipulative materials that would foster literacy development. Montessori (1965) depicted carefully prepared classroom environments intended to promote independent learning, and she recommended that every object supplied in the environment be associated with achieving a specific learning objective.

Piaget (reported in Piaget & Inhelder, 1969) found that children acquire knowledge by interacting with the world or the environment. Ideal learning settings were oriented to real-life situations, and materials were chosen to promote opportunities for children to explore and experiment. Dewey (1966) believed in an interdisciplinary approach in which subject matter or content areas were integrated. He also believed that storing materials in subject-area centers encouraged interest and learning in young children.

More recently, researchers have examined the extent to which physical arrangement of furniture, selection of materials, and the visual–aesthetic quality of a room contribute to teaching and learning (Loughlin & Martin, 1987; Morrow, 1990; Morrow, Reutzel, & Casey, 2006; Morrow & Weinstein, 1986). For example, design of spatial arrangements has been found to affect children's behavior in the classroom. Rooms partitioned into smaller spaces were found to facilitate verbal interaction and cooperative activity among peers more than did rooms with large open spaces. Children in carefully arranged rooms showed more productivity and greater use of language-related activities than did children in randomly arranged rooms (Moore, 1986; Reutzel & Cooter, 2004).

Studies that investigated the role of literacy-enriched dramatic play areas, based on themes being used in the classroom, found that they stimulated increased language and literacy activity and enhanced literacy skills (Morrow, 1990; Neuman & Roskos, 1990, 1992). These researchers also found that use of a dramatic play with story props improved story production and comprehension, including recall of details and ability to sequence and interpret.

Based on theory and research, then, early childhood and elementary classrooms that are designed to provide a literacy-rich environment and optimum literacy development will offer an abundant supply of carefully selected materials that will be housed in literacy centers accessible to children. Literacy development will be integrated with content-area teaching and reflected in materials provided in content-area learning centers. Materials and settings throughout the classroom will be designed to emulate real-life experiences and make literacy meaningful to children. They will be based on information children already possess, and they will be functional so that children see a need and purpose for using literacy to acquire new language and concepts within the variety of literacy and content-area centers.

Unfortunately, the careful preparation of a classroom's physical environment to be print-rich is often overlooked in planning instruction. Teachers and curriculum developers tend to concentrate on instructional and social factors, often giving little consideration to the visual and spatial environment in which teaching and learning occur. In the section that follows, we provide guidelines to support the preparation of effective classroom learning environments.

PREPARING PRINT-RICH LITERACY CLASSROOM ENVIRONMENTS

Studies that have investigated the physical design of classrooms (Morrow, 1990; Neuman, 1999; Neuman & Roskos, 1992) strongly suggest that by purposefully arranging the space and materials, teachers can create physical environments that exert an active, positive, and pervasive influence on literacy learning. Educators must think of their classrooms as places to project a visual atmosphere that communicates a definitive message. The following sections describe the visual presentation and design, based on the research, of a print-rich literacy classroom environment to motivate reading and writing.

Classroom Space

The effective, literacy-rich classroom is often divided into designated spaces for specific literacy learning activities (Neuman & Roskos, 1992). Literacy or content-area learning centers are particularly important spaces. Each literacy or content-area learning center is partially separated from others by furniture that houses its materials. Centers should be labeled and their materials stored on tables, on shelves, in boxes, or on a bulletin board. Each piece of equipment in a center should have its own designated spot so that teachers can direct children to it, and children can easily find and return the item. Early in a school year, a center need hold only a small number of items; new materials may be added gradually as the year progresses. The teacher should introduce the purpose, use, and placement of each item added. In classrooms too small to designate floor space as a particular center, the "center" may be designated by materials contained in a box, posters on the wall, or a basket of items.

The classroom floor plan for a preschool through first grade will also include art, music, block, and drama centers (Morrow et al., 2006). Because the working needs of early childhood classrooms are better met by table surfaces than desks, children should be provided with cubbies for storing individual work. All centers—music, art, block, and drama—should include books and writing materials.

In addition to generating a rich literacy atmosphere and an interdisciplinary approach, the literacy-rich classroom is designed to cater to different teaching methods, organizational strategies, and grouping procedures so that the differences among the children can be accommodated. The centers provide space for independent or social learning, exploration, and self-direction. Tables provide a place for whole-class instruction, as does an open area on the rug where children can sit. The teacher's conference table is a place for individual learning or small-group lessons. All furniture is, of course, movable so that any other needed teaching arrangement can be accommodated. The centers are located to create either quiet, relatively academic areas or places for more active play. The literacy center, for example, which houses the library corner and writing and oral language areas, might be next to the math center because these areas generally house activities that require relative quiet. Alternatively, art, music, dramatic play, woodworking, and block play tend to be noisier activities, so they are placed at the opposite end of the room. The teacher's conference table is situated in a quiet area that allows the teacher a view of the rest of the classroom. While the teacher is involved in small-group or individualized instruction at the conference table, the rest of the class is working independently. The table's location allows the teacher to see all the children even while working with just a few. A classroom floor plan for designing the physical classroom environment used in many nursery schools and kindergartens, and some first and second grades, is shown in Figure 3.1.

Classroom Print

Literacy-rich classrooms are filled with functional print that can be seen easily. There are labels and signs communicating meaningful information and directions (e.g., *Quiet, please,* or *Please put materials away after using them*). There are charts that help students carry out their daily activities (e.g., *Helpers, Daily Routines, Attendance,* and *Calendar;* Morrow, 2002). Labels may identify learning centers, other areas of the room, and materials. A notice board placed prominently in the room may be used to communicate with the children in writing. Experience charts and morning messages are used to display new words generated from themes, recipes used in the classroom, and science experiments conducted. Word walls display high-frequency words, new spelling words, sight words, and words that feature phonics elements. Teachers discuss and use the print in the classroom with the children to ensure that it is noticed. Children are encouraged to read and use words from the print in their writing (Morrow, 2005).

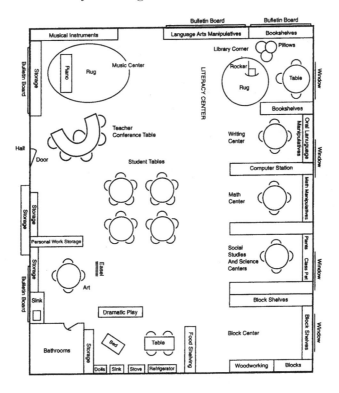

FIGURE 3.1. Classroom floor plan. Reprinted from Morrow (2005). Copyright 2005 by Allyn & Bacon. Reprinted by permission.

The Classroom Literacy Center

The literacy center, which includes the library corner and a writing area, should be the focal point in a classroom. Providing immediate access to literature and writing materials increases the number of children who participate in literacy activities during the school day. The literacy center needs to be obvious and inviting but also should afford privacy and be clearly defined. The areas should accommodate four to five children comfortably. The materials should range in difficulty to meet the needs of individual students. Each set of materials should have its own place, and children are taught to respect all materials. The literacy center should include materials for reading, writing, oral language development, and developing word-study skills.

The library corner is located within the literacy center and can house books in many ways (Reutzel & Fawson, 2002). The most traditional way is to place books on shelves with their spines showing. Shelving books by category and using some sort of coding system introduces children to the idea that books in regular libraries are organized systematically for easy access. Books can be stored in plastic bins and labeled by genre or instructional level (see Figure 3.2). In addition, open-faced shelves or plastic rain gutters permit display of full covers, thus calling attention to featured books about themes being studied; books on these shelves can be rotated every few weeks. Including five to eight books per child, representing three or four grade levels and different genres of children's literature, will ensure that there is something for everyone in the

FIGURE 3.2. Literacy center.

center. There should be folk tales, fairy tales, old favorite classics, novels, biography, magazines, riddle books, cookbooks, picture storybooks, and an equal supply of fiction and nonfiction, as well as multiple copies of popular stories so that children can choose to read the same book together.

The area may also be furnished with a rug and pillows and a rocking chair representing the Literacy Chair of Honor, where the teacher and others may read to the children. This area is where children read for pleasure, read to other children, or present stories that they have written to the class. This area should also include materials for active involvement in storybook reading and storytelling. These might include storytelling manipulatives such as a felt board with story characters, roll movies, puppets, or headsets for listening to taped stories. There might also be a private spot for reading. Teachers have used large cartons from household appliances, painted or covered with contact paper, to provide spaces for children to crawl inside and read. Posters and bulletin boards that celebrate reading may be used to decorate the area. Finally, there should be a method for checking books out of the classroom library so that children can take them home to read on their own or with their parents or siblings.

The writing area is also located within the classroom literacy center. This area requires a table and chairs plus an array of writing materials and utensils, including colored felt-tipped markers, large and small crayons, pencils (both regular and colored), chalk, a chalkboard, and paper in a variety of sizes, kinds, and colors. Materials for word study and spelling might include index cards to record children's "Very Own Words," such as high-frequency words or word patterns they may need to practice. Computers should also be located in the writing area, along with writing folders for each child. Bookmaking materials (e.g., paper, a hole-punch, a stapler, construction paper, blank books keyed to special occasions) motivate children to think of themselves as authors. Bulletin boards may display children's writing, and notice boards provide a place where messages can be exchanged among classmates or between teacher and students.

Content-Area Centers

Effective literacy instructional programs integrate literacy learning with content-area learning. Content-area centers are areas that contain material and resources specific to topics currently under study. The materials are usually manipulative and activity-oriented. They are also designed so that children can use them independently or in small groups.

Content-area centers may include activities related to social studies, science, art, music, math, literacy, or dramatic play. These centers contain materials pertinent to the content area (e.g., globes, maps, microscopes); over time, materials should be added that are specific to topics being studied (e.g., foods or food boxes for a unit on nutrition). Each subject-specific center should also include relevant literacy materials: topic-relevant texts to read or listen to, materials with which to write, and items to talk about. These materials are intended to create interest, develop new vocabulary and concepts, and provide a reason for children to participate in literacy activities.

The social studies center should be especially rich in literacy materials that help children learn about different cultures, families, friends, and the community. Themes may focus on getting along with others, recognizing and appreciating differences and likenesses in friends and family, developing respect for self and others, and developing a community of learners. In addition, social studies centers often include maps, a globe, flags from various countries, photographs or posters depicting community figures, traffic signs, and artifacts from other countries.

The science center needs interesting objects that encourage children to explore and experiment, such as magnets, simple machines, and plants. Other equipment may include an aquarium, terrarium, thermometer, compass, prism, shells, rock collections, stethoscope, kaleidoscope, and microscope (see Figure 3.3).

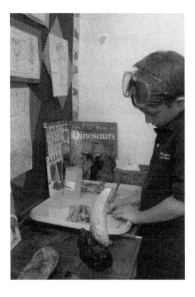

FIGURE 3.3. Content-area learning center.

PROMOTING LITERACY INTERACTIONS
IN PRINT-RICH CLASSROOMS: SIX-WEEK TRAINING

Preparing a print-rich literacy classroom environment is only the first step; as effective teachers, we must also consider how to successfully introduce children into the varied spaces we have created.

At the beginning of the school year these varied literacy spaces in and around the classroom may be fully furnished, designed, and ready for the children to use, but we encourage teachers to resist the temptation to introduce children to all of the centers at once. Instead, we recommend a period of approximately 5–6 weeks of whole-class work during which children are gradually introduced to the purpose of each center and to the expectations for using these spaces and materials.

We urge teachers to spend small amounts of time each day, perhaps 10 minutes, over several weeks explaining expectations, setting limits, and modeling procedures for using and caring for each literacy space and the accompanying literacy tools and materials. Toward the end of this 5- to 6-week introduction and instructional period, we suggest that teachers engage children in role-playing how to enter and move among the spaces of the classroom; how to properly use the materials; and how to clean up and care for the spaces and the literacy tools and materials. And finally, we recommend that teachers post a daily schedule of literacy routines to be reviewed at the start of each day (see Figure 3.4). In the section that follows, we elaborate on the steps that lead to children's effective use of literacy centers.

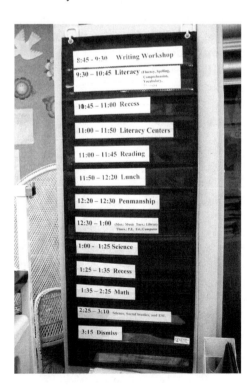

FIGURE 3.4. Daily literacy schedule.

Preparing Children to Use Literacy Spaces and Materials: Explaining, Modeling, and Limit Setting

During the first week of the school year, we suggest using the literacy spaces and materials placed in and around the room only for whole-class, teacher-guided interactions. These may include teacher-led interactive read-alouds, shared readings, and modeled and interactive writing sessions. Also, time during this first week should be spent collecting assessment data on children's ability to follow directions, listen in whole-group settings, and remain on task and focused. Teachers may also gather data on children's literacy-related knowledge of sounds in spoken language, concepts about print, letters, words, fluency, oral language or vocabulary, and comprehension. (See Chapters 5, 6, and 10 for suggestions on how to assess and document early literacy behaviors.) As well, teachers may spend a bit of time learning about children's interests, attitudes, and motivations generally and those specific to reading and writing. (See Chapter 4 for suggestions on how to assess and document motivation and interest.)

By the second week of the school year, we mention to students that in a few weeks they will be working more often in small groups and independently in the spaces designated and set up around the classroom; we explain that there is much they need to learn before they can do so. This introductory comment heightens students' curiosity and motivation to learn the expectations and procedures to eventually enter and engage these spaces and materials. We discuss what each literacy space of the classroom is for, such as a listening area, paired reading nook, alphabet and word work area, a science center, or a writing center. We explain one or two spaces per day during the second week, but we do not let the children enter or use these spaces and materials yet.

In the third week we choose one or two literacy spaces or classroom areas to fully explain, and we model how students are to enter these spaces. For example, on the first day of this third training week, we might model how students should go to the writing area in the classroom. We show children that before going to this space, they need to pick up their writing folders and quietly gather with their peers around the poster that displays the rules for working in the writing area (see Figure 3.5). On the second day, we explain that a team leader will be appointed to lead the small group in a review of the rules and directions each day. We model how this procedure is to be accomplished through a quiet oral reading of the posted rules and the directions for working in the writing area that day. We also model how the team leader is to ask if there are any questions and answer these when possible.

On the third day we model how students should take their places in the writing space and wait for the team leader to distribute any needed materials for completing the displayed task for the day. We also discuss with children the expectation that assigned tasks will be completed in the time allotted. We show children how they are to seat themselves for independent work, using independent workspace cardboard dividers, or at tables for working collaboratively in pairs or as a small group.

On the fourth day we explain the consequences for failure to follow directions and obey the rules. On the last day we model the clean-up process for the selected centers. We use a bell or some other signaling device to let children know that time for using this space has ended; we model how children are to freeze quietly in place; and we explain that the only person moving is the team leader, who gathers up the materials and returns them to their proper storage places. We then again use the bell or signal to

FIGURE 3.5. Children reading directions together.

tell children that they have 15–30 seconds to tidy up their own materials, completed tasks, and seating area within the literacy or content-area space. We end with a final bell or signal to alert children that they are to move to another literacy or content-area learning space or to return to their seats in the classroom.

Training children in procedures for using selected literacy or content-area learning spaces will likely require approximately 10 minutes per day for the entire third week of school. We typically repeat the training process at a slightly accelerated pace over the next 2 weeks (weeks 4 and 5) to introduce children to each of the remaining classroom literacy or content-area learning spaces (see Figure 3.6).

Role-Playing the Use of Literacy Spaces and Materials in the Classroom: Getting Ready to Go!

During the sixth and final week of training, we form small groups with team leaders for role-playing the use of the literacy spaces and materials around the classroom. To begin the role play, we direct students to move from their regular classroom seats to their first assigned literacy or content-area learning space. We also practice moving from one literacy space to another space, using planned rotations during the literacy time block. During this role play, anyone who fails to follow directions exactly causes the entire group to stop and practice the movement and expected behaviors. To minimize management problems later on, we remain firm about meeting expectations as children role-play their use of these spaces and materials. Typically, practicing 10 minutes per day each day for a week is sufficient to familiarize children with the routines. During this 10-minute role play, children should move from their seats into the designated literacy spaces; review and read as a small group the posted rules and daily task directions; get into proper seating arrangements within their designated

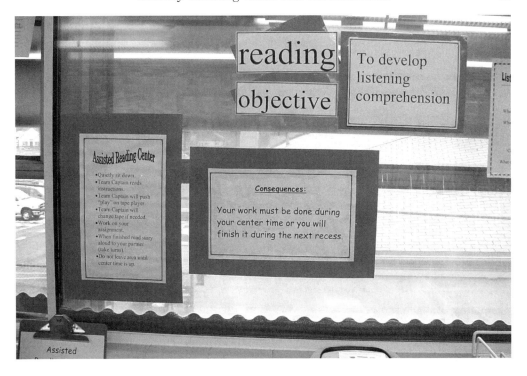

FIGURE 3.6. Literacy center with objectives, rules, and tasks defined.

literacy or content-area learning space, based on the posted task directions; distribute literacy tasks and materials; and practice the clean-up of the literacy space and materials.

Of course, during this time, children become more excited, eager, and motivated to enter these literacy or content-area learning spaces as they engage in the role-playing activities. We have found that using digital photographs of children properly engaged in the various literacy or content-area learning spaces is helpful as a model for children later on as well. One teacher we know simply asks her children if they look like the children in the picture. If not, she asks what they should do about their behavior to align it with the learning activity shown in the photograph.

Minimizing Transition Times and Maximizing Instruction and Practice

Preparing children for efficient movement between activities and into and out of various classroom literacy spaces is essential for minimizing transition times and maximizing literacy instructional time and practice. Here again, our experience has taught us the value of using timers or stopwatches to motivate children to accomplish tasks briskly and without dallying. A worthwhile goal is to reduce transition times between activities and movements to other classroom spaces to a single minute, so that the bulk of classroom time is spent on reading and writing instruction and practice. We use three steps to make this happen:

1. We use a consistent signal, such as a hotel registration bell or turning off the lights, to alert children to stop what they are doing or freeze and listen for directions.
2. We provide brief, well-sequenced, and repetitive oral directions, coupled with written directions displayed on cue cards; children must look, listen, and read to get the directions for what is to be done.
3. We use our signal device once again to alert children to follow the oral and written directions to move to the next classroom literacy center.

RELIABLE AND VALID LITERACY CLASSROOM ASSESSMENT TOOLS

It is often said that what is assessed is valued. This idea is usually applied to the topics and skills in the curriculum. However, given what we now understand about the importance of the literacy environment in helping children to reach optimal levels of achievement, many (e.g., Lipson & Wixson, 2002; Johnston, 1997) argue that assessing the quality of the learning environment is fundamental to understanding children's literacy achievement. In this section we turn to a description of assessments that may be helpful in monitoring and improving the quality of the classroom literacy learning environment.

In the past few years three valid and reliable instruments for measuring the quality of the literacy materials and interactions within early childhood and elementary classrooms have been developed: (1) *Early Language and Literacy Classroom Observation* (Smith, Dickinson, Sangeorge, & Anastasopoulos, 2002); (2) *Classroom Literacy Environmental Profile* (Wolfersberger, Reutzel, Sudweeks, & Fawson, 2004); and (3) *TEX-IN3 Observation System* (Hoffman, Sailors, Duffy, & Beretvas, 2004). In the next section we provide detailed descriptions of each of these assessment tools.

Early Language and Literacy Classroom Observation

Smith and colleagues (2002) developed the Early Language and Literacy Classroom Observation (ELLCO) instrument to provide researchers and practitioners with a comprehensive set of tools for describing the extent to which classrooms provide young children with optimal support for their literacy and language development and growth. The ELLCO toolkit is composed of three interdependent observation components: (1) Literacy Environment Checklist, (2) Classroom Observation and Teacher Interview, and (3) Literacy Activities Rating Scale.

The Literacy Environment Checklist comprises a total of 25 items within five subscales: Book Area, Book Selection, Book Uses, Writing Materials, and Writing Around the Room. Smith et al. reported that rigorous pilot testing of the Literacy Environment Checklist indicated very high levels of interrater reliability when raters were trained and appropriately supervised, as well as high levels of internal consistency among the three book subscales and the two writing subscales, suggesting that these are valid measures of the literacy environment. The authors also reported that the Literacy Environment Checklist is sensitive to changes in classroom environments, but these authors were less sure of this subscale's stability of measurement over time.

The Classroom Observation comprises ratings on a scale of 5 (exemplary) to 1 (deficient) across 16 observable dimensions of classrooms, including organization, contents, technology use, student choice and initiative, management, climate, instruction, availability of literacy materials, literacy instruction, curriculum approaches, diversity, assessment and connecting to families. The Teacher Interview is composed of six questions with associated probes that inquire into various components of the classroom observation scale.

As in the case of the Literacy Environment Checklist, the authors reported very high rates of interrater reliability among raters who were trained and appropriately supervised, and very high internal consistency scores, providing evidence of content validity. The authors also reported that the Classroom Observation Scale is both sensitive to changes in classroom environments and is a stable measurement over time.

The Literacy Activities Rating Scale comprises ratings on two scales. One rates the presence or absence of a particular activity on a dichotomous scale of yes (1) or no (0); the other rates quantitative dimensions of literacy activities on a scale ranging from 0 to 2. There are nine items with separate subscores for book reading and writing as well as a total literacy activities score.

As in the cases of the first two components of this assessment, the authors reported that the Literacy Activities Rating Scale total score has a very high level of interrater reliability among raters who were trained and appropriately supervised, and moderate scores for internal consistency, suggesting that the test is a valid measure of literacy activities in the classroom. The authors reported that the Book Reading subscores of the Literacy Activities Rating Scale were stable over time but that the Writing subscores were less so.

In sum, the ELLCO is a comprehensive, reliable, and valid tool for examining the dimensions of early childhood and early elementary classroom environments that relate to student achievement, as shown in studies of classroom literacy environments.

Classroom Literacy Environmental Profile

Wolfersberger et al. (2004) developed the Classroom Literacy Environmental Profile (CLEP), a tool for examining the "literacy richness" of early childhood and elementary classrooms. Based on a systematic and extensive review of the literature, classroom observations, and teacher focus groups, these researchers identified, defined, and organized into categories the multiple and complex characteristics of literacy-rich classroom environments.

The CLEP is composed of 33 items and two subscales. Subscale 1 (18 items) focuses on the quantity and organization of print materials and literacy tools available in the classroom. Subscale 2 (15 items) focuses on spatial organization and literacy interactions using print materials and literacy tools in the classroom. Each of the 33 items is rated on a 7-point, Likert-type rating scale.

To examine early childhood and elementary language arts classroom literacy environments using subscale 1 of the CLEP, examiners rate the quantity, utility, and appropriateness of literacy-related objects or tools, including the quantity of genres, levels, format, and content of text materials; classroom organization of print; displays of student literacy products; forms of written communication; and availability of writing utensils, writing surfaces, publishing supplies, reference materials, and technology. Using subscale 2, examiners assess storage, organization, and classroom space allocations by size, location, boundaries, and types; the presence of a classroom library; grouping and accessibility of reading and writing tools; invitations and encouragements to participate in literacy events; authentic literacy events, settings; interactions with literacy tools; variety of literacy products produced; and sharing of literacy products.

Pilot testing of the CLEP indicated that raters achieved acceptably low levels of error and high levels of reliability when rating the literacy richness of early childhood and elementary classroom environments. The researchers concluded that the CLEP is a valid and reliable tool for evaluating the print richness of early childhood and elementary classrooms in order to refine, research, and redesign classrooms to foster engaged literacy learning for all children. The CLEP also offers educators "a more calculated approach to the design of literacy enrichments in early childhood and elementary classroom environments" (Neuman & Roskos, 1992, p. 221).

TEX-IN3 Observation System

Hoffman et al. (2004) developed the TEX-IN3 to capture the range and quality of print materials in classrooms; record observations of teachers and children interacting as they used these print materials; and determine the forms, functions, and uses of these print materials by teachers and students. The name, TEX-IN3, is derived from the three subscales found within this complete and comprehensive classroom environment observation system: (1) Text Inventory, (2) Texts In-Use, and (3) Text Interviews (TEX IN x 3 or TEX-IN3).

The Text Inventory component carefully accounts for the available texts present and accessible to students within 17 different text categories, including electronic texts, process texts, games, charts, journals, leveled books, portfolios, reference materials, serials, teacher–student work, and textbooks. Each of the 17 text categories is rated on a four-category rubric using a 5-point scale. Next, the holistic text environment of the classroom is rated using a researcher-designed rubric and 5-point scale, with 5 representing an extremely rich text environment and 1 representing an inadequate text environment.

The Texts In-Use component is based on a 30-minute classroom observation. The observation period is divided into three major elements: a beginning and ending "snapshot" of who is using which texts and under which circumstances, and, in the intervening time, an intensive observation of three "focus children" and their teacher using the texts available in the classroom.

The Teacher Interview begins with the teacher rating the importance of each of the 17 text types using a scale of 1 (low level of importance) to 5 (high level of importance) in the classroom instructional program. Then the teacher rank-orders the 17 text categories from 1 (most valuable) to 17 (least valuable). During these tasks the teacher and interviewer converse about why each rating or ranking is given. At the end of the interview, the interviewer assigns a holistic rating to the teacher interview from 5 (elaborated/enriched understanding) to 1 (no knowledge). Finally, the three focus students observed during the 30-minute observation are interviewed using a series of probing questions intended to elicit the children's descriptions of the print available in the room. At the end, the interviewer rates the students' understanding using the same scale as that used at the end of the teacher's interview.

Pilot testing indicates that the TEX-IN3 has high levels of interrater reliability among pairs of raters. In addition, statistical tests suggest a strong relationship between the subscale scores and students' achievement in reading comprehension, and as such, predict a sizable portion of students' reading comprehension growth. These researchers concluded that "the TEX-IN3 is a useful tool in both evaluation and research settings" (Hoffman et al., 2004, p. 332).

SUMMARY

We began this chapter by painting a vivid portrait of a print-rich literacy classroom. We presented research showing that children's motivation, play, talk, and literacy learning are significantly affected by the quality, planning, and design of the classroom literacy environment that surrounds them on a daily basis. The inclusion of literacy materials arranged for accessibility and use creates an environmental pressure or need for students to behave differently than if such materials were not provided and accessible. Researchers have shown consistently that enriching the literacy environment results in student growth and development in literacy.

Next we described how to supply a classroom with sufficient quantities of literacy-related materials, but we also noted that quantity of literacy materials is an insufficient condition for making classrooms literacy rich. The quality, appropriateness, authenticity, and utility of the literacy materials provided in classrooms must also be carefully considered. We described ways to promote effective literacy interactions within literacy-rich classroom learning spaces, and we advocated use of a 6-week training program to train students through teacher modeling, student role playing, and clear limit setting, to properly use literacy learning spaces and materials.

Finally, we described in detail three currently available classroom environment assessment tools: the ELLCO, the CLEP, and the TEX-IN3. Each of these environmental assessment tools serves a distinct assessment purpose: the ELLCO, for examining early childhood and early elementary classroom literacy environments as well as general teacher instructional characterics; the CLEP, for examining classroom environments (without teachers and children present) for the provisioning of literacy tools, the arrangement and aggregation of literacy tools, and the organization of space for literacy learning; and the TEX-IN3, for understanding how texts are used during classroom interactions among teachers and children. These assessment tools can and should be used periodically by teachers and administrators to evaluate the contents, design, and effectiveness of classroom literacy learning environments. These excellent new assessment tools have been shown to accurately evaluate aspects of classroom literacy environments that predict later student literacy development and achievement.

REFERENCES

Bowman, B. (2003). *Essays in developing and enhancing early literacy skills of African-American children.* Washington, DC: National Black Child Development Institute.

Cambourne, B. (1988). *The whole story: Natural learning and the acquisition of literacy in the classroom.* New York: Ashton Scholastic.

Chall, J. S., Jacobs, V. A., & Baldwin, L W. (1990). *The reading crisis: Why poor children fall behind.* Cambridge, MA: Harvard University Press.

Dewey, J. (1966). *Democracy and education.* New York: First Press.

Dickinson, D. K., Sprague, K., Sayer, A., Miller, C., Clark, N., & Wolf, A. (2000). Classroom factors that foster literacy and social development of children from different language backgrounds. In M. Hopman (Chair), *Dimensions of program quality that foster child development: Reports for 5 years of the Head Start Quality Research Centers.* Poster session presented at the biannual National Head Start Research Conference, Washington, DC.

Froebel, F. (1974). *The education of man.* Clifton, NJ: August A. Kelly.

Goodman, K. S. (1986). *What's whole in whole language?* Ontario, Canada: Scholastic.

Hoffman, J. V., Sailors, M., Duffy, G., & Beretvas, S. N. (2004). The effective classroom literacy environment: Examining the validity of the TEX-IN3 Observation System. *Journal of Literacy Research, 36*(3), 303–334.

Holdaway, D. (1980). *Independence in reading.* New York: Ashton Scholastic.

Johnston, P. (1997). *Knowing literacy: Constructive literacy assessment.* York, ME: Stenhouse.

Lapp, D., & Flood, J. (1993). Are there "real" writers living in your classroom? Implementing a writer-centered classroom. *The Reading Teacher, 47,* 254–258.

Lipson, M. Y., & Wixson, K. K. (2002). *Assessment and instruction of reading and writing difficulties: An interactive approach* (3rd ed.). Boston: Allyn & Bacon.

Loughlin, C. E., & Martin, M. D. (1987). *Supporting literacy: Developing effective learning environments.* New York: Teachers College Press.

Mayfield, M. I. (1992). The classroom environment: A living-in and learning-in space. In L. O. Ollila & M. I. Mayfield (Eds.), *Emerging literacy: Preschool, kindergarten, and primary grades* (pp. 166–195). Boston: Allyn & Bacon.

Montessori, M. (1965). *Maria Montessori—Dr. Montessori's own handbook: A short guide to her ideas and materials.* New York: Schocken Books.

Moore, G. (1986). Effects of the spatial definition of behavior settings on children's behavior: A quasi-experimental field study. *Journal of Environmental Psychology, 6,* 205–231.

Morrow, L. M. (1990). Preparing the classroom environment to promote literacy during play. *Early Childhood Research Quarterly, 5,* 537–554.

Morrow, L. M. (2002). *The literacy center: Contexts for reading and writing* (2nd ed.). York, ME: Stenhouse Publishers.

Morrow, L. M. (2005). *Literacy development in the early years: Helping children read and write* (5th ed.). Boston: Allyn & Bacon.

Morrow, L. M., Reutzel, D. R., & Casey, H. (2006). Organizing and managing language arts teaching: Classroom environments, grouping practices, exemplary instruction. In J. Cooper & C. Evertson (Eds.), *Handbook of classroom management research* (pp. 559–582). Hillsdale, NJ: Erlbaum.

Morrow, L. M., & Weinstein, C. S. (1986). Encouraging voluntary reading: The impact of a literature program on children's use of library corners. *Reading Research Quarterly, 21*(3), 330–346.

Neuman, S. B. (1999). Books make a difference: A study of access to literacy. *Reading Research Quarterly, 34,* 286–311.

Neuman, S. B., & Celano, D. (2001). Access to print in low-income and middle-income communities. *Reading Research Quarterly, 36*(1), 8–27.

Neuman, S. B., & Roskos, K. (1990). The influence of literacy-enriched play settings on preschool-ers' engagement with written language. *National Reading Conference Yearbook, 39*, 179–187.

Neuman, S. B., & Roskos, K. (1992). Literacy objects as cultural tools: Effects on children's literacy behaviors in play. *Reading Research Quarterly, 27*, 202–225.

Neuman, S. B., & Roskos, K. (1993). *Language and literacy learning in the early years: An integrated approach.* New York: Harcourt, Brace Jovanovich.

Noden, H. R., & Vacca, R. T. (1994). *Whole language in middle and secondary classrooms.* New York: HarperCollins.

Piaget, J., & Inhelder, B. (1969). *The psychology of the child.* New York: Basic Books.

Pike, K., Compain, R., & Mumper, J. (1994). *New connections: An integrated approach to literacy.* New York: HarperCollins.

Reutzel, D. R., & Cooter, R. B. (2004). *Teaching children to read: Putting the pieces together* (4th ed.). Upper Saddle River, NJ: Prentice-Hall/Merrill.

Reutzel, D. R., & Fawson, P. C. (2002). *Your classroom library: New ways of giving it more teaching power.* New York: Scholastic.

Roskos, K. A., Christie, J. F., & Richgels, D. J. (2003). The essentials of early literacy instruction. *Young Children, 58*(2), 52–60.

Routman, R. (1991). *Invitations: Changing as teachers and learners K–12.* Portsmouth, NH: Heinemann.

Rusk, R., & Scotland, J. (1979). *Doctrines of the great educators.* New York: St. Martin's Press.

Silber, K. (1973). *Pestalozzi: The man and his work* (3rd ed.). New York: Schocken Books.

Smith, M. W., Dickinson, D. K., Sangeorge, A., & Anastasopoulos, L. (2002). *Early language and literacy classroom observation (ELLCO) toolkit.* Baltimore: Brookes.

Strickland, D., Snow, C., Griffin, P., Burns, M. S., & McNamara, P. (2002). *Preparing our teachers: Opportunities for better reading instruction.* Washington, DC: Joseph Henry Press.

Tomlinson, C. M., & Lynch-Brown, C. (1996). *The essentials of children's literature* (2nd ed.). Boston: Allyn & Bacon.

Tompkins, G. E. (1999). *Language arts: Content and teaching strategies* (4th ed.). Englewood Cliffs, NJ: Prentice-Hall.

U.S. Department of Education. (n.d.). *No child left behind.* Retrieved June 4, 2005, from *www.ed.gov/nclb/landing.jhtml.*

Weinstein, C. S., & Mignano, A. J., Jr. (1996). *Elementary classroom management.* New York: McGraw-Hill.

Wolfersberger, M., Reutzel, D. R., Sudweeks, R., & Fawson, P. F. (2004). Developing and validating the classroom literacy environmental profile (CLEP): A tool for examining the "print richness" of elementary classrooms. *Journal of Literacy Research, 36*(2), 211–272.

CHAPTER 4

Assessing Children's Motivation for Reading and Writing

Linda B. Gambrell
Victoria Ridgeway Gillis

Intrinsic motivation is the link between engagement in literacy activities and proficient reading and writing. Recent research has provided useful information about the characteristics of motivated literacy learners. We know that intrinsically motivated literacy learners (1) choose to read and write, (2) find pleasure in engaging in literacy activities, and (3) consciously apply knowledge and strategies to more deeply comprehend and compose text (Aarnoutse & Schellings, 2003; Guthrie & Wigfield, 2000). We also know that sound literacy instruction in phonics, fluency, vocabulary, and comprehension provides students with the skills and strategies they need to become proficient literacy learners. But, as Cunningham (2005) has so aptly put it, none of this instruction will really matter much if our students "hate to read and do so only when forced!" (p. 90). Therefore, the central issue addressed in this chapter is how teachers can assess literacy motivation in order to provide instruction that will prepare students to read and write with both interest and understanding.

Current theories of motivation focus on learners' goals, values, and beliefs (Deci & Ryan, 1992; Schunk & Zimmerman, 1997; Wigfield, 1997). Consistent with these theories, Guthrie and Wigfield (2000) suggest that literacy motivation consists of students' personal goals, values, and beliefs with regard to the topics, processes, and outcomes of literacy activities. Assessment of literacy motivation is of great importance because research suggests that learners' goals, values, and beliefs guide literacy behavior and influence achievement. In short, we believe that motivation provides the essential foundation for students' strategic literacy learning.

WHY ASSESS LITERACY MOTIVATION?

There are a number of reasons why the assessment of literacy motivation should be a high priority. First, we know that highly motivated literacy learners read more and write more than those who are less motivated to do so. Consequently, highly motivated literacy learners continue to increase in proficiency at literacy tasks, whereas those who are less motivated are more likely to achieve less than their full potential (Guthrie, Wigfield, Metsala, & Cox, 1999). Stanovich (1986) has described this phenomenon as "Matthew effects, after the Gospel According to Matthew" (p. 184), in which the rich get richer, or, in a literacy context, the more motivated literacy learners engage in more literacy activities and, as a consequence, become better readers and writers.

Second, studies have demonstrated that a reciprocal relation exists between literacy motivation and strategy use; in other words, motivation influences the use of strategies, and the use of strategies influences motivation. According to Deci, Vallerand, Pelletier, and Ryan (1991), the development of intrinsic motivation is dependent on students' competence. Therefore, literacy instruction that supports the use of strategies is likely to be empowering and motivating to students. In a year-long study, Guthrie et al. (1996) reported that 100% of the students whose increase in intrinsic motivation also increased their use of strategies; only 50% of the students who were stable or declined in intrinsic motivation increased their reading strategy use. Guthrie and Wigfield (2000) concluded that intrinsic motivation is essential for strategy learning. In addition, this study suggested that the acquisition of literacy strategies and the motivation for using them are likely to be mutually enhancing.

Third, several research studies support the conclusion that there is a critical link between literacy motivation and achievement (Cipielewski & Stanovich, 1992; Purves & Beach, 1972; Guthrie, Schafer, Wang, & Afflerbach, 1995; Walberg & Tsai, 1985). Students who engage in frequent and sustained literacy tasks improve in their ability to comprehend text (Cipielewski & Stanovich, 1992). In a study that comprised a national sample of 9-, 13-, and 17-year-old students, the more highly engaged readers had higher achievement than the less-engaged readers (Campbell, Voelkl, & Donahue, 1997). The results of these studies clearly indicate the need to (1) increase our understanding of how children acquire the motivation to develop into active, engaged readers and writers, and (2) explore ways of assessing literacy motivation in order to provide learning experiences that foster literacy development.

CONSIDERATIONS IN ASSESSING LITERACY MOTIVATION

Researchers who have conducted studies with students during the elementary and middle school years have found consistent and significant differences in literacy motivation with respect to age, interest, and gender. When assessing literacy motivation, it is important to consider the evidence related to each of these factors.

Literacy Motivation across Grade Levels

A consistent finding in the research literature is that literacy motivation declines as children progress through the grades from the elementary level through high school, with the greatest decline occurring from grade 1 to grade 4 (Eccles, Wigfield, & Schiefele, 1998; McKenna, Kear, & Ellsworth, 1995; Oldfather & Dahl, 1994; Wigfield et al., 1997). It appears that younger children are more highly motivated to read and that the motivational level continues to diminish over time as they progress through the grades.

One interesting exception to this linear trend was reported in a cross-cultural study of early literacy motivation conducted by Mazzoni, Gambrell, and Korkeamaki (1999). The most striking finding from this study was that in both the United States and Finland, first graders' reading motivation increased significantly from the beginning of the school year to the end of the year, whereas second graders' reading motivation decreased. In this study, students entered first grade with a high level of reading motivation, and the level of motivation increased during the school year and held constant through the summer months to the beginning of second grade. A statistically significant decrease in motivation occurred from the beginning of second grade to the end of second grade. A possible explanation for this finding is that younger children may not have experienced significant literacy failure or frustration and consequently maintain high levels of literacy motivation throughout first grade. It appears that at about second grade, children's awareness of their own literacy performance increases, likely in response to the evaluative feedback they receive. For some children this growing awareness that they are not as able as some of their peers may lead to a decrease in literacy motivation (Guthrie & Wigfield, 2000). The decrease in motivation that occurs during second grade suggests that this may be a critical time to assess literacy motivation and raises questions about what classroom interventions might support students, particularly struggling readers and writers, in maintaining high levels of literacy motivation.

In addition to evidence of steadily decreasing levels of motivation across the grade levels, it is important to note that a national study conducted by McKenna et al. (1995) investigated the link between motivational level and reading ability level. The results of that study revealed that whereas above-average and average-ability readers' attitudes toward reading remained fairly stable, the attitudes of below-average readers steadily decreased as they progressed through the elementary grades.

Literacy Motivation and Gender

Research on gender differences in reading motivation has been consistent, revealing that girls tend to possess more positive attitudes toward reading than boys (Askov & Fischbach, 1973; McKenna et al., 1995). Given the consistency of the research on gender differences, it would be reasonable to expect that girls would have higher motivation scores than boys on literacy motivation assessments. However, we would urge teachers to keep a longstanding truism in mind: Students are individuals and should be treated as such if we expect to optimize their motivation and learning (Brophy, 2004).

Literacy Motivation and Topic or Task Interest

Interest refers to the disposition to engage in activities such as reading and writing when opportunities arise (Brophy, 2004). Research suggests that students are more motivated when they read materials that they find interesting—that is, materials that elicit heightened attention, concentration, and comprehension (Hidi & Harackiewicz,

2000; Krapp, 2002; Renninger, 2000). Students are more motivated to engage in literacy activities when they have positive affective responses to the content or processes. One way to increase the potential for high levels of literacy motivation is to provide text-to-topic choices, which allow students to pursue their own interests.

Tools for Assessing Literacy Motivation

Educators have become increasingly aware of the importance of literacy motivation, particularly with respect to students' progress in developing high levels of literacy proficiency. Research suggests that intrinsic motivation is associated with higher reading achievement, deeper cognitive processing, greater conceptual understanding, and willingness to persevere when literacy activities are challenging or difficult (Grolnick & Ryan, 1987; Guthrie et al., 1999; Schiefele, 1991; Turner, 1995). Given the importance of intrinsic motivation, several tools have been developed to assess literacy motivation for young children (K–2), elementary children, and middle-grade students.

Tools developed to assess literacy motivation have emphasized a range of constructs and theoretical orientations. Most of these tools also provide some insight into the role of self-concept and the value of literacy as critical constructs of motivation. The self-concept component is supported by a number of research studies that suggest that students who believe they are capable and competent are more likely to outperform those who do not hold such beliefs (Turner, 1995; Wigfield et al., 1997). There is also evidence that students who perceive literacy as valuable and important and who have personally relevant reasons for reading and writing will engage in literacy activities in a more planful and effortful manner (Turner, 1995; Schiefele, 1991). In the section that follows we provide a brief overview of several literacy motivation assessments, examples of items, and references for additional assessment tools at each level.

Assessments of Early Literacy Motivation

A number of considerations come into play in assessing early literacy motivation. First, as mentioned earlier, the scores of young children on literacy motivation assessments tend to be inflated because at this stage they have not yet experienced notable failure or frustration. Second, it is more difficult to administer assessments to young children because they are not yet proficient readers and writers; therefore, most assessments must be administered individually. In the section below, one instrument that does not require the students to be able to read is briefly overviewed, and references for other literacy assessments for preschool through first grade are provided.

The *Me and My Reading Survey* (MMRS; Mazzoni et al., 1999) was designed to assess the reading motivation and behaviors of young children in grades 1 and 2. It consists of 17 items in a multiple-choice format. The items are based on a 2-, 3-, or 4-point response scale. Cronbach's (1951) alpha statistic yielded a reliability coefficient of .72, a value that suggests "good" reliability. This instrument was developed to be used for individual, small-group, and whole-class administration. The teacher or administrator reads the items aloud as children follow along using pictures. For small-group and whole-class administration, children must know and be able to recognize the numbers 1–4. For struggling learners and children below first grade, the survey should be administered individually. Figure 4.1 presents sample items from the survey. See Figure

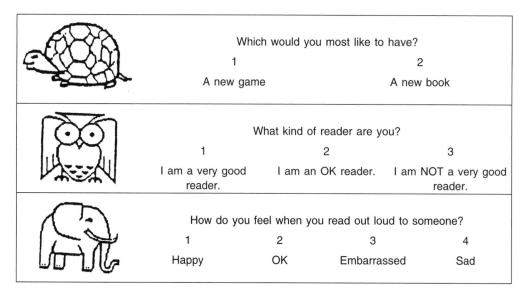

FIGURE 4.1. Sample items from the *Me and My Reading Survey*. From Mazzoni, Gambrell, and Korkeamaki (1999). Copyright 1999 by Routledge. Reprinted by permission.

Saracho, O. N. (1996). The development of the Preschool Reading Attitude Scale. *Child Study Journal, 16*, 113–124.
Baker, L., & Scher, D. (2002). Beginning readers' motivation for reading in relation to parental beliefs and home reading experiences. *Reading Psychology, 23*, 239–269.

FIGURE 4.2. Additional resources for assessing motivation of early readers.

4.2 for additional sources of tools for assessing early literacy motivation that are appropriate for use with preschool, kindergarten, and first-grade children.

Assessments of Literacy Motivation for Elementary-Age Students

Numerous literacy assessment tools are available for use with elementary-age students. In this section we overview an assessment tool that focuses on reading, as well as one of the few that provides information about motivation to write, and we provide references for several other assessment tools that are appropriate for the elementary grades.

The *Motivation to Read Profile* (MRP) has two components: the reading survey and the conversational interview (Gambrell, Palmer, Codling, & Mazzoni, 1996). The reading survey is a self-report, group-administered instrument that is designed to assess two dimensions of motivation: self-concept as a reader and value of reading. The conversational interview, designed for individual administration, provides information about the individual nature of students' reading motivation, such as what books and stories are most interesting, favorite authors, and where and how children locate read-

When I am reading by myself, I understand
- almost everything I read
- some of what I read
- almost none of what I read
- none of what I read

I worry about what other kids think about my reading
- every day
- almost every day
- once in a while
- never

FIGURE 4.3. Sample items from the Motivation to Read Profile reading survey. From Gambrell, Palmer, Codling, and Mazzoni (1996). Copyright 1996 by the International Reading Association. Reprinted by permission.

ing materials that interest them most. There are three sections of the MRP conversational interview: One focuses on the reading of narrative text, one focuses on the reading of informational text, and the third focuses on general reading. The MRP is highly individualized, making it particularly appropriate for inclusion in portfolio assessment. Sample items from each of the two components are presented in Figures 4.3 and 4.4.

Assessment tools that focus on the writing process are rare. One that has been developed for elementary-age children is the *Writer Self-Perception Scale* (WSPS). It is designed to provide information about fourth-, fifth-, and sixth-grade students' attitudes toward writing (Bottomley, Henk, & Melnick, 1998). It is grounded in Bandura's (1977) theory of perceived self-efficacy, which posits that a student's self-perception of

- Narrative—Tell me about the most interesting story or book you have read this week (or even last week). Take a few minutes to think about it. (Wait-time).
     Now tell me about the book or story.

     Probes: What else can you tell me?

     Is there anything else?

- Informational—Why was this book (or article) important to you?

- General—What do you think you have to learn to be a better reader?

FIGURE 4.4. Sample items from the Motivation to Read conversational interview. From Gambrell, Palmer, Codling, and Mazzoni (1996). Copyright 1996 by the International Reading Association. Reprinted by permission.

- General Progress—Writing is easier for me than it used to be.

- Specific Progress—When I write, the sentences and paragraphs fit together better than they used to.

- Observational Comparison—The words I use in my writing are better than the ones other kids use.

- Social Feedback—My classmates would say I write well.

- Physiological States—I am relaxed when I write.

FIGURE 4.5. Sample items from the Writer Self-Perception Scale. From Bottomley, Henk, and Melnick (1998). Copyright 1998 by the International Reading Association. Reprinted by permission.

McKenna, M. C., & Kear, D. J. (1990). Measuring attitude toward reading: A new tool for teachers. *The Reading Teacher, 43,* 626–639.
Wigfield, A. (1997). Children's motivations for reading and reading engagement. In J. T. Guthrie & A. Wigfield (Eds.), *Reading engagement: Motivating readers through integrated instruction* (pp. 14–33). Newark, DE: International Reading Association.

FIGURE 4.6. Additional resources for assessing reading motivation of elementary-age students.

writing ability will affect subsequent writing growth and development. The WSPS is appropriate for classroom, small-group, and individual administration. Students respond to 38 items using a 5-point scale: *strongly agree, agree, undecided, disagree, strongly disagree.* Information is provided in five subareas: general progress, specific progress, observational comparison, social feedback, and physiological states. A sample of test items is presented in Figure 4.5. See Figure 4.6 for additional sources of tools that are appropriate for assessing the literacy motivation of elementary-age students.

Assessments of Literacy Motivation for Middle-Grade Students

Relatively few literacy assessment tools have been specifically designed for use with middle-grade students. Adolescent motivation to read is complicated by a variety of factors, including (1) observed differences between in- and out-of-school literacy activities (Ivey & Broaddus, 2001; Knobel, 2001); (2) the devaluing of out-of-school literacy activities by schools (Nagle, 1999); (3) documented complexities of adolescent readers themselves (Ivey, 1999); (4) the contextual nature of adolescent motivation (Guthrie & Davis, 2003); and (5) indications that adolescent motivation to read decreases for in-school reading but not necessarily for out-of-school reading (Bintz, 1993).

In an effort to better understand adolescent motivation as it relates to literacy, a group of researchers with a common interest in adolescent literacy collaboratively revised the MRP survey and conversational interview (Gambrell et al., 1996) to be more appropriate for adolescents. The resulting *Adolescent Motivation to Read Profile* (AMR; Albright et al., 2004) consists of a group-administered survey and an individually administered conversational interview. In addition, as suggested by Alvermann (2001), questions were added to the conversational interview to include electronic resources; as well, as suggested by Wasserstein (1995), questions were added to investigate students' impressions of schoolwork and projects that are most memorable. These particular questions were designed to understand why some students choose to read and write on their own but do not choose to do so in school (Roe, 1997). Sample items from each section of the AMR are presented in Figures 4.7 and 4.8.

Results of the initial use of the AMR profile indicated that survey responses were influenced by students' conceptualization that reading was an in-school activity, but that literate activities engaged in outside of school did not qualify as reading (Albright et al., 2004). For example, a student who responded that he read "not very often" reported learning important information about new fishing tactics from *Field and Stream*. Another student who considered himself "a poor reader" identified Michael Crichton's book about time travel as the most recent interesting book he had read. Resulting inconsistencies between the survey responses and information shared in the conversational interview led us to conclude that when working with adolescents, survey data should be supplemented by other forms of data collection, including interviews. See Figure 4.9 for sources of other tools for assessing reading motivation that are appropriate for use with middle-grade students.

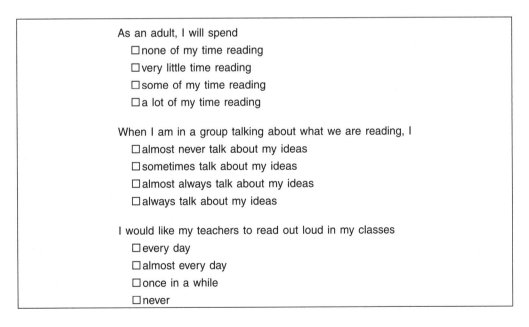

As an adult, I will spend
   ☐ none of my time reading
   ☐ very little time reading
   ☐ some of my time reading
   ☐ a lot of my time reading

When I am in a group talking about what we are reading, I
   ☐ almost never talk about my ideas
   ☐ sometimes talk about my ideas
   ☐ almost always talk about my ideas
   ☐ always talk about my ideas

I would like my teachers to read out loud in my classes
   ☐ every day
   ☐ almost every day
   ☐ once in a while
   ☐ never

FIGURE 4.7. Sample items from the Adolescent Motivation to Read Profile. From Albright et al. (2004). Reprinted by permission of the authors.

Do you have a computer in your home?
  If they answer yes, ask the following questions:
    How much time do you spend on the computer a day?
    What do you usually do?
    What do you like to read when you are on the Internet?
  If they answer no, ask the following questions:
    If you did have a computer in your home, what would you like to do with it?
    Is there anything on the Internet that you would like to be able to read?

- What class do you most like to read in? Why?

- In what class do you feel the reading is the most difficult? Why?

- Do you share and discuss books, magazines, or other reading materials with your friends outside of school? What? How often? Where?

- Do you write letters or email to friends or family? How often?

- Do you belong to any clubs or organizations for which you read and write? Could you explain what kind of reading/writing it is?

FIGURE 4.8. Sample items from the Adolescent Motivation to Read Profile conversational interview. From Albright et al. (2004). Reprinted by permission of the authors.

Guthrie, J. T., & Davis, M. H. (2003). Motivating struggling readers in middle school through an engagement model of classroom practice. *Reading & Writing Quarterly, 19,* 59–85. (Note: Although the complete instrument is not provided in this article, sufficient information is provided so that teachers or researchers could structure their own assessment.)
Martin, A. J. (2001). The Student Motivation Scale: A tool for measuring and enhancing motivation. *Australian Journal of Guidance and Counseling, 11,* 1–20.

FIGURE 4.9. Additional resources for assessing motivation of adolescent students.

CONCLUSION

Because children's literacy motivation plays a significant role in their literacy learning, the assessment of motivation to read and write should be a high priority in the curriculum. Information provided by literacy assessment tools can be used to enhance instruction. Research indicates that children and adolescents are more likely to read and engage in discussions about what they have read when appropriate books are available to them and when they are able to make choices about what they read. Research also indicates that engaged and motivated readers are more likely to use strategies as they read, thus increasing comprehension and achievement. The relationship between literacy motivation and frequency of reading, strategy use, and achievement makes literacy motivation one of the crucial factors in the classroom—one that no teacher can afford to ignore. In this chapter we have presented assessment tools that address literacy motivation for early literacy, elementary grades, and adolescents. Teachers who understand the importance of, and assess, motivation are in a better position to influence students' literacy motivation.

REFERENCES

Aarnoutse, C., & Schellings, G. (2003). Learning reading strategies by triggering reading motivation. *Educational Studies, 29*(4), 387–409.

Albright, L., DeLaney, C. J., Dunston, P. J., Headley, K. N., Moggie, S., Pitcher, S. M., et al. (2004, December). *Adolescent Motivation to Read Profile.* Presented at the 54th National Reading Conference, San Antonio, TX.

Alvermann, D. E. (2001). *Effective literacy instruction for adolescents.* Oak Creek, WI: National Reading Conference. Retrieved February 7, 2005, from *www.nrconline.org/publications/alverwhite2.pdf.*

Askov, E. N., & Fischbach, T. J. (1973). An investigation of primary pupils' attitudes toward reading. *Journal of Experimental Education, 41*, 1–7.

Baker, L., & Scher, D. (2002). Beginning readers' motivation for reading in relation to parental beliefs and home reading experiences. *Reading Psychology, 23*, 239–269.

Bandura, A. (1977). Self-efficacy: Toward a unifying theory of behavioral change. *Psychological Review, 84*, 191–215.

Bintz, W. P. (1993). Resistant readers in secondary education: Some insights and implications. *Journal of Reading, 36*, 604–615.

Bottomley, D. M., Henk, W. A., & Melnick, S. A. (1998). Assessing children's views about themselves as writers using the Writer Self-Perception Scale. *The Reading Teacher, 51*, 286–296.

Brophy, J. (2004). *Motivating students to learn.* Mahwah, NJ: Erlbaum.

Campbell, J. R., Voelkl, K. E., & Donahue, P. L. (1997). *NAEP 1996 trends in academic progress* (NCES Publication No. 97–985). Washington, DC: U.S. Department of Education.

Cipielewski, J., & Stanovich, K. E. (1992). Predicting growth in reading ability from children's exposure to print. *Journal of Experimental Child Psychology, 54*, 74–89.

Cronbach, L. J. (1951). Coefficient alpha and the internal structure of texts. *Psychometrika, 16*, 297–334.

Cunningham, P. (2005). "If they don't read much, how they ever gonna get good?" *The Reading Teacher, 59*(1), 88–90.

Deci, E .L., & Ryan, R. M. (1992). The initiation and regulation of intrinsically motivated learning and achievement. In A. K. Boggiano & T. S. Pittman (Eds.), *Achievement and motivation: A social developmental* perspective (pp. 3–36). Toronto: Cambridge University Press.

Deci, E. L., Vallerand, R. J., Pelletier, L. G., & Ryan, R. M. (1991). Motivation and education: The self-determination perspective. *Educational Psychologist, 26*, 325–346.

Eccles, J. S., Wigfield, A., & Schiefele, U. (1998). Motivation to succeed. In W. Damon (Series Ed.) and N. Eisenberg (Ed.), *Handbook of child psychology: Social, emotional and personality development* (Vol. 3, 5th ed., pp. 189–214). New York: Wiley.

Gambrell, L. B., Palmer, B. M., Codling, R. M., & Mazzoni, S. A. (1996). Assessing motivation to read. *The Reading Teacher, 49*, 518–533.

Grolnick, W. S., & Ryan, R. M. (1987). Autonomy in children's learning: An experimental and individual difference investigation. *Journal of Personality and Social Psychology, 52*, 890–898.

Guthrie, J. T., & Davis, M. H. (2003). Motivating struggling readers in middle school through an engagement model of classroom practice. *Reading and Writing Quarterly, 19*, 59–85.

Guthrie, J. T., Schafer, W. D., Wang, Y. Y., & Afflerbach, P. (1995). Relationships of instruction of reading: An exploration of social, cognitive, and instructional connections. *Reading Research Quarterly, 30*(1), 8–25.

Guthrie, J. T., Van Meter, P., McCann, A. D., Wigfield, A., Bennett, L. M, Poundstone, C. C., et al. (1996). Growth of literacy engagement: Changes in motivations and strategies during concept-oriented reading instruction. *Reading Research Quarterly, 31,* 306–332.

Guthrie, J. T., & Wigfield, A. (2000). Engagement and motivation in reading. In M. L. Kamil, P. B. Mosenthal, P. D. Pearson, & R. Barr (Eds.), *Handbook of reading research* (Vol. 3, pp. 403–422). New York: Longman.

Guthrie, J. T., Wigfield, A., Metsala, J. L., & Cox, K. E. (1999). Motivational and cognitive predictors of text comprehension and reading amount. *Scientific Studies of Reading, 3*(3), 231–256.

Hidi, S., & Harackiewicz, J. (2000). Motivating the academically unmotivated: A critical issue for the 21st century. *Review of Educational Research, 70,* 151–179.

Ivey, G. (1999). A multicase study in the middle school: Complexities among young adolescent readers. *Reading Research Quarterly, 34,* 172–192.

Ivey, G., & Broaddus, K. (2001). "Just plain reading": A survey of what makes students want to read in middle school classrooms. *Reading Research Quarterly, 36,* 350–377.

Knobel, M. (2001). "I'm not a pencil man": How one student challenges our notions of literacy "failure" in school. *Journal of Adolescent and Adult Literacy, 44,* 404–414.

Krapp, A. (2002). An educational–psychological theory of interest and its relation to SDT. In E. L. Deci & R. M. Ryan (Eds.), *Handbook of self-determination research* (pp. 405–427). Rochester, NY: University of Rochester Press.

Martin, A. J. (2001). The Student Motivation Scale: A tool for measuring and enhancing motivation. *Australian Journal of Guidance and Counseling, 11,* 1–20.

Mazzoni, S. A., Gambrell, L. B, & Korkeamaki, R. (1999). A cross-cultural perspective of early literacy motivation. *Journal of Reading Psychology, 20*(3), 237–253.

McKenna, M. C., & Kear, D. J. (1990). Measuring attitude toward reading: A new tool for teachers. *The Reading Teacher, 43,* 626–639.

McKenna, M. C., Kear, D. J., & Ellsworth, R. A. (1995). Children's attitudes toward reading: A national survey. *Reading Research Quarterly, 30,* 934–956.

Oldfather, P., & Dahl, K. (1994). Toward a social constructivist reconceptualization of intrinsic motivation for literacy learning. *Journal of Reading Behavior, 26,* 139–158.

Purves, A. C., & Beach, R. (1972). *Literature and the reader: Research in response to literature, reading interests, and the teaching of literature.* Urbana, IL: National Council of Teachers of English.

Renninger, K. A. (2000). Individual interest and its implications for understanding intrinsic motivation. In C. Sansone & J. Harackiewicz (Eds.), *Intrinsic and extrinsic motivation: The search for optimal motivation and performance* (pp. 373–404). San Diego, CA: Academic Press.

Roe, M. F. (1997). Combining enablement and engagement to assist students who do not read and write well. *Middle School Journal, 28*(2), 35–41.

Saracho, O. N. (1996). The development of the Preschool Reading Attitude Scale. *Child Study Journal, 16,* 113–124.

Schiefele, U. (1991). Interest, learning, and motivation. *Educational Psychologist, 26*(3 & 4), 299–323.

Schunk, D. H., & Zimmerman, B. J. (1997). Developing self-efficacious readers and writers: The role of social and self-regulatory processes. In J. T. Guthrie & A. Wigfield (Eds.), *Reading engagement: Motivating readers through integrated instruction* (pp. 34–50). Newark, DE: International Reading Association.

Stanovich, K. E. (1986). Matthew effects in reading: Some consequences of individual differences in the acquisition of literacy. *Reading Research Quarterly, 21,* 360–406.

Turner, J. C. (1995). The influence of classroom contexts on young children's motivation for literacy. *Reading Research Quarterly, 30,* 410–441.

Walberg, H. J., & Tsai, S. (1985). Correlates of reading achievement and attitude: A national assessment study. *Journal of Educational Research, 78,* 159–167.

Wasserstein, P. (1995). What middle schoolers say about their schoolwork. *Educational Leadership, 53*(1), 41–43.

Wigfield, A. (1997). Children's motivations for reading and reading engagement. In J. T. Guthrie & A. Wigfield (Eds.), *Reading engagement: Motivating readers through integrated instruction* (pp. 14–33). Newark, DE: International Reading Association.

Wigfield, A., Eccles, J. S., Yoon, K. S., Harold, R. D., Arbreton, A. J. A., Freedman-Doan, C., et al. (1997). Change in children's competence beliefs and subjective task values across the elementary school years: A 3–year study. *Journal of Educational Psychology, 89*(3), 451–469.

PART II

Assessing Word Knowledge and Reading Fluency

CHAPTER 5

Language and Literacy Assessment in Preschool

Lea M. McGee

The purpose of this chapter is to describe a comprehensive model of assessment that outlines a systematic approach to measuring language and literacy development in preschool. First, I discuss the essential features of a comprehensive assessment model. Next, I argue that effective assessment in language and literacy is based on a developmental continuum of language and literacy learning that specifies essential outcomes in five foundational areas of language and literacy. For each of these areas I suggest several formal and informal methods of assessment. This discussion provides an important backdrop from which teachers can make decisions about selecting a small set of informal or more formal assessment tools that they will use as a part of their larger assessment plan for program evaluation and screening purposes. Then I discuss issues related to assessing young children 3–5 years old and end the chapter by describing how to integrate ongoing observation of individual children within the balanced assessment plan in order to serve as monitoring assessment. The underlying theme of the chapter is that systematic assessment, including the use of informal and (when required) more formal assessment tools, coupled with regular and frequent observations of children during self-initiated reading and writing activities, provides the best evidence of what children can do and of program effectiveness.

THE ROLE OF ASSESSMENT IN PRESCHOOL: TOWARD A MODEL OF COMPREHENSIVE ASSESSMENT

Assessment has always been a part of preschool, and its ethical and appropriate use has long been of concern in the field of early childhood education (e.g., see Bredekamp & Rosegrant, 1992). Clearly all teaching involves assessing how well children are learning and whether classroom activities are having a positive influence on all areas of children's development. Because learning is defined as the construction of new understandings that arise from a foundation of existing knowledge (Bowman, Donovan, & Burns, 2000), teachers must have a clear understanding of children's current knowledge. Thus, ongoing assessments of children's current conceptual development are a critical component of instructional planning. Most early childhood teachers, at least informally, engage in this cycle of assessment and instruction. When children are not making advancements, given appropriate instruction and classroom activities, teachers consider how best to adjust classroom instruction or consider the need for intervention services. However, fewer early childhood teachers employ a systematic and comprehensive model of assessment in which they collect and analyze data at the level of individual children, but they do participate in analyzing aggregated data across groups of children to make decisions about adjustments in program content, intensity of instruction, and effectiveness of instructional approaches.

A comprehensive and systematic model of assessment would involve a process of collecting, analyzing, and interpreting information about children as they operate in a classroom setting (Epstein, Schweinhart, DeBruin-Parecki, & Robin, 2004). Such a model would also specify what is to be measured (Clay, 1998), informed by an understanding of the broad range of possible language and literacy learning outcomes that might arise during the early childhood years. Finally, a comprehensive assessment model would specify how and when children would be assessed.

In the past, most assessments in preschool consisted almost entirely of teacher observation, and standardized tests were all but banned prior to third grade. However, spurred by requirements in No Child Left Behind and Head Start, preschool children are increasingly being assessed with standardized tests. The current demand for more reliable and valid measures of children's cognitive development—especially language and literacy development—have made the use of these formal assessments more prevalent in today's preschool classrooms. Although all assessments range on a continuum from more formal to informal, standardized tests represent the most formal of all assessments. These tests are administered by trained administrators using standardized directions under standardized conditions. Standardized tests are considered objective because teachers make few or no inferences when scoring results, and the results can be used to make decisions about the performance of groups of children. When used along with other forms of assessments, they can also be used to make decisions about individual children.

Standardized tests used in preschool are usually administered two, or at most three, times during a school year and are more likely, when data are aggregated across groups of children, to be used for program evaluation purposes. For example, the Head Start National Reporting system requires that all Head Start programs administer a set of language, literacy, and numeracy assessments at the beginning and end of the year (U.S. Department of Health and Human Services, 2003). These results are aggregated across groups of children, not individual children, and used to provide feedback for changes in local programs. Teachers in Head Start, as in all preschool programs, are also expected to assess children frequently with more informal measures to ensure that all children are making progress toward achieving appropriate developmental goals. These additional assessments are used to serve two goals: (1) Screening assessments are used to identify initial levels of development and to identify children who may need specific intervention services or more intensive instruction or experiences in particular developmental domains; and (2) monitoring assessments are used to ensure that all children are making adequate progress toward achieving appropriate goals as well and to determine whether adjustments in classroom routines or instruction are suggested for individuals or groups of children (McConnell et al., 1998).

In summary, a comprehensive assessment model would serve several purposes. It would allow teachers to screen children's current level of knowledge and monitor whether instruction and classroom activities are having a positive effect on learning and development. These data could be used to consider ways to adjust classroom routines and instructional activities. The data would also allow teachers to identify children whose progress significantly differs from other children and from expected progress. Finally, data could be aggregated across groups of children to monitor program effectiveness and to determine adjustments at the program level. In order to meet these purposes, a comprehensive assessment program would have eight essential features:

1. A developmentally appropriate description of language and literacy outcomes expected to emerge at the end of preschool, with benchmarks indicating progress in a variety of language and literacy domains.
2. A small number of valid and reliable, perhaps standardized, measures aligned with expected outcomes that could be adapted to meet special needs and populations (e.g., Spanish-speaking children), which are administered at least twice yearly.
3. A procedure to select a smaller number of these valid and reliable measures to be administered quarterly for monitoring purposes.
4. Procedures to ensure that teachers or others are adequately prepared to administer and analyze these measures to maximize validity and reliability.
5. Procedures to systematically collect samples of children's behavior, language, and writing from ongoing classroom activities on a bimonthly or monthly basis.
6. Procedures to ensure that teachers are adequately prepared to observe, record, and analyze data during classroom activities in ways that are integrated with data collected from other sources and used to make instructional decisions about individuals and groups of children.
7. Procedures to aggregate data across children and to use data to make changes in programs.
8. Procedures to communicate data to all stakeholders, including parents, teachers, administrators, and other agencies of concern.

THE HEART OF A COMPREHENSIVE ASSESSMENT PLAN: A DEVELOPMENTAL CONTINUUM OF LANGUAGE AND LITERACY OUTCOMES

Early childhood professionals have long been guided by descriptions of typical development that lay out developmental milestones for various ages of children from infants and toddlers to the end of preschool. Many continua that describe young children's growth in all areas of child development are available (see, e.g., Dodge, Colker, & Heroman, 2001), and many of these include sections on language and literacy development. In addition, the International Reading Association and National Association for the Education of Young Children (1998) have developed a continuum describing children's language and literacy development. Although these continua provide a critical starting point for making decisions about what to measure, my experience has shown that all children do not proceed through a prescribed sequence of developmental milestones as described in any developmental continuum (Clay, 1998). Rather, each child's pathway from emergent to conventional literacy seems to be unique, although broadly speaking, children seem to go through the same general phases of development (see, e.g., McGee & Richgels, 2004).

Although children do not seem to follow precisely the same path through developmental milestones, certain components of early literacy development have been shown to be highly related to later literacy achievement. As researchers have sought to identify the critical components of early literacy that seem to matter in preschool, they have found that children's early development of conventional foundational skills is critical for later success. Researchers have found that before entering kindergarten, a child's level of knowledge in five categories is directly related to later reading and writing success or failure (summarized in Snow, Burns, & Griffin, 1998): (1) alphabet knowledge, (2) phonological and phonemic awareness, (3) phonics and the alphabetic principle, (4) concepts about print and books, and (5) oral comprehension and vocabulary. In the following sections I describe what we know about children's development of these components of language and literacy development. Then I describe a range of methods for assessing these critical components.

ALPHABET KNOWLEDGE

During preschool children begin learning about alphabet letters, although not all preschoolers will learn to recognize all the upper and lower case alphabet letters. Yet, the most successful readers and writers are often those children who enter kindergarten already recognizing most alphabet letters. Thus it is critical that preschool children gain a high level of alphabet knowledge, including the ability to write alphabet letters.

The Development of Alphabet Knowledge

Preschoolers do begin to recognize alphabet letters, and research has shown that 4-year-olds typically know more than half of the alphabet letters by name (Trieman, Sotak, & Bowman, 2001). Preschoolers also learn to write recognizable alphabet letters, although their motor control is still developing and their sense of orientation is still evolving. Therefore, alphabet writing in preschool includes letter reversals and unconventional letter formations often called *mock letters* (McGee & Richgels, 2004). Learning to recognize, name, and write alphabet letters, however, involves several underlying concepts (Bloodgood, 1999), and this knowledge emerges only after children find letters important and meaningful to them.

First, children realize that print, composed of alphabet letters, communicates a message. Most children come to these insights through experiences with print in their homes. Some children acquire this basic understanding when they are as young as 2 or

3 years old, for example, as they talk about Rice Krispies while they eat cereal and gaze at the text on the box. Other children make this insight as they are taught to recognize and write their names. As a part of these experiences, children develop concepts about the purpose of letters. For example, one preschooler, Kristen, at 3 years old, pointed to the letter *K* in *K-Mart* and said, "That's my letter." Like Kristen, many preschoolers may not be able to identify letters, such as *K*, by name; nonetheless, they are aware that letters are used to convey meaningful messages.

Children's growing ability to write their names often parallels their ability to recognize and write letters. For example, Figure 5.1 presents Vin Chinzo's signature written in (a) October, (b) November, (c) December, (d) February, and (e) April during prekindergarten. He began the year recognizing only one alphabet letter (*V*) and wrote his name with a string of letter-like forms. In November he was writing a barely recog-

FIGURE 5.1. Vin Chinzo's signature: (a) October; (b) November; (c) December; (d) February; (e) April.

nizable signature (*Vin*), and in December he could write recognizable letters for his entire name—and recognize 13 alphabet letters by name. In February his teacher invited him to write both his first and last names, which he did, leaving out only a few letters. In April he could write both names in highly recognizable forms; he could also identify 19 upper-case alphabet letters and 16 lower-case ones.

Assessing Alphabet Knowledge

Alphabet knowledge can be assessed informally by presenting children with the upper-case and then the lower-case letters typed in random order on a card. Children point to each letter on the assessment and identify its name, and teachers record which letters children recognize. Standardized forms of alphabet assessment are available, including the alphabet subtests of Clay's (1998) *Observation Survey of Early Literacy Achievement*; Invernizzi, Meier, Swank, and Juel's (1999) *Phonological Awareness Literacy Screening* (PALS-Pre-K); and Good and Kaminski's (2002) *Dynamic Indicators of Basic Early Literacy Skills* (DIBELS). Teachers can also informally assess children's ability to write letters by naming a letter for children to write, and then judging whether the letters are recognizable (some orientation problems are to be expected).

Younger children's concepts about alphabet letters and their ability to write their names can be assessed simply by asking them to write their names. Their signatures can be scored along a 7-point scale (adapted from Bloodgood, 1999; and Hildreth, 1936): (0) no response, (1) scribble, (2) linear scribble, (3) separate units (but no letters formed), (4) mock letters (letter shapes that are not conventional but share some features with actual letters) or mixture of mock letters and few conventional letters, (5) first name generally correct (although all letter formations may not be well formed or have correct orientation), and (6) consistently well-formed name using smaller-sized letters with good legibility. PALS-Pre-K also provides a standardized measure of children's signature writing abilities.

PHONOLOGICAL AND PHONEMIC AWARENESS

Phonological awareness is an overarching concept that includes distinguishing among sounds in the environment as well as sounds in spoken language at the level of words, syllables, and onsets and rimes (Anthony, Lonigan, Driscoll, Phillips, & Burgess, 2003). An onset is every letter in a word that appears before the word's first vowel. The rime is the vowel and every other letter that follows. For example, the word *cat* consists of the onset *c* and the rime *at*; the word *brat* consists of the onset *br* and the same rime *at*. Being able to manipulate onset and rime components means that children can segment speech sounds that are smaller than a syllable. Syllables are easy for young children to segment and blend; in contrast, segmenting and blending sounds smaller than a syllable are difficult tasks (Anthony et al., 2003). Being able to identify or produce rhyming words indicates that children can detect and manipulate onsets and rimes. During preschool some children develop a conscious awareness of rhyming words. However, developing this conscious awareness of rhyming is difficult for many children.

Development of Phonemic Awareness

Phonemic awareness requires children to detect and manipulate the smallest speech sounds in words—individual phonemes. One of the most critical and early phonemic awareness abilities is that of being able to detect and say (e.g., segment or isolate) the beginning phoneme in a spoken word (Morris, Bloodgood, Lomax, & Perney, 2003); for example, being able to say that the phoneme /t/ is the first sound in the spoken word *tire*. Although on their own, most 4-year-olds do not discover phonemic awareness (Lonigan, Burgess, Anthony, & Baker, 1998), with instruction many can learn to identify the beginning and even ending phonemes of spoken words (Byrne & Fielding-Barnsley, 1991). When children can isolate a single phoneme of a spoken word and recognize several alphabet letters, they are ready to learn phonics—the relationship between letters and sounds or phonemes (Johnston, Anderson, & Holligan, 1996).

Assessing Phonological and Phonemic Awareness

Teachers can assess children's phonological sensitivity to rhyme using informal activities such as presenting children with a set of three pictures (king, sun, and ring) and having them select the two pictures that rhyme (Lonigan et al., 1998). Or, children can be asked to select the picture of the word that does not rhyme; this measure is called an *oddity task* because children must select the odd one out (MacLean, Bryant, & Bradley, 1987). Teachers can also ask children to name as many words as they can that rhyme with a target word such as *hat*. A standardized assessment of rhyme is included in *Get It Got It Go!* (Early Childhood Research Institute on Measuring Growth and Development, 1998, 2000). The PALS-Pre-K also includes a standardized rhyme assessment.

Detecting alliteration requires the ability to determine whether two words begin with the same phoneme. This early phonemic awareness insight can be assessed in the same manner as rhyme: having children select pictures that begin with the same phoneme, having them select the picture that does not begin with the same sound as the other words, or by saying words that begin with the same phoneme as a target word. Perhaps one of the most straightforward assessments of phonemic awareness is to ask children to say the beginning sound of orally presented words. There are many standardized assessments of phonemic awareness that use a variety of testing formats to measure children's ability to hear beginning sounds, including DIBELS (Good & Kaminski, 2002), PALS-Pre-K (Invernizzi, Meier, Swank, & Juel, 1999), *Phonological Awareness Test* (PAT; Robertson & Salter, 1997), and *Preschool Comprehensive Test of Phonological and Print Processing* (Pre-CTOPPP; Lonigan, Wagner, Torgesen, & Rashotte, 2002).

Preschool teachers may assess informally children's ability to blend sound segments into words by playing a game of silly words. For example, teachers can say actual words segmented into syllables, onsets and rimes, or even phonemes. First teachers tell children that they will say a silly word and the children are to say the real word. They say the first sound segment, wait 2 seconds, and then say the second sound segment, and so on (Stahl & Murray, 1994). The ability to segment and blend all the phonemes in a word is the most difficult phonemic awareness task (Yopp, 1988), and most preschoolers and many kindergartners have difficulty with this task even after instruction. However, if children can blend words when presented with onsets and rimes, teachers may want to assess if they can do the more difficult task of segmenting words into onsets and rimes or into phonemes. Standardized tests of phonemic awareness often have children blend and segment sound segments as well as match words with the same beginning phonemes. Some tests have children delete phonemes by saying a word such as *brat*, without the /b/ (rat). I do not recommend these assessments be used in preschool because experts argue that children cannot do this task without being able to read conventionally (Blachman, 2000).

PHONICS AND THE ALPHABETIC PRINCIPLE

Phonemic awareness and *phonics* are often confused. Phonemic awareness never includes naming or identifying alphabet letters or their sounds—it only involves hearing the phonemes in spoken words. In fact, phonemic awareness activities could take place in the dark—children merely need to listen to spoken words. Phonics, on the other hand, is the knowledge of how letters are associated with particular sounds or phonemes. Phonics requires the manipulation of alphabet letters as well as phonemes. Thus phonemic awareness is a component of phonics because children must be able to hear and produce phonemes in order to match sounds with letters, but phonics also includes associating letters with sounds whereas phonemic awareness does not.

Development of Phonics and the Alphabetic Principle

Whereas many young children begin learning letter–sound relationships as a part of instruction in preschool or at home, some children discover these relationships all by themselves. They do this when they notice that their lips, teeth, and tongue are in the same places when they say the name of an alphabet letter and when they say a word. For example, when children say the letter name *t* and say the word *teeth*, they notice that their tongue taps the top of their mouths. This discovery leads children to invent spellings for words: *t* spells *teeth* (Morris & Slavin, 2003).

Children who can spell by applying letter–sound knowledge have discovered the alphabetic principle: that the letters in written words represent the sounds in spoken words. However, discovering the alphabetic principle takes more than merely learning to name alphabet letters, acquiring some level of phonemic awareness, and discovering some letter–sound relationships. It requires that children understand that print "says"—that it presents meaningful messages in a systematic fashion—which is through the alphabetic principle. Figure 5.2 presents a child's message written at a preschool writing center; this child has not yet grasped the alphabetic principle. Michael, when asked what he was writing, replied, "This is for my mother. She will like to know that I can write." When asked what it said, he replied, "My mother will be able to read it."

Michael demonstrated both conventional and emerging concepts; he clearly knows some alphabet letters and features that make up letters. He has written a string of letter-like forms with many features of actual letters as well as some recognizable letters. He knows that writing should be meaningful; he has the sign concept (Clay, 1975), the understanding that print signals a message. However, he clearly has not developed the alphabetic principle; indeed his writing does not seem to have words or a specific

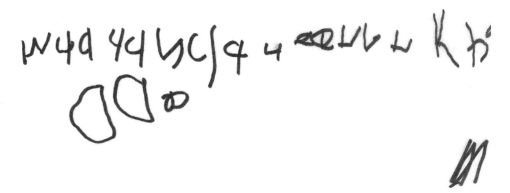

FIGURE 5.2. Michael's note to his mother.

message. His concept about the way that print works is that you have to be a reader (like his mother) in order to read print!

In contrast, another child, writing at the same time in the same writing center, produced the message presented in Figure 5.3. When asked what she was writing, Chalisha replied, "This says 'I colored with my crayons.'" Earlier the teacher had observed Chalisha pick up a crayon and copy the name *Crayola*. Although there are extra letters in her message not related to sounds in the words she intended to write, Chalisha has invented spellings with some letter–sound relationships: she wrote *I* for the word *I*, *c* for the word *colored*, *y* for the word *with*, and copied the word *CRAOLA*, which she believed said *crayons*. Chalisha's writing and her reading demonstrate that she has grasped the alphabetic principle.

Assessing Phonics and Alphabetic Principle

Children's knowledge of the relationship between letters and phonemes can be assessed in a variety of informal tasks. Teachers can show children a picture or say a word and ask them to name the letter that is associated with the beginning sound of that word. A standardized measure of phonics is found in *Woodcock Reading Mastery Tests—Revised* (WRMT-R; American Guidance Service, 1998).

Children's insight into the alphabetic principle and their use of letter–sound relationships can also be assessed by having them spell words. Teachers dictate simple words and analyze which components children spell (including initial consonant, final

FIGURE 5.3. "I colored with my crayons."

consonant, vowels, blends, and digraphs). To assess children's awareness of these phonic elements, we suggest using words such as *van, sun, tip, boat, sky, shop, cheek,* and
drape. Children may spell with random letters, indicating a lack of alphabetic insight;
they might spell with a consonant letter, indicating the onset of the alphabetic principle
and an emerging ability to use letter–sound knowledge; some children may produce
spellings with expected, *conventional* letter–sound relationships (e.g., spelling the word
van with a *v*). Many children use letters that have unconventional, yet logical, relationships to phonemes in the words they are spelling (see Bear, Invernizzi, Templeton, &
Johnston, 2000; Johnston, Invernizzi, & Juel, 1998, for more information about how to
analyze children's invented spellings). For example, one 4-year-old spelled the word
pig pq. Although *p* is the conventionally expected letter for spelling the /p/ phoneme, *g*
rather than *q* is the expected letter to spell the phoneme /g/. However, when children
say the letter name *q,* their mouths make a flap sound in the back of the throat similar to
the flap made when saying the sound /g/. Thus children are using logical connections
with sounds, just not the conventional connection.

CONCEPTS ABOUT PRINT, BOOKS, AND WORDS, AND THE FUNCTIONS OF WRITING

Concepts about print, books, and words include children's awareness of book orientation, directionality, and letter and word concepts as well as their growing awareness of
the different uses of print.

Development of Print and Function Concepts

Children demonstrate book orientation concepts as they browse through a favorite
book. Almost all preschoolers hold books right side up and turn the pages from front to
back as they look at a book on their own. Many preschoolers, when asked, can show a
book's front, back, top, and bottom and demonstrate that left pages are read before
right pages. Few preschool children demonstrate the advanced directionality concepts
involved in tracking (pointing to) printed words from left to right along a line of text
accompanied with a return sweep to the next line of text (Ehri & Sweet, 1991). Preschoolers do, however, often pretend to read by saying the memorized text of a favorite
book as they look at a particular page of text or sweep their finger across the text. Preschoolers also begin to develop concepts about letters and words. Although most preschoolers do not observe the conventions that words are separated by spaces in their
emergent writing or invented spelling, they indicate their awareness of letters and
words by finding words they know (as Chalisha did when she copied the letters in the
word *crayola*) or by writing words using invented spellings involving several letters for
words.

During preschool children also learn how print functions in the lives of their families and in their communities (Purcell-Gates, 1996). Children learn that print helps
memory as they watch mothers and fathers use grocery and to-do lists. They learn that
print signifies ownership as they learn to write signatures on their art projects, and they
learn that print communicates stories and interesting facts as their teachers and parents
read children's books aloud to them. Children often demonstrate this awareness during

FIGURE 5.4. Food order.

play in dramatic play centers such as housekeeping centers. Figure 5.4 presents a food order that Salina wrote while she pretended to be a waitress in a classroom restaurant. The order was for "a peach, orange juice, peanut butter and jelly sandwich, and a cookie." This order demonstrates other concepts about print, including left to right linearity (the text was written in horizontal lines).

Assessing Concept about Words

Concepts about words include children's awareness that words are units of both spoken and written language and that spoken words match with written words in a text. This concept can be informally measured by having children memorize a nursery rhyme and then attempt to "finger point read" the text. Finger point reading is when children say each word of a memorized text while attempting to point to that word in a written text. Teachers can prepare a small booklet to assess this concept. Each page should include two or three lines of text printed in a large font and with larger than normal word spaces, as shown:

Twinkle   twinkle   little   star

How I   wonder   what   you   are

After children memorize the rhyme, teachers introduce the specially prepared book and demonstrate finger point reading. After several teacher demonstrations, children are invited to finger point read on their own. Children who have a concept of word will point to each written word one at a time (self-correcting when they discover mismatches) while they recite each word. Children with a developing concept of word may point to words while reciting syllables or may just point randomly to words left to right while attempting to say the rhyme. Children without a clear concept of word may glide across the line without attempting to point to separate written units, or simply point to the first word repeatedly (adapted from Bloodgood, 1999). Clay's (1998) Observation Survey of Early Literacy Achievement includes a concept-about-print subtest, which is a standardized test of several components of concepts about print, including book orientation, directionality, and letter and word concepts; PALS-Pre-K has a standardized measure of finger point reading.

ORAL COMPREHENSION AND VOCABULARY

Some children enter kindergarten already having acquired several strategies for comprehending books. They sit still and listen attentively, frequently and spontaneously make comments (an effective comprehension strategy is extending and elaborating on information about interesting characters or events), and ask questions (another effective comprehension strategies is asking questions to clarify information). These children have had preschool experiences in which teachers and parents have expected them to listen intently to a book read aloud, answer questions, and make comments. From these book experiences, children build a strong vocabulary and a rich and varied language repertoire. Having a rich and varied vocabulary and being able to understand complex books means that children are likely, later, to be advanced in reading and writing achievement. Thus, during preschool, children need to develop the ability to comprehend, talk about, and retell stories and information from books with some detail and sophisticated vocabulary and language patterns. Being able to construct a thorough understanding of a storybook or informational book requires a variety of abilities, including oral language development, vocabulary knowledge, awareness of the basic structure of stories (concept of story) or informational books, and experience talking about and recalling information from books.

Language and Vocabulary Assessments

Teachers may have access to the services of a speech and language pathologist who can screen children for language delays. Or, teachers may use standardized language tests—such as the *Peabody Picture Vocabulary Test—Revised* (Dunn & Dunn, 1981), *Test of Language Development: Primary* (TOLD; Newcomer & Hammill, 1988), or *Expressive One-Word Picture Vocabulary Test—Revised* (Gardner, 1990)—to gather information about children's vocabulary development or use of complex sentence structure.

Teachers can also prepare informal vocabulary assessments by selecting a set of 10–12 target vocabulary words that are particularly relevant to a theme or set of books to be used during a 2- to 3-week unit. Teachers select one or two book illustrations that provide opportunities for children to use many of these target vocabulary words or phrases and ask them to tell what is happening in the illustrations. Teachers note whether children use any of the target vocabulary as they talk about the book illustrations (Senechal, 1997). Alternatively, children can be asked to retell informational or storybooks as teachers check off a list of the target vocabulary words that children might be expected to use in their retellings (Leung, 1992).

Assessing Story and Informational Book Retellings

Retelling checklists are informal assessments of the amount and accuracy of children's recall. Teachers compose checklists by writing a list, using short phrases, of the major events in the story or informational book. As children retell a text, teachers match the gist of the recount with the checklist. Over time, children should be able to recount more information from both informational books and storybooks (Pelligrini & Galda, 1982), and their retellings should follow the order of events as they are presented in the book (Duke & Kays, 1998; Newkirk, 1989; Purcell-Gates, McIntyre, & Freppon, 1995). Children's retellings usually shift from being mere recollections of few ideas presented in random order to detailed accounts with explanations.

EFFECTIVE ASSESSMENT PRACTICES

Caution is needed when administering and interpreting all assessment results. Standardized tests and other formal tests can be especially difficult to administer to young children in ways that yield reliable and valid results. Three-, four-, and five-year-olds are still in nascent stages of language development and may have difficulty expressing what they do know. They may not understand directions, be able to sustain attention for long periods, or be able to remain purposeful throughout several tasks. Further, individual children differ greatly from one another even when they are considered in normal developmental pathways. Thus assessments of young children may not be highly reliable or valid and may not reflect what children do know. For these reasons, teachers must be thoroughly familiar with administration guidelines in order to minimize the possible misinterpretations that might arise because of issues of appropriateness, validity, and reliability.

Developing an Assessment Plan

Systematic assessment is achieved when teachers are knowledgeable about the particular literacy concepts to be assessed, based on a model of development that includes the five foundational language and literacy components described earlier. Teachers first select a small set of valid and reliable assessment tools that will provide information about children's development of those concepts. I recommend selecting a battery of short and easy-to-administer and score formal assessments (e.g., see *Early Literacy Knowledge Assessment* (ELKA) in McGee & Richgels, 2003; McGee & Morrow, 2005) or informal teacher-developed tasks such as those described in this chapter. Next, teachers schedule a time to administer all assessments (usually early fall and late spring) to make sure information is gathered in a timely manner. These assessments can serve the purpose of both program evaluation and screening. Teachers may select a subset of all the measures given fall and spring to administer quarterly to use for monitoring purposes. For example, assessments of alphabet knowledge would be useful at the end of first and second quarters, and assessments of phonemic awareness would be useful at the end of second and third quarters.

Finally, teachers make a schedule that allows systematic observation of all children as they participate in a variety of classroom activities. One plan is to schedule observations each Tuesday and Thursday. The first week of the month the teacher would designate three or four children for observation on Tuesday and three or four children on Thursday. During center time, outside play, and mealtimes, the teacher would observe each of the designated children for approximately 10–15 minutes and take anecdotal notes. During the second, third, and fourth Tuesdays and Thursdays of the month, other children would be observed. Once all the children have been observed, the cycle of observation would resume again.

Deciding What to Observe

A comprehensive assessment model helps teachers combine information gathered from both formal and informal assessments and from observations of children during self-selected activities. Thus there should be a plan for collecting observations that can be used to enhance information gathered in more formal assessments. As children engage in literacy activities in their play, teachers make decisions about which activities to record. Teachers record activities that document ongoing or new levels of development in alphabet knowledge, phonological and phonemic awareness, alphabetic principle and letter sound knowledge, concepts about print, and vocabulary and comprehension. Teachers may observe children in the library center as they browse through books and pretend to read. Some children may be pretending to retell stories, and others merely flick through pages of a book without sustaining attention on any one story. As children engage in these behaviors, teachers may ask children to pretend to read or tell teachers what is going on in the story. Observations such as these provide teachers with information about children's vocabulary and comprehension development as well as with information on how to intervene with individual children to push their literacy development forward. For example, teachers would note which children may need special invitations to sit and reread a story with the teacher in the book center in order to obtain more focused practice and opportunity to engage in recounting favorite stories or information books.

Teachers may observe children as they pretend to read and write in dramatic play centers such as a classroom restaurant. These centers provide children with frequent opportunities to write in a variety of genres. Children may write menus in the restaurant center and take telephone messages in the housekeeping center. Teachers can collect written samples as well as write anecdotal notes about these interactions. As a part of these observations, teachers note children's language and the particular ways in which they pretend to use writing and reading materials. These observations provide information about children's concepts of print and awareness of print functions. Some children may participate in lengthy and complex play episodes in which they embed the use of reading and writing in functionally appropriate ways, whereas other children may merely handle materials without actually including them as a part of their play. Such observations would indicate which children had awareness of a wide variety of print uses and those who had limited concepts. Such observations would help teachers identify children who could benefit from participating in dramatic play centers while teachers model the use of reading and writing tools as they play with these particular children.

Samples of children's writing should be collected frequently. These samples provide insight into children's growing writing development and literacy insights. Some children's attempts to write may consist of uncontrolled scribbles, indicating that they may not have acquired the motor schemes necessary to produce lines, dots, and circles (McGee & Richgels, 2004). Some children may attempt to draw people by making large circular heads that sprout lines for arms and legs, indicating their awareness of the symbolic potential in drawing. Frequently children experiment with writing their signatures and attempt to draw alphabet letters and other objects. Some children's name writing may consist of mock cursive writing or random written marks, whereas others may write several recognizable, although not perfectly formed, letters as they write their names. Most preschoolers tend to ignore word spaces when they pretend to write; some may demonstrate their discovery of letter–sound relationships and begin to invent spellings. Each of these behaviors provides a window into children's developing literacy concepts and suggests activities in which teachers might engage in order to nudge children's development forward.

In order to ensure observation across the wide range of possible language and literacy concepts, teachers can deliberately place particular materials in related centers and then observe how children use those materials. For example, to capture a naturalistic observation of children's knowledge and use of phonemic awareness, teachers can place rhyming word pictures in a pocket chart or place a book with farm animal pictures in the writing center. Teachers can sit in these centers and observe children as they select and use these materials or invite children to play in those centers. Children may arrange rhyming word pictures in meaningful groups such as animals, objects, and people—indicating that rhyme is not a salient feature yet for them. Or, children may decide to write about the farm animals and can be encouraged to listen for the first sound and select a letter to use to spell the sound—indicating an awareness of beginning phonemes, the ability to segment or isolate a beginning phoneme, and knowledge of letter–sound relationships.

Keeping Records

Teachers need a method of recording assessment data (the anecdotal notes), analyzing the notes, and writing interpretations about what the observations revealed. Teachers can divide one notebook into sections to record notes and interpretations for each child or keep each child's assessment information in a separate folder. Anecdotal notes should be placed in the assessment notebook or folder immediately after they are collected to reduce the opportunity to misplace information. Most teachers use dated stickies on which to write anecdotal notes during observations and then later tape these sticky notes in the folder or notebook. One preschool teacher uses time after school on Tuesday and Thursday afternoons to keep her assessment notebook up to date. She dates and makes copies of anecdotal notes that she wrote during her observation of each child and tapes them securely in her notebook. She takes a few minutes to analyze what the observations mean by quickly reading through the previous month's observations, consulting her commercial continuum of language and literacy development, and jotting down a few insights about the significance of what she has observed.

Refining Observational Skills and Analyzing Anecdotal Notes

Observing young children is the most authentic of all assessment strategies that teachers can use. However, in order for observations to provide reliable and valid information, anecdotal notes must be detailed and accurate, without judgments or evaluations (Rhodes & Nathenson-Mejia, 1992). Anecdotal notes provide an accurate picture of what children were doing and saying in a classroom event and should capture those events even when read several weeks later. Teachers describe the classroom setting of an event and the children's critical actions; they also record what children say as much as possible. The object is to write an account of what is seen and heard without making inferences about meaning.

Analyzing the significance of the behaviors and language recorded in anecdotal notes takes place later as teachers reflect on the underlying cognitive strategies and understandings suggested by the event (Clay, 1998). One teacher wrote an anecdotal note about a play event that occurred in the restaurant center as three children pretended to order food. The anecdotal note described the setting and the three children's behavior and language. The teacher used this note to analyze what one of the children, Salina, knew. As the children played, Salina pretended to be the waitress and took a food order from her friend (Figure 5.4 presents Salina's written food order). After she had pretended to serve the food and clear the table, she presented her friends with a check (shown in Figure 5.5). The teacher collected both writing samples (presented in Figures 5.4 and 5.5) and placed them in her assessment notebook. Figure 5.6 presents her anecdotal notes and her later reflections.

To analyze this event, the teacher drew upon her knowledge of language and literacy development to write a tentative hypothesis about Salina's literacy development. She wrote this hypothesis (which is also shown in Figure 5.6) in her assessment notebook. First, the teacher recognized that Salina (1) knew the behaviors and language used by waitresses, (2) clearly intended for her writing to be meaningful, and (3) demonstrated linearity in the food order writing sample. Salina wrote in a different format when she composed the check, using a list-like vertical arrangement; she used scribble writing and a series of O-shaped forms without producing any recognizable letters. The teacher combined this insight with knowledge she had about a previous assessment of Salina's alphabet recognition to note that although Salina can identify many alphabet letters, she chose to use pretend writing rather than alphabet letters during the dramatic play.

FIGURE 5.5. Bill for lunch order.

Salina, Shanika, and Katisha play in the restaurant center. Salina has on apron, holds pencil, and pad, says, "What you ordering?" Shanika says, "A peach, orange juice, peanut butter and jelly sandwich, and a cookie." Salina pretends to write, goes to house center and pretends to cook, brings dishes, and serves the girls. The girls gossip about their boyfriends as they eat. Salina asks, "You finished?" and she clears the table. She goes into the house center and writes a "bill" and brings it to the table. She puts it on the table and says, "You pay this."

Reflections: Salina knows the language and behavior of waitress and uses writing functionally. Her writing on the food order shows linearity, and her writing on the bill displays understanding of the vertical presentation of numbers. She chooses to use scribble writing rather than writing with alphabet letters. I may need to assess her growing competence in writing letters.

FIGURE 5.6. Anecdotal notes and reflections.

Using Insights to Plan Responsive Instruction

After teachers have written reflections that interpret children's literacy concepts, they should use this information to make decisions about instructional activities that will nudge children forward in their literacy learning. Teachers should consider adjustments they might make in instructional activities, materials and activities placed in centers, and classroom routines that will help children take the next steps along the developmental continuum. For example, after observing Salina play in the restaurant center, the teacher decided that she would place alphabet cards in the writing center to use as an informal assessment to check Salina's progress in writing letters; the teacher is aware that Salina recognizes letters, but she wants more information on whether Salina is also learning to write those letters. She planned to intensify her instruction in alphabet writing by planning several writing activities to be used in small-group instruction for several children over the next few weeks.

SUMMARY

Assessing young children's language and literacy development has long been a critical component of early childhood programs. Comprehensive assessment models are planned to meet specific goals and purposes and draw upon thoughtful observation of children and careful reflection in order to construct hypotheses about children's underlying language and literacy concepts. These observations should be rounded out by a consideration of the results gathered from quarterly assessments that systematically sample children's development of five foundational literacy concepts: language and vocabulary, concepts about print, alphabet letter knowledge, phonemic awareness, and knowledge of letter–sound relationships and the alphabetic principle.

As teachers assess individual children, the best practice is to form tentative conclusions about that child's language development and literacy awareness. These tentative conclusions should be refined through ongoing, multiple assessments that include a combination of observation, standardized or formal tests, informal assessments (e.g., teacher-developed tasks, checklists), and samples of children's writing. Thus a comprehensive assessment model is continuous, planned, and guided by knowledge of literacy development. It provides insights into children's underlying cognitive concepts and strategies, is used to make plans for future instruction, and informs decisions about program and classroom adaptations. When used carefully, this variety of assessment data can fulfill three purposes: (1) to make instructional decisions about individual children, (2) to identify children who may have special needs or require intervention services, and (3) to monitor program effectiveness.

REFERENCES

American Guidance Service. (1998). *Woodcock Reading Mastery Test—Revised Normative Update* (WRMT-R/NU). Circle Pines, MN: American Guidance Service. Available at *www. agsnet.com/*.

Anthony, J. L., Lonigan, C. J., Driscoll, K., Phillips, B. M., & Burgess, S. R. (2003). Phonological sensitivity: A quasi-parallel progression of word structure units and cognitive operations. *Reading Research Quarterly, 38,* 470–487.

Bear, D. R., Invernizzi, M., Templeton, S., & Johnston, F. (2000). *Words their way: Word study for phonics, vocabulary, and spelling instruction.* Columbus, OH: Merrill.

Blachman, B. A. (2000). Phonological awareness. In M. Kamil, P. Rosenthal, P. D. Pearson, & R. Barr (Eds.), *Handbook of reading research* (Vol. 3, pp. 483–502). Mahwah, NJ: Erlbaum.

Bloodgood, J. W. (1999). What's in a name?: Children's name writing and literacy acquisition. *Reading Research Quarterly, 34,* 342–367.

Bowman, B. T., Donovan, M. S., & Burns, M. S. (Eds.). (2000). *Eager to learn: Educating our preschoolers.* Washington, DC: National Academy Press.

Bredekamp, S., & Rosegrant, T. (Eds.). (1992). *Reaching potentials: Appropriate curriculum and assessment for young people* (Vol. 1). Washington, DC: National Association of Education for Young People.

Byrne, B., & Fielding-Barnsley, R. (1991). Evaluation of a program to teach phonemic awareness to young children. *Journal of Educational Psychology, 83*(4), 104–111.

Clay, M. M. (1975). *What did I write?* Portsmouth, ME: Heinemann.

Clay, M. M. (1998). *By different paths to common outcomes.* Portland, ME: Stenhouse.

Dodge, D. T., Colker, L., & Heroman, C. (2001). *The creative curriculum developmental continuum for ages 3–5, English version.* Washington, DC: Teaching Strategies.

Duke, N. K., & Kays, J. (1998). "Can I say 'once upon a time'?": Kindergarten children developing knowledge of information book language. *Early Childhood Research Quarterly, 13,* 295–318.

Dunn, L., & Dunn, L. (1981). *Peabody Picture Vocabulary Test—Revised.* Circle Pines, NM: American Guidance Service. Available at *www.cps.nova.edu/~cpphelp/PPVT-R.html*.

Early Childhood Research Institute on Measuring Growth and Development. (1998, 2000). *Individual growth and development indicators for preschool children.* Minneapolis: Center for Early Education and Development, University of Minnesota. Available at *http://ggg.umn.edu/*.

Ehri, L., & Sweet, J. (1991). Finger-point reading of memorized text: What enables beginners to process the print? *Reading Research Quarterly, 15,* 442–462.

Epstein, A. S., Schweinhart, L. J., DeBruin-Parecki, A., & Robin, K. B. (2004). *Preschool assessment: A guide to developing a balanced approach.* Rutgers, NJ: State University of New Jersey, National Institute for Early Education Research.

Gardner, M. (1990). *Expressive One-Word Picture Vocabulary Test—Revised.* Novato, CA: Academic Therapy.

Good, R. H., III, & Kaminski, R. A. (2002). *Dynamic indicators of basic early literacy skills* (6th ed.). Eugene, OR: University of Oregon. Available at *www.dibels.uoregon.edu*.

Hildreth, G. (1936). Developmental sequences in name writing. *Child Development, 7,* 291–303.

International Reading Association and National Association for the Education of Young Children. (1998). Learning to read and write: Developmentally appropriate practices for young children. *The Reading Teacher, 52,* 193–216.

Invernizzi, M., Meier, J., Swank, L., & Juel, C. (1999). *Phonological awareness literacy screening (PALS-PK).* Charlottesville, VA: University of Virginia. Available at *www.curry.edschool.virginia.edu/go/pals/.*

Johnston, F. R., Invernizzi, M., & Juel, C. (1998). *Book buddies: Guidelines for volunteer tutors of emergent and early readers.* New York: Guilford Press.

Johnston, R. S., Anderson, M., & Holligan, C. (1996). Knowledge of the alphabet and explicit awareness of phonemes in pre-readers: The nature of the relationship. *Reading and Writing: An Interdisciplinary Journal, 8,* 217–234.

Leung, C. B. (1992). Effects of word-related variables on vocabulary growth through repeated read-aloud events. In C. Kinzer & D. Leu (Eds.), *Literacy research, theory, and practice: Views from many perspectives* (pp. 491–498). Chicago: National Reading Conference.

Lonigan, C. J., Burgess, S. R., Anthony, J. L., & Baker, T. A. (1998). Development of phonological sensitivity in 2- to 5-year-old children. *Journal of Educational Psychology, 90,* 294–311.

Lonigan, C. J., Wagner, R. K., Torgesen, J. K., & Rashotte, C. A. (2002). *Preschool comprehensive test of phonological and print processing (Pre-CTOPPP).* Department of Psychology, Florida State University.

Maclean, M., Bryant, P., & Bradley, L. (1987). Rhymes, nursery rhymes, and reading in early childhood. *Merrill-Parker Quarterly, 33,* 255–281.

McConnell, S., McEvoy, M., Carta, J., Greenwood, C. R., Kaminski, R., Good, R. H., et al. (1998). *Research and development of individual growth and development Indicators for children between birth to age eight.* Technical Report No. 4. Minneapolis: University of Minnesota, Early Childhood Research Institute on Measuring Growth and Development.

McGee, L. M., & Morrow, L. M. (2005). *Teaching literacy in kindergarten.* New York: Guilford Press.

McGee, L. M., & Richgels, D. (2003). *Designing early literacy programs: Strategies for at-risk preschool and kindergarten children.* New York: Guilford Press.

McGee, L. M., & Richgels, D. (2004). *Literacy's beginnings: Supporting young readers and writers* (4th ed.). Boston: Allyn & Bacon.

Morris, D., Bloodgood, J., Lomax, R., & Perney, J. (2003). Developmental steps in learning to read: A longitudinal study in kindergarten and first grade. *Reading Research Quarterly, 38,* 302–328.

Morris, D., & Slavin, R. (Eds.). (2003). *Every child reading.* Boston: Allyn & Bacon.

Newcomer, P., & Hamill, D. (1988). *Test of Language Development–2, Primary.* Austin, TX: PRO-ED.

Newkirk, T. (1989). *More than stories: The range of children's writing.* Portsmouth, NH: Heinemann.

Pellegrini, A. D., & Galda, L. (1982). The effects of thematic-fantasy play training on the development of children's story comprehension. *American Educational Research Journal, 19,* 443–452.

Purcell-Gates, V. (1996). Stories, coupons, and the *TV Guide*: Relationships between home literacy experiences and emergent literacy knowledge. *Reading Research Quarterly, 31,* 406–428.

Purcell-Gates, V., McIntyre, E., & Freppon, P. A. (1995). Learning written storybook language in school: A comparison of low-SES children in skills-based and whole language classrooms. *American Educational Research Journal, 32,* 659–685.

Rhodes, L., & Nathenson-Mejia, S. (1992). Anecdotal-records: A powerful tool for ongoing literacy assessment. *Reading Teacher, 45,* 502–509.

Robertson, C., & Salter, W. (1997). *Phonological awareness test.* East Moline, IL: Lingui-Systems. Available at *www.linguisystems.com.*

Senechal, M. (1997). The differential effect of storybook reading on preschoolers' acquisition of expressive and receptive vocabulary. *Journal of Child Language, 24,* 123–138.

Snow, C. E., Burns, S. M., & Griffin, P. (Eds.). (1998). *Preventing reading difficulties in young children.* Washington, DC: National Academy Press.

Stahl, S. A., & Murray, B. A. (1994). Defining phonological awareness and its relationship to early reading. *Journal of Educational Psychology, 86,* 221–234.

Treiman, R., Sotak, L., & Bowman, M. (2001). The roles of letter names and letter sounds in connecting print and speech. *Memory and Cognition, 29,* 860–873.

U.S. Department of Health and Human Services. (2003). The national reporting system: What is it and how will it work? *Head Start Bulletin, 76.* Available at *www.headstartinfo.org/publications/ hsbulletin76/cont-76.htm.*

Yopp, H. K. (1988). The validity and reliability of phonemic awareness tests. *Reading Research Quarterly, 23,* 159–177.

CHAPTER 6

Assessing Word Recognition

David Chard
Sarah McDonagh
Sangeun Lee
Virginia Reece

By reading this book, you are exercising numerous complex processes that allow you to communicate with a long list of contributing authors. One of the most astonishing processes is the uniquely human skill of being able to communicate through abstract printed symbols (Adams, 1990). In a broad sense, an understanding of texts connotes more than being able to pronounce individual words in print (Baumann & Kame'enui, 2004). It also includes knowing something about that word, its meaning, and its relation with other words in the context in which it is read. But word recognition begins with being able to recognize the word or decode it from its printed form (Adams, 1990). Word recognition is the ability to read words, an act that sounds deceptively simple. Unfortunately, it's *not* as simple as it sounds.

The fact that most people read words with ease sometimes causes us to assume that the skill develops naturally, much like speech. However, word recognition does not develop naturally but instead relies on conventions (i.e., letter–sound relationships) that must be taught. Specifically, students must be shown how to (1) look at letters or letter combinations in words, (2) identify the sounds that correspond to those letters or letter combinations, and (3) blend the sounds together to pronounce the word. Additionally, students must match their pronunciation of the blended sounds with a word that is already in their oral vocabulary. In other words, strong word recognition depends on the reader being able to get the correct pronunciation (or a close approximation) of the word and having the vocabulary knowledge to make sense of it.

Despite the complexity of the word recognition process, many students learn how to do it well. But for those who do not, their poorly developed word recognition has dire consequences (Torgesen, 1998; Stanovich, 1980), including lack of exposure to new words, underdeveloped reading fluency, and inadequate reading comprehension (Pikulski & Chard, 2005). Stanovich (1986) popularized a metaphor to explain the consequence of these individual differences in word recognition skill; he used a biblical reference to the Book of Matthew, known as the *Matthew effect*, to propose that the "rich get richer and the poor get poorer" as a consequence of exposure to and engagement with print. Cunningham and Stanovich (1998) argue that poor word readers do not find reading rewarding and, consequently, do not read enough to learn new words and practice familiar words. As a result, they do not develop strong vocabularies and are not able to understand what they read. In contrast, proficient readers enjoy reading and have access to far more complex texts—and, as such, to rich sources of vocabulary and content knowledge (Cunningham & Stanovich, 1998; Nagy & Herman, 1987).

Proficient word recognition is established by applying a reliable, step-by-step strategy for recognizing familiar words and figuring out unfamiliar words (Chard & Osborn, 1999). Readers who have such a strategy are able to read a wide range of print and electronic text. Whether they are reading a surfing magazine, fantasy book, or dinosaur cards, they are rewarded by their ability to understand the text and a desire to read more. In short, when readers have a strategy for word recognition, they enjoy reading and read more. When they read more, they become better readers (Cunningham & Stanovich, 1998).

This chapter focuses on strategies for assessing word recognition development in children in kindergarten through grade 2. We anchor our discussion in prevailing theories of word recognition development, and we propose that teachers consider four different purposes for word recognition assessment: screening, diagnosis, progress monitoring, and outcomes. Specific examples of each type of assessment are described and illustrated. Finally, we discuss the use of word recognition assessments with populations of diverse learners.

PREVAILING THEORIES
OF WORD RECOGNITION DEVELOPMENT

We subscribe to three theories relevant to the development of proficient word recognition. These theories combine to help us understand (1) the phases through which readers progress in their development (Ehri, 1995, 1997, 1998, 2005), (2) how automaticity with word recognition may be achieved (Logan, 1997), and (3) the impact this development has on more sophisticated aspects of reading (Perfetti, 1985).

How Do Students Learn to Recognize Words?

Before children can learn to read words well, they must meet four prerequisite conditions (Chard, Simmons, & Kame'enui, 1998). They must:

- Acquire phonemic awareness.
- Recognize that print can be used to communicate.
- Recognize the letters of the alphabet.
- Understand the alphabetic principle: the notion that words are made of letters that represent sounds.

These prerequisite conditions are reflected in Ehri's (1995, 1997, 1998, 2005) phase model of word recognition development, which includes the following phases: pre-alphabetic, partial alphabetic, fully alphabetic, consolidated alphabetic, and automatic. Table 6.1 describes each phase and identifies the approximate age and grade level at which children typically reach that phase. The final column lists implications of each phase for assessment.

Ehri's phase model culminates in what she refers to as "sight word reading." This phase is achieved by (1) progressing through the earlier phases and (2) having sufficient exposure to words through frequent reading. Logan (1997) supports and extends the idea that word recognition must be automatic and is dependent on the amount of practice, the level of consistency in the task environment, and the number of relevant instances of the task recorded in memory. As the reader's knowledge base expands and becomes accurate, performance becomes reliant on memory retrieval rather than problem solving (Logan, 1997). In other words, if a particular word is read frequently enough, the cumulative practice with that word results in an increased likelihood that the word will be recognized again and that the time required to recognize the word will decrease.

TABLE 6.1. Ehri's Phases of Reading Development and Their Implications for Assessment

Phase of reading development	Description of student knowledge	Typical age/ grade level	Implications for assessment
Prealphabetic	Emerging understanding of the alphabetic principle; recognize words by letter shape.	3–6 years/ pre-K–K	Assess students' knowledge of • *Alphabet knowledge* • Common *letter–sound relationships*
Partial alphabetic	Beginning to grasp connections between letters and sounds and use connections to read simple words (e.g., /c/ and /t/ in *cat*).	5–8 years/ K–1	Assess students' knowledge of • Common *letter–sound relationships* • Blending *regular words* and *nonwords*
Fully alphabetic	Increasingly familiar with most letter–sound relationships; sounding out unfamiliar words; instantly recognizing some familiar words.	6–8 years/ late K–2	Assess students' knowledge of • *Nonword decoding* • Word reading (e.g., CVC, CVCe, CCVC) • *Reading in simple connected texts*
Consolidated alphabetic	Students begin to economize by recognizing word chunks (e.g., *-ight*) and using these patterns to read unfamiliar words more quickly.	7 years– adulthood/ grade 2 and beyond	Assess students' knowledge of • *Advanced word recognition skills* (e.g., CCVCC) • Fluency in *connected texts*
Automatic	Students instantly recognize words and apply advanced decoding strategies and confirm using context.	Intermediate grades– adulthood	Assess students' fluency in *connected texts*

Though our focus in this chapter is on the process of learning to recognize words and specific strategies for assessing word recognition, we are mindful that word recognition is a means to understanding text. The connection between word recognition and reading comprehension is represented in Perfetti's (1985) "verbal efficiency theory." Perfetti (1985) adopts a resource capacity view of the relationship between word recognition and comprehension whereby he suggests that lower-level reading processes such as word recognition must reach a minimum performance level before higher-level processes (e.g., making inferences) can be performed simultaneously during reading. In other words, if a reader spends all of his or her time focused on transforming the printed symbols to speech, he or she has little cognitive energy remaining to think about what the word means and how it relates to the words around it.

These theories remind us that there is a cohesive sequence to word recognition development and that readers may have trouble if they have not received instruction and assessment that reflect this sequence. Too often, children who are struggling with word recognition receive interventions that focus on using syntax and context when they really need to overcome the challenge of using their knowledge of letters and sounds to pronounce the words.

In the next section we describe four purposes for assessment and provide some examples of specific assessments that can be used to achieve these purposes. Additionally, each type of assessment is illustrated in the context of a specific first-grade student who is likely to experience later reading difficulties if his or her needs are not addressed.

Purposes of Assessment

Assessment is commonly defined as the "process of collecting data for the purpose of making decisions about individuals and groups" (Salvia & Ysseldyke, 2004, p. 5). If we broaden our perspective of assessment, we can consider the utility of assessment data at a system level (i.e., state, district, school) and from an instructional perspective (i.e., grade, class, group, and individual student). In both cases, the quality of the decisions made depend on the use of data from technically adequate assessments—that is, those that are reliable, valid, and focus on essential skills within a given domain. Put simply, if a test is *reliable*, we know that the test score is stable across test administration on a different day, with a different tester, and on a minimally different set of test items. If a test is *valid*, we know that the test accurately measures what it is designed to measure. And if a test *focuses on essential skills* within a given domain, we know that it is assessing skills that are important in a specific area of learning. Information pertaining to the technical adequacy of a specific assessment is generally located in the administration and scoring guide of a test manual.

The technical adequacy of the assessments we use to make educational decisions often varies greatly. Standardized measures of reading may have excellent reliability and validity but present very limited information for instructional planning (Salvia & Ysseldyke, 2004). In contrast, informal measures that may be very useful in the classroom may not be very reliable. As a general rule, when making high-stakes decisions such as placement in special programs, it is imperative to ensure that your data are derived from several technically adequate assessments that measure student performance across multiple domains. In making daily instructional decisions, the technical adequacy of the assessments you use is less important. What is more important is that you are able to modify the assessments quickly based on additional information you glean during instruction.

In addition to understanding how the technical adequacy of assessments affects our interpretation of the resulting data, it is important to consider the types of decisions that can be made with different word recognition assessments. As noted previously, word recognition assessments can be used for four important purposes: screening, diagnosis, progress monitoring, and outcomes. In the sections that follow, we describe each of these purposes, word recognition assessments that can be used to achieve each purpose, and a case study of how specific assessments help a teacher make high-stakes and instructional decisions for a student experiencing difficulties developing word recognition.

Screening

The intent of a word recognition screening measure is to quickly determine which students might experience difficulties developing word recognition skills at a later time. Screening assessments are brief and administered to all students early in the school year or when new students transfer in during the school year. These assessments are used to assess student proficiency with letter–sound correspondence and decoding and to assist teachers in (1) identifying students at risk for future word recognition difficulties, and (2) making instructional grouping and support decisions. Strong technical adequacy of assessments used to determine a student's relative risk status for future word recognition difficulties is essential. An example of assessing word recognition for the purpose of screening follows.

Lani is in first grade at Northside Elementary School. At the beginning of the school year Lani's teacher sought to identify students at risk for word recognition difficulties. Because screening decisions help to determine how much support Lani will receive in her reading instruction, her teacher turned to a screening measure that has documented technical adequacy, the *Dynamic Indicators of Basic Early Literacy Skills—Nonsense Word Fluency* subtest (DIBELS-NWF; Kaminski & Good, 1996). The DIBELS-NWF subtest is used to determine if a reader can apply decoding strategies when there is no support provided from context or word familiarity. Students are given 1 minute to read a list of single-syllable nonwords or to identify the letter–sound correspondences that make up those nonwords (see Figure 6.1 for an example). A student's final score consists of the total number of letter–sound correspondences or nonwords read correctly in 1 minute and provides a relative indicator of student reading risk (measures, administration and scoring procedures, and benchmark goals are available at *www.dibels.uoregon.edu*). The DIBELS-NWF subtest is an example of one screening tool designed to assess word recognition. Additional examples of screening measures are included in Table 6.2.

Benchmark scores have been established for this subtest based on the performance of thousands of children across the United States. The benchmarks help us predict whether a student needs support, over and above typical classroom instruction, to become a proficient reader. Results from the screening assessment revealed that Lani was able to correctly identify 17 letter–sound correspondences in 1 minute, placing her below the beginning of the year benchmark of 24 correct letter–sound correspondences

wub	doj	ik	vus	nuk
ul	zel	feb	wuj	hiz
min	ros	kub	jaf	duz
faj	ad	ked	ig	el
loj	et	yat	ol	tov
uf	ral	ep	kab	vif
tic	dev	dop	zac	doc
tik	sij	zoj	mig	zut
foj	ib	jud	zek	vov
ruz	huf	sib	ak	jec

FIGURE 6.1. Example of nonsense word fluency measure. From Good and Kaminski (2003). Copyright 2003 by Sopris West Educational Services. Reprinted by permission.

TABLE 6.2. Additional Examples of Assessments Useful for Various Purposes

Assessment purpose	Examples
Screening	Nonwords • *Test of Word Reading Efficiency*, Phonemic Decoding Efficiency subtest (Torgesen, Wagner, & Rashotte, 1999) • *Woodcock Reading Mastery Test—Revised*, Word Attack subtest (Woodcock, 2000) • *Woodcock Johnson III Test of Achievement*, Word Attack subtest (Woodcock, McGrew, & Mather, 2001) Real words • *Test of Word Reading Efficiency*, Sight Word Efficiency subtest (Torgesen et al., 1999) • *Woodcock Reading Mastery Test—Revised*, Word Identification subtest (Woodcock, 2000) • *Word Identification Fluency* test (Fuchs, Fuchs, & Compton, 2004)
Diagnosis	• *Basic Phonics Skills Test* (BPST; Shefelbine, 1996) • *Early Reading Diagnostic Assessment*, Letter Recognition and Pseudoword Decoding subtests (Smith et al., 2000) • *Texas Primary Reading Inventory* (Center for Academic Reading Skills, 1999) • *Woodcock Reading Mastery Test—Revised* (Woodcock, 2000)
Progress monitoring	• *DIBELS* Letter Naming, Nonsense Word and Oral Reading Fluency subtests (Kaminski & Good, 1996) • *Test of Word Reading Efficiency*, Phonemic Decoding Efficiency and Sight Word Efficiency subtests (Torgesen, Wagner, & Rashotte, 1999) • *Word Identification Fluency* test (Fuchs, Fuchs, & Compton, 2004)
Outcomes	• *DIBELS* Letter Naming Fluency, Nonsense Word Fluency and Oral Reading Fluency subtests (Kaminski & Good, 1998) • *Early Reading Diagnostic Assessment*, Letter Recognition and Pseudoword Decoding subtests (Psychological Corporation, 2000) • *Iowa Test of Basic Skills*, Word Analysis, Reading Words and Spelling subtests (Hoover et al., 2001) • *Slosson Oral Reading Test* (Slosson & Nicholson, 1999) • *Stanford Achievement Test—10th Edition*, Word Reading and Word Study Skills subtests (Harcourt, Brace Educational Measurement, 1997)

per minute and at some risk for future difficulties in developing word recognition skills. Lani is in the phase of word recognition development that Ehri refers to as *partial alphabetic.*

Because screening measures are designed for efficiency, they do not assess a wide range of skills. Once it is determined that a student such as Lani needs extra assistance, it is important to more fully assess his or her knowledge and skills and identify areas in which additional instruction is needed. For this purpose, the teacher should consider diagnostic assessments.

Diagnosis

After screening, or at any time during the school year, teachers may need more detailed diagnostic information for a particular student to plan instruction. Diagnostic assessments provide a detailed picture of student performance in a specific domain area. These assessments generally take more time to administer than a screening or progress monitoring assessment. There are many diagnostic tests designed to help target students' word recognition needs more precisely. Most include many of the same components, including:

- Matching sounds corresponding to a sequence of letters.
- Reading a series of increasingly difficult regular nonwords or real words.
- Reading a series of increasingly difficult irregular words.
- Reading a series of increasingly difficult connected text passages.

Although there are many commercially available diagnostic assessments for word recognition that have documented technical adequacy, we recommend caution in deciding to use many of them. Diagnostic testing can be time consuming, expensive, and may provide little information for instructional planning. Rather than spend a great deal of time administering and scoring diagnostic word recognition measures that might not be useful to guide instructional decisions, we recommend that you use only those measures that (1) provide additional information beyond that provided through screening, and (2) provide information directly applicable to instructional planning and decision making. A discussion of some examples of informal and formal diagnostic assessments follows.

Figure 6.2 illustrates an example of an informal diagnostic word recognition assessment. We recommend creating a student booklet of the key words and administering the assessment by asking a student to read the words aloud. Each numbered word represents a specific phonic element or word part, indicated by the letters in italicized font. For example, if a child can read #87, *invention*, it is safe to assume that he or she recognizes the word part -*tion*. The items on this informal diagnostic assessment are sequenced in a manner that will help determine where instruction should begin. The point at which a student begins to struggle gives you a sense of where to begin instruction. For example, if the student is unable to read #54 *cart,* an intervention lesson on the *r*-controlled vowel *ar* may be beneficial.

After careful examination of Lani's screening data, her teacher decided to use the Word Recognition Assessment (Figure 6.2) to identify Lani's specific knowledge and skills. She found that Lani was able to identify the sounds for the first 12 items (vowel

Word Recognition Assessment								
Name _____			Grade _____			Age _____		
Sounds			Words			Words		
#	Item	Response	#	Item	Response	#	Item	Response
1	a		35	flag		69	tap*ed*	
2	m		36	drop		70	hop*ing*	
3	t		37	stamp		71	ti*mer*	
4	s		38	strap		72	*kn*ock	
5	l		39	split		73	boi*l*	
6	f		40	skunk		74	enj*oy*	
7	d		Advanced Word Analysis			75	st*ew*	
8	r		41	ba*th*		76	gra*ph*	
9	o		42	hunt*er*		77	*wr*ap	
10	g		43	test*ing*		78	ha*un*t	
11	l		44	*sh*op		79	ha*wk*	
12	h		45	land*ed*		80	*con*fuse	
13	u		46	lick*ed*		81	pay*ment*	
14	c		47	miss*ed*		82	*dis*tant	
15	b		48	*wh*en		83	enjoy*able*	
16	n		49	*qu*iz		84	use*less*	
17	k		50	fo*ld*		85	dark*ness*	
18	e		51	sunn*y*		86	pro*tect*	
19	v		52	fast*est*		87	inven*tion*	
20	p		53	lo*an*		88	sens*ible*	
21	y		54	ca*rt*		89	pack*age*	
22	j		55	f*ine*		90	mis*sion*	
23	x		56	h*ope*		91	sil*ence*	
24	w		57	ca*ne*		92	self*ish*	
25	q		58	n*eat*		93	*pre*dict	
26	z		59	h*oop*		94	*com*pare	
Regular Words			60	cand*le*		95	mill*ion*	
27	it		61	m*eet*		96	vent*ure*	
28	am		62	pa*in*		97	detec*tive*	
29	mad		63	lun*ch*		98	ac*cuse*	
30	him		64	po*rt*		99	joy*ous*	
31	must		65	pra*y*		100	pa*nic*	
32	flag		66	pr*oud*		101	*for*ward	
33	drop		67	thi*rs*t		102	real*ize*	
34	hand		68	cu*rb*		103	art*ist*	

FIGURE 6.2. Sample monitoring form for word recognition skills. Adapted from Carnine, Silbert, Kame'enui, and Tarver (2004). Copyright 2004 by Prentice-Hall. Adapted by permission.

and consonant sounds), item #18 (short *e*), and regular words from #27 through #31. After considering Lani's needs based on this assessment, her teacher was able to group her with four other children in class with similar word recognition skills to work collaboratively with a Title I teacher to plan for supplemental lessons they will receive for 15 minutes per session three times a week. Given her risk level, as identified by the screener, Lani's teachers recognized that it is important to regularly assess her progress in word recognition to make sure that she is mastering key knowledge and skills. Monitoring student progress is a third very important purpose of word recognition assessment.

Progress Monitoring

Following initial screening, planning, grouping, and instruction, it is necessary to monitor student progress throughout the school year to ensure instructional effectiveness and to plan for future instruction. Progress monitoring assessments are brief and administered during the school year to monitor student progress (1) toward foundational goals in establishing word recognition, and (2) in word recognition in instructional-level materials. Assessments used to establish student progress toward foundational reading goals in word recognition are formal, technically adequate progress monitoring assessments that compare student progress to locally or nationally representative norms. Examples of formal progress monitoring assessments for word recognition are included in Table 6.2. Assessments used to monitor student progress in word recognition in instructional-level materials can be referred to as informal progress monitoring assessments. These assessments need not be studied for their technical adequacy, nor do they map to representative norms for word recognition. Examples of informal progress monitoring assessments include tools such as checklists to gauge students' word growth as they read letter cards, reading of word lists and decodable books, writing and spelling samples, in-program placement tests and in-program assessments.

Figure 6.3 illustrates one example of an informal progress monitoring tool that might be used to assess word recognition—specifically, taught affixes. In this example, instruction would focus on teaching the affix *at* and then building words from *at*. Following initial instruction, and after students have had sufficient modeling, guided and independent practice, and review, the teacher would have the students read the decodable passage in Figure 6.3. The teacher would follow along while the students

Nat, the Cat, and the Rat

Nat has a cat.

The cat is fat.

Nat and the cat sit on the mat.

Nat pats the cat.

The cat sees a rat.

The cat runs to the rat.

FIGURE 6.3. Sample informal progress monitoring tool: decodable text.

read, monitoring accuracy and fluency with word recognition. If the students are able to identify words at a rate of one word correct for every 1.5 seconds, with a criterion of 95% accuracy or higher, the teacher can safely assume that the students are proficient with building words from *at*.

Now we return to Lani and her teacher's plan for progress monitoring. Lani's initial screening results revealed that she was at *some risk* for difficulties in developing word recognition skills. As a consequence, the teacher provided supplemental instruction (15 minutes per day, 3 days per week) focused on developing Lani's word recognition. In order to determine the effectiveness of the instructional intervention in improving Lani's word recognition, the teacher decided to monitor Lani's progress one time per month using the DIBELS-NWF measure. This measure serves multiple purposes: screening, progress monitoring, and formal progress monitoring. By the middle of the school year Lani's score on the DIBELS-NWF measure was 42, placing her below the middle of the year benchmark of 50, indicating that her performance still fell within the *some risk* range for future difficulties in developing word recognition skills. Lani's performance had improved during the year, but her progress was not sufficient to place her in the consolidated phase of word learning (Ehri, 1995, 1997, 1998, 2005).

In order to gain additional information pertaining to Lani's performance during instruction, her teacher decided to use informal progress monitoring. The teacher implemented a commercially produced instructional program to address Lani's difficulties in developing word recognition skills. The program featured informal progress monitoring assessments every 10 lessons to determine (1) student mastery of taught content, (2) appropriate instructional placement, and (3) generalization of skills to unfamiliar materials. Lani's performance data revealed that she had consistently scored at a level of 95% accuracy or higher on her previous five progress monitoring assessments, indicating that her placement in the instructional program was appropriate. Lani's formal progress monitoring assessment indicated that the level of instructional intensity currently provided was not sufficient to accelerate her progress. Consequently, it was determined that Lani should receive additional support in word recognition development five times per week rather than three.

Outcome

Assessments used to establish whether students achieve expected levels of academic performance by the end of the school year are generally referred to as *outcome assessments*. Data from outcome assessments may be used by teachers and administrators to (1) evaluate overall instructional effectiveness and (2) document student progress at the end of the year. The information generated by outcome assessments may confirm the findings from the screening, progress monitoring, and diagnostic assessments collected during the school year, or establish that changes to the instructional program that were made as a consequence of these assessments were effective. Outcome assessments must be technically adequate to yield trustworthy results from which to make appropriate decisions. Examples of outcome assessments for word recognition are included in Table 6.2.

On concluding the school year, Lani's teacher administered the DIBELS-NWF and Oral Reading Fluency measures to all her students to determine her overall instructional effectiveness and to document her students' overall growth in word recognition.

Lani correctly identified 67 letter sounds per minute on the NWF measure, exceeding the middle of the year benchmark of 50 letter sounds per minute, and she read at a rate of 52 words correct per minute on the Oral Reading Fluency measure, well beyond the first-grade end-of-year benchmark of 40 words correct per minute. Her performance across measures at the end of the school year indicated that Lani was now at *low risk* for reading difficulties and that she was on track for developing her skills in word recognition.

In considering the purposes of assessment and how they are applied in practice, it is evident that assessment has the potential to provide answers to one global question for teachers: "How effective is my instruction?" Lani's teacher implemented a systematic approach to assessment throughout the school year. She screened all students in her class early in the school year using a technically adequate measure of word recognition. She used informal diagnostic assessment to pinpoint specific areas of need for students, such as Lani, identified on the screening instrument as at risk for later difficulties. In addition, she monitored progress toward grade-level expectations and progress within instructional-level materials, and she used her outcome assessment data to evaluate her overall teaching effectiveness. Adopting this process enabled the teacher to identify the proficiency of her students in terms of word recognition and to plan and modify her instruction responsively.

WORD RECOGNITION ASSESSMENT AND STUDENTS WITH LEARNING DISABILITIES

Not all children follow Ehri's (2005) developmental phases and easily develop their word recognition to a level of automaticity (Cunningham & Stanovich, 1998; Logan, 1997). One group of students that has significant difficulties with word reading is students with learning disabilities (LDs). These students experience concomitant challenges and struggles with fluency, developing new vocabulary, and in understanding authors' meaning. These difficulties reinforce the importance of early identification of students with reading problems and the provision of systematic, explicit intervention (McCray, Vaughn, & Neal, 2001; Torgesen, 1998).

Traditional models of LD identification require the documentation of a significant discrepancy between a child's achievement and aptitude. Unfortunately, these models postpone special instruction until the child is "age 9 or older" (Vaughn, Linan-Thompson, & Hickman, 2003, p. 392). However, by this point, word reading problems of students with LD have become more difficult to overcome than if they were addressed at an earlier age. One approach to preventing this delay of instructional support is to use a response-to-intervention model (RTI), adopting alternative criteria for LD identification that include unexplained low achievement or minimal response to instruction (Vaughn et al., 2003; Wagner, Francis, & Morris, 2005). RTI employs a system-wide model for prevention of academic failure for all students by implementing high-quality, research-based instruction in the general classroom setting. Frequently, RTI consists of a multiple-tier model of instruction that is predicated on documented effective practices and increasing intensity across tiers and established across a school. This multiple-tier model of increasing intensity systematically manipulates variables such as time, instructional programs, grouping structures, and personnel to ensure optimal outcomes for students as they progress through the tiers of instruction. Systematic collection of screening, diagnostic, progress monitoring, and outcome data, as we have described earlier in this chapter, is an integral component of the RTI model (National Research Center on Learning Disabilities, 2005).

The purposeful and systematic use of measures to assess student word recognition is a critical feature in the process of identifying and evaluating the effectiveness of instruction overall in the RTI model. The system of measures can facilitate the implementation of the RTI model to provide prevention and intervention services in an early phase of reading development (Simmons et al., 2000). If Lani's teacher, for example, had not adopted the systematic assessment process and had not planned her instruction in a responsive way, several of her students, including Lani, may have been identified as having LDs in second or third grade, as they still struggled with decoding.

Recent studies suggest that with systematic assessment and instruction, fewer children are referred for special education for word reading difficulties (Harn, Chard, Kame'enui, & MacConnell, 2005; Vaughn, Linan-Thompson, & Hickman, 2003). However, for those who need additional support despite effective and supported instruction, it is necessary to manipulate instructional variables to increase the intensity of instruction. These variables include reducing group size (Berninger et al., 2002; O'Connor, 2000), increasing the duration of instruction (Simmons, Kame'enui, Good, & Chard, 2001; Berninger et al., 2002), and increasing the amount of scaffolded coached reading (Harn et al., 2005).

Most students with LDs have significant problems in phonological processing and in other aspects of language processing (Catts & Hogan, 2003). Therefore, in addition to the system of word recognition assessments described earlier, it is important to use other language measures to help identify students' specific learning needs (Catts & Hogan, 2003; Torgesen, 1998). Further description of the support needed for students with LD is beyond the scope of this chapter.

ASSESSING WORD RECOGNITION IN ENGLISH LEARNERS

English language learners (ELLs) often experience difficulties in learning to read words. These difficulties sometimes go beyond elementary school, influencing students' success in reading in academic content areas. However, it is very complex to identify whether ELLs are experiencing reading difficulties while their language and literacy skills in a second language are still under development. Therefore, it is often difficult to plan and provide appropriate instructional services for them at the right time (McCardle, Mele-McCarthy, Cutting, Leos, & D'Emilio, 2005). However, with regard to the development of word reading skills, assessments need not differ considerably from the assessments we would use with monolingual English readers.

Mason, Stahl, Au, and Herman (2003) assert that we can best ascertain children's understanding of words "from the perspective of developing sensitivities to the English language" (p. 914). This perspective suggests that it is critical for practitioners to gain a "big picture" of ELLs' level of sensitivities to English before, or at the time of, using any screening, diagnostic, progress monitoring, and outcome measures of English word recognition skills. The development of sensitivity to the English language, particularly English orthography, may initially be influenced by the nature of ELLs' native language (both written and spoken) and continuously be developed or shaped by the additive formal and/or informal experiences with English. For example, young Arab children who have little knowledge or experience with English print may not know that they should read an English word from left to right, instead of from right to left. Chinese children who have just started learning the names of English letters may not know that individual letters do not carry meaning. With increased English language experience, their growing level of sensitivity to English and its print conventions will facilitate their word recognition growth (Mason et al., 2003).

For children who learn to read languages with predictable rules of grapheme–phoneme correspondence, such as Italian, Arabic, Spanish, and German (Denton, Hasbrouck, Weaver, & Riccio, 2000; Goswami, 2002; Lipka, Siegel, & Vukovic, 2005), the letter sound learning process is rapid. In contrast, finding the regularities of the language may be a slow process for children who are learning to read a language such as English, which has more complex and inconsistent orthographical rules (Goswami, 2002). These findings imply that an ELL whose first language has a consistent orthography might not have any difficulty in learning to read that language, but might have some difficulties in learning to read English (Wade-Woolley & Siegel, 1997; Lipka et al., 2005). Emerging research evidence suggests that, in general, ELLs and monolingual children do not differ on reading development patterns in English (Denton et al., 2000; Lipka et al., 2005). It is helpful for practitioners to be aware of, and sensitive to, the different orthographical features of ELLs' primary languages when interpreting assessment results and making instructional decisions.

In summary, the measurement instruments described earlier to assess word recognition are useful for ELLs in that they can help us measure their skill development with phonemic awareness, phonics, and phonological recoding. However, the results should be interpreted with caution. First, because most assessments in English were not validated with ELLs in their norm sample, their technical adequacy for ELLs has not been established. In addition, ELLs need to be assessed for their language proficiency in both English and their first language (McCardle, Mele-McCarthy, & Leos, 2005). Although their word reading skills (e.g., letter sound knowledge) may be developing similarly to those of their monolingual English peers, it is possible that their knowledge of word meanings is not.

CONCLUSION

In his recent book *The Blank Slate*, psychologist Steven Pinker wrote: "Education is neither writing on a blank slate nor allowing the child's nobility to come into flower. Rather, education is a technology that tries to make up for what the human mind is innately bad at" (2002, p. 222). Word recognition is an important convention that the human mind must be educated to do. For many children, the complexities of word recognition become a barrier to accessing the meaning of texts. In this chapter we have described several assessments that can be used to (1) predict and detect word recognition difficulties, (2) identify specific difficulties, and (3) plan, monitor, and evaluate instruction. When used with explicit and planful instruction, these assessments can assist teachers in enhancing their instructional effectiveness for all developing readers.

REFERENCES

Adams, M. J. (1990). *Beginning to read: Thinking and learning about print.* Cambridge, MA: MIT Press.

Baumann, J. F., & Kame'enui, E. J. (Eds.). (2004). *Vocabulary instruction: Research to practice.* New York: Guilford Press.

Berninger, V. W., Abbott, R. D., Vermeulen, K., Ogier, S., Brooksher, R., Zook, D., et al. (2002). Comparison of faster and slower responders to early intervention in reading: Differentiating features of their language profiles. *Learning Disability Quarterly, 25,* 59–76.

Carnine, D. W., Silbert, J., Kame'enui, E. J., & Tarver, S. G. (2004). *Direct instruction reading.* New York: Prentice-Hall.

Catts, H. W., & Hogan, T. P. (2003). Language basis of reading disabilities and implications for early identification and remediation. *Reading Psychology, 24,* 223–246.

Center for Academic Reading Skills. (1999). *Texas Primary Reading Inventory.* Austin, TX: Texas Education Agency.

Chard, D. J., & Osborn, J. (1999). Phonics and word recognition instruction in early reading programs: Guidelines for accessibility. *Learning Disabilities Research and Practice, 14,* 107–117.

Chard, D. J., Simmons, D. C., & Kame'enui, E. J. (1998). Word recognition: Research bases. In D. C. Simmons & E. J. Kame'enui (Eds.), *What reading research tells us about children with diverse learning needs: The bases and the basics* (pp. 141–168). Hillsdale, NJ: Erlbaum.

Cunningham, A. E., & Stanovich, K. (1998). What reading does for the mind. *American Educator, 22,* 8–15.

Denton, C. A., Hasbrouck, J. E., Weaver, L. R., & Riccio, C. A. (2000). What do we know about phonological awareness in Spanish? *Reading Psychology, 21,* 335–352.

Ehri, L. C. (1995). Stages of development in learning to read words by sight. *Journal of Research in Reading, 18,* 116–125.

Ehri, L. C. (1997). Sight word learning in normal readers and dyslexics. In B. Blachman (Ed.), *Foundations of reading acquisition and dyslexia* (pp. 163–189). Mahwah, NJ: Erlbaum.

Ehri, L. C. (1998). Research on learning to read and spell: A personal–historical perspective. *Scientific Studies of Reading, 2,* 97–114.

Ehri, L. C. (2005). Learning to read words: Theory, findings, and issues. *Scientific Studies of Reading, 9*(2), 167–188.

Fuchs, L. S., Fuchs, D., & Compton, D. L. (2004). Monitoring early reading development in first grade: Word identification fluency versus nonsense word fluency. *Exceptional Children, 71*(1), 7–21.

Good, R. H., & Kaminski, R. A. (2003). *DIBELS: Dynamic indicators of basic early literacy skills* (6th ed.). Longmont, CO: Sopris West.

Goswami, U. (2002). Phonology, reading development, and dyslexia: A cross-linguistic perspective. *Annals of Dyslexia, 52,* 141–163.

Harcourt, Brace Educational Measurement. (1997). *Stanford Achievement Test—10th edition.* Orlando, FL: Harcourt Brace.

Harn, B., Chard, D. J., Kame'enui, E. J., & MacConnell, K. (2005, July). *Accelerating learning rates: Instructional and curricular features of intensive third tier intervention efforts with second graders.* Paper presented at the annual meeting of the Office of Special Education Programs Project Director's Conference, Washington, DC.

Hoover, H., Dunbar, S., Frisbie, D., Oberley, K., Ordman, V., Naylor, G., et al. (2001). *Iowa Tests of Basic Skills.* Itasca, IL: Riverside.

Kaminski, R. A., & Good, R. H. (1996). Toward a technology for assessing basic early literacy skills. *School Psychology Review, 25,* 215–227.

Kaminski, R. A., & Good, R. H. (1998). Use of curriculum-based measurement to assess early literacy: Dynamic indicators of basic early literacy skills. In M. Shinn (Ed.), *Advances in curriculum-based measurement and its use in a problem-solving model* (pp. 113–142). New York: Guilford Press.

Lipka, O., Siegel, L. S., & Vukovic, R. (2005). The literacy skills of English language learners in Canada. *Learning Disabilities Research and Practice, 20*(1), 39–49.

Logan, G. D. (1997). Automaticity and reading: Perspectives from the instance theory of automatization. *Reading and Writing Quarterly, 13*(2), 123–146.

Mason, J. M., Stahl, S. A., Au, K. H., & Herman, P. A. (2003). Reading: Children's developing knowledge of words. In J. Flood, J. M. Jensen, D. Lapp, & J. R. Squires (Eds.), *Handbook of research on teaching the English language arts* (pp. 914–930). Mahwah, NJ: Erlbaum.

McCardle, P., Mele-McCarthy, J., Cutting, L., Leos, K., & D'Emilio, T. (2005). Learning disabilities in English language learners: Identifying the issues. *Learning Disabilities Research and Practice, 20*(1), 1–5.

McCardle, P., Mele-McCarthy, J., & Leos, K. (2005). English language learners and learning disabilities: Research agenda and implications for practice. *Learning Disabilities and Practice, 20*(1), 68–78.

McCray, A. D., Vaughn, S., & Neal, L. I. (2001). Not all students learn to read by third grade: Middle school students speak out about their reading disabilities. *Journal of Special Education, 35*, 17–30.

Nagy, W. E., & Herman, P. A. (1987). Breadth and depth of vocabulary knowledge: Implications for acquisition and instruction. In M. G. McKeown & M. E. Curtis (Eds.), *The nature of vocabulary acquisition* (pp. 19–35). Hillsdale, NJ: Erlbaum.

National Research Center on Learning Disabilities. (2005). *Core concepts of RTI.* Retrieved March 16, 2006, from *www.nrcld.org/research/rti/concepts.shtml.*

O'Connor, R. (2000). Increasing the intensity of intervention in kindergarten and first grade. *Learning Disabilities Research and Practice, 15*(1), 43–54.

Perfetti, C. A. (1985). *Reading ability.* New York: Oxford University Press.

Pikulski, J. J., & Chard, D. J. (2005). Fluency: Bridge between decoding and reading comprehension. *The Reading Teacher, 58*, 510–519.

Pinker, S. (2002). *The blank slate.* New York: Putnam.

Psychological Corporation. (2000). *Early Reading Diagnostic Assessment.* Orlando, FL: Author.

Salvia, J., & Ysseldyke, J. E. (2004). *Assessment in special and inclusive education.* Boston: Houghton Mifflin.

Shefelbine, J. (1996). *Basic Phonics Skills Test.* Sacramento: California State University.

Simmons, D. C., Kame'enui, E. J., Good, R. H., & Chard, D. J. (2001). *Focus and nature of primary, secondary, and tertiary prevention: CIRCUITS model* [Technical report]. Eugene, OR: Center for Teaching and Learning.

Simmons, D. C., Kame'enui, E. J., Good, R. H., Harn, B. A., Cole, C., & Braun, D. (2000). Building, implementing, and sustaining a beginning reading model: School by school and lessons learned. *Oregon School Study Council Bulletin, 43*(3), 1–30.

Slosson, R. L., & Nicholson, C. L. (1990). *Slosson Oral Reading Test.* East Aurora, NY: Slosson Educational Publishers.

Stanovich, K. E. (1980). Toward an interactive–compensatory model of individual differences in the development of reading fluency. *Reading Research Quarterly, 16*, 32–71.

Stanovich, K. E. (1986). Matthew effects in reading: Some consequences of individual differences in the acquisition of literacy. *Reading Research Quarterly, 21*, 360–407.

Torgesen, J. K. (1998). Catch them before they fall: Identification and assessment to prevent reading failure in young children. *American Educator, 22*, 32–39.

Torgesen, J. K., Wagner, R. K., & Rashotte, C. A. (1999). *TOWRE: Test of Word Reading Efficiency.* Austin, TX: PRO-ED.

Vaughan, S., Linan-Thompson, S., & Hickman, P. (2003). Response to instruction as a means of identifying students with reading/learning disabilities. *Exceptional Children, 69,* 391–409.

Wade-Woolley, L., & Siegel, L. S. (1997). The spelling performance of ESL and native speakers of English as a function of reading skill. *Reading and Writing, 9,* 387–406.

Wagner, R. K., Francis, D. J., & Morris, R. D. (2005). Identifying English language learners with learning disabilities: Key challenges and possible approaches. *Learning Disabilities Research and Practice, 20*(1), 6–15.

Woodcock, R. W. (2000). *Woodcock Reading Mastery Test–Revised.* Circle Pines, MN: American Guidance Service.

Woodcock, R. W., McGrew, K. S., & Mather, N. (2001). *Woodcock–Johnson III Tests of Achievement.* Itasca, IL: Riverside.

CHAPTER 7

Effective Oral Reading Assessment (or Why Round Robin Reading Doesn't Cut It)

Melanie R. Kuhn

Over the past several years, fluency has shifted from being a "neglected" (Allington, 1983a, p. 556) component of reading development to one of reading education's "hot topics" (Cassidy & Cassidy, 2004/2005, p. 1). This move is well deserved, given that fluency is a key element in the development of skilled reading and a contributing factor to reading comprehension (Kuhn & Stahl, 2003; National Reading Panel, 2000). As fluency becomes increasingly prominent within the literacy curriculum, it becomes equally important to identify appropriate assessment tools for use in concert with that instruction—measures that will help identify which students are developing into fluent readers and which students need additional support. The purpose of this chapter is to outline effective approaches for assessing a multifaceted component of reading. Before focusing on assessment, however, it is important to identify what it means to be a fluent reader and what effective fluency instruction entails.

WHAT IS FLUENT READING?

In order to be considered a fluent reader, a learner needs to have made the transition from reading that is word by word and monotonous to reading that is smooth and expressive (Kuhn & Stahl, 2003; National Reading Panel, 2000). In other words, rather than expending a large amount of effort identifying the words they encounter in text, students have to develop accurate and automatic word recognition (e.g., Adams, 1990;

LeBerge & Samuels, 1974). Further, fluent readers need to be able to transfer prosodic elements, such as appropriate pitch, stress and phrasing, from oral language to written text (e.g., Erekson, 2003; Schreiber, 1991).

Fluent reading contributes to a learner's ability to construct meaning from text in two ways. First, automatic word recognition allows learners to focus on a text's meaning rather than on the decoding of words (e.g., LeBerge & Samuels, 1974). As long as students have to spend significant amounts of attention on word identification, it is unlikely that they will have enough attention remaining to concentrate on the meaning. However, as word recognition becomes automatic, the attention that was previously used for decoding is freed up and can be used for comprehension instead. Second, readers' use of appropriate prosody allows them to develop accurate interpretations of written language by applying aspects of oral language, such as expression and appropriate phrasing, to text (e.g., Dowhower, 1991; Schreiber, 1991). In turn, their accurate interpretations allow them to understand the shades of meaning in a text and to derive pleasure from their reading (think how uninspiring it is to listen to a word-by-word reader or one who reads in a monotonous manner!). Finally, as students become increasingly fluent, they develop growing competence with their reading, which, in turn, allows them to move on to more challenging material and to become increasingly independent learners (e.g., Stanovich, 1986)—that is, readers who are capable of learning from the texts they are reading (Chall, 1996).

FOUR PRINCIPLES FOR DEVELOPING READING FLUENCY

In order to implement effective assessments, it is also important to discuss briefly those elements that make for effective—and ineffective—oral reading instruction. Such an understanding can help not only to assist learners in their literacy development, but also to guide the evaluation of their reading. Rasinski (2003) has identified four principles that underlie good fluency instruction. First, he suggests that teachers provide a model of expressive reading by reading aloud. Expressive oral reading of enjoyable texts provides learners with an example of what their reading should ultimately sound like. It also engages learners and encourages the realization that reading consists of more than simply identifying words. As well, when a broad range of texts (including nonfiction and poetry) is read aloud, students are introduced to new genres and new concepts. Some readers will find such material more appealing than they do a traditional story and are more likely to be drawn to reading on their own as a result (Duke & Bennett-Armistead, 2003).

The second principle involves the provision of support or assistance as learners make the transition to fluency. Such support can be provided through choral, echo, partner, or paired reading and gives learners access to material that would otherwise be inaccessible. This scaffolding helps guide students through whatever difficulties they encounter during their reading and assists them in moving beyond word-by-word reading to an automatic and prosodic reading of texts. Third, effective fluency instruction provides students with ample opportunities to practice reading connected text. Such practice helps students read smoothly and expressively by allowing them to apply what they have learned about word recognition in context. Further, reviews of research (Kuhn & Stahl, 2003; National Reading Panel, 2000) and recent studies (e.g., Stahl & Heubach, 2005) confirm that such practice is key in developing students' overall reading ability.

Fourth, it is important to teach students the use of appropriate phrasing through direct feedback (e.g., explaining how the words should be grouped in a given sentence) and by indicating how inappropriate phrasing can muddle the meaning of a text. By integrating these principles into the literacy curriculum, it is possible to help learners make the transition from laborious word recognition and unexpressive renditions of text to reading that is "fluid, flowing and facile" (Dowhower, 1987, p. 390).

INEFFECTIVE ORAL READING INSTRUCTION

Although there are a number of effective ways to integrate the above principles into practice (e.g., repeated reading, echo reading) when thinking about oral reading, the primary approach that still comes to mind for many educators is that of round robin reading (Rasinski & Hoffman, 2003). Despite the fact that it is generally considered ineffective as an instructional procedure (Allington, 1983a, 1983b; Ash & Kuhn, 2006; Optiz & Rasinski, 1998), it remains a common component in many classrooms in at least one of its guises (popcorn, popsicle, combat, and round robin reading, itself). There are a number of reasons for this popularity. According to a recent survey (Ash & Kuhn, 2006), round robin reading is seen by teachers as a way to develop students' fluency, a way to make difficult text accessible, a way to ensure that each student has the opportunity (or is required) to read at least a portion of the text, and, perhaps most importantly from the perspective of this chapter, a way to assess students' oral reading development.

Unfortunately, round robin reading not only fails to aid learners in their reading development, it can actually contribute to disfluent reading practices among students. For example, the practice of round robin reading takes a connected text and causes students to focus on disconnected parts. Further, when disfluent readers are called upon to read a given passage aloud, they provide other learners with a poor example of what oral reading should sound like. This is especially problematic when students are grouped according to ability, and disfluent readers serve as one another's only model of oral reading. Further, when learners are provided with limited opportunities for practice—for example, one paragraph out of every 15 or 20—as is common with any form of round robin reading, conditions are created that actually make it unlikely for students to demonstrate significant improvement in their reading. Similarly, it is unlikely that most students will perform a "cold" reading of a text well, particularly when they are reading it in front of their peers. Finally, although it is seen as a way of determining students' progress in terms of fluency and word recognition development, it fails to serve as an effective measure of oral reading growth for the reasons presented above. If the goal is to see students' optimal oral reading performance on an unpracticed text, it is more likely that a one-on-one setting would be conducive to achieving that aim. Ultimately, the growth that a teacher hopes to see as a result of round robin reading is actually *less* likely to occur precisely because of its use as an instructional or evaluative approach.

ASSESSING FLUENT READING

Although round robin reading is ineffective at both teaching and assessing oral reading, there are several measures that provide valid evaluations of students' fluency. Such assessments are important for several reasons (McKenna & Stahl, 2003; Rasinski, 2003). They allow you to see how fluently your students are reading, and they allow you to match students with texts by determining their independent, instructional, and frustration levels. Over time, a series of oral reading assessments will allow you to identify your students' growth—or lack of growth—both individually and as a class. Additionally, assessments can help to inform your instruction by answering a range of questions:

> Do my students need fluency-oriented literacy instruction?
>
> Should I consider using such instruction with all of my students, or is it more appropriate for a smaller group of learners who do not seem to be making the transition to fluent reading?
>
> Is the instructional approach I'm currently using helping my students become skilled and expressive oral readers, or should I consider using an alternative?

Taken together, fluency assessment can help to ensure that there is a good match between your instruction and the goals you are setting for the students in your classroom as well as help you evaluate your students' progress to date.

Accurate and Automatic Word Recognition

Given the importance of valid oral reading assessments, it is useful to know that there are multiple ways to evaluate students' oral reading. The first of these approaches is the most commonly used measure and is perhaps the easiest to implement as well. It involves determining the students' reading rate along with their percentage of correct versus incorrect words. These two aspects of a learner's oral reading are usually combined into a single measure known as the number of correct words read per minute (cwpm). By establishing this figure, it becomes possible to determine the accuracy (correct words) and rate (the number of words read per minute) of an individual reader.

Since it is relatively easy to establish these figures, reading rate and accuracy are routinely used to evaluate whether students' fluency development is on track. The students' cwpm figure can be established in several ways. First, it is possible to determine cwpm rate by asking students to read aloud for 1 minute from the beginning of a selected text. Students can be asked to read either from a text that is part of the classroom literacy curriculum or from a text that is chosen specifically for assessment purposes (e.g., a 100–200-word passage identified as being at a specific reading level, such as those presented by Fountas & Pinnell, 1996, or Gunning, 1998, could be used). The former allows teachers to see how well their students are performing on their day-to-day instructional material, and the latter helps teachers determine the appropriate reading level for their students (e.g., to determine levels for flexible grouping). In a modification of this approach, the teacher can ask a student to read aloud from a given text for several minutes before taking a 1-minute rating (Valencia et al., 2005). This "prereading" serves as a "warm-up" period for the students, allowing them to become comfortable with the material they are reading before being assessed. A third option is to take a number of 1-minute readings (I would suggest three) and average the ratings across the passages. If you choose to do this, however, I suggest either selecting several passages from the same text or identifying passages from equivalently leveled texts in order to maximize the reliability of your ratings.

Once you have established the students' cwpm ratings, how can you determine whether they are making adequate progress in terms of their fluency development? Fortunately, there are a number of excellent norms that provide cwpm guidelines for students. These present a range of what can be expected for readers both across grade levels and at various time points within a given grade (usually spring, winter and fall). The norms presented in Table 7.1 are available in the public domain. Additional guidelines include those developed by Hasbrouck and Tindal (2006) and Howe and Shinn (2001).

When comparing the cwpm rates established for your students with the norms presented here, it is important to keep two points in mind. First, these norms represent an average. If you have a few students who fall significantly below this average, it is a sign that additional instruction, either as part of a one-on-one or an intensive small group setting, is warranted. Appropriate strategies for such instruction can include reading while listening (e.g., Chomsky, 1978), repeated reading (e.g., Dahl, 1979; Samuels, 1979), and fluency-oriented oral instruction (Kuhn, 2004). However, if large numbers of students are not approaching these guidelines, it is likely that fluency instruction that can be used with the entire class should be considered. Commonly used practices include paired repeated reading (Koskinen & Blum, 1986), Fluency-Oriented Reading Instruction, or Wide Reading (Kuhn et al., in press).

Second, it is often the case that students lose ground over the summer—a fact that is reflected in the norms presented here. Note that the cwpm norms for the spring of a given grade are generally higher than the norms presented for the following fall (e.g., the cwpm norm for spring of second grade is 94, whereas the norm for fall of third grade is 79). Although this decrease should not be surprising, it should reinforce the importance of encouraging student reading over the summer in order to minimize such losses. Allington (2005) presented data indicating that although students from low socioeconomic status (SES) and middle-to-high SES backgrounds made generally equivalent gains over the course of a school year, these gains were more likely to evaporate over the summer for students from lower SES backgrounds than were the gains

TABLE 7.1. Oral Reading Fluency Target Rate Norms

Grade	Fall (wcpm)	Winter (wcpm)	Spring (wcpm)
1		10–30	30–60
2	30–60	50–80	70–100
3	50–90	70–100	80–110
4	70–110	80–120	100–140
5	80–120	100–140	110–150
6	100–140	110–150	120–160
7	110–150	120–160	130–170
8	120–160	130–170	140–180

Note. Downloaded August 31, 2005, from www.prel.org/products/re_/assessing-fluency.htm.

for their more economically advantaged peers. Given the structure of the school year, this backsliding can likely best be countered through the creation of engaged readers, that is, readers who willingly pick up reading material for their own pleasure. Because skilled readers are more likely to be engaged readers, it follows that, by assisting students with their fluency development, we are assisting them in becoming engaged readers as well.

Prosodic Reading

When considering fluency assessment, it is important to think not only in terms of accurate and automatic word recognition, but also in terms of prosody. A recent review of studies measuring fluent reading (Kuhn & Stahl, 2003) indicated that there has been a heavy concentration on rate and accuracy, to a large extent because they are the more tangible elements of fluency. That is, it is comparatively easy to measure the rate at which a student is reading and the number of words that are read correctly and incorrectly in each passage with a high degree of accuracy. Although automaticity and accuracy are important components of fluent reading, they do not capture the entire picture. An equally significant aspect of reading fluency involves features such as expression and appropriate phrasing that, when taken together, comprise prosodic reading. However, it is also the case that these elements are harder to measure than the components discussed above, because they are less concrete. Fortunately, as is the case with the cwpm norms cited earlier, there are several excellent scales designed for a more global evaluation of fluency, including a scale created by Allington and Brown (Allington, 1983a), the Multidimensional Fluency Scale by Zutell and Rasinksi (1991), and that of the National Center for Education Statistics (1995).

The scale presented here, the National Assessment of Educational Progess (NAEP) Oral Reading Fluency Scale (National Center for Education Statistics, 1995), is designed to evaluate students' oral reading across four levels (see Figure 7.1). The NAEP is a national evaluation of the country's fourth, eighth, and twelfth graders' academic achievement and serves as a periodic indicator (it is given approximately every 4 years)

Level 4	Reads primarily in larger, meaningful phrase groups. Although some regressions, repetitions, and deviations from text may be present, those do not appear to detract from the overall structure of the story. Preservation of the author's syntax is consistent. Some or most of the story is read with expressive interpretation.
Level 3	Reads primarily in three- or four-word phrase groups. Some smaller groupings may be present. However, the majority of phrasing seems appropriate and preserves the syntax of the author. Little or no expressive interpretation is present.
Level 2	Reads primarily in two-word phrases with some three- or four-word groupings. Some word-by-word reading may be present. Word groupings may seem awkward and unrelated to larger context of sentence or passage.
Level 1	Reads primarily word by word. Occasionally two-word or three-word phrases may occur, but these are infrequent and/or do not preserve meaningful syntax.

FIGURE 7.1. National Assessment of Educational Progress's Oral Reading Fluency Scale. From National Center for Education Statistics (1995).

of these students' standing on a range of measures, including fluency (Graves, Juel, & Graves, 2001). The scale incorporates evaluations of pace, smoothness, phrasing, and expression in a generalized measure of prosodic oral reading, thereby allowing the listener to assess children's oral reading across four levels. These levels range from reading that is, at the most basic level, primarily word by word and lacks both a sense of expression and the appropriate use of syntax, and advances to reading that incorporates all of the attributes that comprise a fluent rendering of text.

It is important to recognize that the results from the fluency scales are more nuanced and will, therefore, show greater variation as the result of the students' grade level, than are the comparable guidelines for rate and accuracy. For example, it is not unusual for first graders to read in a word-by-word manner (NAEP level 1). As they progress through first grade and into second, they should start shifting to two-word phrases; however, this shift is likely to be accompanied with little or no expression (NAEP level 2). As students progress through second grade, their reading should begin to incorporate more appropriate phrasing and start to take on elements of expression. Ideally, by the end of the second and continuing into the third grade, students' reading should begin to incorporate appropriate phrasing and adequate expression (moving through NAEP level 3 and onto NAEP level 4). Again, these are guidelines, and some learners will move through these levels more quickly. However, students who are not meeting these goals will likely benefit from additional fluency instruction. Of course, this transition is more likely to occur when your literacy instruction models the qualities of fluent reading *and* when students are encouraged to develop these traits in their own reading. Further, it is important to note that students in the fourth grade—and beyond—whose reading of grade-level material does not reach a level 4 on the NAEP scale would also likely benefit from direct instruction in either some, or all, aspects of reading fluency.

The use of the NAEP scale, or one of its alternatives, allows the teacher to establish a fuller picture of students' oral reading than would be the case with just a cwpm rating. As a result, it becomes apparent when a student, or a class, needs to have the less tangible elements of fluency, such as expression, emphasized as part of their reading instruction. Because both of the evaluations can be conducted relatively quickly, I strongly suggest that both be implemented to establish a broader understanding of students' oral reading abilities. As with rate and accuracy measures, the NAEP Oral Reading Fluency Scale (National Center for Education Statistics, 1995) and similar measures can be used with the texts that are part of the literacy curriculum or with texts that are selected specifically for evaluation purposes.

CONDUCTING FLUENCY ASSESSMENT: GENERALIZATIONS

When assessing students' oral reading fluency both in terms of cwpm and their use of appropriate prosody, there are three considerations worth bearing in mind. First, it is important that the students' evaluations are conducted on a "cold" reading of the selected text; in other words, they should not have had the opportunity to practice reading the material previously. Although it is the case that, for instructional purposes, students should not be called upon to read a passage aloud unless they have had ample opportunity for practice, the same does not hold true for assessment. Although this may seem to be an obvious point, I emphasize it because of its salience: If an accurate picture of your students' oral reading is to be attained during the assessment, it is necessary that their reading be conducted using a text that they have not encountered previously.

Second, although you may wish to conduct oral reading assessments to determine students' instructional level, it is also important that your students be evaluated on grade-level material—or text that you would expect to be appropriate for your grade's literacy instruction—whenever possible. Although reading instruction often uses materials at your students' instructional level, this is not always the case. Further, content-area instruction usually involves reading grade-level material as opposed to instructional-level text. In order to determine how well your students can handle text designed for their grade level, it is necessary to evaluate them on such material. However, the goal of this exercise is not to subject students to an experience in which they are inevitably going to fail. If you know that your students will not be able to handle such material at all, start the assessment at a level you believe is appropriate for them and continue with more challenging material, until the students are either disfluent in their reading or performing below your expectations for a given passage (e.g., their reading becomes choppy, or there is a high percentage of miscues). This guideline should provide you with a sense not only of the text level at which the students are performing, but also the degree to which fluency-oriented instruction is indicated for your students.

Finally, although it is possible to determine the reader's accuracy, automaticity, and prosody levels simply by listening to her or him, I suggest making a tape recording of each student's reading, at least until you become comfortable with the rating scales that you are using. Because you will probably listen to each student's reading only for a few minutes, you should be able to fit all your students' samples onto a single 60- or 90-minute tape. This recording will provide you with a more accurate analysis of your students' reading in two ways. First, it will allow you to go back to your students' rendering of a passage and confirm their miscues. Second, it will allow you to relisten to the prosodic elements of the text, such as phrasing, in order to confirm your rating on the NAEP scale or its equivalent. Because these latter elements are more difficulty to quantify, it is especially beneficial to confirm these scores by listening to your students' reading a second time.

WHICH STUDENTS NEED FLUENCY ASSESSMENT?

As part of the broader discussion surrounding fluency assessment, it is important to consider which students need to be evaluated. Traditionally, fluency has been regarded as the purview of second and third grade (Chall, 1996). Prior to second grade, most print-oriented literacy instruction focuses either on concepts of print (pre-K and kindergarten) or word recognition (first grade). By the time students reach second grade, there is a shift in this focus. At this point, instruction should be designed to assist students in consolidating their decoding knowledge, thereby making their word recognition automatic. This consolidation can best be achieved through the supported reading of connected text. Further, the integration of prosodic elements into the students' reading of texts needs to be emphasized. As a result of this instructional focus, it makes sense to assess students' fluency in the second and third grades. However, fluency assessment is also appropriate from the middle or end of first grade to determine whether students are beginning to make the transition from strictly word-by-word reading to two-, or even the occasional three-, word phrases and to see if their cwpm rates are developing as would be expected.

Finally, the belief that students will be able to read grade-level material with a good degree of fluency by the time they are in the fourth grade, thereby allowing them to use reading as a means of acquiring previously unknown knowledge, is one of the major objectives of literacy instruction (Chall, 1996). However, it is often the case that students who are struggling readers in the fourth grade and beyond demonstrate a lack of fluency as well as difficulties with decoding and comprehension. When such learners are encountered, it is important to assess their oral reading both by comparing their cwpm rates to one of the norms and by using a fluency scale. Although a gap exists between these learners' literacy skills and those of their peers, research indicates that fluency-oriented instruction can help such learners develop their overall reading performance within a relatively short period of time (Dowhower, 1989, 1994; Kuhn & Stahl, 2003; National Reading Panel, 2000), thereby helping them to move more closely to the reading levels considered appropriate for their age.

DETERMINING STUDENTS' READING LEVELS

A different, but equally valid, goal for oral reading assessment involves determining individual student's independent, instructional, and frustration levels. In order to identify these levels for an individual student, it is useful to begin with the traditional percentage of correct words for a given passage; that is, 98% or higher for independent reading level, 95–98% for instructional reading level, and below 95% for frustration level texts (Betts, 1946). However, it is useful to incorporate the rate and prosodic elements of oral reading discussed above for a broader understanding of these levels. That is, students may have high levels of accuracy but read exceedingly slowly, or they may have appropriate rate but poor phrasing. In cases such as these, students will benefit from a view of instructional level that takes factors beyond accuracy into account. It is also worth repeating that students can benefit from reading instruction that uses challenging texts if adequate scaffolding is provided (Kuhn et al., in press).

REPEATED READINGS AND FLUENCY ASSESSMENT

In addition to using assessments to evaluate students' oral reading on an intermittent basis and to determine instructional levels, students' growth can be measured as part of a repeated readings procedure. There are several approaches that use repetition as part of a fluency-oriented literacy curriculum, not only for individuals (repeated readings, e.g., Dowhower, 1989; Samuels, 1979), but also for dyads (paired repeated reading, e.g., Koskinen & Blum, 1986) and groups of students or classrooms (e.g., the Oral Recitation Lesson by Hoffman, 1987, and Fluency-Oriented Reading Instruction, or FORI, by Stahl & Heubach, 2005). When using these approaches, teachers—or the students themselves—can keep track of the progress that is being made for a given text by

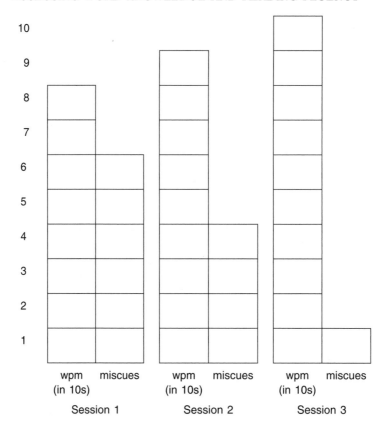

FIGURE 7.2. Tracking changes across repetitions. From Ash and Hagood (2000). Reprinted by permission of the authors.

recording increases in reading rate and decreases in the number of miscues across a series of repetitions. By recording these figures, students can see their own reading improve—a highly motivating scenario for students who have encountered difficulties with their reading in the past. Note that when employing a repeated reading approach, the bulk of the growth occurs between three and five repetitions (Reutzel, 2003). Should a student fail to see progress by the fifth repetition, it is an indication that the given text is too challenging and that it should be replaced with one closer to the student's instructional level (see Dowhower, 1989, or Rasinski, 2003, for a full description of the repeated readings procedure). Finally, Ash and Hagood (2000) have developed an easy-to-complete way of tracking the changes in a students' reading development across repetitions (see Figure 7.2).

CONCLUSIONS

Because fluency is being increasingly integrated into the literacy curriculum, it is important that teachers have a clear sense of what it is and how it should be evaluated. The assessments presented in this chapter should help to achieve these goals. By implementing these measures, you can determine which of your students would benefit from fluency-oriented instructional approaches. Further, when given over time, these assessments allow students' progress to be documented. Such a combination allows teachers to target their instruction to the students who most need it and ensures that these students make the progress necessary to become fluent readers.

REFERENCES

Adams, M. J. (1990). *Beginning to read: Thinking and learning about print*. Cambridge, MA: MIT Press.

Allington, R. L. (1983a). Fluency: The neglected reading goal. *The Reading Teacher, 36*, 556–561.

Allington, R. L. (1983b). The reading instruction provided readers of differing abilities. *Elementary School Journal, 83*, 95–107.

Allington, R. L. (2005, June). *What do good literacy program's look like?* Paper presented at the International Reading Association's urban deans' network, Washington, DC.

Ash, G., & Hagood, M. (2000, May). *This song goes out to Miss Gwynne and Miss Margaret*. Paper presented at the annual meeting of the International Reading Association, Indianapolis, IN.

Ash, G. E., & Kuhn, M. R. (2006). Meaningful oral and silent reading in the elementary and middle school classroom: Breaking the round robin reading addiction. In T. Rasinski, C. Blachowicz, & K. Lems (Eds.), *Fluency instruction: Research-based best practices* (pp. 155–172). New York: Guilford Press.

Betts, E. A. (1946). *Foundations of reading instruction*. New York: American Book.

Cassidy, J., & Cassidy, D. (2004/2005). What's hot, what's not for 2005. *Reading Today, 22*, 1.

Chall, J. S. (1996). *Stages of reading development*. Orlando, FL: Harcourt, Brace.

Chomsky, C. (1978). When you still can't read in third grade?: After decoding, what? In S. J. Samuels (Ed.), *What research has to say about reading instruction* (pp. 13– 30). Newark, DE: International Reading Association.

Dahl, P. R. (1979). An experimental program for teaching high speed word recognition and comprehension skills. In J. E. Button, T. Lovitt, & T. Rowland (Eds.), *Communications research in learning disabilities and mental retardation* (pp. 33–65). Baltimore: University Park Press.

Dowhower, S. L. (1987). Effects of repeated reading on second-grade transitional readers' fluency and comprehension. *Reading Research Quarterly, 22*, 389–406.

Dowhower, S. L. (1989). Repeated reading: Research into practice. *The Reading Teacher, 42*, 502–507.

Dowhower, S. L. (1991). Speaking of prosody: Fluency's unattended bedfellow. *Theory into Practice, 30*(3), 158–164.

Dowhower, S. L. (1994). Repeated reading revisited: Research into practice. *Reading and Writing Quarterly, 10*, 343–358.

Duke, N. K., & Bennett-Armistead, V. S. (2003). *Reading and writing informational text in the primary grades: Research-based practices*. New York: Scholastic Press.

Erekson, J. (2003, May). *Prosody: The problem of expression in fluency*. Paper presented at the Preconference Institute #15 of the International Reading Association annual meeting, Orlando, FL.

Fountas, I. C., & Pinnell, G. S. (1996). *Guided reading: Good first teaching for all children*. Portsmouth, NH: Heinemann.

Graves, M. F., Juel, C., & Graves, B. B. (2001). *Teaching reading in the 21st century* (2nd ed.). Boston: Allyn & Bacon.

Gunning, T. G. (1998). *Best books for beginning readers*. Boston: Allyn & Bacon.

Hasbrouck, J., & Tindal, G. (2006). Oral reading fluency norms: A valuable assessment tool for reading teachers. *The Reading Teacher, 59*, 636–644.

Hoffman, J. (1987). Rethinking the role of oral reading. *Elementary School Journal, 87*, 367–373.

Howe, K. B., & Shinn, M. M. (2001). *Standard reading assessment passages (RAPS) for use in general outcome measurements: A manual describing development and technical features.* Eden Prairie, MN: Edformations.

Koskinen, P. S., & Blum, I. H. (1986). Paired repeated reading: A classroom strategy for developing fluent reading. *The Reading Teacher, 40*, 70–75.

Kuhn, M. R. (2004). Helping students become accurate, expressive readers: Fluency instruction for small groups. *The Reading Teacher, 58*, 338–344.

Kuhn, M. R., Schwanenflugel, P., Morris, R. D., Morrow, L. M., Stahl, S. A. (*in memoriam*), Woo, D., et al. (in press). Teaching children to become fluent and automatic readers. *Journal of Literacy Research.*

Kuhn, M. R., & Stahl, S. (2003). Fluency: A review of developmental and remedial strategies. *Journal of Educational Psychology, 95*, 1–19.

LeBerge, D., & Samuels, S. (1974). Toward a theory of automatic information processing in reading. *Cognitive Psychology, 6*, 293–323.

McKenna, M. C., & Stahl, S. A. (2003). *Assessment for reading instruction.* New York: Guilford Press.

National Center for Education Statistics. (1995). NAEP's oral reading fluency scale. *Listening to Children Read Aloud, 15*, Washington, DC: U.S. Department of Education.

National Reading Panel. (2000). *Teaching children to read: An evidence-based assessment of the scientific research literature on reading and its implications for reading instruction. Reports of the subgroups.* Bethesda, MD: National Institutes of Health. Available at *www.nichd.nih.gov/publications/nrp/.*

Optiz, M. F., & Rasinski, T. V. (1998). *Good-bye round robin: 25 effective oral reading strategies.* Portsmouth, NH: Heinemann.

Rasinksi, T. V. (2003). *The fluent reader: Oral reading strategies for building word recognition, fluency, and comprehension.* New York: Scholastic.

Rasinski, T. V., & Hoffman, J. V. (Eds.) (2003). Theory and research into practice: Oral reading in the school curriculum. *Reading Research Quarterly, 38*, 510–522.

Reutzel, D. R. (2003, May). *Fluency: What is it? How to assess it? How to develop it!* Paper presented at the Preconference Institute #15 of the International Reading Association annual meeting, Orlando, FL.

Samuels, S. J. (1979). The method of repeated readings. *The Reading Teacher, 32*, 403–408.

Schreiber, P. A. (1991). Understanding prosody's role in reading acquisition. *Theory into Practice, 30*(3), 158–164.

Stahl, S. A., & Heubach, K. M. (2005). Fluency-oriented reading instruction. *Journal of Literacy Research, 37*, 25–60.

Stanovich, K. E. (1986). Matthew effects in reading: Some consequences of individual differences in the acquisition of literacy. *Reading Research Quarterly, 21*, 360–407.

Valencia, S. W., Smith, A., Reece, A., Newman, H., Wixson, K., & Li, M. (2005, June). *The rush for oral reading fluency: Issues of assessment and implications for instruction.* Paper presented at the Berkeley Summer Literacy Institute, University of California, Berkeley.

Zutell, J., & Rasinski, T. V. (1991). Training teachers to attend to their students' oral reading fluency. *Theory into Practice, 30*, 211–217.

CHAPTER 8

Assessing Students' Spelling Knowledge

RELATIONSHIPS TO READING AND WRITING

Shane Templeton
Donald R. Bear
Sandra Madura

English spelling, that most troublesome torture of wits.
—HOOLE (1660)

English orthography is not a failed phonetic transcription system, invented out of madness or perversity . . . [rather] a more complex and more regular relationship, wherein phonemes and morphemes play leading roles.
—VENEZKY (1999)

Since the 1970s, research has revealed that students' spelling performance is a mirror of their knowledge of words (Templeton & Bear, 1992; Ehri, 1997; Perfetti, 1997). This knowledge underlies both writing words *and* reading words. Spelling or orthographic knowledge is no longer merely a convention of writing, therefore, but also a critical foundation for word identification in reading. In addition, in the intermediate grades and beyond, spelling knowledge is a significant cornerstone of vocabulary development (Templeton, 2004). In his classic work *Learning to Read and Spell: The Child's Knowledge of Words* (1981), Edmund Henderson compellingly advanced the argument that through the analysis of students' spelling, we may obtain the best insight into their knowledge of words. More recently, Charles Perfetti (1997) observed that the best way to assess the nature of an individual's lexical knowledge is to administer a well-constructed spelling test. Assessing students' spelling knowledge has emerged, therefore, as a cornerstone of reading and writing assessment. Because of the importance of the knowledge of word structure in learning to read and in growing and maintaining reading competence, the more we know about a student's knowledge of word structure, the more precisely we are able to determine where that student falls along the continuum of literacy development, and the better able we are, therefore, to provide appropriate instructional engagements with words (Bear, Invernizzi, Templeton, & Johnston, 2004; Templeton, 2004a).

In this chapter we (1) briefly summarize the nature of the spelling system of English and the significant research underlying a developmental model of spelling knowledge and how this knowledge relates to writing and reading; (2) offer representative case studies of students in grades 1, 3, and 5 in which spelling assessment guides instructional planning; and (3) describe what instruction may look like for these students.

THE NATURE OF THE SPELLING SYSTEM AND RESEARCH IN SPELLING DEVELOPMENT

The spelling system of English is far more regular than many literacy educators—and most of the lay public, for that matter—assume. As we illustrate, this regularity exists at the levels of alphabet, pattern, and meaning. The introductory quote from Venezky captures this perspective, and in his comprehensive description of American English spelling, Cummings (1988) commented that "it seems probable that a better understanding of the American English orthographic system *would lead us toward a better teaching of literacy*" (p. 463, emphasis added). In part for this reason, we provide a very brief overview of the system. Over time, students are capable of learning this system, moving from the exploration of how sounds are represented to the exploration of how meaningful parts of words—morphemes—are represented. Earlier in development, students primarily learn how to spell *sounds*; later in development, they learn primarily how to spell *meaning* (Hughes & Searle, 1997; Templeton, 1983, 2004b).

The alphabetic principle of English spelling refers to the basic left-to-right match between letters and sounds, illustrated in words such as *tap* and *spin*. The pattern principle operates both within and between syllables. Within syllables, the pattern principle governs long vowel spellings such as *tape* (the silent *e* signals a long vowel) and *day* (the *ay* spelling for the long *a* sound is determined by the *position* of the sound; at the end of words it is usually spelled *ay*). The pattern principle also governs many consonant spellings such as the /j/ in *badge* and *cage* (the vowel sound preceding the /j/ determines whether the spelling is *dge* or just *ge*) and the /ch/ at the end of syllables as in *coach* or *snitch* (the vowel sound preceding the /ch/ determines whether the spelling is *ch* or *tch*). Between syllables, the pattern principle operates to determine whether one or more consonant letters occur at the juncture of syllables; *hopping* has two consonants at the syllable juncture because of the short vowel pattern in the base word *hop* (otherwise, the word would be *hoping*), whereas *human* has one consonant at the syllable juncture because of the long vowel in the first syllable.

The *meaning* principle is quite powerful in that it applies to most of the words in the English language: Words that are related in meaning are often related in spelling as well, despite changes in sound (Templeton, 1983, 2004b). For example, the related words *define*, *definition*, and *definitive* share the common spelling *defin*, despite changes in the pronunciation of this base when different suffixes are added—they *look* similar, in other words. Contrast this with a system in which we attempt to represent sounds more consistently—*duhfayn*, *defunishun*, *duhfinutiv*—in which the spelling of the base would change to reflect the change in pronunciation—*duhfayn*, *defun*, *duhfin*—the words no longer *look* similar. Within the spelling system itself and within the learner's brain, as Venezky (1999) aptly observed, "Visual identity of word parts takes precedence over letter-sound simplicity" (p. 197).

What are the instructional implications of a spelling system of this nature? The research in developmental spelling and in how children learn to read words has shed considerable light on this question. We understand that learning how the English spelling system works is a *developmental* and *conceptual* process in which, over time, students may learn the balance between sound and meaning (Invernizzi & Hayes, 2004; Templeton, 2003; Templeton & Morris, 2000). As students develop this understanding, they also learn the regularity of the spelling system in terms of alphabet, pattern, and meaning principles. As students explore each new principle or "layer," earlier understandings are incorporated and reorganized "so that a reader/writer may implicitly as well as explicitly access this underlying knowledge when encoding words in writing and decoding words in reading" (Templeton, 2003, p. 740).

Studies conducted by Morris and his colleagues (Morris, Blanton, Blanton, Nowacek, & Perney, 1995; Morris, Blanton, Blanton, & Perney, 1995; Morris, Nelson, & Perney, 1986) have demonstrated the critical importance for instruction of establishing where students fall along a developmental continuum of word knowledge. Over the course of a year, Morris et al. (1995) compared the spelling performance of students who were placed appropriately for spelling instruction with students who were not; in Morris et al.'s terminology, the students who were placed appropriately studied words at their *spelling instructional level* as opposed to students who studied words at their *spelling frustration level*. There were no additional adjustments for instruction; in both groups, students simply worked through the pages of their spelling basal lesson over the course of each week. Compared to students attempting to work at their spelling frustration level, students placed at their spelling instructional level were better able to spell words correctly in writing as well as abstract and apply spelling patterns. Once students have moved beyond the alphabetic layer of the spelling system and are exploring within word patterns, the words that they examine should be words that they have already encountered in their reading—which explains Morris et al.'s results. Students placed at their spelling frustration level were attempting simply to memorize words that were not yet securely in their reading sight word vocabularies. Morris et al. used the McGuffey Qualitative Spelling Inventory, which was developed under the direction of Edmund Henderson at the McGuffey Reading Center at the University of Virginia; most subsequent qualitative inventories have been derived from, or built upon, this original McGuffey inventory.

Although appropriate spelling level is critically important, equally important is the quality of engagement with words that students experience. Recent research addressing beginning and transitional readers and writers (e.g., Allal, 1997; Bear & Helman, 2004; Berninger, Vaughan, & Abbot, 2000; Ehri & Wilce, 1987; Ellis & Cataldo, 1990; Ehri, 1997; Graham, 2000; Iversen & Tunmer, 1993; Joseph, 2000; Juel & Minden-Cupp, 2000; Madura, 1998; Santa & Hoien, 1999; Templeton, 2004a) as well as intermediate and advanced readers and writers (e.g., Allal, 1997; Derwing, Smith, & Wiebe, 1995; Fowler & Liberman, 1995; Henry, 1989, 1993; Leong, 1998; Smith, 1998; Templeton, 2004b) supports more active exploration of words, looking for spelling patterns, and applying these insights to writing and to reading.

THE NATURE AND DEVELOPMENT OF A QUALITATIVE SPELLING INVENTORY

We referred above to the use by Morris et al. of the McGuffey Qualitative Spelling Inventory. This original assessment has been refined through subsequent research and development (e.g., Bear, 1992; Bear et al., 2004; Edwards, 2003; Ganske, 1999; Invernizzi, 1992; Invernizzi, Meier, & Juel, 2003; Schlagal, 1992; Zutell, 1992). Other inventories, such as the one developed by Masterson, Apel, and Wasowicz (2002), are similarly grounded in a developmental framework. These qualitative assessments are constructed to capture students' knowledge of the orthographic features of English, beginning at the alphabetic level and moving from the pattern level to the meaning or morphological level. The words on these lists are carefully chosen to probe for the spelling features that would indicate in which stage of spelling students are positioned. Many districts use these developmental spelling inventories as reliable measures to monitor students' growth in word knowledge and to plan word-study instruction. Feature guides have also been devised to assist scoring and determine a spelling stage and in placing students in groups for instruction (see, e.g., Bear et al., 2004; Ganske, 2000). The *Phonological Awareness Literacy Survey* (PALS) assessment is an example of a standardized measure that depends heavily on the spelling score in determining its standardized score, in turn assisting teachers in establishing word-study groups (Invernizzi et al., 2003). There is a consistent high positive correlation between these developmentally grounded inventories and word recognition ability and reading (e.g., Bear, 1992; Ehri, 1997; Zutell, 1992; Zutell & Rasinski, 1989). For example, in a study of over 300 eighth and tenth graders, a correlation of .80 was found between students' spelling and reading comprehension scores on a standardized reading test (Edwards, 2003). This reciprocal relationship between reading and writing holds at all grade levels (Bear, 1992).

There are a number of ways to score students' spelling. Spellings may be analyzed developmentally by examining the key features and then determining a spelling stage for each student. The feature guides in Figures 8.2, 8.5, and 8.8, which are ongoing versions of guides we are continually in the process of revising and refining, represent features explored by most learners in first, third, and fifth grades, respectively (Bear et al., 2004; Templeton & Bear, 2006). The two levels of column heads note the continuum of stages and features. The bottom-most row (Totals) and right-hand columns note features correct in relation to words correct; because of space limitations we do not explore this relationship in this chapter, though it is well documented elsewhere, as are the implications for interpreting this relationship (Bear et al., 2004; Ganske, 2000). Having determined a spelling stage for students, teachers then select appropriate word-study activities, in which students explore words that reflect the spelling features that should be learned at each stage. In this regard, over the last few years several teacher resources have been published in which activities and developmentally appropriate words are provided (e.g., Bear et al., 2004; Fresch & Wheaton, 2004; Ganske, 2000; Pinnell & Fountas, 1998). Some major educational publishers have also incorporated this information into the development of reading and spelling basal programs. In selecting reading materials, teachers develop a sense of the word knowledge students bring to various levels of materials, and finally, with these analyses of spelling, teachers also think about how to group students for reading instruction (Bear & Venner, 2003).

Qualitative assessments for a number of other languages have also been developed: Spanish (Bear et al., 2004; Consortium on Reading Excellence, 1999; Estes & Richards, 2002; Fashola, Drum, Mayer, & Kang, 1996; Ferroli & Krajenta 1990; Temple, 1978); Chinese (Shen & Bear, 1990); and French (Gill, 1980).

CASE STUDIES: ANALYZING STUDENTS' SPELLING, ITS RELATION TO WRITING AND READING, AND PLANNING INSTRUCTION

To illustrate how the assessment of students' spelling knowledge relates to writing and reading, we offer three brief case studies of students in grades 1, 3, and 5. These children attend a small elementary school in the Western United States. The school educates approximately 440 students on a traditional school calendar. The demographics for the school reveal a population in the lower socioeconomic range (3.2% African American, 4.4% Asian/Pacific Islander, 40.6 Hispanic, 3.0 Native American/Alaskan Native, and 48.8% European American); 49% of the students receive free or reduced breakfast and lunch services, and 29% speak English as a second language.

First Grade: Carlo

Carlo is a quiet child with an easy manner and a strong sense of family. When writing in his journal, he often retells exciting events from family outings. During read-aloud sessions at school, Carlo places himself carefully at the foot of his teachers so as not to miss any details from the illustrations. It is important to note that Carlo's primary language is Tagalog, a language spoken by 17 million people from a Philippine culture. On the Qualitative Spelling Inventory (Figure 8.1) Carlo has missed three features at the late alphabetic phase, and when we look at his spelling of within-word pattern features, particularly long vowel patterns, we see only two instances of including a silent *e*: one in the correct spelling of *shade*, the other, an erroneous addition in HUGEING (*hugging*). Notably, however, he has also spelled *pool* correctly. It is interesting that most short vowel spellings are correct with the exception of NAT (*net*), in which the A for a short *e* sound is a very common spelling at this level. He has a fair command of consonant digraphs and blends. Carlo spelled 80% of the 20 words correctly, a score at the higher end of the first-grade level of instruction. His feature analysis (Figure 8.2) reveals that he falls within the late alphabetic phase. Comparing this analysis to his composition (Figure 8.3), we see that he has spelled a number of two-syllable words correctly, a function of frequency (*daddy*, *Ilene* [his sister]), and is not far off the mark

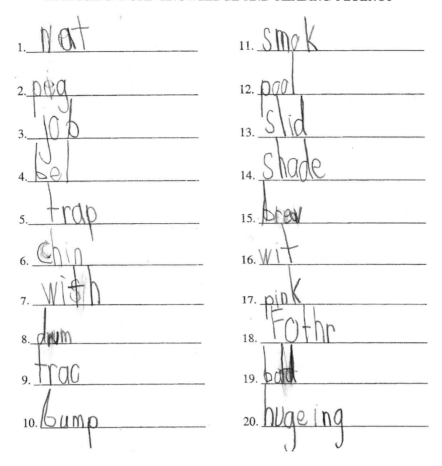

FIGURE 8.1. Qualitative Spelling Inventory, grade 1: Carlo.

with some others (MAMMY for *mommy*). His spelling of *birthday* as BRSTAY and *with* as WIT may reflect the fact that there is no /th/ sound in Tagalog.

Carlo's Word Study

Given Carlo's spelling of some within-word pattern features correctly, we may be tempted to begin his spelling instruction at early within-word pattern. Because he is still uncertain about some alphabetic-level features, however—as indicated by his spelling inventory and his writing—it is better, as we have noted, to begin one level down, at the late alphabetic. He will experience success in his work with these features while also being allowed the opportunity to consolidate his understandings of features at this level.

The teacher indicated that Carlo's guided reading instructional level is F; this is equivalent to early primer level. At this level, Carlo is experiencing a large number of words that follow and reinforce the alphabetic layer, as well as a number that reflect within-word pattern features such as vowel–consonant–silent *e* and vowel digraphs. With continued reading experience, words that include these latter types of features

Level I Qualitative Spelling Inventory Feature Analysis.

Student: _Carlo_ Teacher: _____ Grade: _1_ Date(s): _4-8_

Directions: Check the features spelled correctly. Note the first column where the student first missed two features.

CHECK SPELLING PHASE: [□ EARLY □ MIDDLE ☑ LATE] □ EMERGENT ☑ ALPHABETIC □ WITHIN-WORD PATTERN □ SYLLABLES & AFFIXES

Phases →	EMERGENT		ALPHABETIC			WITHIN-WORD PATTERN	SYLLABLES & AFFIXES	Feature Points	Words Spelled Correctly
	LATE	EARLY	MIDDLE	LATE	EARLY MIDDLE LATE	EARLY MIDDLE		Features: 35 (47)
									Words: 10 (25)
									Total: 45 (72)
Features →	Beginning & ending consonants	Short vowels	Beginning & final consonant digraphs & blends	Long vowel patterns and Other vowel patterns	Less frequent vowel patterns, Prefixes & suffixes, Inflectional endings, Common syllable patterns, Unaccented syllables			
1 net	✓n ✓t	e					2	0
2 pig	✓p ✓g	✓i					3	1
3 job	✓j ✓b	✓o					3	1
4 bell	✓b	✓e	ll				2	0
5 trap		✓a	✓tr				2	1
6 chin	✓n	✓i	✓ch				3	1
7 with	✓w		✓th				2	1
8 drum	✓m	✓u	✓dr				3	1
9 track		✓a	✓tr ck				2	0
10 bump	✓b		✓mp				2	1
11 smoke			✓sm	oke			1	0
12 pool	✓p			✓ oo			3	1
13 slide	✓d		✓sl	ide			2	0
14 shade				✓ ade			1	1
15 brave	✓v			ave			1	0
16 white			wh	ite			0	0
17 pink			✓nk				1	0
18 father	✓f				er		1	0
19 batted					tt ed		0	0
20 hugging					gg ✓ing		1	0
Totals →	8 (8) 8 (8)	7 (8)	6 (7) 3 (5)	2 (6)	1 (5)		35 (47)	10 (25)

FIGURE 8.2. Qualitative Spelling Inventory feature analysis: Carlo.

119

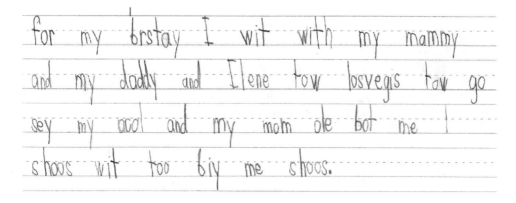

FIGURE 8.3. Carlo's composition.

will become part of Carlo's sight vocabulary—words that, when he sees them in isolation, he will be able to identify immediately. Over time, the teacher's discussion of these patterns—for example, how to use the "silent *e*" feature to decode unfamiliar words in reading—as well as Carlo's continued exercise of his spelling knowledge through writing will result in these more advanced patterns appearing with greater frequency in his writing. His "using but confusing" these patterns is our indicator that he now has sufficient underlying spelling knowledge to analyze, learn, and apply these more advanced patterns (Bear et al., 2004).

For Carlo and other students at this developmental level, word-study instruction begins with the basic consonant–vowel–consonant (CVC) pattern. For example, in a word-sort or word-categorization activity, the teacher provides the three key words *hat*, *net*, and *chin*. Carlo has a number of words written on small chips or cards that he places under the appropriate key word. In his word-study group, Carlo will also discuss how blends and digraphs are CVC-pattern words, as in *thin*. Carlo will then move to the study of how a number of final consonant sounds are spelled, as, for example, the *ck* in *track* (which he spelled TRAC), the final *th*, as in *with*, and the *nt* in *went*. The study of short vowel patterns will serve him when he studies the inflectional endings in words such as *hugging* (spelled HUGEING) and *batted* (spelled BATD). Carlo will then make comparisons between short and long vowel sounds and spelling patterns and study the basic consonant–vowel–consonant–silent *e* (CVC*e*)—the silent *e* pattern—across long vowels from *cake* to *mule*.

Third Grade: Jared

Jared is a verbally adept 9-year-old boy who loves to read and to write. On most assignments he eagerly composes two and three pages more than other students. Jared's favorite subject is science, and he selects nonfiction titles for most of his independent reading selections. Jared's errors occur with significant frequency at the late within-word pattern phase; by the end of third grade, most students have reached this level of spelling development. Students in this phase explore vowel patterns in single-syllable words that occur less frequently than the more straightforward and frequent long- and

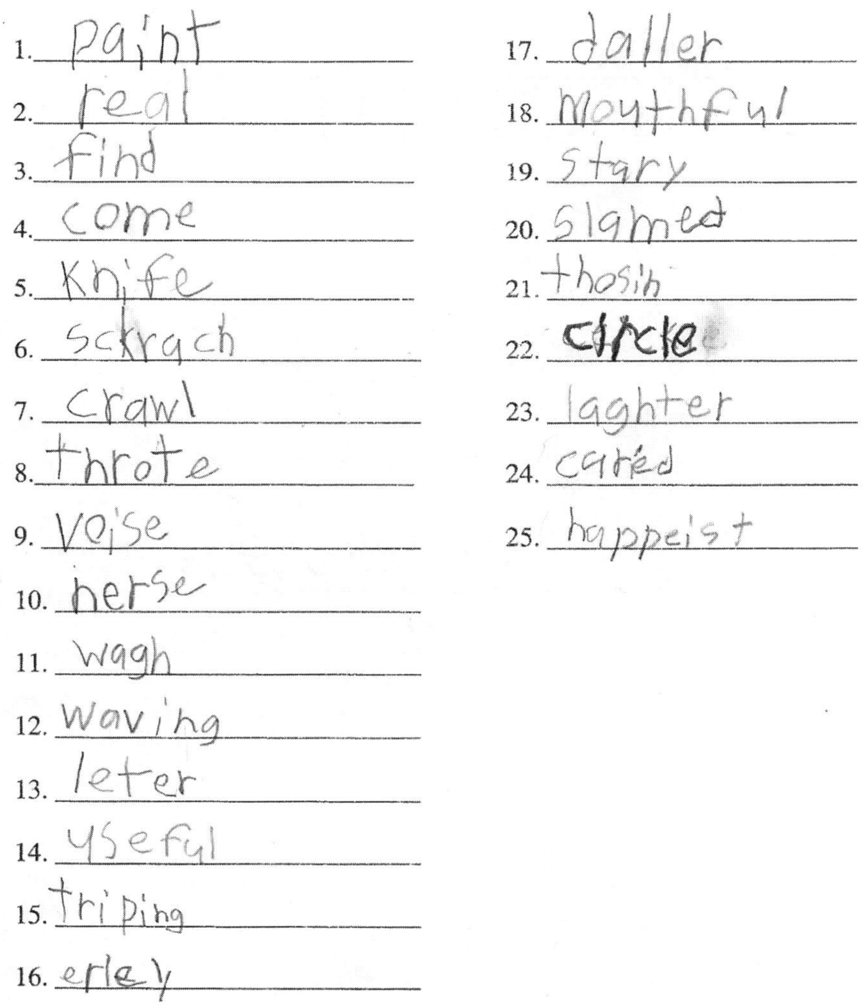

1. paint
2. real
3. find
4. come
5. knife
6. sckrach
7. crawl
8. throte
9. voise
10. herse
11. wagh
12. waving
13. leter
14. yseful
15. triping
16. erley

17. daller
18. mouthful
19. stary
20. slamed
21. thosih
22. circle
23. laghter
24. cared
25. happeist

FIGURE 8.4. Qualitative Spelling Inventory, grade 3: Jared.

short-vowel patterns. Notably, some of Jared's errors (see Figure 8.4) reveal that he falls back on the more frequently occurring vowel patterns (the vowel–consonant–silent *e* spelling of COME for *comb* and THROTE for *throat*). On the other hand, he has spelled the diphthongs /oy/ and /ow/ correctly in the words *voice* and *mouthful*. His score of 32% on this third-grade inventory indicates that he should study single-syllable word patterns before moving to the two-syllable words, those tested in the second half of this inventory. Beginning third-grade spelling programs would most likely contain the words that he needs to study in sorting.

We have included half of Jared's response to a writing prompt that asked students to imagine what it would be like to be given a lot of money and what they would do

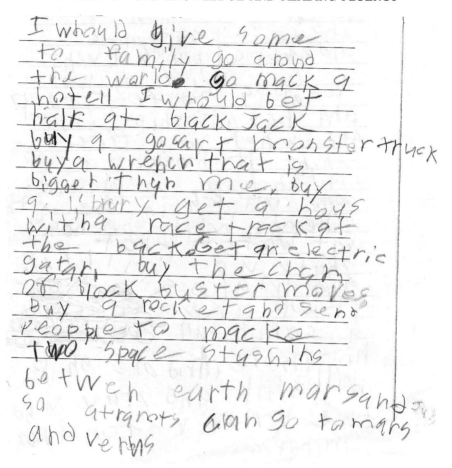

FIGURE 8.5. Jared's composition.

were that to happen (see Figure 8.5). He writes with a verve that is most encouraging. In his writing, it is important to note that Jared's errors reflect his level of spelling knowledge, as indicated by his performance on the spelling assessment. For example, his spelling of *make* is at first glance odd; he had actually been spelling this word correctly earlier in the year. At this point, however, his errors reveal that he is experimenting with the final /k/ spelling, which varies depending on whether it is preceded by a long vowel or a short vowel: He spells *make* both MACK and MACKE. His spelling of BETWEN for *between* foretells the type of spelling instruction that will be addressed when he moves into the examination of the spelling of two-syllable words: Specifically, using what he has learned about the spelling of vowels in single-syllable words to help him spell the same vowel sounds in two-syllable words.

The teacher indicated that Jared's guided reading levels fluctuate between N and O, which are solidly third-grade level. His spelling instructional level, in other words, corresponds to his reading instructional level—as is the case with most students. It bears repeating that although a student's *spelling* instructional level and his or her *reading* instructional level may both be late third grade, this does not mean that new words encountered in reading are the same words that are used for spelling instruction: As Morris et al.'s research confirmed, only words that have been experienced in reading several times will later become words for spelling instruction.

Jared's Word Study

Two strands of word study should be pursued: the study of beginning and final consonant blends and digraphs and some of the less frequent vowel patterns for short- and long-vowel sounds. As suggested by the feature analysis (Figure 8.6), Jared will study some of the more difficult digraphs and triple letter blends such as *thr*oat and w*atch*. In his word-study notebook, Jared might make a list of words that end in *ght* and then look within these words at the vowels (e.g., *bought*, *caught*). Word sorts would examine these vowel patterns that are less frequent or more complex. A sort with the key words *school*, *mouse*, and *mouth* would occur early in his examination of vowel patterns. In board games following a sports theme such as soccer, football, or baseball, Jared would make matches for these spelling patterns. For example, he could earn a first down when he matches *brought* and *thought* for their vowel and consonant pattern matches (Bear et al., 2004).

Fifth Grade: Suzette

Eleven-year-old Suzette is a highly motivated, intuitive learner. She thrives on being able to talk about what she reads and readily records her opinions and feelings on paper. Her exuberance in discussing text-to-self, text-to-text, and text-to-world connections becomes most apparent when what she reads has high emotional appeal. Suzette spelled 70% of the words on the fifth-grade inventory correctly, indicating that her instructional level is indeed fifth grade (see Figure 8.7). The feature analysis (Figure 8.8) indicates that Suzette is in the early part of the derivational relations stage. Suzette has learned to spell one- and two-syllable words correctly, including complex vowel patterns found in words such as *scowl*, *pounce*, and *poison*. She has misspelled a number of prefixes and suffixes (PURMISSION for *permission*, RESPONSEABLE for *responsible*). There were a number of erasures and write-overs in her spelling sample, which may reflect some uncertainty in spelling several of the words on the fifth-grade list.

Based on the relationship between reading and spelling, we would expect that Suzette would be a solid intermediate reader, capable of reading books such as *Charlotte's Web* with good fluency. Indeed, the teacher reports that her classroom reading and test scores indicate that she reads at a solid fifth-grade level. Though Suzette's writing sample (Figure 8.9) filled an entire page and was a pleasant enough account of her feelings about the month of May, the construction and use of language as well as word choice were unadventuresome, with correct spelling of all words except for several apostrophe deletions. We would look to other writing samples for spelling errors and to see if she continues to be so safe in her use of vocabulary and word choice.

Level III Qualitative Spelling Inventory Feature Analysis.
Student: _Jared_   Teacher: _____   Grade: _3_   Date(s): _4-2_

Directions: Check the features spelled correctly. Note the first column where the student first missed two features.

CHECK SPELLING PHASE: [□ EARLY □ MIDDLE ☑ LATE]   □ ALPHABETIC   ☑ WITHIN-WORD PATTERN   □ SYLLABLES & AFFIXES

Features: 45 (65)
Words: 9 (25)
Total: 54 (90)

Phases → Features ↓	ALPHABETIC EARLY — Beginning & ending consonants	ALPHABETIC MIDDLE — Short vowels	ALPHABETIC MIDDLE — Beginning & final consonant digraphs & blends	ALPHABETIC LATE — (digraphs & blends)	WITHIN-WORD PATTERN EARLY — Long vowel patterns	WITHIN-WORD PATTERN MIDDLE/LATE — Other vowel patterns	SYLLABLES & AFFIXES EARLY/MIDDLE — Less frequent vowel patterns, Prefixes & suffixes, Inflectional endings, Common syllable patterns, Unaccented syllables	Feature Points	Words Spelled Correctly
1 paint	✓p ✓t			✓nt	✓ai			4	1
2 real	✓r ✓l				✓ea			3	1
3 find	✓f			✓nd				2	1
4 comb	✓c			mb				1	0
5 knife	✓f		✓kn		✓i_e			3	1
6 scratch		✓a	scr	tch				1	0
7 crawl			✓cr			✓aw		2	1
8 throat			✓thr		oa			1	0
9 voice	✓v c					✓oi		2	0
10 nurse						ur ✓e		1	0
11 weigh						eigh		0	0
12 waving		✓e				✓a (no e)	✓ing	2	0
13 letter							tt ✓er	2	1
14 useful							✓ful (not full)	1	0
15 tripping		✓i	✓tr				pp ✓ing	3	0
16 early						ear	y	0	0
17 dollar		o					✓ll ar	1	0
18 mouthful				✓th		✓ou		2	1
19 starry		✓a	✓st				rr ✓y	3	0
20 slammed		✓a	✓sl				mm ✓ed	3	0
21 thousand			✓th	nd		ou		1	0
22 circle		✓i					✓le	2	1
23 laughter						aught	✓er	2	0
24 carried		✓a					rr ✓ied	2	0
25 happiest		✓a					✓pp iest	2	0
Totals →	8 (9)	8 (9)	7 (8)	3 (6)	3 (4)	5 (10)	11 (19)	45 (65)	9 (25)

FIGURE 8.6. Qualitative Spelling Inventory feature analysis: Jared.

124

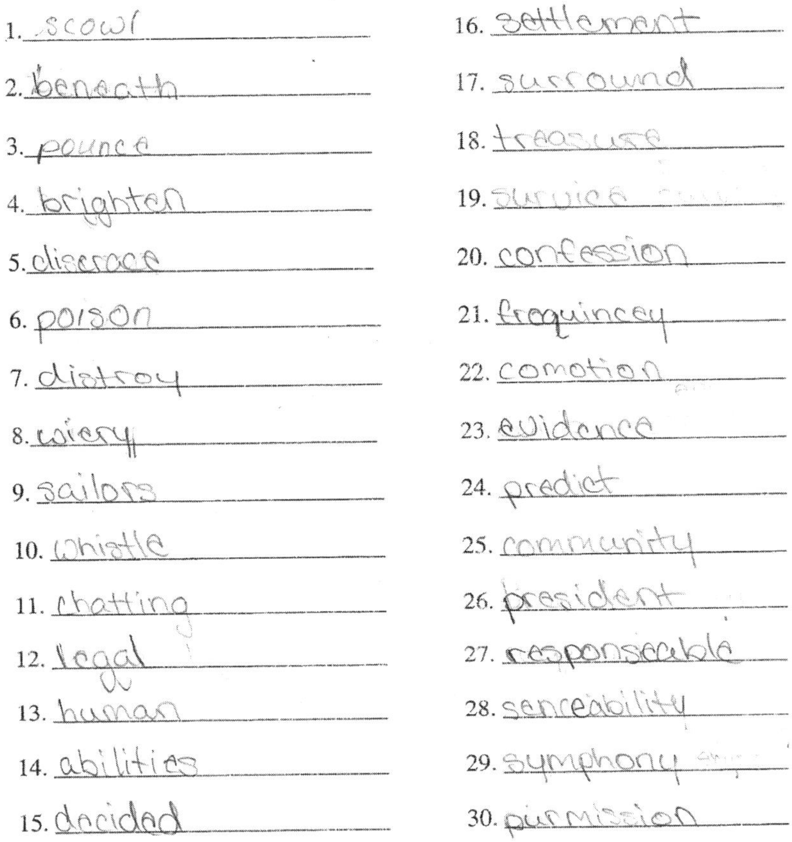

1. scowl
2. beneath
3. pounce
4. brighten
5. disgrace
6. poison
7. distroy
8. wiery
9. sailors
10. whistle
11. chatting
12. legal
13. human
14. abilities
15. decided

16. settlement
17. surround
18. treasure
19. survice
20. confession
21. frequincey
22. comotion
23. evidence
24. predict
25. community
26. president
27. responseable
28. senceability
29. symphony
30. purmission

FIGURE 8.7. Qualitative Spelling Inventory, grade 5: Suzette.

Suzette's Word Study

The fifth-grade level is a good place to begin instruction, because at this level Suzette will study the more difficult prefixes and suffixes and learn how meaning is represented in word structure. Morphology, the study of the meaning aspects of words, will be the focus of her spelling and vocabulary study. Suzette will be asked to go on word hunts to collect words that begin with the same prefixes and suffixes as the words in her core list or group for that week. She will explore how words are related in their bases and roots, as, for example, in the word pairs *magic/magician*, *crime/criminal*, *compose/composition*, and *legal/legality*. The dictionary and easy etymological or word history references become vital sources for her as she compiles lists of related words in her word-study notebook. For example, after a sorting activity in which Suzette matches base words with their derivatives—for example, *sane* and *sanity*, *preside* and *president*—she would write the sort in her notebook and then continue to hunt for words in her reading that she can add to the various lists; for example, words that end in *–ity* or *–ency*.

Level V Qualitative Spelling Inventory Feature Analysis.

Student: _Suzette_   Teacher: _____   Grade: _5_   Date(s): _4–8_

Directions: Check the features spelled correctly. Note the first column where the student first missed two features.

CHECK SPELLING PHASE: [☑EARLY ☐ MIDDLE ☐ LATE] ☐ALPHABETIC ☐WITHIN-WORD PATTERN ☐SYLLABLES & AFFIXES ☑DERIVATIONAL PATTERNS

Totals Correct — Features: 61 (73); Words: 20 (30); Total: 81 (103)

Phases →	ALPHABETIC Late	WITHIN-WORD PATTERN Early	WITHIN-WORD PATTERN Middle	WITHIN-WORD PATTERN Late	SYLLABLES & AFFIXES Early	SYLLABLES & AFFIXES Middle	SYLLABLES & AFFIXES Late	DERIVATIONAL RELATIONS Early	DERIVATIONAL RELATIONS Middle	Feature Points	Words Spelled Correctly
Features	Beginning & ending consonant digraphs & blends	Long vowel patterns & vowel patterns		Other vowel patterns	Less frequent vowel patterns, Prefixes & suffixes, Inflectional endings, Common syllable patterns, Unaccented syllables		Complex prefixes & suffixes, Less frequent unaccented final syllables	Spelling-meaning connection in base & derived words, Greek & Latin word parts, Absorbed prefixes			
1 scowl	✓ sc			✓ ow						2	1
2 beneath	✓ th	✓ ea				✓ be				3	1
3 pounce			✓ ounce							1	1
4 brighten	✓ br	✓ ght			✓ en					3	0
5 disgrace	gr	✓ ace					✓ dis			2	0
6 poison				✓ oi	✓ on					2	1
7 destroy	✓ str			✓ oy			de			2	0
8 weary				ear	✓ y					1	0
9 sailors		✓ ai			✓ s (final)	✓ or				3	1
10 whistle	✓ wh					✓ tle				2	1
11 chatting	✓ ch				✓ tt	✓ ing				3	1
12 legal						✓ al			✓ leg	2	1
13 human		✓ u				✓ man				2	1
14 abilities						✓ ies			✓ abilit	2	1
15 decided					✓ ed	✓ cid		✓ de		3	1
16 settlement					✓ tt	✓ le ✓ ment				3	1
17 surround	✓ nd			✓ ou		✓ rr				3	1
18 treasure	✓ tr			✓ ea			✓ ure			3	1
19 service							✓ ice	serv		1	0
20 confession							✓ ion	✓ con	✓ fess	3	1
21 frequency						y			frequenc	1	0
22 commotion							✓ tion		com (both ms)	1	0
23 evidence								✓ ence	✓ evid	2	1
24 predict							✓ pre	✓ dict		2	1
25 community						✓ ity			✓ commun	2	1
26 president							✓ pre	✓ ent	✓ sid	3	1
27 responsible							✓ re	ible	✓ spons	3	1
28 sensibility						✓ ity		ibil		2	0
29 symphonies						ies		✓ sym	✓ phon	2	0
30 permission							per ✓ sion			1	0
Totals →	8 (9)	5 (5)	6 (7)	7 (7)		13 (15)	9 (11)	5 (8)	9 (11)	61 (73)	20 (30)

FIGURE 8.8. Qualitative Spelling Inventory feature analysis: Suzette.

126

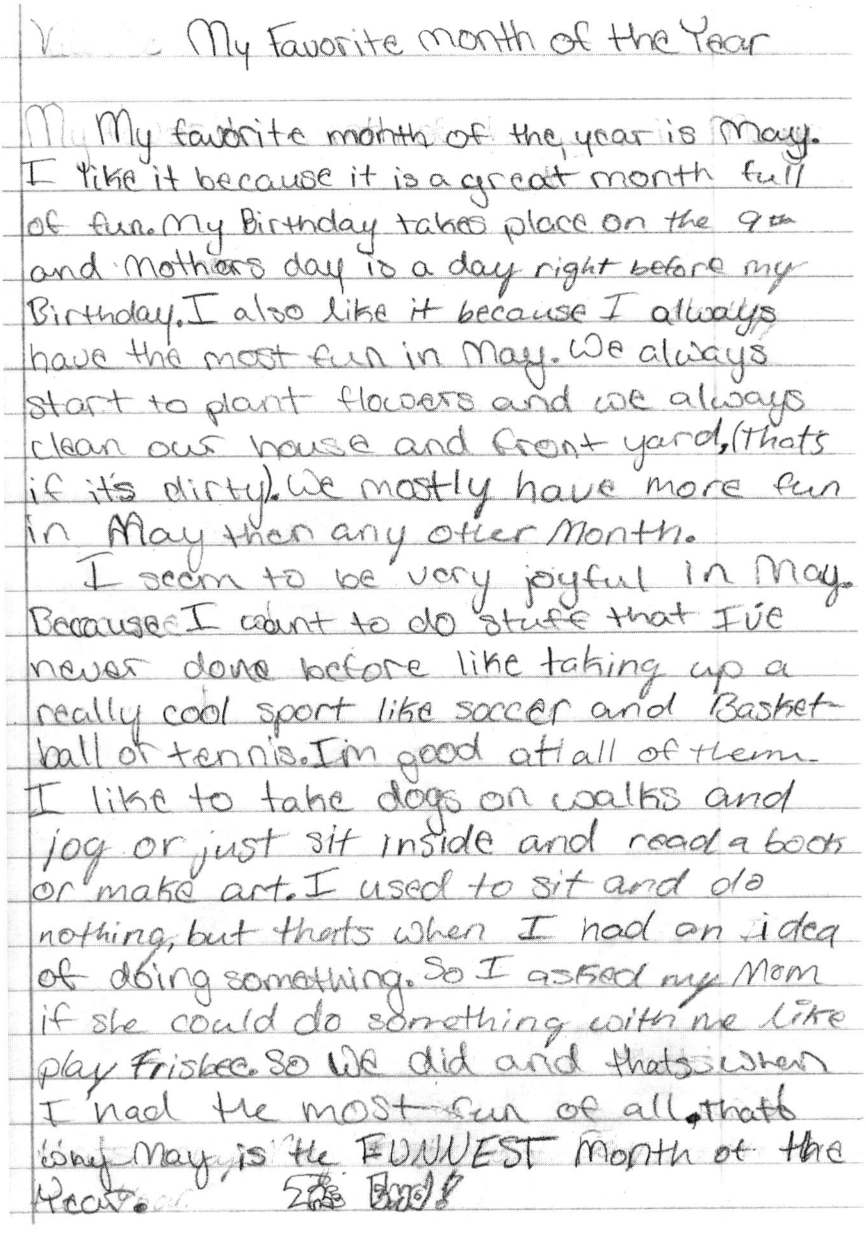

My Favorite month of the Year

My My favorite month of the year is May.
I like it because it is a great month full
of fun. My Birthday takes place on the 9th
and mothers day is a day right before my
Birthday. I also like it because I always
have the most fun in May. We always
start to plant flowers and we always
clean our house and front yard, (thats
if it's dirty). We mostly have more fun
in May then any other Month.
    I seem to be very joyful in May.
Becauses I want to do stuff that I've
never done before like taking up a
really cool sport like soccer and Basketball or tennis. I'm good at all of them.
I like to take dogs on walks and
jog or just sit inside and read a book
or make art. I used to sit and do
nothing, but thats when I had an idea
of doing something. So I asked my Mom
if she could do something with me like
play Frisbee. So We did and thats when
I had the most fun of all. thats
why May is the FUNNEST month of the
Year. The End!

FIGURE 8.9. Suzette's composition.

CONCLUSIONS

The spelling and writing by Carlo, Jared, and Suzette illustrate the relationships among reading, writing, and spelling. We hope that the foregoing discussion of word study, writing, and reading provides a sense of how spelling assessment is used to inform our thinking about developmentally appropriate word study, as well as our thinking about integrated literacy instruction and grouping more broadly.

What we have learned from studying spelling is that spelling is not "a failed phonetic system," nor does the study of spelling torture wits. Quite the opposite: The study of words leads students to greater wit by enriching their vocabularies and advancing their thinking. In our teaching, the study of the relationships among reading, writing, and spelling advances our wit and leads to better understanding of how to teach phonics, vocabulary, and spelling.

REFERENCES

Allal, L. (1997). Learning to spell in the classroom. In C. A. Perfetti & L. Reiben (Eds.), *Learning to spell: Research, theory, and practice across languages* (pp. 129–150). Mahwah, NJ: Erlbaum.

Bear, D. R. (1992). The prosody of oral reading and stages of word knowledge. In S. Templeton & D. R. Bear (Eds.), *Development of orthographic knowledge and the foundations of literacy: A memorial festschrift for Edmund H. Henderson.* Hillsdale, NJ: Erlbaum.

Bear, D. R., & Helman, L. (2004). Word study for vocabulary development in the early stages of literacy learning: Ecological perspectives and leaning English. In J. F. Baumann & E. J. Kame'enui (Eds.), *Vocabulary instruction: Research to practice* (pp. 139–158). New York: Guilford Press.

Bear, D. R., Invernizzi, M., Templeton, S., & Johnston, F. (2004). *Words their way: Word study for phonics, spelling, and vocabulary development* (3rd ed.). Englewood Cliffs, NJ: Merrill/Prentice-Hall.

Bear, D. R., & Venner, D. (2003, December). *How teachers use developmental spelling inventories to organize reading and spelling instruction.* Paper presented at the 53rd Annual National Reading Conference, Scottsdale, AZ.

Berninger, V. W., Vaughan, K., & Abbott, R. D. (2000). Language-based spelling instruction: Teaching children to make multiple connections between spoken and written words. *Learning Disability Quarterly, 23,* 117–135.

Consortium on Reading Excellence. (1999). ESL spelling inventory. In *Assessing reading: Multiple measures for kindergarten through eighth grade.* Novato, CA: Arena Press.

Cummings, D. W. (1988). *American English spelling.* Baltimore: Johns Hopkins University Press.

Derwing, B. L., Smith, M. L., Wiebe, G. E. (1995). On the role of spelling in morpheme recognition: Experimental studies with children and adults. In L. B. Feldman (Ed.), *Morphological aspects of language processing* (pp. 3–27). Hillsdale, NJ: Erlbaum.

Edwards, W. (2003). *Charting the orthographic knowledge of intermediate and advanced readers and the relationship between recognition and production of orthographic patterns.* Unpublished doctoral dissertation, University of Nevada, Reno.

Ehri, L. C. (1997). Learning to read and learning to spell are one and the same, almost. In C. A. Perfetti, L. Rieben, & M. Fayol (Eds.), *Learning to spell: Research, theory, and practice across languages* (pp. 237–269). Mahwah, NJ: Erlbaum.

Ehri, L. C., & Wilce, L. (1987). Does learning to spell help beginners learn to read words? *Reading Research Quarterly, 22*, 47–65.

Ellis, N., & Cataldo, S. (1990). The role of spelling in learning to read. *Language and Education, 4*, 1–28.

Estes, T., & Richards, H. (2002). Knowledge of orthographic features in Spanish among bilingual children. *Bilingual Research Journal, 26*, 295–307.

Fashola, O. S., Drum, P. A., Mayer, R. E., & Kang, S. (1996). A cognitive theory of orthographic transitioning: Predictable errors in how Spanish-speaking children spell English words. *American Educational Research Journal, 33*, 825–843.

Ferroli, L., & Krajenta, M. (1990). Validating a Spanish developmental spelling test. *Journal of the National Association for Bilingual Education, 14*, 41–61.

Fowler, A. E., & Liberman, I. Y. (1995). The role of phonology and orthography in morphological awareness. In L. B. Feldman (Ed.), *Morphological aspects of language processing* (pp. 157–188). Hillsdale, NJ: Erlbaum.

Fresch, M., & Wheaton, A. (2004). *The spelling list and word study resource book*. New York: Scholastic.

Ganske, K. (1999). The Developmental Spelling Analysis: A measure of orthographic knowledge. *Educational Assessment, 6*, 41–70.

Ganske, K. (2000). *Word journeys*. New York: Guilford Press.

Gill, C. E. (1980). An analysis of spelling errors in French. *Dissertation Abstracts International, 41*(09), 33924.

Graham, S. (2000). Should the natural learning approach replace spelling instruction? *Journal of Educational Psychology, 92*, 235–247.

Henderson, E. H. (1981). *Learning to read and spell: The child's knowledge of words*. DeKalb, IL: Northern Illinois Press.

Henry, M. K. (1989). Children's word structure knowledge: Implications for decoding and spelling instruction. *Reading and Writing, 1*, 135–152.

Henry, M. K. (1993). Morphological structure: Latin and Greek roots and affixes as upper grade code strategies. *Reading and Writing, 5*, 227–241.

Hoole, C. (1660/1973). *A new discovery of the old art of teaching schoole*. London: Scolar Press.

Hughes, M., & Searle, D. (1997). *The violent "e" and other tricky sounds: Learning to spell from kindergarten through grade 6*. Portsmouth, NH: Stenhouse.

Invernizzi, M. (1992). The vowel and what follows: A phonological frame of orthographic analysis. In S. Templeton & D. R. Bear (Eds.), *Development of orthographic knowledge and the foundations of literacy: A memorial festschrift for Edmund H. Henderson* (pp. 106–136). Hillsdale, NJ: Erlbaum.

Invernizzi, M., & Hayes, L. (2004). Developmental-spelling research: A systematic imperative. *Reading Research Quarterly, 39*, 216–228.

Invernizzi, M., Meier, J., & Juel, C. (2003). *PALS 1–3: Phonological Awareness Literacy Screening* (4th ed.). Charlottesville, VA: University Printing Services.

Iversen, S., & Tunmer, W. E. (1993). Phonological processing skills and the Reading Recovery Program. *Journal of Educational Psychology, 85*, 112–126.

Joseph, L. M. (2000). Developing first graders' phonemic awareness, word identification and spelling: A comparison of two contemporary phonic instructional approaches. *Reading Research and Instruction, 39*, 160–169.

Juel, C., & Minden-Cupp, C. (2000). Learning to read words: Linguistic units and instructional strategies. *Reading Research Quarterly, 35*, 458–492.

Leong, C. K. (1998). Strategies used by 9– to 12–year-old children in written spelling. In C. Hulme & R. M. Joshi (Eds.), *Reading and spelling: Development and disorders* (pp. 421–432). Mahwah, NJ: Erlbaum.

Madura, S. (1998). An artistic element: Four transitional readers and writers respond to the picture books of Patricia Polacco and Gerald McDermott. In T. Shanahan & F. V. R. Rodriguez-Brown (Eds.), *National reading conference yearbook 47* (pp. 366–376). Chicago: National Reading Conference.

Masterson, J. L., Apel, K., & Wasowicz, J. (2002). *SPELL Examiner's Manual.* Evanston, IL: Learning by Design.

Morris, D., Blanton, L., Blanton, W. E., Nowacek, J., & Perney, J. (1995). Teaching low-achieving spellers at their "instructional level." *Elementary School Journal, 96*, 163–178.

Morris, D., Blanton, L., Blanton, W., & Perney, J. (1995). Spelling instruction and achievement in six classrooms. *Elementary School Journal, 96*, 145–162.

Morris, D., Nelson, L., & Perney, J. (1986). Exploring the concept of "spelling instruction level" through the analysis of error-types. *Elementary School Journal, 87*, 181–200.

Perfetti, C. A. (1997). The psycholinguistics of spelling and reading. In C. A. Perfetti, L. Rieben, & M. Fayol (Eds.), *Learning to spell: Research, theory, and practice across languages* (pp. 21–38). Mahwah, NJ: Erlbaum.

Pinnell, G., & Fountas, I. (1998). *Word matters.* Portsmouth, NH: Heinemann.

Santa, C. M., & Hoien, T. (1999). An assessment of Early Steps: A program for early intervention of reading problems. *Reading Research Quarterly, 33*, 338–355.

Schlagal, R. C. (1992). Patterns of orthographic development into the intermediate grades. In S. Templeton & D. R. Bear (Eds.), *Development of orthographic knowledge and the foundations of literacy: A memorial festschrift for Edmund H. Henderson* (pp. 31–52). Hillsdale, NJ: Erlbaum.

Shen, H., & Bear, D. R. (2000). The development of orthographic skills in Chinese children. *Reading and Writing: An Interdisciplinary Journal, 13*, 197–236.

Smith, M. L. (1998). Sense and sensitivity: An investigation into fifth-grade children's knowledge of English derivational morphology and its relationship to vocabulary and reading ability. *Dissertation Abstracts International, 59*(4-A), 1111 (University Microfilms No. AAM9830072).

Temple, C. A. (1978). An analysis of spelling errors in Spanish. *Dissertation Abstracts International, 40-02A*, 0721.

Templeton, S. (1983). Using the spelling/meaning connection to develop word knowledge in older students. *Journal of Reading, 27*, 8–14.

Templeton, S. (2003). Spelling. In J. Flood, D. Lapp, J. R. Squire, & J. M. Jensen (Eds.), *Handbook of research on teaching the English language arts* (2nd ed., pp. 738–751). Mahwah, NJ: Erlbaum.

Templeton, S. (2004a). Instructional approaches to spelling: The window on students' word knowledge in reading and writing. In L. Wilkinson & E. Silliman (Eds.), *Language and literacy learning: Collaboration between speech language pathologists and classroom teachers* (pp. 273–291). New York: Guilford Press.

Templeton, S. (2004b). The vocabulary–spelling connection: Orthographic development and morphological knowledge at the intermediate grades and beyond. In J. F. Baumann & E. J. Kame'enui (Eds.), *Vocabulary instruction: Research to practice* (pp. 118–138). New York: Guilford Press.

Templeton, S., & Bear, D. R. (Eds.). (1992). *Development of orthographic knowledge and the foundations of literacy: A memorial festschrift for Edmund H. Henderson.* Hillsdale, NJ: Erlbaum.

Templeton, S., & Bear, D. R. (2006). *Spelling and vocabulary.* Boston: Houghton Mifflin.

Templeton, S., & Morris, D. (2000). Spelling. In M. Kamil, P. Mosenthal, P. D. Pearson, & R. Barr (Eds.), *Handbook of reading research* (Vol. 3, pp. 525–543). Mahwah, NJ: Erlbaum.

Venezky, R. (1999). *The American way of spelling: The structure and origins of American English orthography.* New York: Guilford Press.

Zutell, J. (1992). An integrated view of word knowledge: Correlational studies of the relation-ships among spelling, reading, and conceptual development. In S. Templeton & D. R. Bear (Eds.), *Development of orthographic knowledge and the foundations of literacy: A memorial festschrift for Edmund H. Henderson* (pp. 213–230). Hillsdale, NJ: Erlbaum.

Zutell, J., & Rasinski, T. (1989). Reading and spelling connections in third and fifth grade stu-dents. *Reading Psychology, 10*(2), 137–155.

PART III

Assessing Comprehension and Composition

Assessing Vocabulary

EXAMINING KNOWLEDGE ABOUT WORDS AND ABOUT WORD LEARNING

Janis M. Harmon
Wanda B. Hedrick
Lina Soares
Michelle Gress

On Friday, Ms. Garza administered the weekly vocabulary test to her fifth-grade reading class. The test looked like this:

Match the following words with the correct definitions:

____ 1. scowled	a.	To move or stir slightly
____ 2. budge	b.	To know that something is believable
____ 3. disappointed	c.	To feel self-conscious
____ 4. misunderstanding	d.	To wrinkle the brow as an expression of anger
____ 5. embarrassed	e.	A failure to understand something
____ 6. reproachfully	f.	To fail to satisfy the hope or desire of
____ 7. convinced	g.	Expressing disapproval of

Fill in the blanks with the correct word.

8. The students stared _____ at the teacher when she told them they would not be able to go outside for recess.

9. Tom was _____ that Ricky was the one who took his candy bar.

10. The _____ over who won the prize caused the girls to become angry with one another.

Marcy missed 8 out of the 10 questions, Sammy missed 5, and John answered all of them correctly. What do these results tell Ms. Garza about what Marcy, Sammy, and John have learned about these words? Does Marcy's score indicate that she can hold her own with the words in most contexts? Does it mean that the two she missed will create comprehension difficulties whenever she encounters them in her reading? Does Sammy's score mean that he has little understanding of half the words and therefore will have serious comprehension problems when these words appear in the texts he reads? What about John? Does his score mean that he has internalized the word meanings and is well equipped to use the words in his speaking, writing, reading, and listening? Is it possible that John memorized all the definitions and really does not have an understanding of how to use some of the words? Is it possible that he already knew the words? What about the instruction that Ms. Garza provided? Does this exam reflect the ways in which she taught the words?

Although weekly vocabulary tests in the form of matching exercises, multiple-choice questions, and fill-in-the-blank statements leave us with many unanswered questions about what the results might mean, they remain the norm in many classrooms (Allen, 1999). The test formats themselves are not necessarily problematic. In fact, multiple-choice questions and matching tasks can be very useful in providing information about what students are learning. However, if the content of these assessment tasks does not require students to demonstrate word knowledge beyond simple definitions, then their performances on the tasks do not help us identify what our students really understand about the word meanings and about appropriate usage of the words.

The purpose of this chapter is to describe effective strategies for assessment of vocabulary knowledge. Throughout the chapter, we work from a basic premise: that the ultimate goal of teaching vocabulary is to help students to become independent word learners across different disciplines. First, we present what we currently know about effective vocabulary instruction, and we relate this information to the features of effective vocabulary assessment. We then provide examples of the ways in which teachers integrate these ideas within the context of ongoing instruction—examples that provide clear alternatives to the test that Marcy, Sammy, and John took in Ms. Garza's class.

EFFECTIVE VOCABULARY INSTRUCTION

Teachers across various grade levels and from different content areas agree that teaching vocabulary is a very important part of their instructional program, and they also understand that teaching vocabulary successfully is not an easy, simple task. This realization is verified in the wealth of research on vocabulary learning and teaching. Numerous studies have shown that vocabulary acquisition is a complex process that involves multiple dimensions and issues (see research reviews by Baumann, Kame'enui, & Ash, 2003, and Blachowicz & Fisher, 2000). Nagy and Scott (2000) identify five components that can help us understand this complexity: (1) realizing that word learning is incremental—we build stronger understandings of words with each successive encounter with the word; (2) knowing that some words have multiple meanings that are unique to specific subject areas; (3) knowing that there are multiple dimensions to knowing a word, such as knowing how to use it orally and in written form, knowing related words, and knowing about the structure of the word in terms of affixes and roots; (4) knowing how words are connected to other words and how these connections help us develop a richer and deeper understanding of a word; and (5) knowing the difference between function words and meaning-bearing words and the functions they serve in written texts. These components not only illustrate the complexity of word learning but also suggest the need for different instructional practices as well as assessment techniques.

We acknowledge that vocabulary learning is no simple matter and requires sound instructional practices. But what does research specifically tell us about effective vocabulary instruction? Stahl and Fairbanks (1986) identified three distinctive features of effective vocabulary instruction: integration, repetition, and meaningful use. Integrative practices provide opportunities for students to be actively involved in word learning as they connect new word meanings with other known and related concepts. The feature of integration requires in-depth word processing as students make associations with related words through classifying and categorizing, identify synonyms and antonyms, and gain an understanding of different contexts in which words can be used appropriately.

The second feature, repetition, means that students need multiple opportunities to use the words in varying contexts and in varying ways. They need sufficient practice with the words in order to internalize word meanings and claim ownership. These multiple exposures are closely tied to the third feature, meaningful use, in that students need to actively apply the meanings of words in situations that go beyond the definitional level of word knowledge and beyond the use of a single meaning or a single context. Meaningful use is also closely tied to integration in that meaningful tasks require that students relate the words to other concepts and situations. Exposure to these higher-level, cognitive word-processing tasks will, in turn, optimize students' chances for internalizing word meanings. Informative vocabulary assessment practices are grounded in the features of effective vocabulary instruction. In other words, like good vocabulary instruction, good vocabulary assessment must also move beyond the definitional level to assess the extent to which students can successfully apply word meanings in appropriate contexts—tasks that involve the instructional features of integration and meaningful use.

EFFECTIVE VOCABULARY ASSESSMENT PRACTICES

Effective vocabulary assessment is closely interwoven in all phases of productive vocabulary instruction. We begin this section by identifying and explaining assessment principles that are tightly aligned in what we know about effective vocabulary instruction.

Assess Words Students Need to Know

Johnson (2001) argues that we must think carefully about words we target for instruction. Word selections may be assessed by keeping in mind the following questions:

- How important is the word? Does the reader need to know this word to understand a text?
- How useful is the word? Is this a word that appears frequently in multiple contexts?

The sources for words we choose to teach may include narrative or expository texts related to a particular unit of study; lists of words generated by students from outside of school experiences; or contrived lists containing the word structures and terminology we are required to teach from state-mandated curriculum lists (Johnson, 2001).

Use Assessment Tools That Capture What It Means to Know a Word

To assess students' understanding of particular words, we must understand what "knowing" a word involves. Being able to provide or recognize a definition in a matching exercise may tell us little about our students' word knowledge. As Blachowicz (1999) so aptly states:

> We need to recognize the distinction between word knowledge as traditionally conceived (and measured) and the cultural or general knowledge that may be necessary for understanding a given text. This distinction is somewhat analogous to the difference between a dictionary and an encyclopedia, between a definition and a full-fledged concept. Nevertheless, it is through words that readers gain access to their relevant stores of knowledge—their mental encyclopedias as well as their mental dictionaries—and through them that we assess that knowledge in diagnosing comprehension difficulties. (p. 214)

Knowing a word means knowing not only the meaning, but knowing the contexts in which that word is used; it means knowing related words and ideas; it means knowing when and where to use the word. Therefore, to assess word knowledge, we need to consider the behaviors and actions that demonstrate what it means to know a word. Assessment tasks might include asking students to (1) provide synonyms and/or antonyms of words; (2) categorize words under appropriate headings; (3) use the words in oral or written contexts that provide clear evidence of knowledge of word meanings (Baumann et al., 2003).

Use Assessment Techniques That Reflect Different Dimensions of Word Knowledge

Word learning is a gradual process that occurs across multiple encounters with words in a variety of contexts (Baumann et al., 2003). With each successive encounter with a word, we learn a little more about its meaning and continue to develop a richer and more complete understanding of it. At any point in time, we find that we know words at varying levels or dimensions, resulting in differences in the quality and comprehensiveness of our understanding of particular words. We may have a general understanding of the meanings of some words that serves us sufficiently in understanding what we read. For other words, however, we may have a more thorough and extensive understanding of their meanings, and these meanings enable us to not only understand what we read or listen to, but also to use the words in writing and speaking.

These variations in levels of word knowledge are important considerations for informative vocabulary assessment. Effective assessment techniques reflect the level of word knowledge needed for performing particular tasks. Therefore, planning assessment requires careful examination of the multiple dimensions of the target words and of the ways we expect students to use them. If students need to acquire only a generalized understanding of what a word means, then our assessment tools should reflect this broad meaning as opposed to a more in-depth, all-inclusive meaning. If, on the other hand, students need a thorough understanding of a word because the concept it represents is crucial for understanding a text, then the assessment should capture this richer knowledge. For English language learners (ELLs), this method of assessing vocabulary might also have the effect of giving "learners the incentive to deepen their knowledge of lexical items, or to develop effective communication strategies to deal with gaps in their vocabulary knowledge" (Read & Chapelle, 2001, p. 23).

Use Vocabulary Assessment Procedures That Are Systematic, Organized, and Ongoing

Vocabulary assessment techniques, similar to other aspects of literacy, should be systematic, organized, and ongoing (Lipson & Wixson, 1997). These techniques help us gather useful information about students' developing vocabulary knowledge in the contexts of authentic and ongoing classroom activities. Furthermore, gathering data about vocabulary learning must be an ongoing process that can capture the incremental nature of word learning. In this way we acknowledge the different dimensions of word knowledge, avoid distorted pictures of what students really know about targeted vocabulary, and become more responsive to the needs of all students, particularly students with diverse cultural and linguistic backgrounds.

Frey and Hiebert (2003) describe teacher-based assessments in terms of three general assessment techniques—teacher observations, student–teacher dialogues, and artifacts or samples of student work—all of which apply to assessing vocabulary learning and teaching. First, our close observations of student reactions to vocabulary instruction can be very telling. How students react to direct, "student-friendly" explanations of word meanings tied to rich instructional contexts can serve as a barometer for subsequent lessons (Beck, McKeown, & Kucan, 2002). Moreover, students' active participation in class discussions about the words is another source of assessment data, especially when the discussions involve meaningful use of words. Finally, vocabulary assessment also involves samples of work illustrating students' level of knowledge about the words. The work samples can include illustrations, mappings, creative writings, documentation of role-play demonstrations, and even teacher-developed assessments that reflect the type of instruction used.

Ultimately, our goal is to help students become independent language users of the words we teach, and these rich sources of assessment data—observations, dialogues, and work samples—can help us determine student progress toward this goal. Furthermore, assessing student learning in the context of instruction can help us examine the relationship between the type of instructional activity and the degree of student learning, and by so doing, we can turn the assessment lens on our teaching: Are we providing students the types of opportunities that predictably lead to the depth of knowledge we seek for them? This question may be of special importance in the assessment of ELLs, who are especially in need of rich contextual experiences to help them retain the large number of new vocabulary words they need to acquire. In fact, we know that memory is strongly correlated with the meaningfulness of the learning experience (Willingham, 2005). When teachers gather data as students learn, they can gauge appropriateness of the type of instruction provided for the ELLs.

Use Assessment Tools That Reflect the Type of Instruction Used

Effective vocabulary instruction helps students understand how and when to use certain words in specific contexts and offers them multiple opportunities to actively use new words in meaningful ways. This type of instruction is addressed by Beck et al. (2002) through detailed descriptions and rich examples of what they call "robust" vocabulary instruction. Their research-based instructional strategies and procedures emphasize active student engagement in challenging tasks that focus primarily on significant and purposeful applications of word meanings in appropriate contexts. For example, one of their activities asks students to associate targeted words with a related word or idea (e.g., "Which word goes with a professional tennis player?" [*vigorous*]). In another activity students must complete a sentence using what they know about a word's meaning in order to do so (e.g., "The father *reluctantly* handed the car keys to his son because . . . ").

When we implement these instructional practices, we must also assess students' word learning accomplishments in ways that match this type of instruction. If we assessed word learning by merely asking students to match the words with their definitions or to define the words, we would obtain information only at a low level of cognitive processing. That is, some students may provide appropriate responses by simply memorizing definitions without acquiring a clear or deep understanding of word meaning. The information obtained from such an assessment would not tell us the level of word knowledge the students have acquired, nor would it tell us how well the students can apply the words in real contexts. Instead, assessment techniques should mirror the high-level thinking activities used during instruction.

Incorporate Student Self-Assessment Practices

One final aspect of effective vocabulary assessment is student self-assessment, a practice that is beneficial in several ways. First, it enhances students' metacognitive ability by increasing their awareness of new and unfamiliar words. Second, self-assessment creates opportunities for students to think critically about what they know and do not know about the challenging vocabulary they encounter in their readings. In doing so, they become more cognizant of the situational contexts in which the words are used and of the language or grammatical functions that the words can serve. In addition, students consider the independent word-learning strategies they possess and how these strategies can help them figure out the meanings of the unfamiliar words (Harmon, 1998). Finally, self-assessment allows us to adjust instruction to fill in the gaps that we notice as students grapple with active word usage.

ASSESSMENT ACTIVITIES

In this section we offer several specific examples of ways in which these assessment principles might be applied in the context of a typical classroom. These examples include (1) assessment of explicitly taught vocabulary intended to support comprehension of a designated text, such as a short story; (2) assessment of students' self-selected vocabulary; (3) assessment of a cooperative learning activity, "Wordsmith" (Daniels, 2002); and (4) assessment of independent word-learning strategies.

Assessment of Explicitly Taught Vocabulary

Teaching vocabulary to support comprehension of a specified text is a common and important instructional practice. Based upon the existing research and recommendations of noted experts in the field (Beck et al., 2002; Frey & Hiebert, 2003; Vacca & Vacca, 2005), we have developed a basic vocabulary lesson framework that highlights particular assessment practices. These practices can be applied to different texts. Our example is based upon "The Necklace," a short story by Guy de Maupassant. It is a story about a frustrated wife, Mme. Loisel, who envies her wealthier friends and yearns for a higher station in life. When she and her husband are invited to a party, she borrows a diamond necklace from a friend and, unfortunately, loses it. As a result, the couple goes into debt to replace the necklace, and they spend the next 10 years in abject poverty to repay their loans. It is only then that Mme. Loisel discovers that the diamond necklace was only an inexpensive replica. Because this story lends itself to the study of character development, we selected vocabulary words that represented the feelings, emotions, and experiences of the characters.

The instructional framework highlights before-, during-, and after-reading activities with the accompanying assessments (Vacca & Vacca, 2005). Refer to Figure 9.1 for an overview of the framework. In the before-reading phase, the teacher uses direct instructional procedures to explain word meanings. The accompanying assessments include close observations of students' reactions to the word explanations and instructional contexts. As the teacher and the students explore other contexts and related ideas about the words, the teacher carefully monitors student responses to the prompts via student–teacher dialogues.

The during-reading phase requires students to pay attention to the ways in which the author uses the targeted words. Students assess their own understanding of the words by monitoring their meaning constructions in the context of the story line. In addition, the teacher encourages the students to refer to outside resources, such as dictionaries or vocabulary logs, to clarify word meanings. The teacher then observes which students make use of this strategy.

In the after-reading phase, student–teacher dialogues provide important assessment information as the teacher and students relate the words to story ideas during class discussion. These specific prompts allow students to connect the targeted words to the important story ideas that the teacher has highlighted for the lesson. Once again, the teacher can reinforce word learning through prompts that require students to use the words in meaningful contexts. The prompts can require either oral or written responses from the students. Finally, if grades are necessary, the teacher can develop a written assessment based upon the types of prompts used during instruction.

"The Necklace"

	Instruction (adapted from Beck et al., 2002)	Assessment (based upon techniques described by Frey & Hiebert, 2003)

Before Reading	1. Teacher selects words
	   Character development
	      lofty humiliating
	      disconsolate overwhelmed
	      anxiety anguish
	      deprivation odious
	   Other words
	      superb
	      frugal
		1. **Teacher assesses word** list to determine which words to emphasize; teacher narrows word list, highlighting words with a specific focus.

	2. Teacher presents words to students.
	
	Teacher presents comprehensible definitions and instructional contexts to students.
	Example:
	   lofty—describes actions when people think they are better than someone else; *arrogant*; *proud*; *snobbish*; *conceited*
	
	   Sandy acted like she was better than the girls in the club. Her *lofty* attitude was so irritating to Janey that she would not invite Sandy to her Halloween party.
		2. **Teacher observations**
		
		Teacher assesses understanding by asking who might be familiar with the terms; teacher observes students to see if they understand the definitions and contexts.

	3. Explore other contexts and related ideas of the terms.
	   Example:
	     Which word goes with a conceited person?
	     Describe a time when you might feel *overwhelmed*.
		3. **Student–teacher dialogues**
		Teacher notes student responses to these prompts.

During Reading	4. Focus attention on the way in which the author uses the words.	4. **Students self-monitor** their understanding of the text and the ways in which the author uses the terms.
	5. Refer to dictionary or word logs for meanings.	5. **Teacher observations** Teacher notes student use of the dictionary and/or word logs during reading.

(continued)

FIGURE 9.1. "The Necklace" lesson plan.

| After Reading | 6. Relate words to story ideas.
Example:
How did Mme. Loisel feel about *lofty* women who were wealthy? How did she feel about not being rich? If she were rich, do you think she would have a *lofty* attitude about people who were not as well off as she? | 6. **Student–teacher dialogues**
Teacher notes student responses to these questions; correct responses indicate an understanding of vocabulary as well as story comprehension. |
| | 7. Reinforce and extend word meanings through meaningful use of prompts.
Examples:
Could an *odious* task cause you great *anguish?*
The old man standing in front of the post office had a *disconsolate* look on his face because _____. | 7. **Student–teacher dialogues**

8. **Samples of student work**
Graded teacher-developed assessment based upon types of prompts used during instruction. |

FIGURE 9.1. *(continued)*

Assessment of Students' Self-Selected Vocabulary

To promote active engagement and personal ownership of word learning, Michelle (a classroom teacher and coauthor of this chapter) uses the "vocabulary squares" activity throughout the school year with her eighth-grade students. This activity is an adaptation of Haggard's (1986) vocabulary self-collection strategy in which words to study and learn are selected by the students. Students in Michelle's classes work in groups to find words that they believe everyone should know. Sources for the words can be the texts they are reading, conversations with others, electronic media, and other outside-of-school contexts. Similar to Haggard's strategy, the students share their words with the class and provide a rationale for learning the words. Michelle writes all the words on the board, selects two words she wants the students to learn, and then directs her students to nominate and vote to select two other words. Once the four words are targeted, Michelle leads the class in rich discussions and meaningful activities to illustrate semantic and syntactical uses of the words. The students complete a four-square map for each term to support and reinforce their learning. Figure 9.2 provides the procedures for implementing this strategy and a student example of a four-square sheet.

To assess student word learning, Michelle uses two assessment tools: student self-assessments and weekly vocabulary tests. The student self-assessments, as illustrated in Figure 9.3, enable students to think metacognitively about the work they have completed in the four squares. By taking this personal stance when examining their work, students decide whether or not they need further explanation from the teacher or from peers. This process enables them to take charge of their own learning and to become more strategic as they work toward becoming more independent word learners. Figure 9.3 is an example of one student's self-assessment of her work with four words. Marisela is uncertain about the word *intervene* but believes that she has a good under-

1. Students individually select four words to learn from in-school or out-of-school sources.

2. Students address the following self-assessment questions:

   Where did I find the word?

   Why do I think the word is a good one for everyone to know?

3. Student groups discuss their words and decide which words to share with the whole class.

4. Teacher and whole class discuss the word selections of each group; words are displayed on the chalkboard.

5. Teacher selects two high-utility words from the list on the chalkboard.

6. The class votes to select two more words for the week.

7. Students complete a four-square data sheet for each word.

Word	Word meaning Part of speech Sample sentence
Illustration	Nonexample
Practice sentence	

FIGURE 9.2. Procedures for vocabulary squares activity.

standing of the other three words. From this self-assessment, Michelle knows that she must clarify the meaning of *intervene* for Marisela and provide more rich examples of how the word can be used.

The weekly vocabulary tests are based upon the four words selected by the students. Given that Michelle teaches five sections of reading, this approach requires writing five different texts because each class section has different word lists. However, Michelle has created a template that helps her develop questions systematically. Each test is worth 12 points and includes four major sections: sentence completions, meaningful use, a language-use chart, and a section where students generate their own use of a self-selected term. She bases her questions on the types of meaningful prompts that she uses during instruction and is careful to develop different contexts and questions for the tests. Because the tests parallel instruction, students know what to expect and how to prepare. Figure 9.4 provides an example of Marisela's answers to one weekly test. We note that she appears to understand the word *intervene*, but she apparently does not understand the function of the word *extravagant*. Because several students in the class also appear confused about the functions of the tested words, Michelle will develop her next lesson based on this information.

Name: Marisela   Class Period: 7th

Word #1: despicable			
To what extent do I agree with the following statements? Check one column.			
	not really	**somewhat**	**very much**
I understand what the word means by the definition.			✓
My illustration helps me remember the word's meaning.	✓		
My nonexample makes me think more deeply about the word's meaning.		✓	
My sentence is a good example of what I know about this word.	✓		
I understand who would use this word, when and where it might be used, and how to use it correctly.		✓	

Examine your responses. Then check the statement that applies.

    __✓__ I know this word and can easily use it in my reading, writing, speaking, and listening.

    ____ I need more explanation about this word.

Word #2: console			
To what extent do I agree with the following statements? Check one column.			
	not really	**somewhat**	**very much**
I understand what the word means by the definition.			✓
My illustration helps me remember the word's meaning.			✓
My nonexample makes me think more deeply about the word's meaning.			✓
My sentence is a good example of what I know about this word.		✓	
I understand who would use this word, when and where it might be used, and how to use it correctly.		✓	

Examine your responses. Then check the statement that applies.

    __✓__ I know this word and can easily use it in my reading, writing, speaking, and listening.

    ____ I need more explanation about this word.

Word #3: intervene			
To what extent do I agree with the following statements? Check one column.			
	not really	**somewhat**	**very much**
I understand what the word means by the definition.		✓	
My illustration helps me remember the word's meaning.		✓	
My nonexample makes me think more deeply about the word's meaning.	✓		

(continued)

FIGURE 9.3. Vocabulary squares self-assessment.

My sentence is a good example of what I know about this word.	✓		
I understand who would use this word, when and where it might be used, and how to use it correctly.	✓		
Examine your responses. Then check the statement that applies. ____ I know this word and can easily use it in my reading, writing, speaking, and listening. ✓ I need more explanation about this word.			

Word #4: extravagant			
To what extent do I agree with the following statements? Check one column.			
	not really	**somewhat**	**very much**
I understand what the word means by the definition.		✓	
My illustration helps me remember the word's meaning.		✓	
My nonexample makes me think more deeply about the word's meaning.			✓
My sentence is a good example of what I know about this word.		✓	
I understand who would use this word, when and where it might be used, and how to use it correctly.		✓	
Examine your responses. Then check the statement that applies. ✓ I know this word and can easily use it in my reading, writing, speaking, and listening. ____ I need more explanation about this word.			

FIGURE 9.3. *(continued)*

Assessment of a Cooperative Learning Activity

Lina (a teacher of middle school students identified as gifted and talented and a co-author of this chapter) has found that meaningful vocabulary assessments are linked to activities that allow young adolescents to experience their vocabulary and take control of their own learning. One activity Lina uses to evaluate her students' knowledge of their vocabulary is literature circles. The discussion group format she uses is a variation of Daniel's (2002) literature circles and typically involves reading groups of four to six members who have designated responsibilities. To actively involve students in their own vocabulary development, Lina uses the role of wordsmith (Newell, 2003) in her literature circles. A student who is the wordsmith is required to self-select words from texts to teach to members of his or her literature group. It is a role that challenges students to form a deeper understanding of vocabulary by examining unfamiliar words or familiar words that are used in different ways. The objective of a Wordsmith is to lead group members in a variety of vocabulary strategies to expand students' reading, writing, listening, and speaking vocabularies.

The wordsmiths have several responsibilities. First, they must gather information about the self-selected words, including word meanings, derivations, different forms

Student: Marisela

Sentence Completions. Complete each sentence in a way that shows you understand the meaning of the italicized word.

1. Maria's response to her father's question was *despicable* because <u>of how she replied in a rude way.</u>
2. During his re-election campaign, the president had to defend his *extravagant* spending of federal money because <u>he spent too much money.</u>

Meaningful Use. Answer the following questions with a "yes," "no," or "it depends" answer. Then write a statement to support your answer.

3. Would you want a *despicable* person to be your friend?
   No, because they could be mean to you and others.
4. Would buying a Hummer be considered an *extravagant* purchase?
   It depends because some people don't care about spending a lot money on an expensive car.
5. Are teachers likely to *intervene* when two students start arguing?
   Yes, because they always get into everybody's business.
6. Would you expect a *despicable* person to *console* you if you just lost your wallet?
   No, because they are vile and they will give you the wrong advice.

Check the description that fits each word.

Word	Describes something or someone; describes how you do something or how you feel	Names objects or things or something people do	Shows action of what people or things can do
despicable	✓		
extravagant		✓	
intervene			✓
console			✓

Select one word from the list that you know you are comfortable using in your speaking and writing. Then do one of the following:

1. List two situations in which you would use the word.
   In an argument; take a little kid's money.
2. Write a sentence with the word. The sentence must have enough clues in it to let me know that you know the word. For example, a sentence such as "She is *krunk*" does not tell me that you know what the word means. A more appropriate sentence would be "Kathy is so *krunk* because she always wears the coolest clothes."
   The despicable girl always plays mean, dirty tricks on her little brother to make him cry.

FIGURE 9.4. Example of weekly vocabulary test.

and uses, dictionary pronunciation, and parts of speech. Second, after presenting their word choices to the group, each wordsmith interviews the members to assess their knowledge of the words and then to determine effective strategies to help them gain an understanding of the word choices. The interview is a brief question-and-answer period and follows each wordsmith's introduction of the words. Wordsmith questions are unique to each student but generically include:

"Do you understand the meanings of the words?"
"What can I do to help you develop a stronger understanding of the words?"
"Would you like for me to use the word in a sentence?"

To assess group members' word knowledge, each wordsmith may suggest that members write poems, create analogies, develop games, or convert words into pictures. Finally, wordsmiths write a self-evaluation to reflect on their instructional/assessment strategies and then report their findings to the whole class. Figure 9.5 contains an example of the self-evaluation. Lina uses these evaluations as a springboard for further vocabulary assessment.

Self-Assessment

Explain why the role of *wordsmith* is significant to a literature circle.
The role of wordsmith is significant to a literature circle because when you find a word that you don't know or you have a question about, the wordsmith helps you and your group discuss and decide together what that word means.

Explain why you chose the words to teach to your group members.
I chose the words to teach to my group members because either they were unfamiliar or familiar but used in a different way. Either way, our group was able to discuss and figure out the meaning of each word by examining the words in context. I specifically chose the word *cordial* because I was only familiar with how a cordial is consumed in our house. I was completely unaware that *cordial* can also mean friendly and sincere. I also chose the word *brackish* because I like the sound of that word. The word has a salty sense about it.

Explain how the role of wordsmith increased your understanding of the words the author used in the reading selection.
The role of wordsmith increased my understanding of the words the author used because while being wordsmith, I had to learn what the words meant in order to teach them to my group. As I was studying the words, I got a better understanding of each word.

Which of the activities worked best for your group members while learning the words?
The activity that worked best for my group members was Tic-Tac-Toe. Tic-Tac-Toe helped our group learn the words and their meanings because in order to play well, you had to memorize the word and all its meanings, and that helps you on the final test if you know the words well.

Future plans to improve the role of *wordsmith*.
Future plans to improve the role of wordsmith would be to create more games that help students learn the words and their meanings, such as Concentration. I think one possibility would be to draw the words to pictures, like suggested, but draw the words in context.

FIGURE 9.5. Role of wordsmith in book discussion groups.

Lina targets her final assessments to coincide with each group's completion of their texts. Each group is given a portfolio of performance assessment activities that are multidimensional and connect to her students' interests. These assessment activities reflect students' reading, viewing, listening, speaking, and writing vocabularies. Each member of the reading group chooses a required number of activities from the portfolio and completes the activities within a specific time and according to the holistic rubrics Lina provides (see an example of a rubric in Figure 9.6). For example, students may choose to graphically organize their words through semantic mapping (Johnson & Pearson, 1984; Nagy, 1988), in which each vocabulary word is categorized in relationship to key topics. Key words are placed at the top of the organizer, and related words are connected to the key words. Students may also choose to graphically organize their words by creating word webs. In this activity, each vocabulary word is shown as the center of the wheel, and then synonyms or antonyms form the spokes of the wheel. Additional portfolio activities involve developing games, creating art, preparing media presentations, composing poetry, and performing skits and documentaries. All activities focus on using the vocabulary words from their particular study. As a culminating

DEMONSTRATION OF STUDENT'S COMPREHENSION OF VOCABULARY WORK

6 = exceptional degree of understanding of words
> in-depth understanding, thorough, accurate information that elucidates, insightful interpretations, all significant details provided

5 = excellent degree of understanding of words
> perceptive, strong understanding, accurate information throughout, well-supported interpretations, many significant details

4 = proficient degree of understanding of words
> competent understanding, satisfactorily accurate information, interpretations adequately supported, sufficient significant details provided

3 = minimal degree of understanding of words
> simplistic understanding, accurate information but sometimes confusing, interpretations minimally supported, few significant details provided

2 = limited understanding of words
> incomplete, limited attempt to understand, inaccurate information, interpretations not apparent, very limited and/or insignificant details provided

1-missing degree of understanding of words
> NO attempt to demonstrate understanding
> OR missed the mark completely

Percent Conversion

6 = 95–100
5 = 90–94
3 = 85–89
3 = 80–84
2 = 76–79
1 = Below 76

FIGURE 9.6. Wordsmith rubric. Adapted from North Carolina Department of Public Instruction.

activity, Lina prepares four multiple-choice tests to strategically evaluate the word knowledge of the members of each reading circle. The four assessments test words in the contexts of the literature studied, rather than as an unrelated list.

Assessment of Independent Word-Learning Strategies

If our goal is to help students become independent word learners, then we must teach word-learning strategies and metacognitive skills. At some point we must assess the independent word-learning strategies of students to determine which ones they use and which ones need to be taught. The think-aloud procedure (Pressley & Afflerbach, 1995) is one important assessment technique to help us understand the strategies individual students use independently to construct word meanings while reading authentic texts. This assessment is conducted with individual students during independent reading; the teacher asks students to stop when they come to an unfamiliar word and to think aloud as they figure out the word's meaning. The teacher uses generic prompts, such as "Tell me more" and "What makes you say that?" to encourage elaboration of responses. The teacher uses the form provided in Figure 9.7 to note strategies she observes the student implementing.

Finally, to become independent word learners, students must also become metacognitively aware of the strategies available to them as they encounter unfamiliar words in their reading. We use the following self-monitoring questions to help students think more deeply and more critically about their word knowledge and about the strategies they use when they encounter unfamiliar words in their reading (Harmon, 2000, p. 525):

- Do I know this word?
- Do I need to know this word to understand what I am reading?
- If I think this word is important, what do I already know about it?
- What does the word have to do with what I am reading? What is it referring to?
- How is it used in the sentence? Does it describe or show action?
- Do I see any word parts that make sense?
- Do I know enough about this word?
- Do I need to know more information?
- How can I find out more about this word? Should I ask someone or use the dictionary?

CONCLUSION

In this chapter we have described critical vocabulary assessment features and provided several examples of vocabulary assessment practices that can be implemented with upper elementary and middle school students. These examples illustrate the close relationship between assessment and instruction and also indicate how vocabulary assessment tasks can be configured in a variety ways to reflect the instructional practices used in learning words and related concepts. We close by noting Nagy and Scott's (2000) assertion that "the quality of vocabulary instruction must . . . be judged, not just on whether it produces immediate gains in students' understanding of specific words,

Words									
Examines local context:									
sentence containing the word									
before the word									
after the word									
Refers to distant contexts									
Other locations									
Makes connections that refer to:									
immediate story events									
knowledge of story line									
ideas beyond the text									
language structures									
author's style of writing									
Other connections									
Uses word-level strategies:									
sounding out									
structural analysis									
word appearance									
Other word-level strategies									
Uses dictionary									
Other outside sources									
Relies on syntax									
Focuses on relevant information									
Determines plausible word meanings									
Other maneuvers									

Comments:

FIGURE 9.7. Chart for assessing independent word-learning strategies. From Harmon (2000). Copyright 2000 by the International Reading Association. Reprinted by permission.

but also on whether it communicates an accurate picture of the nature of word knowl-edge and reasonable expectations about the word learning process" (p. 281). We hold that assessment practices must also reflect an "accurate picture" to capture students' understandings about their vocabulary learning—learning that goes beyond word meanings and includes how, when, and where to use newly learned words appropri-ately. It is through this metalinguistic and metacognitive awareness that students even-tually acquire ownership of new words.

REFERENCES

Allen, J. (1999). *Words, words, words: Teaching vocabulary in grades 4–12*. York, ME: Stenhouse.

Baumann, J. F., Kame'enui, E. J., & Ash, G. E. (2003). Research on vocabulary instruction: Voltaire redux. In J. Flood, D. Lapp, J. R. Squire, & J. M. Jensen (Eds.), *Handbook of research on teaching the English language arts* (2nd ed., pp. 752–785). Mahwah, NJ: Erlbaum.

Beck, I. L., McKeown, M. G., & Kucan, L. (2002). *Bringing words to life*. New York: Guilford Press.

Blachowicz, C. L. Z. (1999). Vocabulary in dynamic reading assessment: Two case studies. *Journal of Reading Psychology, 20*, 213–236.

Blachowicz, C. L. Z., & Fisher, P. (2000). Vocabulary instruction. In M. L. Kamil, P. B. Mosenthal, P. D. Pearson, & R. Barr (Eds.), *Handbook of reading research* (Vol. 3, pp. 503–523). Mahwah, NJ: Erlbaum.

Daniels, H. (2002). *Literature circles: Voice and choice in book clubs and reading groups* (2nd ed.). York, ME: Stenhouse.

Frey, N., & Hiebert, E. H. (2003). Teacher-based assessment of literacy learning. In J. Flood, D. Lapp, J. R. Squire, & J. M. Jensen (Eds.), *Handbook of research on teaching the English language arts* (2nd ed., pp. 608–618). Mahwah, NJ: Erlbaum.

Haggard, M. R. (1986). The vocabulary self-collection strategy: Using student interest and world knowledge to enhance vocabulary growth. *Journal of Reading, 29*, 634–642.

Harmon, J. M. (1998). Constructing word meanings: Strategies and perceptions of four middle school learners. *Journal of Literacy Research, 30*(4), 561–599.

Harmon, J. M. (2000). Assessing and supporting independent word learning strategies. *Journal of Adolescent and Adult Literacy, 43*(6), 518–527.

Johnson, D. D. (2001). *Vocabulary in the elementary and middle school*. Boston: Allyn & Bacon.

Johnson, D. D., & Pearson, P. D. (1984). *Teaching reading vocabulary* (2nd ed.). New York: Holt, Rinehart & Winston.

Lipson, M. Y., & Wixson, K. K. (1997). *Assessment and instruction of reading and writing disability: An interactive approach* (2nd ed.). New York: Longman.

Nagy, W. E. (1988). *Teaching vocabulary to improve reading comprehension*. Newark, DE: Interna-tional Reading Association.

Nagy, W. E., & Scott, J. A. (2000). Vocabulary processes. In M. L. Kamil, P. B. Mosenthal, P. D. Pearson, & R. Barr (Eds.), *Handbook of reading research* (Vol. 3, pp. 269–284). Mahwah, NJ: Erlbaum.

Newell, Y. (2003). *Using the 21st century bloom's taxonomy within collaborative reading groups*. Paper presented at the regional meeting of the North Carolina Association for the Gifted and Tal-ented, Winston-Salem, NC.

North Carolina Department of Public Education. (2004). *Honors and Pre-AP curriculum* (rev. ed.). Raleigh, NC: Author.

Pressley, M., & Afflerbach, P. (1995). *Verbal protocols of reading: The nature of constructively respon-sive reading*. Hillsdale, NJ: Erlbaum.

Read, J., & Chapelle, C. A. (2001) A framework for second language vocabulary assessment. *Language Testing, 18*, 1–32.

Stahl, S., & Fairbanks, M. (1986). The effects of vocabulary instruction: A model-based meta-analysis. *Review of Educational Research, 56*(1), 72–110.

Vacca, R. T., & Vacca, J. L. (2005). *Content area reading: Literacy and learning across the curriculum* (8th ed.). Boston: Pearson.

Willingham, D. T. (2005). Do visual, auditory and kinesthetic learners need visual, auditory, and kinesthetic instruction? *American Educator, 29*, 31–35, 44.

Zumwalt, M. (2003). Words of fortune. *The Reading Teacher, 56*(5), 439–441.

CHAPTER 10

Assessing Literary Understandings through Book Talk

Nancy L. Roser

with *Charles Fuhrken* and *Peggy Semingson*

Little more than two decades ago a flurry of attention put children's books squarely in the center of many elementary school literacy programs. Across the country, the number of "real books" on classroom shelves proliferated. "Real books" was the label kids gave to tradebooks—those picture books, novels, poems, short stories, and information texts initially published by trade houses, crafted by well-regarded authors and illustrators, and produced with varying trim sizes, fonts, and designs. Unlike textbooks or basal programs, tradebooks are not designed to teach literacy. Rather, like all creative products, they are designed for pleasure, imagination, and thought.

Concurrent with this emphasis on authentic texts for children came a host of questions about how children learn to make literary sense of their sensible books. So researchers, too, produced a flurry of activity. Poised with tape recorders and video cameras, they captured the conversations of children who were reading and listening to this infusion of literature in their classrooms. The researchers gathered the written and drawn artifacts that children produced in response and watched as children enacted meanings. It wasn't long before research began to describe how readers of all ages responded to books, and proclaim that, regardless of age, kids were remarkably thoughtful about literature: They could (when given opportunity) generate themes, interpret illustrations, make connections across texts, notice author craft, and, with experience and guidance, talk ever more insightfully about books (Eeds & Wells, 1989; Galda, 1982; Hickman, 1981; Kiefer, 1983; Lehr, 1988; Many, 1991; McGee, 1992; Martinez & Roser, 1985).

Of course, teachers (and parents) always knew that even young children are remarkably good at sense making (Baghban, 1984; Golden, Meiners, & Lewis, 1992;

Martinez, Roser, & Dooley, 2004; Meek, 1988; Yaden, Smolkin, & Conlon, 1989; White, 1954), especially when offered good books, time to read, and opportunities to talk. But teachers were learning new ways to incorporate structures and invitations for children's literary meaning making. They offered children expanded classroom libraries, invitations into classroom literature circles, open-ended response journals, opportunities to represent their ideas through the arts, and literature unit study—all indicators of more time to consider books carefully (Daniels, 2001; Hancock, 1993a, 1993b; Martinez & Teale, 1988; Roser, Hoffman, Labbo, & Farest, 1992; Short & Pierce, 1990; Whitin, 1994; Worthy, 1996).

Yet before those interested in language, literature, and literacy could pull together what was being learned from the proliferation of children's literature, book talk, and journals in classrooms came a confluence of policy, test scores, research findings, and citizen groups prodding a shift in teachers' attention toward different concerns—including phonological awareness, accurate decoding, fluency, and vocabulary. There have also been bids for a larger role for informational texts (rather than a steady diet of story) in classrooms (e.g., Duke, 2004; Smolkin & Donovan, 2001). If the lines that form outside particular sessions at professional conferences or the topics appearing in journals are an indication, there are currently louder claims for teachers' attention than the meanings their children construct from literary experiences.

Yet, despite all the tugs on teachers' attention, literature study has neither evaporated from, nor saturated, the school day. Children are still talking and writing about books in classrooms, although their teachers feel increasingly concerned that time set aside for book clubs, independent reading, reading aloud, and book talk affect the benchmarks and measures that demonstrate success to external audiences. Perhaps more than ever before, teachers should be both convinced and convincing that each child's emerging sense of story, each child's growing literary understandings, and each child's way of approaching and constructing meanings are of great significance to their literate lives. Teachers already committed to the placement of literature in the curriculum are positioned best to observe and interpret how each reader in a classroom works toward achieving meanings.

Each of us is constantly in the act of observing. Assessment depends upon interpreting our observations—and that's hard. There's an old story about a man who got a job sorting potatoes. "Just put 'em in three piles," his boss told him, "big uns, li'l uns, and mediums." After several hours, the boss came back to find little work done, and the man pondering a single potato. "I can tell the 'big uns' and the 'li'l uns' easy enough," he explained. "It's the 'mediums' that's giving me fits." We who teach understand the dilemma. It is often easiest to differentiate the extremes—to identify those readers/writers who offer profound abstractions across pieces of literature from those who have not yet displayed affinity for books. But in between are the mediums. Yet, with each literature event, *each* reader/listener/writer moves toward greater understanding. It is precisely by assessing (observing and interpreting) what children say and do with their understandings that we are able to scaffold and support their growth (Donovan & Smolkin, 2002; Kamberelis & Bovino, 1999; Maloch, 2002; Roser & Martinez, 1985; Morrow, 1988).

Somehow the notion of children's books and assessments seem an unlikely pairing. People who love books the most seem to barely use the word. We looked for the term *assessment* in the subject index of those hefty children's literature textbooks used in teacher preparation courses. What did we find? That the term *assonance* is always there—but only once did we find *assessment*. Both teachers and children's authors bemoan the kinds of intrusions that traditional teaching/testing inflicts on children's literature in classrooms (Babbitt, 1990; Serafini, 2003). Children's author Jon Scieszka (2005) jokes in the preface to a new collection of short stories guaranteed to appeal to boys, *Guys Write for Guys Read*, that the "guys" should pay attention as they read the stories because they'll be asked to "complete the quiz at the end of each section" and then "write an essay" (p. 11). That's a kind of "ouch humor" to those of us who continue to assess children's reading by counting pages, recording scores, and prescribing journal entries. "Just kidding," Scieszka then adds, noting that his book is "not required reading. It's reading to find what you like" (p. 11). We argue that "reading to find what you like" and even "reading for fun" are legitimate goals of literature/literacy programs. And, as with any legitimate goal, there should be manageable ways to tell whether we're getting there—ways to observe, record, inform teaching, and give feedback (other than quizzes at the end of each section) (Purves, 1986).

This chapter considers some central goals of literature programs and offers ways for determining whether kids are moving toward those goals. It is intended to help teachers listen and look carefully at children's book talk (and responsive writing/ drawing) so as to make decisions about how children are approaching literature, and what their responses reveal about their literary experiences and understandings. There aren't many readily available inventories or checklists designed to help teachers gauge growth in children's literary meaning making (Hoyt, 1999; Many, Gerla, Wiseman, & Ellis, 1995; Morrow, 1990; Paradis, Chatton, Boswell, Smith, & Yovich, 1991; Paris & Hoffman, 2004). As a result, we've attempted to draw composite pictures of children's insights from investigations of students' book talk, responsive writing, and drawings. That is, we searched the tables of contents of 12 literacy and literature journals published in the last quarter century, identifying studies that described children's oral, written, and symbolic insights into literature. We also looked to classic text-length contributions toward understanding children's growing sense of story (e.g., Applebee, 1978; Cochran-Smith, 1984; Dyson, 1989; Kiefer, 1995; Lehr, 1991; McMahon, Raphael, Goatley, & Pardo, 1997; Wells, 1986). Across studies, we watched for the documentation of similar findings or discussion of recurring phenomena in children's responses, even though the researchers might have entered the discourse with different questions and labeled the features differently. From these similarities across studies, then, we arrayed some recurring features of readers'/writers' literary insights that might be useful to others who want to examine, document, and make decisions about talk and writing. But first, let's consider how literary meaning making looks—so we can know it when we see it.

MAKING SENSE OF LITERATURE

Langer (1995) describes the dynamic process of making sense of text as one of building "envisionments"—or the sense a reader (or writer or speaker) has of the text at any given point. Envisionment-building theory rests on the transactional theories of Rosenblatt (1978, 1985), Iser (1978), and others. The theory contends that, based on personal, cultural, and text experiences, individuals continuously build and then rebuild meanings as they approach a text, deal with uncertainties, consider and reconsider possibilities, and even continue to rethink issues when the reading is finished. Langer offers four vantage points from which teachers can ascertain what students' talk and writing signal about how they are developing and refining meanings.

She labels the first stance "being out and stepping in" (Langer, 1995, p. 16). It encompasses those instances when a reader's personal radar screen spins to pick up the clues as to what kind of text this is, who's involved in it, and what seems to be going on. Clues are gathered from the text's format, style, and structure, as well as from the experiences the reader brings. The reader builds tentative hypotheses about character, plot, and time. Langer explains that this is often the stance readers take as they approach texts, but it's also the position of fallback when they become confused or derailed (i.e., stepping back to rethink the developing sense of the whole). Teachers know that their students are engaged in this clue gathering, clarifying stage of talk and writing when their hypotheses and hunches unfold: "I think Noah just might be a *little* cocky" (during fifth-graders' discussion of Chapter One of *The View from Saturday*; Konigsberg, 1996). So, "being out and stepping in" is a gathering, entry-type stance— that can occur at any time.

Langer's second envisionment category/stance, "being in and moving through" (p. 17), is registered by readers immersed in the story world they are helping to create. Positioned inside the story, readers draw from their own experiences and the text to live through the characters' dilemmas, consider the possibilities for actions, and reframe their expectations as new events arise. From within the story, the talk sounds like: "He shouldn't do it"; "That king is so MEAN"; "I wonder if she knows"; or "Oh, no!!" We asked a college English professor (one with a pipe and sweater vest) if he could ever turn off the critic in his head long enough to live fully inside a literary text— especially on the first read. He replied that he could not—that he was constantly aware of the crafting of the text even while immersed in the plot. By contrast, children's story talk seems to indicate that most can (and do) thoroughly immerse themselves in text, sometimes "stepping in" so completely that the text-world–real-world division is made permeable or "transparent" (Sipe, 2000a, p. 267).

The third way Langer describes the construction of meaning is what she calls "stepping out and rethinking" (p. 17). From this position on texts, readers move back from the story world to consider its effects on their own lives. For example: "I wish that I, too, could slow to consider life one teaspoonful at a time" (a book club member's response to Julian's character in *A View from Saturday*; Konigsberg, 1996). Langer calls it a time when readers use their developing understanding of the text to rethink their positions and ideas.

The fourth category of Langer's envisionment process, "stepping out and objectifying the experience" (p. 18), is a stance that describes a kind of distancing from the inside-the-story relationship with text, permitting reflection on the work itself and the meanings we are making. It is most likely in this stance that readers consider the text as a work of art—an aesthetic creation. Their talk may show that they are no longer living the story's events but rather considering (or basking in) the art itself: "I love when he goes: 'Oooo' " (5-year-old responding to *The Ghost-Eye Tree*; Martin & Archambault,

1985); or "Do you think Roald Dahl hates kids?" (10-year-old responding to *Witches*; Dahl, 1983).

Teachers who pay attention to their children's talk and writing about texts (whether approaching, immersed within, connecting with, or critically objectifying) can determine how and when a particular reader's vantage point shifts. Further, any reader who seems to "homestead" in one stance can be coaxed to consider the story from a different view. For example, children whose talk stays at concrete levels (even after repeated exposures to the text) can be offered text with layered meanings, time for rereading, a teacher "curator" (Eeds & Peterson, 1991), and/or a discussion group. Teachers can watch for children's first glimmer of appreciation of a text's surprising language or plot twist, indicating that they may be ready to look more closely at some aspect of the story's crafting. Conversely, children who quickly assume the outsider/critical stance, announcing only "I like it" or "I don't like it," can be guided into stories that grip them and then encouraged to consider that story from the character's perspective. Overall, talk about text roams across the stances—and probably should.

Sipe's (2000a) research into young children's responses produced a grounded theory for considering young children's stances, actions, and the literary understandings they demonstrate while using texts to fulfill different functions (see Figure 10.1). His

Aspects of literary understanding	Stance How children situate themselves in relation to texts	Action What children do with texts	Function How texts function
Analytical	(a) Within texts,	children analyze,	using texts as objects.
	Dealing with the text as an object or cultural product. Children stay within the text and make comments that reflect an analytical stance.		
Intertextual	(b) Across texts,	children link or relate,	using texts as context.
	Relating the text being read to other cultural products. The text is understood in the context of other texts, functioning as an element in a matrix of interrelated texts.		
Personal	(c) To or from texts,	children personalize,	using texts as stimuli.
	Connecting the text to one's own life, moving either from the life to the text or from the text to one's life. The text acts as a stimulus for a personal connection.		
Transparent	(d) Through texts,	children merge with texts,	using texts as their identity.
	Entering the world of the story and becoming one with it. The story world becomes (momentarily) identical with and transparent to the children's world.		
Performative	(e) On texts,	children perform or signify,	using texts as platforms.
	Entering the text world and manipulating it for one's own purposes. The text functions as a platform for children's creativity, becoming a playground for a carnivalesque romp.		

FIGURE 10.1. Sipe's five aspects of literary understanding, interrelated by stance, action, and fiction. From Sipe (2000a). Copyright 2000 by the International Reading Association. Reprinted by permission.

chart describes children's literary meaning making with picture books as operating in five domains (Sipe, 2000a, 2000b). From the *analytic* domain, children interpret and make sense of the text from within (somewhat similar to Langer's stance 2—"being in and moving through"). Nearly one out of ten children responded to storybooks in Sipe's research with *intertextual* comments, defined as drawing on their familiarity with related texts (movies, television, and other books) to interpret stories. Sipe separated this kind of intertextual connection from children's *personal* connections—that is, their talk that linked the story with their lives (comparable to Langer's stance 3—"stepping back and rethinking"). *Transparent* responses gave evidence of the "power" of the text to draw the reader in such that the children's talk flitted easily between the walls of the story and the children's lives (again, like Langer's stance 2). Finally, Sipe identified *performative* responses as those in which children creatively and playfully enacted, elaborated, and manipulated the text. This, too, seems a within-text kind of consideration, indicating that young children's primary pleasure and occupation with literature comes from being absorbed by it—a particular function of childhood "do" rather than grown-up "say"—but performance, of course, could reach for any aspect of story and for any level of learner.

In a similar way, Cochran-Smith's (1984) work with preschool children showed that children's sense making with story included readying themselves for reading, making life connections with the text, and making text connections with their lives. The children's story talk revealed the "inside the story/ outside the story" shifts that Langer and Sipe also describe. Cochran-Smith noted that most storyreading episodes had interactions of all three types in no particular sequence.

Although not all researchers have labeled or categorized children's talk in the same ways, or even agreed completely about what they described, nearly all have noted rich patterns of insight, inference, and connection (both personal and intertextual). Some have positioned the cognitive demands of meaning making against the aesthetic backdrop of text (e.g., Galda, 1982; Many & Wiseman, 1992; McGee, 1992; Purves, 1993); others have carefully described the contexts (social, physical, instructional) that elicit and build on children's individual and collective best (e.g., Battle, 1995; Cox & Many, 1992; Latshaw, 1991; Leal, 1993; Oyler & Barry, 1996; Purcell-Gates, 1991; Rowe, 1998; Short, Kauffman, Kaser, Kahn, & Crawford, 1999). Collectively, these descriptions form a sound base for observing and deducing what children are contemplating and working to understand through their book talk and responsive writing. Assessment of children's book responses seems to center on the questions: What's going on here between children and text? How are the children (at this moment) working to make sense of the story? Are they living in the action? Linking it with their lives? Finding its dilemmas en route to wrestling with its larger issues and layers? Are they sensitive to a central character's dilemma and leaning on it to follow/construct plot? Does the children's talk/writing reveal wonderings, projections, deliberations, connections? Are they stepping back from the story to say things such as: "That seems so foolish," or "I never thought of that." Are they reaching across texts: "This is so much like how Marty felt in *Shiloh*" (Naylor, 1991)? Are they leaning on literature as an art form that helps them consider their place in the world? How children make and amend hypotheses, contemplate the effects of the text, and grow ever more discerning of the artistry of authors and illustrators are understandings that teachers can observe over time.

The Focus and Forms of Story Talk

Focus of Talk

Although talk is certainly not the first or only response children make to literature (Hickman, 1981), it is the most prevalent way in which readers get to reveal and construct their meanings. In traditionally taught literature classes, teachers supplied their students with interpretations before they could make their own discoveries of the art form; in today's classroom, by contrast, many teachers choose to do what Miller (1980) calls "practice restraint": "That time is the moment when the student begins, independently, to appreciate, to perceive the work as it is, to make vital connections between the work and the self or between the work and the rest of the world" (p. 11). Restraint and a knowing teacher make two big contributions to what Peterson and Eeds (1990) describe as the "grand conversation" (from Eeds & Wells, 1989), a collaborative group making meaning(s) together. From such group talk, teachers are continuously making decisions (assessments) about children's stance, associations, ability to support from text, and literary experience. Peterson and Eeds suggest that a legitimate goal of the literature curriculum is helping readers come to an understanding of how literate people discover depths of meanings and use literary talk to leverage meaning making. The elements of literature that appear in Figure 10.2 are familiar aspects of the lexicon of litera-

Setting (place/time) 　setting identification 　setting description 　setting interpretation	**Mood** **Style** Conversational Ornate
Character Identification/interpretation 　traits/attributes 　actions 　feelings/thoughts 　relationships 　dilemmas/conflicts 　goals/motives 　change	Dialect Devices 　figurative language 　imagery 　symbols/metaphors 　puns 　hyperbole **Theme(s)/messages**
Plot Identification/interpretation 　details 　events 　narrative order (chronology, flashback, time lapse) 　conflict 　turning point 　resolution 　suspense 　foreshadowing	**Artistry of the illustration** Identification/interpretation 　details 　techniques 　design features **Bookmakers' craft** Authored/illustrated Titled Design/layout

FIGURE 10.2. Focus of literacy talk.

ture instruction. Two points are worth reiterating: The first is that the ability to label literary elements is not the same as making meaning. The second is that we who guide discussions can serve as knowing curators for heightened literary understanding by (1) knowing the text (and the potential of the text) that children discuss; (2) listening to receive their fledgling insights expressed in their own ways; and then (3) offering (gently) terms that can clad, build from, and stretch their understanding.

For example, fourth-grader Zach concluded after a chapter of *Make Way for Sam Houston* (Fritz, 1986), "Sam Houston's life was in a knot."

"That's a metaphor Zach made," his teacher responded. "Zach is finding the similarities between two things that seem different. How can a life be like a knot?"

Even while she was receiving Zach's talk, she was scaffolding his understanding. Teachers' support can help label and clarify what readers seem ready to see and use. Eeds and Peterson term these supports with the focus of literary talk as "shooting literary arrows."

Across texts, teachers can notice both the elements of literature and the ways those elements are being used in book talk. Figure 10.2 arrays a typical construal of a "knowledge core" of elementary school literature study, but let's consider them instead as elements of literature that can help focus talk.

Forms of Talk

Across observers of students' responses, there has been attention to development, that is, to the increased complexity of students' responses over time (Applebee, 1978; Beach & Wendler, 1986). In a study of over 300 first- through eighth-graders' perceptions of character in the same short story, we (Martinez, Keehn, Roser, Harmon, & O'Neal, 2002) described younger children's character talk as surface-focused—on character features and actions rather than qualities, goals, changes, or relationships. Older readers, however, talked predominantly about characters' internal qualities—their motives and changes. Applebee (1978) noted that generalizing from the reading was a skill that developed later rather than earlier, and Purves (1993) described interpreting as the skill of a more mature reader. In her study of children's awareness of themes, Lehr (1988) noted that children's ability to generate abstract thematic statements correlated with their experience with literature and with age. Sipe and Ghiso (2005) described the ways in which children develop increasingly insightful meanings from close inspection of illustrations. All of these insights contribute to ways of watching for and scaffolding children's insights. For example, when Hillocks and Ludlow (1984) produced a taxonomy of "skills in interpreting fiction," they argued that basic literal comprehension must precede inference because "if readers cannot retrieve information that is stated directly in the text, they will not be able to make inferences from that information" (p. 8).

In a loose way, Figure 10.3 collects information from these studies and others in an attempt to represent the forms talk may take as children become increasingly experienced with literary talk. Of course, it would be both too simple (and inaccurate) to say that the figure represents a hierarchy, or that all children develop from "noticing/labeling" to "generalizing," but in some ways these verbs describe a fair range of responsive talk from toddlers to graduate students, with the toddlers clus-

What respondents to text may be doing	Examples
Noticing/labeling	"What are those things?" (35-month-old in response to *A Boy Went Out to Gather Pears*; Hoffman, 1965, as cited in Crago, 1993, p. 219).
Describing	"He doesn't always use layered tissue paper. It looks like sometimes he cuts out heavier paper, paper he's painted all over. See here, you can see the brush strokes" (7-year-old in response to Eric Carle's art; Madura, 1995, p. 115).
Recalling (explicit information)/retelling	" . . . and it's about snakes and all these animals and it has all these dark pages. It's about a monkey who killed an owlet and the monkey killed the owlet because the branch fell because the hawk" (second grader in response to *Why Mosquitoes Buzz in People's Ears*; Aardema, 1975, as cited in McCormack, 1997, p. 34).
Wondering	"I wonder why Sam was so dedicated to doing things big" (9-year-old in response to *Make Way for Sam Houston*; Fritz, 1986, as cited in Roser & Keehn, 2002, p. 419).
Connecting	"When um I think of cats, sometimes, Miss Gaynor's [her teacher] got a soft jumper, like one, when I stroke her I think she's a cat sometimes" (8-year-old in response to the poem, "My Old Cat"; Summers, 1982, as cited in Foreman-Peck, 1985, p. 203).
Conjecturing (hypothesizing, inferring)	"That guy, the person that wrote the story, mighta been an astronaut or something" (third grader in response to *How to Dig a Hole to the Other Side of the World*; McNulty, 1979, as cited in Leal, 1993, p. 114).
Comparing	"When it shows the picture of the kids, Rapunzel has the kids, in the other stories they were wrapped up in blankets and they were babies" (First or second grader responding to *Rapunzel* variants; Sipe, 2001, p. 340).
Elaborating	"Well, the man and the woman, they're a lot younger in this one. So maybe, maybe when they were younger they lived in the city and they made the gingerbread boy, and he got eaten up, and then when they got older they retired to the country and they tried again" (primary grader in response to Richard Egielski's city-set version of *The Gingerbread Boy*; Egielski, 1997, as cited in Sipe, 2000b, p. 85).
Summarizing	"Yep. They took him as far as they could, and after that he came back again, and they decided to put him in the zoo" (third grader in response to *The Biggest Bear*; Ward, 1952, as cited in Hade, 1991, p. 11).
Interpreting	"The shadow was the anti-god, the bad side of him" (sixth grader in response to *A Wizard of Earthsea*; Le Guin, 1968, as cited in Cullinan, Harwood, & Galda, p. 35).
Analyzing	"The darker the color is, the slower the words are" (second grader in response to *The Whale's Song*; Sheldon, 1997, as cited in Sipe, 2000a, p. 265).
Generalizing	It makes me just sick when people moan about having a big nose and taking it out on other people...because if they read this book they would be thankful for what they have right" (14-year-old in response to *The Elephant Man*; Treves, 1980, as cited in Foreman-Peck, 1985, p. 203).

FIGURE 10.3. Forms of talk about books and illustration.

tered at the top of the chart and proficient, experienced literary readers filling the bottom categories.

What Children's Book Talk Reveals about Their Understandings

One of the critically important implications of Vygotsky's (1978) theory of the social construction of knowledge has been an underscoring of the value of talk as children work together to make sense of text (e.g., Gavelek & Raphael, 1996; Wiencek & O'Flahavan, 1994). That is, literary meaning making is strengthened through its social construction. Aidan Chambers (1996) understands this point well. Chambers suggests inviting children to talk together to make meaning in response to three specific prompts: (1) talk about what they notice or appreciate; (2) talk about what puzzles or concerns them; and (3) talk about the patterns they see or the connections they draw. These open-ended invitations, eliciting talk about the text through the readers' collected experiences, can lead to shifts in perspectives and new meanings.

We have used a simple chart (see Figure 10.4) to literally "cross" Chambers' three ways to invite book talk with three stances readers may take on the aesthetic of the text (Cianciolo, 1982, citing Miller, 1980), such that the three invitations to share meanings intersect with three ways of considering text. Cianciolo's three stances on text include (1) living in the story world (considering the story as event); (2) stepping out of the story to reflect (considering the text as a crafted object); and (3) considering the story's themes and layered meanings (considering the text as message). By placing an example of book talk into each of the cells, we can examine how children's meaning making can be considered in relation to the invitations and vantage points of talk. Encouraged to share their ideas, images, and noticings, for example, children's comments may focus on the story world—its details, character, and action (e.g., "The Strawberry Snatcher has mushrooms growing under his feet"). With increasing experience, readers may also be able to connect abstract messages across texts, indicating that "[these two stories] show that anyone can be a hero or heroine."

So, how does the chart contribute to assessment? Early in the school year or on their first venture into a text, readers' talk may cluster toward the upper left cells in this table. With experience, familiarity, and instruction, readers' talk may range more broadly across cells, with the most experienced readers even contributing talk in the lower right-hand cells, for example, linking abstract themes across texts. Carrying a chart like this to literature circle and making tally marks as talk progresses would show the range and focus of children's responses.

What Students Tell Us about Their Literary Understanding When They Write

To understand what writers know and do, teachers and researchers sit beside them— observing, listening, and conferring. When students write in response to what they read, we learn still more about their literary insights. By observing their processes and reading their products, teachers and researchers have agreed that literary awareness is both made evident and strengthened when readers write (in judicious doses). For those reasons, perhaps, response journals are instantiated in classrooms—serving as invita-

Invitations to respond / Considering the work	Noticings	Puzzlements	Connections
Story as event	"The Strawberry Snatcher has mushrooms growing under his feet" (7-year-old in response to *The Grey Lady and the Strawberry Snatcher*; Bang, 1980, as cited in Kiefer, 1983, p. 17). "I think the reason that he [William] smashed the mirror is because he didn't go all that way to carry out evil" (10-year-old in response to *The Castle in the Attic*; Winthrop, 1985, as cited in Martinez & Roser, 1994, p. 323).	"It doesn't make sense. The Pain and the Great One" (6-year-old in response to *The Pain and the Great One*; Blume, 1985, as cited in McGee, Courtney, & Lomax, 1994, p. 521). "I know mosquitoes have no brains—not much brains. But I don't know why they just buzz in people's ears" (second grader in response to *Why Mosquitoes Buzz in People's Ears*; Aardema, 1975, as cited in McCormack, 1997, p. 39). "I got a, I got a question. How could, uh, Thanh and [Park] . . . be brothers and sisters? I don't get it" (fifth grader in response to *Park's Quest*; Paterson, 1989, as cited in Raphael, Brock, & Wallace, 1997, p. 190).	"I always do it [pretend, as does the protagonist, to be asleep] when my dad wakes me up" (6-year-old in response to *The Castle in the Attic*; Winthrop, 1985, as cited in unpublished classroom transcript). "If I was Little Red Riding Hood, and, um, the wolf asked me where Grandma's was, I'd say, 'She's in New York and 100 miles away'" (Primary grader in response to Little Red Riding Hood; Sipe, 2002, p. 478). "In *Meteor* [Polacco, 1996], it's really a lot like *James and the Giant Peach* [Dahl, 1961] because they ended sort of the same. . . . In *James* . . . all the insects got jobs and in *Meteor* they were good at something they weren't before" (transitional primary reader in response to *Meteor* and *James and the Giant Peach*; Madura, 1995, p. 373).
Story as crafted object	"Look, it kinda goes weesh umm" (first- or second-grade student comparing two styles of art; Kiefer, 1983, p. 17). I noticed that they spelled some words different in the book and I noticed that they wrote different in the book than we do (8-year-old in response to *Winnie the Pooh*; Milne, 1926/1974, as cited in Kelly, 1990, p. 469).	"Is Annie a brown girl like me? . . . think the lady and Annie both hasta be white, because see, Leo Lionni likes the color brown. If Annie and that lady . . . are brown, he's going to show us that" (5-year-old in response to *Geraldine the Music Mouse*; Lionni, 1979, as cited in Paley, 1997, p. 71). "I wonder why she thought of the name	"The colors that Ezra Jack Keats draws with are dark. His colors are different from the kind Tomie dePaola uses because they are light" (5-year-old in response to two illustrators; Roser et al., 1992, p. 51). "I think if I can see how some authors write, I can try to write like they do" (8-year-old in response to author/illustrator studies in a multiage classroom; Madura, 1995, p. 112).

	"This is a 'yummy story'" (6-year-old in response to *James and the Giant Peach*; Dahl, 1961, as cited in Wollman-Bonilla & Werchadlo, 1995, p. 566). "The illustrator and the author are probably making another stupid book" (kindergartner in response to *The Stinky Cheese Man*; Scieszka, 1992, as cited in Sipe, 2002, p. 482).	Pictures, 1918?" (fifth grader in response to *Pictures, 1918*; Ingold, 1998, as cited in Roser et al., 2000, p. 272). "I was wondering in this book, how could the writer do that? How could you kind of plan going forwards and backwards and forwards and backward. I was just wondering if the author thought ahead of . . . just the basic plot" (sixth grader in response to *The View from Saturday*; Konigsburg, 1996, as cited in Gustavson, 2000, p. 25).	"Maybe Mr. Slobodkin read those old stories about giants and decided to write a new one with a friendly giant instead of an old one. And Mr. Thurber probably liked the stories with the evil giants better, so he made up the giant Hunder" (third or fourth grader responding to *The Amiable Giant* [Slobodkin, 1955] and *The Great Quillow*; Thurber, 1994, as cited in Moss, 1996, p. 220).
Story as message(s)	"Even if you love them, you always have to let somebody go" (5-year-old in response to *The Castle in the Attic*; Winthrop, 1985, as cited in Martinez & Roser, 1994, p. 322). "Everyone's different, and you shouldn't be jealous" (11-year-old in response to *Tico and the Golden Wings*; Lionni, 1964, as cited in Hickman, 1981, p. 351).	"I used to think if you're not scared of anything, you're brave. But maybe it's just the opposite" (primary child in response to *The Tunnel*; Browne, 1990, as cited in Moss, 1996, p. 140). "In order to keep the first one you gotta break the second one. Sorta hard" (7-year-old in response to "Three Strong Women," from a collection edited by Phelps, 1978, as cited in Trousdale, 1995, p. 178). "Well, it could have been, now that I think about it, that she was the bridge to Terabithia" (sixth grader in response to *The Bridge to Terabithia*; Paterson, 1977, as cited in Cullinan, Harwood, & Galda, 1983, p. 35).	"I think they were all looking for something. Like the Rooster wanted to see what the world was like. The boy wanted his cat. The Ladybug was looking for people to show how tough she was" (7-year-old connecting books by Eric Carle; Madura, 1995, p. 114). "These two stories are about real kids . . . like us. . . . It shows that anyone can be a hero or heroine . . . like Kyle said before" (primary child responding to *The Tunnel* [Browne, 1990] and *Jess Was the Brave One* [Little, 1991]; Moss, 1996, p. 141).

FIGURE 10.4. Ways of inviting, observing, and assessing responses to literature.

tions for children to write what they think, feel, or wonder about the texts they are reading. Some researchers have discovered that when students are given time to write a thought or two *before* discussion, that thought is preserved; further, time to think and write (e.g., what a student wishes to *say*) gives the writer entrée into the book talk (Martinez, Roser, Hoffman, & Battle, 1992). Based on findings from research on children's journals, in Figure 10.5 we have compiled descriptors of literary understanding that writers reveal (e.g., Hancock, 1993a, 1993b; Kamberelis & Bovino, 1999; Kelly, 1990; Wollman-Bonilla, 1989; Wollman-Bonilla & Werchadlo, 1995, 1999).

Journal writer	Response task	Journal excerpt	What the teacher can observe for
Beginning (or inexperienced) writers	Invited to respond to a picture book	*Irene showed graet ceriz and love in what she had done for her preshis mother. I know that Irene was scard. I was lost in a stor and I had to tell my mom the hole store. I admier her ceriz. Irene Irene I like Irene* (second grader writing in response to *Brave Irene*; Steig, 1986, as cited in Roser, 1994, p. 92).	Makes general evaluative statements "I like _____." Lists interesting ideas (to writer). Recounts an event that appeals. Records story events more cohesively (linearly, with connections). Adds personal connections. Considers the story's meanings. Makes judgments about a character or the work.
More experienced (or older) writers	Writing in response to a novel	*I really think what Harry is doing staying with girl so he can eat, take a fue tishues and spi on the people. And I think that at the begginning, Tucker took it a bit wierd, like througing a fit over a fried [friend] but then again they are good friends* (fourth grader writing in response to *Tucker's Countryside*; Selden, 1969, as cited in Wollman-Bonilla, 1989, p. 115).	Writes what they understand about the story. Makes some inferences about characters. Writes conjectures about the events. Offer their confusions and misconceptions. Begins to add justification for notions and interpretations. Indicates awareness of story craft, including specialized registers.
Most experienced (or mature) writers	Writing in response to a novel or other literary text	*Brian shouldn't be sitting there thinking he should be out there working. Finding food and shelter . . . Brian should be using his mind to make some crafty little gizmo to start a fire, catch an animal, or to get food. He should try to find anything that comes into his mind as a desperation tactic* (sixth-grade student writing in response to *Hatchet*; Paulsen, 1987, as cited in Hancock, 1993b, p. 472).	Produce evidence of the emotional response to text (including satisfaction and evaluative language). Bring a broader understanding of the world when considering text. Reveal their own wrestlings with moral/ethical dimensions of text. Seem to project an entrenched stake in the story's outcome. Pull from multiple sources (within and outside the text) to justify evaluative/ inferential comments. Show awareness of the author's craft appreciatively, comparatively, or critically.

FIGURE 10.5. Observing (and learning from) children's written responses.

What Drawings and Visual Images Reveal about Literary Understanding

When children are presented with one of the most typical tasks of schooling—to draw what they are thinking about a story—another window opens to their understanding. Too often, perhaps, we have viewed drawings as decorative attachments to the writing, or as a task that fills the ragged edges of transition times. Yet the drawings themselves (and the talk that surrounds them) yield deep insights into children's meaning making (e.g., Dyson, 1989). When students draw their understandings of the themes and messages of the texts with images and symbols, they both show and learn what meanings they are trying to represent (Harste, Short, & Burke, 1988; Hubbard, Winterbourne, & Ostrow, 1996; Whitin, 2005; Wilhelm, 1995). From students' individual and collaborative visual responses, teachers can begin to interpret their students' grasp and growth (see Figure 10.6).

Recordkeeping Systems

Simple, dependable record systems must ultimately come from classrooms—from teachers' own informed identification of the telling features of burgeoning literary thought—their own goals for literature study. A widely used and frequently adapted checklist of the features of talk surrounding books (Peterson & Eeds, 1990) is reproduced in Figure 10.7. Tompkins and McGee (1993) offer a simple checklist for monitoring a child's book talk in Figure 10.8; and Sebesta, Monson, and Senn (1995) have produced a hierarchy of aesthetic response for grades 4–10 (Figure 10.9). Reminding us to keep records that have purpose, can be efficiently collected, and are manageable, in sum, Calkins, Hartman, and White (2005) write: "Records that pull a sampling of words from a conversation and plop them on a form someone has asked us to fill in can actually displace more meaningful interactions and more significant information collection" (p. 37).

CONCLUSIONS

At the outset of this chapter, we pointed toward an influx of books into classrooms across recent decades, and the instructional accommodations that resulted—including more time to talk. Looking back, Petrosky's (1980) call to action seems prescient:

> We need to talk with each other about what we see and how we feel and think about what we experience. Children are no different. Books are worlds. Books are experiences. Children need to talk with each other and with teachers about their encounters with those worlds, those experiences. We would do well to minimize our expectations of quick answers and fast responses. Meaning comes slowly. Beginning response is a mediated process and not always coherent. (p. 155)

In the intervening years, we have learned a great deal about how literary conversations both socialize students into a particular discourse and reveal their thinking. We have seen for ourselves that students who can support their developing ideas with both text evidence and experience deepen their understandings. We have seen, too, how a book-

Drawing	What the child said about the drawing
The Lightning Poem Bright Purple zig-zag in the Sky! I am scard of Flash Explosions. I like air loud! Long white and blue Rumble!	José, age 9, was in his third month of learning English. Poetry seemed the natural medium for his quick, lively temperament and his motivation to write in English. In response to *Doodle Dandies* by J. Patrick Lewis (1998), he produced jagged language that mimicked powerful lightning. When his teacher splurged and made him two color copies, he wrapped one for his father's birthday present. The next day he said, "My dad, he cried."
token	Chris (age 7), wrote excitedly in response to Chapter 15 of *The Castle in the Attic* (Winthrop, 1985), the chapter in which the wicked wizard Alastor was knocked off mark by the gymnastic feats of the young protagonist, William: "William defeated Alistor!" Chris wrote. "William cratd the mirror! William got Alistor's torkn [token]!" Chris's drawing showed even more grasp of the story actions and details (plus his intertextual borrowings of style from the video game *Dragonball Z*).

Observing and learning from children's symbols/images

Images/symbols	What the student says about the sketch	What the teacher can learn from the sketch
11-year-old David's picture of Jonah as Atlas* (in response to *The Giver* [Lowry, 1993])	"Jonas is like Atlas having to carry the weight of the world because Jonas has to carry all of the memories of the world since the beginning of time—war, the bad things, the good things" (Wolf, 2004, p. 248).	Deep understanding of texts depends upon a grasp of the central problem—the character's goals and dilemmas. The use of Atlas as an analogy for Jonah's psychological load represents an intertextual link, as well as evidence of the artist's grasp of a character's struggles.
Eighth-grader Rebekah's representation of Liddie's heart (in response to *Liddie* [Paterson, 1991]). Description: A heart with a jagged line through it. Inside are illustrations that correspond with the written words "sadness," "strength," "loneliness," "fear," and "courage."	Rebekah's "character heart," filled with symbols of Liddie's hard life in 19th-century textile mills, was outlined in a broad yellow band. Questioned by her classmates about the significance of the color, Rebekah responded that she had not intended to "mean anything." But classmates had ideas—about warmth and goodness, or Liddie's need for a protective shell, or the yellow ribbons of wartime that symbolized "coming home" (Whitin, 1996, pp. 34–36).	Rebekah's choice to represent a central character's traits and feelings reflected a defensible grasp of the character. But when her classmates contributed their ideas for interpreting her sketch, they helped Rebekah consider symbolic interpretations of themes or messages.

FIGURE 10.6. Learning from children's drawings. *Illustration from Wolf (2004). Copyright 2004 by Lawrence Erlbaum Associates, Inc. Reprinted by permission.

I. Enjoyment/Involvement

	often	occasionally	rarely
• Is aware of a variety of reading materials and can select those he or she enjoys reading.	_____	_____	_____
• Enjoys looking at pictures in picture story books.	_____	_____	_____
• Responds with emotion to text: laughs, cries, smiles.	_____	_____	_____
• Can get "lost" in a book.	_____	_____	_____
• Chooses to read during free time.	_____	_____	_____
• Wants to go on reading when time is up.	_____	_____	_____
• Shares reading experiences with classmates.	_____	_____	_____
• Has books on hand to read.	_____	_____	_____
• Chooses books in different genres.	_____	_____	_____

II. Making Personal Connections

	often	occasionally	rarely
• Seeks meaning in both pictures and the text in picture storybooks.	_____	_____	_____
• Can identify the work of authors that he or she enjoys.	_____	_____	_____
• Sees literature as a way of knowing about the world.	_____	_____	_____
• Draws on personal experiences in constructing meaning.	_____	_____	_____
• Draws on earlier reading experiences in making meaning from a text.	_____	_____	_____

III. Interpretation/Making Meaning

	often	occasionally	rarely
• Gets beyond "I like" in talking about story.	_____	_____	_____
• Makes comparisons between the works of individual authors and compares the work of different authors.	_____	_____	_____
• Appreciates the value of pictures in picture storybooks and uses them to interpret story meaning.	_____	_____	_____
• Asks questions and seeks out the help of others to clarify meaning.	_____	_____	_____
• Makes reasonable predictions about what will happen in story.	_____	_____	_____

FIGURE 10.7. Response to literature checklist. From Peterson and Eeds (1990). Copyright 1990 by the authors. Reprinted by permission.

Student's Name: _Annie_____

Name of the Book or Poem: _Hey, Al_____

Other members of the Group: _Chris, Ryan, John, Alice_____

Product: What the student said   **Comments:**

✓ Recalled story events and characters

   Made global evaluations of story

✓ Made thematic statements ———————— _better as a janitor_

   Evaluated a character

✓ Interred a characters' feelings, thoughts, ———— _Al's not afraid anymore_

   motivations, traits

✓ Inferred about events ———————— _it was gonna be okay_

                                                when they got back

   Made reference to other literature

   Made reference to personal experience

   Shared personal reactions

   Made thematic statements

   Commented about structure of text

   Commented about author or illustrator

✓ Commented about the author's craft ———— _could be noting symbol of yellow color/happy_

✓ Commented about the illustrations ———— _notice foreshadowing of hand in picture_

   Commented about language of text

Process: How the student participated   **Comments:**

✓ Asked questions

✓ Made hypotheses ———————— _thought all birds were people before_

   Gave positive feedback to others

   Acknowledged comments of others

   Called for clarification, support

   Challenged thinking of others

   Spoke one at a time

FIGURE 10.8. Analysis of Annie's participation in a grand conversation. From Tompkins and McGee (1993). Copyright 1993 by Pearson Education. Reprinted by permission.

A taxonomy of aesthetic response

	Minimal	Moderate	Complete
0. Efferent response. Example: "The main characters in the story are the talking mule, the talking dog, the boy, and his father."	_____	_____	_____

Stage 1 : Evocation

1. *Relive the experience:* reexperience what happened as you read; includes acting out, telling, rereading a part that you, the reader, choose to reread. Example: "When the mule spoke it was a surprise. I was thinking it was going to be a magical or in some way a special mule."	_____	_____	_____
2. *Imagine or picture* characters, setting, or events from the selection; elaborate on the basic idea. Example: "The son was so scared that he almost had a heart attack. He screamed as loud as he could. Then he ran as far as he could."	_____	_____	_____

Stage 2: Alternatives (comparing, contrasting the original evocation)

3. *Apply own experience:* reconsider response by relating self. Example: "This is a picture of all the people telling Bill what to do and where to go because it reminds me of my brother and everyone telling him what to do and him telling them NO!"	_____	_____	_____
4. *Apply other reading or media to the work:* e.g. comparing folk tales. Example: "This story reminds me of a story I was told when I was little about a King who had a chair that talked and nobody would believe him. . . ."	_____	_____	_____
5. *Apply other readers' views (as in book discussions) or reexamine your own views.* Example: "I really liked the story. It was unpredictable and humorous. . . . It was surprising when the dog started talking, too. . . . It would be great to be able to talk to animals and have them talk back."	_____	_____	_____
6. *Reexamine text from other perspectives:* including hypothesizing, considering another point of view, extrapolating. Example: "I wonder why the mule hadn't talked before now? Why did he wait so long to say he was sick of being yelled at?"			

Stage 3: Reflective thinking (thematic level, requiring generalization and application)

7. *Interpretation:* generalize about the meaning of the literary experience, with application to the reader's own life, hence extending #3 to application. Example: "Finding out what animals thought would change the world. There may not be anymore eating beef or poultry. Yikes! I love a good leg of chicken."	_____	_____	_____

Stage 4: Evaluation (classified only as aesthetic if the above categories have been met)

8. *Evaluating what you got from the transaction.* Example: *"If I were the boy I wouldn't trip out. I would go and talk to the animals. What harm can talking to a mule do? Most people chat with their pets anyways. It wouldn't make much difference if the pet talked back. It would actually be nice."*	_____	_____	_____
9. *Evaluating the "goodness" of the work itself:* in regard to criteria set by the reader. Example: "I think this story really does not have any other point beside the fact that things are not always what they seem. Writing about this donkey might be a lot easier if the story was longer and more thought provoking."	_____	_____	_____

FIGURE 10.9. A hierarchy to assess reading response with middle- and upper-grade students. From Sebesta, Monson, and Senn (1995). Copyright 1995 by the International Reading Association. Reprinted by permission.

talking group stretches and challenges those initial insights—and that teachers' close observations can include what "transactions" readers construct within groups. The assessments of literary meaning making that best inform teaching, give useful feedback to students, help parents understand how their kids are making sense of texts (from inside and outside), and ultimately convince external audiences depend upon close and careful observation of talk, writing, drawing, enactments, and other forms of meaningful response.

Literature is an inviting medium, both in content and structure, in which all students can find a place. To ensure the accuracy of that statement, though, notions of "what counts" in assessments may need to change.

REFERENCES

Applebee, A. N. (1978). *The child's concept of story: Ages two to seventeen.* Chicago: University of Chicago Press.

Babbitt, N. (1990). Protecting children's literature. *The Horn Book, 66*(1), 696–703.

Baghban, M. (1984). *Our daughter learns to read and write.* Newark, DE: International Reading Association.

Battle, J. (1995). Collaborative story talk in a bilingual kindergarten. In N. L. Roser & M. G. Martinez (Eds.), *Book talk and beyond: Children and teachers respond to literature* (pp. 157–167). Newark, DE: International Reading Association.

Beach, R., & Wendler, L. (1987). Developmental differences in response to a story. *Research in the Teaching of English, 21*(3), 286–297.

Calkins, L., Hartman, A., & White, Z. (2005). *One to one: The art of conferring with young writers.* Portsmouth, NH: Heinemann.

Chambers, A. (1996). *Tell me: Children, reading, and talk.* York, ME: Stenhouse.

Cianciolo, P. (1982). Responding to literature as a work of art—an aesthetic experience. *Language Arts, 59*(3), 259–264, 295.

Cochran-Smith, M. (1984). *The making of a reader.* Norwood, NJ: Ablex.

Cox, C., & Many, J. (1992). Toward an understanding of the aesthetic response to literature. *Language Arts, 69,* 28–33.

Crago, M. (1993). Creating and comprehending the fantastic: A case study of a child from twenty to thirty-five months. *Children's Literature in Education, 24*(3), 209–222.

Cullinan, B. E., Harwood, K. T., & Galda, L. (1983). The reader and the story: Comprehension and response. *Journal of Research and Development, 16*(3), 29–38.

Daniels, H. (2001). *Literature circles: Voice and choice in book clubs and reading groups.* Portland, ME: Stenhouse.

Donovan, C. A., & Smolkin, L. B. (2002). Children's genre knowledge: An examination of K–5 students' performance on multiple tasks providing differing levels of scaffolding. *Reading Research Quarterly, 37*(4), 428–465.

Duke, N. (2004). The case for informational text. *Educational Leadership, 61*(6), 40–44.

Dyson, A. H. (1989). *Multiple worlds of child writers: Friends learning to write.* New York: Teachers College Press.

Eeds, M., & Peterson, R. (1991). Teacher as curator: Learning to talk about literature. *The Reading Teacher, 45*(2), 118–126.

Eeds, M., & Wells, D. (1989). Grand conversations: An exploration of meaning construction in literature study groups. *Research in the Teaching of English, 23*(1), 4–29.

Foreman-Peck, L. (1985). Evaluating children's talk about literature: A theoretical perspective. *Children's Literature in Education, 16*(4), 203–218.

Galda, L. (1982). Assuming the spectator stance: An examination of the responses of three young readers. *Research in the Teaching of English, 16,* 1–20.

Gavelek, J. R., & Raphael, T. E. (1996). Changing talk about text: New roles for teachers and students. *Language Arts, 73,* 182–192.

Golden, J. M., Meiners, A., & Lewis, S. (1992). The growth of story meaning. *Language Arts, 69,* 22–27.

Gustavson, L. (2000). Normalizing the text: What is being said, what is not and why in students' conversations of E. L. Konigsburg's *The View from Saturday. Journal of Children's Literature, 26*(1), 18–31.

Hade, D. D. (1991). Being literary in a literature-based classroom. *Children's Literature in Education, 22*(1), 1–17.

Hancock, M. R. (1993a). Exploring the meaning-making process through the content of literature response journals: A case study investigation. *Research in the Teaching of English, 27,* 335–368.

Hancock, M. R. (1993b). Exploring and extending personal response through literature journals. *The Reading Teacher, 46,* 466–474.

Harste, J. C., Short, K. G., & Burke, C. (1988). *Creating classrooms for authors: The reading–writing connection.* Portsmouth, NH: Heinemann.

Hickman, J. (1981). A new perspective on response to literature: Research in an elementary school setting. *Research in the Teaching of English, 15,* 343–354.

Hillocks, G., & Ludlow, L. (1984). A taxonomy of skills in reading and interpreting fiction. *American Educational Research Journal, 21*(1), 7–24.

Hoyt, L. (1999). *Revisit, reflect, retell: Strategies for improving reading comprehension.* Portsmouth, NH: Heinemann.

Hubbard, R., Winterbourne, N., & Ostrow, J. (1996). Visual responses to literature: Imagination through images. *The New Advocate, 9*(4), 309–323.

Iser, W. (1978). *The act of reading: A theory of aesthetic response.* Baltimore: Johns Hopkins University Press.

Kamberelis, G., & Bovino, T. (1999). Cultural artifacts as scaffold for genre development. *Reading Research Quarterly, 34*(2), 138–170.

Kelly, P. R. (1990). Guiding young students' response to literature. *The Reading Teacher, 43,* 464–470.

Kiefer, B. (1983). The responses of children in a combination first/second grade classroom to picture books in a variety of artistic styles. *Journal of Research and Development in Education, 16*(3), 14–20.

Kiefer, B. (1995). *The potential of picturebooks: From visual literacy to aesthetic understanding.* Englewood Cliffs, NJ: Merrill.

Langer, J. A. (1995). *Envisioning literature: Literary understanding and literature instruction.* New York: Teachers College Press.

Latshaw, J. L. K. (1991). Middle grade students' response to Canadian realistic fiction for young adults. *Canadian Journal of Education, 16*(2), 168–183.

Leal, D. J. (1993). The power of literary peer-group discussions: How children collaboratively negotiate meanings. *The Reading Teacher, 47*(2), 114–120.

Lehr, S. S. (1988). The child's developing sense of theme as a response to literature. *Reading Research Quarterly, 23,* 337–357.

Lehr, S. S. (1991). *The child's developing sense of theme: Responses to literature.* New York: Teachers College Press.

Madura, S. (1995). The line and texture of aesthetic response: Primary children study authors and illustrators. *The Reading Teacher, 49*(2), 110–118.

Maloch, B. (2002). Scaffolding student talk: One teacher's role in literature discussion groups. *Reading Research Quarterly, 37*(1), 94–112.

Many, J. E. (1991). The effects of stance and age level on children's literary responses. *Journal of Reading Behavior, 23,* 61–85.

Many, J. E., Gerla, J. K., Wiseman, D. L., & Ellis, L. (1995). Transactional criticism and aesthetic literary experiences: Examining complex responses in light of the teacher's purpose. *Reading Horizons, 36*(2), 166–186.

Many, J. E., & Wiseman, D. L. (1992). The effects of teaching approach on third-grade students' response to literature. *Journal of Reading Behavior, 24*(3), 265–287.

Martinez, M. G., Keehn, S., Roser, N., Harmon, J., & O'Neal, S. (2002). An exploration of children's understanding of character in grades 1–8. In D. L. Schallert, C. M. Fairbanks, J. Worthy, B. Maloch, & J. V. Hoffman (Eds.), *51st yearbook of the National Reading Conference* (pp. 310–320). Oak Creek, WI: National Reading Conference.

Martinez, M. G., & Roser, N. (1985). Read it again: The value of repeated readings during storytime. *The Reading Teacher, 38,* 782–786.

Martinez, M. G., & Roser, N. L. (1994). Children's responses to a chapter book across grade levels: Implications for sustained texts. In C. Kinzer & D. J. Leu (Eds.), *Multidimensional aspects of literacy practice: 43rd yearbook of the National Reading Conference* (pp. 317–324). Chicago: National Reading Conference.

Martinez, M. G., Roser, N., & Dooley, C. (2004). Young children's literary meaning making. In N. Hall, J. Larson, & J. Marsh (Eds.), *Handbook of early childhood literacy* (pp. 222–234). London: Sage.

Martinez, M. G., Roser, N. L., Hoffman, J. V., & Battle, J. (1992). Fostering better book discussions through response logs and a response framework: A case description. In C. K. Kinzer & D. J. Leu (Eds.), *Literacy research, theory, and practice: Views from many perspectives: 41st yearbook of the National Reading Conference* (pp. 303–311). Chicago: National Reading Conference.

Martinez, M. G., & Teale, W. (1988). Reading in a kindergarten classroom library. *The Reading Teacher, 41,* 568–573.

McCormack, R. (1997). Eavesdropping on second graders' peer talk about African trickster tales. In J. R. Paratore & R. L. McCormack (Eds.), *Peer talk in the classroom: Learning from research* (pp. 26–44). Newark, DE: International Reading Association.

McGee, L. (1992). An exploration of meaning construction in first graders' grand conversations. In C. K. Kinzer & D. J. Leu (Eds.), *Literacy research, theory, and practice: Views from many perspectives: 41st yearbook of the National Reading Conference* (pp. 177–186). Chicago: National Reading Conference.

McGee, L., Courtney, L., & Lomax, R. G. (1994). Teachers' roles in first graders' grand conversations. In C. K. Kinzer & D. J. Leu (Eds.), *Multidimensional aspects of literacy research, theory, and practice: 43rd yearbook of the National Reading Conference* (pp. 517–526). Chicago: National Reading Conference.

McMahon, S., Raphael, T., Goatley, V., & Pardo, L. (Eds.). (1997). *The book club connection: Literacy learning and classroom talk.* New York: Teachers College Press.

Meek, M. (1988). *How texts teach what readers learn.* South Woodchester, Stroud, UK: Thimble Press.

Miller, B. E. (1980). *Teaching the art of literature.* Urbana, IL: National Council of Teachers of English.

Morrow, L. M. (1988). Young children's responses to one-to-one story reading in school settings. *Reading Research Quarterly, 23,* 89–107.

Morrow, L. M. (1990). *Assessing children's understanding of story through their construction and reconstruction of narrative.* In L. M. Morrow & J. K. Smith (Eds.), *Assessment for instruction in early literacy* (pp. 110–134). Englewood Cliffs, NJ: Prentice-Hall.

Moss, J. F. (1996). *Teaching literature in the elementary school: A thematic approach.* Norwood, MA: Christopher-Gordon.

Oyler, C., & Barry, A. (1996). Intertextual connections in read-alouds of information books. *Language Arts, 73*, 324–329.

Paley, V. (1997). *The girl with the brown crayon.* Cambridge, MA: Harvard University Press.

Paradis, E. E., Chatton, B., Boswell, A., Smith, M., & Yovich, S. (1991). Accountability: Assessing comprehension during literature discussion. *The Reading Teacher, 45*(1), 8–17.

Paris, S. G., & Hoffman, J. V. (2004). Reading assessments in kindergarten through third grade: Findings from the Center for the Improvement of Early Reading Achievement. *Elementary School Journal, 105*(2), 199–217.

Peterson, R., & Eeds, M. (1990). *Grand conversations: Literature groups in action.* New York: Scholastic.

Petrosky, A. R. (1980). The inferences we make: Children and literature. *Language Arts, 57*(2), 149–156.

Purcell-Gates, V. (1991). On the outside looking in: A study of remedial readers' meaning-making while reading literature. *Journal of Reading Behavior, 23*(2), 235–253.

Purves, A. (1986). ERIC/RCS report: Testing in literature. *Language Arts, 63*(3), 320–323.

Purves, A. (1993). Toward a reevaluation of reader response and school literature. *Language Arts, 70*, 348–361.

Raphael, T. E., Brock, C. H., & Wallace, S. M. (1997). Encouraging quality peer talk with diverse students in mainstream classrooms: Learning from and with teachers. In J. R. Paratore & R. L. McCormack (Eds.), *Peer talk in the classroom: Learning from research* (pp. 176–206). Newark, DE: International Reading Association.

Rosenblatt, L. (1978). *The reader, the text, the poem: The transactional theory of the literary work.* Carbondale, IL: Southern Illinois University Press.

Rosenblatt, L. (1985). The transactional theory of the literary work: Implications for research. In C. R. Cooper (Ed.), *Researching response to literature and the teaching of literature* (pp. 33–53). Norwood, NJ: Ablex.

Roser, N. L. (1994). From literature to literacy: A new direction for young learners. In J. Flood & J. A. Langer (Eds.), *Literature instruction: Practice and policy* (pp. 71–108). New York: Scholastic.

Roser, N. L., Hoffman, J. V., Labbo, L., & Farest, C. (1992). Language charts: A record of story time talk. *Language Arts, 69*, 44–52.

Roser, N. L., & Keehn, S. (2002). Fostering thought, talk, and inquiry: Linking literature and social studies. *The Reading Teacher, 55*(5), 416–426.

Roser, N. L., & Martinez, M. (1985). Roles adults play in preschoolers' response to literature. *Language Arts, 62*, 485–490.

Rowe, D. W. (1998). The literate potentials of book-related dramatic play. *Reading Research Quarterly, 33*(1), 10–35.

Sebesta, S. L., Monson, D. L., & Senn, H. D. (1995). A hierarchy to assess reading response. *Journal of Reading, 38*(6), 444–450.

Serafini, F. (2003, February). Informing our practice: Modernist, transactional, and critical perspectives on children's literature and reading instruction. *Reading Online, 6*(6). Retrieved September 3, 2005, from *www.readingonline.org/articles/art_index.asp?HREF=serafini/index.html.*

Short, K. G., Kauffman, G., Kaser, S., Kahn, L., & Crawford, K. (1999). Teacher watching: Examining teacher talk in literature circles. *Language Arts, 76*, 377–385.

Short, K. G., & Pierce, K. M. (1990). *Talking about books: Creating literate communities.* Portsmouth, NH: Heinemann.

Sipe, L. R. (2000a). The construction of literary understanding by first and second graders in oral response to picture storybook read-alouds. *Reading Research Quarterly, 35*(2), 252–275.

Sipe, L. R. (2000b). "Those two gingerbread boys could be brothers": How children use intertextual connections during storybook read-alouds. *Children's Literature in Education, 31*(2), 73–90.

Sipe, L. R. (2001). A palimpsest of stories: Young children's construction of intertextual links among fairytale variants. *Reading Research and Instruction, 40*(4), 333–352.

Sipe, L. R. (2002). Talking back and taking over: Young children's expressive engagement during storybook read-alouds. *The Reading Teacher, 55*(5), 476–483.

Sipe, L. R., & Ghiso, M. P. (2005). Looking closely at characters: How illustrations support children's understandings. In N. L. Roser & M. G. Martinez (Eds.), *What a character! Character study as a guide to meaning making in grades K–8* (pp. 134–153). Newark, DE: International Reading Association.

Smolkin, L., & Donovan, C. A. (2001). The contexts of comprehension: The informational book read aloud, comprehension acquisition, and comprehension instruction in a first-grade classroom. *Elementary School Journal, 102*(2), 97–122.

Tompkins, G. E., & McGee, L. M. (1993). *Teaching reading with literature: Case studies for action plans.* New York: Merrill.

Trousdale, A.M. (1995). I'd rather be normal: A young girl's responses to "feminist" fairy tales. *The New Advocate, 8*(3), 167–182.

Vykotsky, L. S. (1978). *Mind in society.* Cambridge, MA: Harvard University Press.

Wells, G. (1986). *The meaning-makers: Children learning language and using language to learn.* Portsmouth, NH: Heinemann.

White, D. (1954). *Books before five.* New York: Oxford University Press.

Whitin, P. (1994). Opening potential: Visual response to literature. *Language Arts, 71*, 101–107.

Whitin, P. (1996). *Sketching stories, stretching minds: Responding visually to literature.* Portsmouth, NH: Heinemann.

Whitin, P. (2005). The interplay of text, talk, and visual representation in expanding literary interpretation. *Research in the Teaching of English, 39*(4), 365–397.

Wiencek, J., & O'Flahavan, J. F. (1994). From teacher-led to peer discussions about literature: Suggestions for making the shift. *Language Arts, 71*, 488–498.

Wilhelm, J. (1995). Reading is seeing: Using visual response to improve the literary reading of reluctant readers. *Journal of Reading Behavior, 27*(4), 467–503.

Wolf, S. A. (2004). *Interpreting literature with children.* Mahwah, NJ: Erlbaum.

Wollman-Bonilla, J. E. (1989). Reading journals: Invitations to participate in literature. *The Reading Teacher, 43*, 112–120.

Wollman-Bonilla, J. E., & Werchadlo, B. (1995). Literature-response journals in a first-grade classroom. *Language Arts, 72*, 562–570.

Wollman-Bonilla, J. E., & Werchadlo, B. (1999). Teacher and peer roles in scaffolding first graders' responses to literature. *The Reading Teacher, 52*(6), 598–608.

Worthy, J. (1996). Removing barriers to voluntary reading for reluctant readers: The role of school and classroom libraries. *Language Arts, 73*, 483–492.

Yaden, D. B., Smolkin, L. B., & Conlon, A. (1989). Preschoolers' questions about pictures, print conventions, and story text during reading aloud at home. *Reading Research Quarterly, 24*(2), 188–214.

CHILDREN'S BOOKS

Aardema, V. (1975). *Why mosquitoes buzz in people's ears.* New York: Dial Press

Bang, M. (1980). *The grey lady and the strawberry snatcher.* New York: Four Winds Press.

Blume, J. (1985). *The pain and the great one.* Scarsdale, NY: Bradbury.

Browne, A. (1990). *The tunnel.* New York: Knopf.

Dahl, R. (1961). *James and the giant peach.* New York: Knopf.

Dahl, R. (1983). *Witches.* New York: Farrar, Straus & Giroux.

Egielski, R. (1997). *The gingerbread boy.* New York: HarperCollins.

Fritz, J. (1986). *Make way for Sam Houston*. New York: Putnam.

Hoffmann, F. (1965). *A boy went out to gather pears*. London: Oxford University Press.

Ingold, J. (1998). *Pictures 1918*. San Diego, CA: Harcourt.

Koningsberg, E. L. (1996). *The view from Saturday*. New York: Atheneum.

Le Guin, U. K. (1968). *A wizard of Earthsea*. Berkeley, CA: Parnassus Press.

Lewis, J. P. (1998). *Doodle dandies: Poems that take shape*. New York: Atheneum.

Lionni, L. (1964). *Tico and the golden wings*. New York: Pantheon.

Lionni, L. (1979). *Geraldine the music mouse*. New York: Pantheon.

Little, J. (1991). *Jess was the brave one*. New York: Viking.

Lowry, L. (1993). *The giver*. Boston: Houghton-Mifflin.

Martin, B. Jr., & Archambault, J. (1985). *The ghost-eye tree*. New York: Henry Holt.

McNulty, F. (1979). *How to dig a hole to the other side of the world*. New York: Harper & Row.

Milne, A. A. (1974). *Winnie the Pooh*. New York: Dutton. (Original work published 1926)

Naylor, P. (1991). *Shiloh*. New York: Atheneum.

Paterson, K. (1977). *The bridge to Terabithia*. New York: Crowell.

Paterson, K. (1989). *Park's quest*. New York: Puffin.

Paterson, K. (1991). *Liddie*. New York: Viking Penguin.

Paulsen, G. (1987). *Hatchet*. New York: Bradbury Press.

Phelps, E. J. (Ed.). (1978). *Tatterhood and other tales*. Old Westbury, NY: Feminist Press.

Polacco, P. (1996). *Meteor*. New York: Putnam.

Scieszka, J. (1992). *The stinky cheese man*. New York: Viking.

Scieszka, J. (Ed.). (2005). *Guys write for guys read*. New York: Viking.

Selden, G. (1969). *Tucker's countryside*. New York: Farrar, Straus & Giroux.

Sheldon, D. (1997). *The whale's song*. New York: Puffin.

Slobodkin, L. (1955). *The amiable giant*. New York: Vanguard Press.

Steig, W. (1986). *Brave Irene*. New York: Farrar, Straus & Giroux.

Summers, H. (1982). My old cat. In *The burning book and other poems*. Sussex, UK: Book Guild.

Thurber, J. (1994). *The great quillow*. San Diego, CA: Harcourt.

Treves, F. (1980). *The elephant man and other reminiscences*. London: Allen.

Ward, L. (1952). *The biggest bear*. Boston: Houghton-Mifflin.

Winthrop, E. (1985). *The castle in the attic*. New York: Bantam.

CHAPTER 11

Assessing Strategic Reading

Peter Afflerbach
Heather Ruetschlin
Sharon Russell

We begin this chapter with consideration of the term *strategic reading*. There is ample evidence that the teaching and learning of reading strategies benefit developing student readers (Pressley, 2000). In classrooms, readers who predict the content and form of text, derive word meanings from context, summarize text, and monitor the process and progress of constructing meaning are demonstrating important strategy use. Our conceptualization of reading includes these important strategies, for they contribute to success in reading and related tasks. Yet, we believe that successful reading comprises more than a collection of individual reading strategies.

We conceptualize strategic reading not only in relation to the content of what we read and understand, but also in relation to how we use what we learn from reading. Strategic reading is guided by the reader's overarching goals and purposes, and supported by plans that link these goals and purposes to specific reading strategies (Paris, Wasik, & Turner, 1991; Pressley & Afflerbach, 1995). Strategic readers understand the value of strategies and the active role that they must take in using them. Strategies are employed in service of understanding text, and strategic readers are talented at applying that which is learned from text in reading-related tasks.

In addition, we understand becoming a strategic reader to be a developmental phenomenon (Alexander, 2005). Accordingly, it is important that our instruction and assessment reflect the growth trajectories of developing readers. Through modeling, explanation, and discussion, teachers help students develop an understanding of the nature of reading strategies and how they are useful, from constructing literal meaning to critically evaluating text content. That students develop gradually as strategic readers requires us to approach the teaching, learning, and assessment of strategies in like manner. Instruction succeeds when teachers assess their students' current level of strategic reading and are able to address their anticipated levels of accomplishment with instructional materials and procedures (Palincsar & Brown, 1984).

Finally, we believe that strategic reading includes (but goes beyond) the goal of literal and inferential comprehension of text. In information-dense societies, the ability to make critical and evaluative judgments about texts, authors, and their purposes is central to successful reading in and out of school (Fehring & Green, 2001). Students must develop reading strategies that help them determine the accuracy and trustworthiness of texts. They must uncover and understand the biases and agendas that influence how texts are created and read. Reading strategies are central to this effort.

WHY ARE STRATEGIES IMPORTANT TO READING AND SCHOOL SUCCESS?

Developing readers need strategies to effectively interact with texts, construct meaning, and apply what is learned from reading to various tasks, in school and out. These readers, through appropriate instruction and assessment, can build repertoires of strategies that are utilized in different acts of reading. Strategic reading helps students construct literal and inferential understanding of text (Kintsch, 2000), as well as critical and evaluative understanding of authors, texts, and their purposes. Yet, indications are that many students lack strategic reading ability (Perie & Moran, 2005). These students struggle to construct meaning from text, rarely enjoy reading, and may fail to realize their potential. There is clear need for assessment that helps us understand the nature of students' strategic reading development and helps us foster their progress with this essential skill.

THE COEVOLUTION OF KNOWLEDGE ABOUT READING STRATEGIES AND READING ASSESSMENT

Our understanding of reading and the strategies used by successful readers is continually evolving (Thorndike, 1917; Snow, 2002). Research provides new and confirmatory knowledge about how reading "works," and reading theories change in relation to this knowledge, thereby providing an important dynamic in how we conceptualize, teach, and assess reading. Currently, we are the beneficiaries of considerable research knowledge that contributes to detailed reading strategy instruction. As we learn more about the nature of reading strategies, including generating and monitoring predictions, making inferences, summarizing and synthesizing text information, and critiquing the author's arguments, this knowledge can inform effective reading instruction. We believe that current research and theory offer new insights into the nature of the strategies and stances that students use as they create critical understanding in the classroom in particular content domains (VanSledright, 2002).

The evolution of knowledge about strategic reading is paralleled by the evolution in research and theory in educational measurement (Pellegrino, Chudowsky, & Glaser,

2001). We believe that this is a fortuitous situation: The accumulating knowledge of strategies and reading assessment places us in a strong position from which to develop and use effective measures of strategic reading. Our knowledge about both strategies and assessment must be combined to create the most useful measures, be they checklists, teacher questioning routines, performance assessments, or think-alouds.

The effective assessment of reading strategies must be an informed combination of formative and summative assessment. Unfortunately, as noted in several other chapters in this volume, the current pressure to meet adequate yearly progress in accordance with No Child Left Behind legislation results in the overemphasis of single summative assessments in reading. High-stakes test scores are one indicator of what teachers and students have accomplished, yet they provide only "thin" information about students' strategies (Davis, 1998). That is, tests from which we may infer students' use of reading strategies comprise reading and assessment items that are contrived in nature, focused on the products of reading strategies (rather than the reading strategies themselves), and temporally removed from teachers' decision making and teaching. The summative information produced by such tests must be complemented with the formative assessment of reading strategies—assessment that contributes to teachable moments that shape students' ongoing strategic reading development and success. Formative reading assessment not only measures and describes strategic reading development, it has the potential to positively influence this development by serving as a model of how developing readers might begin to assess themselves.

In summary, this is an era of challenge and promise related to the development and use of effective reading assessment. Assessments of students' strategic reading development should influence instruction and learning so that students are increasingly capable of understanding and using complex information. The tension between high-stakes testing and classroom-based assessments (and the disparate distribution of school resources to the former) is unlikely to abate, and our efforts to construct high-quality classroom assessments of strategic reading should be a priority. Effective assessments derive from the use of state-of-the-art knowledge. In this chapter we illustrate how effective teachers use their knowledge of research and theory, along with a suitable array of assessment materials and procedures, to meet the challenge of assessing strategic reading.

CASES OF IMPORTANT READING STRATEGIES AND EFFECTIVE READING STRATEGY ASSESSMENTS

Following are three case studies of assessing the development of students' strategic reading. Our cases are intended to reflect a range of diversities that include specific reading strategies that we believe to be important, the representative content areas in which strategic reading and assessment take place, the students who are developing as strategic readers, and the manner in which strategic reading can be assessed. Each of the three cases is purposefully centered on classroom-based assessment that is embedded in instruction. Each case describes assessment that offers teachers and students important information about reading strategy progress, along with the opportunity to influence that progress.

Case 1: Using Checklists to Assess Students' Critical Reading of Advertisements

Students need diverse reading strategies to be successful in reading, in and out of school. Children are confronted with text messages each time they read magazines, surf the Internet, or turn on the television. Advertisers acknowledge that children are an invaluable market for everything from video games to peanut butter (Linn, 2004) and have begun to penetrate school walls through the distribution of school materials and the sponsorship of school programs. Daily, students face situations in school for which they need critical reading strategies to determine the purpose of texts, question the authors' authority, and uncover underlying messages the texts might carry.

Because advertising is intended to influence consumers' thinking and behavior, we believe that the texts of advertising offer an available and familiar means by which students can further develop their critical reading strategies. In the following case, Alison uses a checklist to assess her students' critical reading development, and her students work with the same checklist to learn and practice their strategies to critically read advertisements. The checklist is used across the school year; it is intended that, through regular use, the items contained in the checklist become internalized and are used as needed in students' critical reading and assessment routines.

Alison teaches in a university-sponsored summer reading clinic. Through effective assessment, she determines that her third- through fifth-grade students are able to answer basic literal and inferential questions about what they read, but they have difficulty making complex, critical judgments about texts. She decides that popular print advertisements are an appropriate venue for students to begin using checklists to critically examine texts. Alison's assumption is that using advertisements will allow her students to put more effort into strategic, critical reading because they are less likely to be overwhelmed with lengthy passages, largely unfamiliar content, or decoding challenges. She focuses on advertisements that have a limited amount of text but are rich in content that is familiar to the students. Alison intends this lesson to help her students reach the instructional goals of extending their thinking about a variety of texts and supporting their claims related to the authority of text with evidence from the text or other sources. Alison's assessment of her students' reading strategies is intertwined with her instruction as she (1) observes how students connect the texts to their existing knowledge, (2) evaluates the complexity of their strategic thinking as they use the checklist, and (3) monitors their discussions about the texts.

To orient her students to checklist assessment, Alison helps them understand why readers use checklists to critically think about texts. She discusses why the checklist's evaluative questions are important. She tells students that her checklist represents a "set of good questions to ask about what we read when we read," and then models the use of the checklist with a sample advertisement. She reminds students that critical reading often depends on readers' ability to connect the text to their relevant prior knowledge. With her students, she talks about the purposes of advertisements, shares personal experiences with advertisements, and questions whether it is always clear what product is being marketed in advertisements. Once she has engaged her students' background knowledge about the purposes of advertising, she introduces the checklist that will help them critically evaluate advertisements (see Figure 11.1). We note that the checklist presents a consistent, two-part task: Students must attend to a prompt for the

_____ When I read this advertisement, I think about what I already know about this topic.

An example of when I did this was when _____

_____

_____ When I read this advertisement, I think about who wrote this and whether they have the authority to tell me this information.

I decided that this author DOES or DOES NOT (circle one) have the authority to tell me this information because _____

_____

_____

_____ When I read this advertisement, I think about the author's purpose in writing it.

I decided that the author's purpose was _____

_____

_____ When I read this advertisement, I think about the things that the text did not tell me exactly, but that the author still meant for me to understand.

An example of when I did this was when _____

_____

FIGURE 11.1. Critical reading strategy checklist for advertisements.

use of a particular strategy and then use the strategy related to the prompt. For example, the third item on the checklist prompts students to report if they are thinking about the author's purpose, followed by the task of determining and stating what that purpose is.

After showing students the checklist and explaining her purpose for using it, Alison fills out the checklist while she "thinks aloud" about a Cartoon Network advertisement. This advertisement features characters from the show *Teen Titans* running with a child on a bicycle. The slogan reads, "Get up, get active: Action and adventure—something you can do with the TV turned off" (Cartoon Network, 2005). Alison chooses this advertisement as a text to model critical reading strategies because it involves content that is familiar to students, is sponsored by a television station that is well known to children, and focuses on a seemingly noncontroversial issue. As Alison asks herself questions from the checklist, her students observe the questioning technique that they are expected to learn and use.

The following excerpt details how Alison models her thinking about the third and fourth checkpoints.

"When I first saw this, I saw 'Get up, get active!' and saw the kid on the bike and I thought that this is an advertisement about playing outside. Then I saw, 'Action and adventure—something you can do with the TV turned off,' and then I thought, 'Cool, they are trying to get kids to watch less TV.' But I got down here [points to bottom of advertisement where it lists the sponsor—Cartoon Network], and it made me question the Cartoon Network's purpose in creating this advertisement. It seems weird to me that a television network would want kids to watch less TV. Then I thought, well, they are linking too much television watching to overweight kids. Maybe the Cartoon Network's lawyers made the station sponsor this advertisement to create the impression that they are supporting active life-styles. Or maybe the advertisement is really saying, go out and be active, but if you are inside watching TV, tune in to the Cartoon Network!"

In talking through these points, Alison models how she builds on her existing knowledge to help her make predictions about the advertisement's purpose and the underlying messages in the text, and to question the advertisement's motives.

In the effort to help them build their reading strategies, Alison uses a series of lessons in which students are asked to use the checklist with increasing independence. She chooses a "got milk?" advertisement (retrieved from *www.whymilk.com*) because she believes that it meets the following criteria: Most students are familiar with the "got milk?" advertising campaign, the text of the ad is relatively short and focused on familiar content, and the text contains few decoding challenges. The familiarity of the advertisement text helps Alison scaffold the critical reading task for students and allows them to invest more energy in using the checklist to think about this advertisement in a new, more critical, way.

The advertisement she chooses honors Ekema Okafor, a professional basketball player, as the "got milk?" Rookie of the Year (America's Milk Processors, 2005). As planned, the checklist serves as a prompt for students to think strategically and to use particular reading strategies. Students first use their checklists to record what they already know about the topics of this advertisement and as a source of ideas, such as Okafor is "a rookie," "a new player," "a good basketball player," and milk is "healthy," "good for you," and "collected on farms." As she observes her students' written responses, Alison determines that she does not need to spend more time activating their background knowledge on these topics because they already possess knowledge that they can use to develop a critical reading approach to this text. From the start, the checklist serves the purposes of providing Alison with important information, shaping her instructional decision making, and prompting students' strategy use.

One focus of Alison's lesson is the determination of who pays for advertising. This task can be complicated, especially in the case of the "got milk?" advertisement. The "got milk?" advertising campaign, complete with milk mustaches, is paid for by dairy farmers, all of whom are required to contribute to the federal Dairy Promotion Program. The price of milk often reflects the approximately 2¢ per gallon that U.S. dairy farmers must pay to this program. In effect, then, the "got milk?" ad campaign is subsidized by hidden consumer charges. We believe that such hidden funding is an important subtext of the "got milk?" advertisement, and as such, is a legitimate issue to pursue in school as students continue to develop critical reading strategies to "uncover" the means through which advertisement texts are developed, disseminated, and financed.

It is not surprising that Alison's students are not aware of the funding source for the advertisement, and they immediately name the National Basketball Association (NBA) as a sponsor on their checklists. Concerned that her students do not recognize the Dairy Promotion Program of America's Milk Processors as the true sponsor of the advertisement, Alison initiates a discussion that prompts students to think about the role of America's Milk Processors. Alison recognizes that her students are not yet critically thinking about who paid for this advertisement. To push her students to think beyond the text, she decides to have them use the checklist to question the authority of the sponsors, using the second item. Her students conclude that America's Milk Processors are qualified to inform them about the healthy components of milk, and they support their opinions with justifications on their checklists. For example, one student responds, "I decided that this author does have the authority to tell me this information because they're in the practice where they're surrounded by milk." In evaluating her students' responses, Alison concludes that they were able to assess, independently and critically, this sponsor's authority on the topic. She anticipates that continued reading strategy development and ability to read critically will result from the checklist assessment.

The next question on Alison's checklist has students evaluate the sponsor's purposes for supporting this advertisement. She is surprised to find that her students focus on the NBA's purposes for supporting this product. She decides that the inferences her students are making regarding the NBA's involvement in a milk advertisement are important, and she is impressed when her students record on their checklists that the NBA might be participating in this advertisement as a ploy to "make money" or to "get people to fill the seats at games." Although these may not be the real reasons the NBA is involved with this advertisement, Alison realizes that her students are extending their thinking beyond the literal text. They are demonstrating critical reading by generating theories about the advertisement, aided by the checklist assessment. Further practice with reading critically will help them refine the predictions and assumptions that they make about texts.

Alison uses the final checkpoint to further her students' development in being able to read texts critically. Specifically, she asks her students to think about the inferences they could draw from this advertisement by "reading between the lines." In the following excerpt, students record the inferences they were making and then share their thoughts in a class discussion.

ALISON: What are the underlying messages that the authors want you to understand when you see this advertisement?

TASHA: If you drink milk, you can become a good basketball player.

DAVE: Pro athletes drink milk.

ALISON: And what do we know about pro athletes?

DAVE: They are healthy . . .

RANDY: And strong.

FRANCIE: Whenever I see a milk ad, I never see a baseball player or a hockey player, I always see basketball players. And I think it is because of the muscles. They are also telling you if you drink milk, you can become a basketball player.

RANDY: I think they are telling you, if you want to be a basketball player and drink milk, then you can shoot better.

ALISON: Yeah they might be trying to say if you drink milk, you can be like him.

Alison is pleased with her students' inferences regarding the hidden messages in this text. The checklist provides her with opportunities to examine and assess students' critical reading strategy use. Moreover, the checklist serves as an effective tool for guiding students' thinking, prompting the application of critical reading strategies, and helping students organize their thoughts.

The checklist also allows Alison to document students' use of the critical reading strategies needed for understanding advertisements and to observe an increase in the complexity of their thinking over the course of the lesson. Alison is able to conclude from her classroom observations that, with guidance, her students are developing the ability to read advertisements critically. Her classroom assessments during this and other lessons remind her that to cultivate students' ability to read texts critically and independently, she needs to provide opportunities for practice. She will gradually reduce the amount of scaffolding she provides to help students work through the checklist.

The benefits of teaching children to read critically and assessing their progress toward this complex level of thinking are invaluable. In order to be active citizens in today's society, children need to be able to deconstruct the many media messages that they encounter each day. It is our responsibility to provide students with appropriate strategy instruction and to continually assess their progress toward becoming independent critical readers. Checklists provide students with a questioning framework and prompt for strategic reading, and they provide teachers with detailed information on critical reading and strategy development. With ample practice, the contents of the checklist and the stance toward texts and authors that it encourages can be used independently.

Case 2: Teacher Assessment of Student's Verbal Responses to Text-Based Questions

Historically, classroom questioning has been used to evaluate reading comprehension, as opposed to helping students learn to read strategically (Beck, McKeown, Sandora, Kucan, & Worthy, 1996). Using questions to assess students' strategy growth can be combined with instruction that helps struggling readers learn to ask strategic questions. Sarah teaches reading in a low-performing school, working with small groups of adolescents who struggle with reading. Many of the students are recent immigrants to the United States, and their English proficiency is limited. She knows that helping her students learn how to answer teachers' questions, how to make text-based inferences, and how to question the text and think critically are requisite strategies for their success in high school (Bean, 2000). Her instructional goals for these students are (1) to assist them in understanding informational text and (2) to monitor comprehension through direct instruction in questioning. Ultimately, she hopes that her students will be able to use her modeling as a means of applying questioning strategies that will help them understand the texts they read more fully (Sullivan, Mastropieri, & Scruggs, 1996).

Sarah believes that instruction-embedded assessment and ongoing analysis of students' reading strategies and responses to questions about text provide a crucial indicator of student progress. She also believes that this type of assessment best occurs in a classroom environment where students are willing to take risks as readers. Instructional questioning is central to the formative assessment of strategic reading abilities because student responses suggest the cognitive processes they are using to make meaning from text. As well, these responses illustrate how students integrate prior knowledge with knowledge gleaned from text (Taboada, 2003).

Sarah meets with a group of five students 40 minutes daily. Because her students have limited decoding skills, for this single lesson, she chooses to use a short expository text about wolves with about four simple sentences per page. For example, the four sentences on the first page of the short informational text, *Wolves* (Smith, 1997), are: "A wolf is a kind of wild dog. Wolves have big feet and long legs. Wolves grow thick fur in winter. Wolves can bark, growl, and howl" (p. 1). Her teaching experience tells her that the photographs that accompany the text will help stimulate student interest. Her goal is for her students to learn to understand and answer literal as well as inferential questions in English and to begin to create their own questions about text. Sarah uses her instruction-embedded assessment to continue to build knowledge of her students' strategic reading progress and to guide instruction.

Sarah's initial assessment focus is on the predictions students make about the text. In their prereading discussion, students preview the text and discuss the title, the cover, and the photographs. Students predict that the text is about a type of animal called a wolf, that the author will tell them about how wolves hunt, how they care for their young, and that there are different types of wolves. As students engage in this prereading discussion, Sarah is able to assess their background knowledge.

Following their prereading discussion, Sarah guides the students through each section of text by writing on sentence strips a question for them to answer as they read. After each question is posed, the students read the question, and then silently read a specified chunk of text to answer the question. Sarah uses student responses from the first question she poses to determine whether her students possess literal comprehension of the selection and how their background knowledge affects their comprehension.

Sarah's initial written question is "How does the author describe wolves?" This question prompts the following interaction with her student, Rui:

RUI: (*reading from text*) They have thick fur and long legs.

SARAH: Hmm. Let's back up and start with what a wolf is. What is a wolf?

RUI: It's a wild dog.

SARAH: If it is wild . . . (*interrupted*)

RUI: Like snakes.

Sarah's assessment begins when Rui answers, "Wolves have thick fur and long legs." She immediately assesses that although Rui's answer contains important information, it lacks a full description. Instead, Rui uses two pieces of information about wolves from the middle of the text. At this point, Sarah's background knowledge of students is crucial to her assessment. She knows that this student's grasp of the English language as well as his background knowledge about wolves are limited, so she clarifies her question (i.e., "What is a wolf?"). In effect, Sarah adapts her teaching to the student's current level of understanding and strategy use, as indicated by responses to questions. Then Rui responds that wolves are wild animals, "like snakes." Sarah assesses this response and determines that he is using related background knowledge as a strategy to create a definition for wolf.

Sarah is able to use her accumulating knowledge of how her students are processing text to add a new challenge she believes will be instructionally appropriate. Her second question remains focused on literal comprehension but adds the challenge of asking students to think about *how* to use text to answer literal questions using question–answer relationships (QARs). QARs are a teaching method that help readers understand the relationship between questions, where the corresponding answers can be found in the text, and consequently how to answer different types of questions. Sarah uses three categories of QARs: (1) text-explicit questions, with answers stated directly in the text; (2) text-implicit questions that require the reader to integrate information from various sources in the text; and (3) script-implicit questions that require the reader to draw upon personal background knowledge (Raphael & Wonnacott, 1985). Sarah uses QARs to help her students understand how to use textual information to answer different types of text-based questions because she knows that, in order for them to understand how to learn from text, they must acquire self-questioning techniques. She also knows that they will glean more content-based information when they are taught how to use questioning as a text-processing strategy (Olson, Duffy, & Mack, 1985). She believes that using QARs will help accomplish this goal. Sarah's students labeled the three levels of questions (1) Right There, (2) Text and Me, and (3) On My Own (Raphael & Wonnacott, 1985).

Sarah's next written question is "What is a pack"? This question prompts the following interaction with a student named Andre:

SARAH: A group of wolves (*repeats student's answer*). Is that a level 1, 2, or 3 answer?

ANDRE: Two.

SARAH: Why do you say it's a 2?

ANDRE: One.

SARAH: Why is it a 1?

ANDRE: Right there.

In this example, Sarah's assessment relates to, but is not focused on, the original question "What is a pack?" She wants to help students determine *how* they used text to answer the question. After students locate the sentence that defines wolf packs, Sarah asks for the QAR level. When Andre says "2," she assumes he does not understand how he used the text to answer the question. She follows up by asking "why" because she knows that scaffolded prompts encourage students to think about relationships present in text. The intention of her prompt is to move his thinking. Andre changes his answer and tells her it is a 1, a "Right There" question. Sarah assesses his response and concludes that he made the connection between the question and its corresponding QAR level.

Through instruction-embedded assessment across the lesson, Sarah determines that, with scaffolding, her students can successfully use QARs to answer literal questions. She believes she can add a new challenge by adding inferential questions and then helping students to understand the QAR level. She quickly moves to making inferences because she knows that inferential comprehension requires deeper text processing, more thorough reading of the text, and encourages higher-level thinking while still requiring literal understanding (Davey & McBride, 1986). The text provides individual pieces of information on things wolves do in packs. Sarah wants students to relate this information to the advantages of living in packs, so she creates a question that requires students to infer this point from the information provided. Sarah's written question is "Why would wolf packs do things together?" It prompts the following conversation:

LUIS: I got it. They like to work together because they like to share their food.

SARAH: That tells me *what* they do. Think about *why* they would do that.

LUIS: Because they are like brothers. They are family.

SARAH: They are like a family. What do families do?

LUIS: Share together.

SARAH: They share together and that helps them what?

LUIS: That helps them live.

Here Sarah assesses her students' ability to answer the inferential question. One of the students, Luis, provides a literal answer first. Her assessment is that he either did not understand the question or did not understand how to use text to answer an inferential question. She prompts him to think about *why*. When Luis makes the connection to brothers and families, Sarah realizes he is drawing upon his background knowledge to answer the question. Because background knowledge is essential to the eventual creation of self-generated questions (Taboada, 2003), Sarah uses the background knowledge he provides to create the next scaffold. He then completes the inference. Once they arrive at the answer to the inferential question, Sarah wants to determine if her students can use QARs to ascertain *how* they arrived at the inference about why wolf packs would live together. Using the students' terminology for QARs, she decides to add a question.

SARAH: Is that a 1, a 2, or a 3?

TONY: It's all in your mind.

SARAH: Is it all in your mind? It [the book] doesn't give you any clues?

RUI: Oh, it is a 1. It is right there in the book.

SARAH: Is it right there? Does the book say "Wolves live in groups to survive?" What clues does the book give you?

RUI: They like to share.

SARAH: It tells you that they *do* share. It doesn't tell you *why*. You have to take what's in the book—*they share food and water* and decide the *why* part in your brain.

RUI: Two.

SARAH: That's a 2—the clues in the book plus what's in your head, right?

Tony responds with "It's all in your mind." Sarah's assessment is that he did not understand how the inference about why packs live together relates to the information found in the text. She immediately prompts him to focus on the text by asking what clues it provides. Because a different student (Rui) indicates that the question is literal, Sarah assesses that the students need a more specific scaffold to guide their thinking. She offers an example of what the text would have to include for the question to be literal. Rui is then able to provide a partial clue (i.e., "They like to share"). Sarah assesses that he is beginning to understand how to pull information from text to make an inference, but that he does not completely understand. She uses Rui's response to explain how to use textual information to answer an inferential question. After her explanation, Rui answers correctly. Sarah assesses that, with her scaffolds, students are beginning to understand the strategy of making text-based inferences, and she spends more practice time on this throughout the lesson.

Toward the end of the lesson, Sarah's students begin to ask their own questions. Sarah knows that engaging in the process of self-questioning during reading is an important milestone for her students. When readers use the strategy of generating their own questions, they become more actively and deeply involved in the processing of text. They must inspect text, identify ideas, formulate questions they want to have answered, and connect text parts together or to their own background knowledge. Self-questioning may also imply a personal interest in the topic as well as self-regulation of learning (Dillon, 1990). Student-generated questioning as an avenue for learning may be one of the most effective strategies proficient readers employ (Rosenshine, Meister, & Chapman, 1996).

The questions Sarah's students ask are all text-based but important for a number of reasons. One student begins by asking why various species of wild dogs have different names. Another student examines the photos and asks if wolves and foxes are the same animal. A third asks about coyotes. Sarah decides that the students are starting to take responsibility for creating their own questions. Because this is one of her overall goals for helping students to develop strategic reading proficiency, she allows the lesson to follow the students' line of questioning. Sarah's knowledge of her students, combined with what she has learned, play an important role in her assessment of this situation. Because Sarah wants a risk-free environment, particularly for her second-language learners, she feels it is crucial to respond immediately and is pleased that they are willing to ask questions. Further, she sees that students are beginning to use her modeling of question asking as a text-negotiation tool to pose their own questions.

As students' abilities increase, Sarah continues to use her assessment of their responses and her growing understanding of how they process text to guide instruction. She adds new challenges as she scaffolds their progression through text. Sarah is constantly analyzing her students' responses and is always conscious of the need to assist her students successfully, so that each new challenge adds to their growing understanding of how to negotiate expository text.

Case 3: Performance Assessments in Fifth Grade and Reading Like Historians

Our evolving understanding of how students develop as readers should help us identify and teach important reading strategies that are germane to particular content domains (Alexander, 2005; VanSledright, 2002). In history, strategies help readers develop literal and inferential understanding of text. Reading history, however, can require complex critical reading strategies that involve more than constructing meaning from text and then remembering it. Reading like a historian demands that students use critical reading strategies accompanied by the important knowledge that written history is *one* account of "what happened" (Wineburg, 1991). Different authors' historical accounts may be more or less accurate, more or less trustworthy, or more or less removed in time and space from the actual history that is described. Thus students who "read like historians" use strategies to determine the trustworthiness, accuracy, and reliability of the historical texts they read.

Part of the strategic challenge for these readers is figuring out where the text "comes from." Reading strategies help readers meet this challenge, as they determine the primary- or secondary-source status of history texts. Student readers who can recognize a colonist's original diary entry and distinguish it from a textbook author's account of colonial America possess valuable information that is a direct result of reading strategically in history. Knowing who wrote a text, when the text was written, why it was written, and under what circumstances helps the student-as-historian construct literal, inferential, and critical understanding of history.

Strategies such as determining source-text status are necessary in Steve's fifth-grade history classroom, but they are not sufficient for successful reading. We noted in our chapter introduction that good strategy use is informed (and, in some cases, coordinated) by readers' plans and goals. Students who aspire to read like historians must use particular strategies in concert with a strategic approach to reading history. In Steve's classroom, student readers must approach reading history with an appropriate stance: They must have an inclination to read critically and they must be comfortable doing so. This is no small accomplishment, because Steve's students (like most students) develop as readers in school contexts that focus on the primacy of text.

Steve's students must move beyond the idea that what is written and read is to be learned and remembered, to understand that written history can be critically examined. Different authors may tell history differently. These authors may have different (and competing) agendas for their writing, and authors and texts represent selective samplings of the universe of information related to particular histories. In essence, history reading strategies are prompted and enabled by students' understanding that reading history critically is not only acceptable but necessary.

Given the goals for teaching and learning in Steve's classroom, assessment of reading strategies is given considerable time and effort. Steve understands that his students' ability to read like historians is facilitated by strategies and mind-sets. The teaching and learning goals for reading history in fifth grade include the establishment of a critical stance with which to read history and the strategy of determining if history texts are primary or secondary sources of history information. The goals are carefully aligned with the construct of reading like an historian and the state standards for history. To meet these goals, Steve uses checklists and students' think-alouds for assessment.

How do students develop critical stances toward the history texts they encounter, especially when literal understanding and memorization of text are stressed in other subjects in school? To address this question from both an assessment and instruction perspective, Steve uses a checklist, illustrated in Figure 11.2. The checklist serves two

____ I think about what it means to "read like a historian."

____ I consider this text an invitation to investigate the integrity of the author's/text's claims and evidence.

____ I investigate and try to determine the source status of this text.

____ I think about why the author wrote this account of history.

____ I consider this text to be one account of an event in history.

____ If possible, I compare this account of history to a contrasting account.

____ I attempt to make a judgment about the accuracy and reliability of the author's account of history.

____ If possible, I try to reconcile two or more accounts of history.

FIGURE 11.2. Checklist for student critical stance toward reading history.

important purposes. First, it directs students to important features of their critical reading task, including the use of a questioning stance toward text. The checklist prompts students to adopt the particular mindset that is needed when reading like a historian. Steve uses the results of students' checklists to check the success of his instruction that focuses on students' ability and willingness to question texts and authors—to think and read like historians.

A second important purpose of the checklist is the development of independent student assessment (Afflerbach, 2002). Students who internalize the contents and spirit of the checklist (or particular items on the checklist) are capable of reading critically without the physical presence of the printed checklist, and without Steve's consistent reminding. It is also Steve's hope that the questioning attitude promoted with the use of the checklist will assist students in critical reading in other content areas and reading tasks. As reading strategies develop, we expect that students will gradually assume control and responsibility for using them, based on their informed understanding of the text, task, and context.

The checklist allows Steve to determine if his students are adopting an appropriate stance toward history reading. Steve's strategic approach to strategy assessment requires that students' use of the checklist is followed (and complemented) by a series of think aloud assessments as they read history texts: students' verbalizations of what they are doing as they read. When the checklist and think-alouds are combined, they comprise an assessment instrument that offers a unique window into the strategies that readers report using. Steve begins the teaching year with an introduction to think-alouds for students. He models thinking aloud for students as he uses critical reading strategies. For example, he directs students' attention to history-text features using an overhead projector and marking pen. Students observe the strategic identification of cues to determine source-text status, while they listen to his think-aloud account of strategy use.

The think-aloud protocols help Steve determine if the strategic reading instruction regarding primary- versus secondary-source status of texts is successful. This instruction focuses on students' strategic searches for cues that help uncover history source-text status. The cues include special vocabulary, the syntax and author's style of writing, spelling (archaic or contemporary), the author's presence and voice in text, header material in text (e.g., author name, place and date written, where text "comes from"), the type of text, and the age of the text. Using these cues, students may focus on spelling and syntax and determine that a text is a primary-source text. For example, the following excerpt, from the diary of a colonial governor of Jamestown (Hakim, 1993), contains unusual spelling and syntax: " . . . hunger which no man can truly describe but he who hath tasted the bitterness, thereof" (p. 32).

As the semester progresses, Steve expects that students will gradually internalize the process for identifying source-text cues that he models, and that they will develop the ability to think aloud about their reading strategies. This think-aloud procedure then offers Steve an opportunity to focus on reading strategy assessment. To illustrate this process, consider Drew's (a fifth grader in Steve's class) think-aloud as he reads an original newspaper article from colonial America. The article includes the date of publication and spelling cues:

> "I'm thinking that this might be a primary-source text because of several cues here. First, the date is 1766 so I focus on that. I'll be looking to see if there is any other stuff to support that idea. And then I come to this phrase 'hath given,' which makes me again think primary-source text because you just don't see that kind of word in stuff written around today. So I'm thinking that this might really be a primary text, written back in 1766. And then, oh yeah, here it is . . . there is another cue here—the spelling of this word 'wee.' "

To read like historians, the fifth graders must learn and use strategies that allow them to make primary- and secondary-source text distinctions. In this case, Drew is able to determine that the text is a primary source document (a newspaper published in 1766) because he strategically locates and uses cues that include the given date of the newspaper and unfamiliar spelling. The process orientation of Drew's think-aloud influences the nature of the inferences Steve can make from this assessment. That is, the window on strategic reading provided by think-alouds gives a relatively direct account of how Drew searches for and uses cues in text. Rather than making an inference about Drew's strategic reading from assessment product information, this assessment focuses on the processes themselves, as strategies are used to help construct critical understanding. Steve determines that Drew is successful in using two different cues to determine the status of the history source text.

SUMMARY AND CONCLUSIONS

The three cases presented in this chapter suggest how teachers' classroom-based assessment can provide a measure and description of students' strategic reading development. The assessment materials and procedures used include teachers' questioning routines that evoke student responses, checklists that assess and encourage the use of reading strategies, and think-aloud procedures that provide a window on the reading strategies themselves. Based on the three cases, we propose that classroom assessments of reading strategies serve several important purposes:

- First, they can provide detailed information about students' current level of development as strategic readers, be it the ability to construct literal meaning from simple text, determine the authority of information in an advertisement, or adopt a questioning stance and locate cues in history text. Through the cycle of teaching, assessing, and reflecting that is a hallmark of effective instruction, assessment provides teachers with detailed information about the effectiveness of strategy instruction and students' progress in strategy use. Accomplished teachers use the assessment information to shape their instruction efforts.

- Second, assessment can help form students' strategic reading behavior. Teachers can use strategy assessment to model the types of questions, routines, and foci that students must eventually adopt to be independent, successful readers. Independent, strategic readers benefit from assessment that teaches them how to do assessment themselves. Teachers can use this approach to teaching assessment of strategies by making the often abstract concept of assessment concrete for their students. This is accomplished through instruction that makes assessment thinking comprehensible, assessment routines visible, and the practice of assessing strategies useful. Teachers should provide a classroom environment that supports the student risk taking that is demanded by forays into self-assessment.

- Third, the closeness of assessment to instruction results in instructionally useful information. This is an obvious but sometimes overlooked feature of each of these strategy assessments: The assessments fit well with the strategy to be assessed. The use of checklists, teacher questioning, and think-alouds is embedded in normal routines of the classroom. As such, the assessment is authentic. It is not disruptive. In fact, it is supportive, occurring as an expected feature of teaching and learning.

- Fourth, the reading strategy assessments are used in a developmental sense: They are intended to encourage students' strategy development as they assess it. The assessments focus on students' reading strategies in their process form, providing rich information about those processes and their relative success. Compared to summative reading tests, these assessments are well positioned to provide formative feedback throughout the school year. Teachers can use this information immediately to amend or continue strategy instruction. The assessments provide information that a particular strategy is in use with particular students, or that more work is needed for the strategy to become a useful component of the student's reading repertoire.

We note that our cases revolve around teachers who are accomplished at classroom-based assessments of students' reading strategies. Although a considerable number of teachers are capable of conducting the assessments described in this chapter, it is unfortunate that many teachers do not receive training or support in their efforts to become valid and reliable assessors of students' reading development. Thus it is important to advocate not only for particular forms of assessment but also for professional development that helps teachers meet the stringent criteria that are demanded by any worthwhile assessment. Important reliability and validity issues accompany each form of assessment. As we consider such critical reading assessments, we must ascertain that our assessments meet clear standards for reliability and validity. Professional development for teachers who are becoming adept at assessing strategies is of utmost importance.

REFERENCES

Afflerbach, P. (2002). Teaching reading self-assessment strategies. In C. Block & M. Pressley (Eds.), *Comprehension instruction: Research-based best practices* (pp. 96–111). New York: Guilford Press.

Alexander, P. (2005). *The path to competence: A lifespan developmental perspective on reading.* Retrieved February 4, 2006, from *www.nrconline.org/.*

America's Milk Processors. (2005, July). Got milk? Rookie of the Year. *Sports Illustrated for Kids,* p. 36.

Bean, T. W. (2000). Reading in the content areas: Social constructivist dimensions. In R. Barr, M. L. Kamil, P. B. Mosenthal, & P. D. Pearson (Eds.), *Handbook of reading research* (Vol. 2, pp. 629–644). New York: Longman.

Beck, I. L., McKeown, M. G., Sandora, C. A., Kucan, L., & Worthy, J. (1996). Questioning the author: A year-long classroom implementation to engage students with text. *Elementary School Journal, 96,* 385–414.

Cartoon Network. (2005, June/July). Get up, get active. *National Geographic Kids,* p. 5.

Davey, B., & McBride, S. (1986). Effects of question-generation training on reading comprehension. *Journal of Educational Psychology, 78,* 256–262.

Davis, A. (1998). *The limits of educational assessment.* Oxford, UK: Blackwell.

Dillon, J. T. (1990). *The practice of questioning.* New York: Routledge.

Fehring, H., & Green, P. (2001). *Critical literacy.* Newark, DE: International Reading Association.

Kintsch, W. (2000) *Comprehension: A paradigm for cognition.* New York: Cambridge University Press.

Linn, S. (2004). *Consuming kids: The hostile takeover of childhood.* New York: New Press.

Olson, G. M., Duffy, S. A., & Mack, R. L. (1985). Active comprehension: Teaching a process of reading comprehension and its effects on reading achievement. *The Reading Teacher, 39,* 24–31.

Palincsar, A. S., & Brown, A. L. (1984). Reciprocal teaching of comprehension-fostering and comprehension-monitoring activities. *Cognition and Instruction, 1,* 117–175.

Paris, S., Wasik, B., & Turner, J. (1991). The development of strategic readers. In R. Barr, M. Kamil, P. Mosenthal, & P. Pearson (Eds.), *Handbook of reading research* (Vol. 2, pp. 609–640). Hillsdale, NJ: Erlbaum.

Pellegrino, J. W., Chudowsky, N., & Glaser, S. (Eds.). (2001). *Knowing what students know: The science and design of educational assessment.* Washington, DC: National Research Center.

Perie, M., & Moran, R. (2005). *NAEP 2004 trends in academic progress: Three decades of student performance.* Washington, DC: U.S. Department of Education, National Center for Educational Statistics.

Pressley, M. (2000). What should comprehension instruction be the instruction of? In M. L. Kamil, P. B. Mosenthal, P. D. Pearson, & R. Barr (Eds.), *Handbook of reading research* (Vol. 3, pp. 545–561). Mahwah, NJ: Erlbaum.

Pressley, M., & Afflerbach, P. (1995). *Verbal protocols of reading: The nature of constructively responsive reading.* Hilldale, NJ: Erlbaum.

Raphael, T., & Wonnacott, C. (1985). Heightening fourth grade students' sensitivity to sources of information for answering comprehension questions. *Reading Research Quarterly, 20,* 282–296.

Rosenshine, B., Meister, C., & Chapman, S. (1996). Teaching students to generate questions: A review of the intervention studies. *Review of Educational Research, 66,* 181–221.

Snow, C. (2002). *Reading for understanding: Toward an R&D program in reading comprehension.* Washington, DC: Rand.

Sullivan, G. S., Mastropieri, M. A., & Scruggs, T. E. (1996). Reading and remembering: Coaching thinking with students with learning disabilities. *Journal of Special Education, 29,* 310–322.

Taboada, A. M. (2003). The association of student questioning with reading comprehension. *Dissertation Abstracts International* (UMI 3107270).

Thorndike, E. (1917). Reading as reasoning: A study of mistakes in paragraph reading. *Journal of Educational Research, 8*, 323–332.

Wineburg, S. (1991). On the reading of historical texts: Notes on the breach between school and academy. *American Educational Research Journal, 28*, 495–520.

VanSledright, B. (2002). Confronting history's interpretive paradox while teaching fifth graders to investigate the past. *American Educational Research Journal, 39*, 1089–1115.

CHILDREN'S BOOKS

Hakim, J. (1993). *A history of US: Making thirteen colonies.* New York: Oxford University Press.

Smith, M. K. (1997). *Wolves.* Austin, TX: Steck-Vaughn.

CHAPTER 12

Assessing Students' Understanding of Informational Text in Intermediate- and Middle-Level Classrooms

Karen D. Wood
D. Bruce Taylor
Brenda Drye
M. Joyce Brigman

As literacy reinvents itself in the face of ever-changing media and technological influences (Alvermann & Hagood, 2000; Luke & Elkins, 1998), likewise assessment needs to follow suit, taking a new look at the demands of informational text and the ways in which teachers can evaluate students' proficiencies and areas of need as they engage with new technologies (Johnson & Kress, 2003; Johnston & Costello, 2005).

The No Child Left Behind legislation frequently uses the term "formative assessment." Yet Chappula (2005) contends that there is great risk that it will be misunderstood as "testing that is done often" with the end goal of "forming higher test scores." That is not how we envision formative assessment in this chapter, nor is it how it was intended to be viewed. Formative assessment involves instructional and evaluative practices that are used frequently and authentically by classroom teachers to gain information about the ever-evolving needs of individual students. It can and should be used by students themselves to help them focus on what they know and still need to learn.

In this chapter we focus on what Valencia and Wixson (2000) refer to as the microlevel of assessment. Unlike the macrolevels of assessment that collect broad, quantitative data to note trends and determine policy in a school, system, or state, data collected at the microlevel are qualitative in nature and include rubrics, informal observation, anecdotal records, as well as self- and peer evaluations (Boyd-Batstone, 2004).

We describe research-based methods for assessing students' understanding of informational text and then illustrate their application across the subject areas typical of the intermediate and middle school curriculum. Modifications of actual teacher-developed assessment devices are shown along with representative samples of student performance. Because of the validation given such strategies as retelling and summarizing (Allington, 2002; National Reading Panel Report, 2000; Pressley, 2002), we outline methods of evaluating students' ability to retell, put information in their own words, and summarize, select, and synthesize the most significant concepts from multiple sources of information (print and nonprint). We also provide examples of self- and peer assessment of literacy experiences across the subject areas.

We present vignettes of three classrooms in which teachers in grades 4, 6, and 8 use a variety of tools to assess student learning with informational texts: a science unit on weather and hurricanes and social studies units on the Cold War and the Civil War and slavery. We examine the microlevel assessment practices of these teachers within these units and share the strategies and tools for assessing student learning that proved effective.

THE NEED FOR FLEXIBILITY: A FOURTH-GRADE UNIT ON WEATHER AND HURRICANES

Each year Kristina, a fourth-grade teacher, uses a variety of texts to teach students about hurricanes as part of a unit on weather. In preparation for her unit on hurricanes, Kristina looks for ways to assess what her students know prior to beginning the unit as well as what they have learned at the end of the unit. Research has clearly shown that determining, eliciting, and evaluating students' prior knowledge before a topic is studied is one of the best ways to begin improving students' comprehension (Allington, 2005; Pressley, 2000, 2002). By evaluating what students already know or think they know about a topic, teachers learn when, where, and how much information to add to their existing lesson plan.

Kristina uses a modified anticipation guide (Figure 12.1) to assess what students know about hurricanes, to help her answer students' initial questions, and to clear up misconceptions. She modified the anticipation guide so that it can be used by students to discuss the topic—hurricanes—in small groups. This movement from individual assessment to group interaction and discussion provides for more active learning and allows her to assess students' growth in knowledge about hurricanes throughout that process. Students discuss each of the eight statements on the anticipation guide, and then they work together to reach a consensus for each. The most important part of the anticipation guide, as a tool for finding out what students know before reading as well as solidifying their understanding after reading, is the group or paired discussion and interaction. Studies on the sociocultural dimensions of learning have clearly shown benefits for allowing students to share their knowledge with one another (Alvermann, 2002; Blanton, Wood, & Taylor, in press; Luria, 1985; Vygotsky, 1978). These discussion approaches have a long history of effectiveness in helping students evaluate their own thinking in relation to others and in helping teachers evaluate what students know and have learned (Wilkinson & Reninger, 2005).

ANTICIPATION GUIDE FOR *HURRICANES: EARTH'S MIGHTIEST STORMS*

To begin our unit on hurricanes, please read the following statements. If you think that the statement is true, please place a "T" in the blank. If you think that the statement is false, please place an "F" in the blank. Once you have completed responding to these statements, you will get in your assigned cooperative group to discuss and reach a consensus. As you read *Hurricanes: Earth's Mightiest Storms*, please write the page number from the text that provides information for you to correctly answer the questions from the anticipation guide.

Before Reading	After Reading	Page Reference		Group Consensus
____	1. Hurricanes only develop in the Pacific Ocean.			1. ____
	1. ____	1. ____		
____	2. Hurricane Hugo caused more damage and deaths than any hurricane.			2. ____
	2. ____	2. ____		
____	3. In El Niño years, more hurricanes develop.			3. ____
	3. ____	3. ____		
____	4. A hurricane in the Atlantic Ocean is called a typhoon.			4. ____
	4. ____	4. ____		
____	5. Most hurricane damage is due to the wave surge.			5. ____
	5. ____	5. ____		
____	6. The center of the hurricane is called the "eye."			6. ____
	6. ____	6. ____		
____	7. The center of the hurricane is the worst part of the hurricane.			7. ____
	7. ____	7. ____		
____	8. A hurricane stays together for a long period of time once it reaches land.			8. ____
	8. ____	8. ____		

FIGURE 12.1. Anticipation guide for hurricane unit.

Once students have reached or neared a consensus about the statements on the anticipation guide, they discuss their thinking with the entire class. While engaged in this discussion process in the prereading stage, Kristina observed that many of the groups thought that the center of the hurricane was the most dangerous part (see statement number 7). Kristina made a note to herself to be sure to address this topic thoroughly during and after the reading of the texts. Kristina's approach illustrates what Johnston and Costello (2005) contend is the essence of formative assessment: noticing the fine details of literate behavior, of what students know and do not know, and planning instruction accordingly. Effective teachers, as a matter of routine, use these observations to question whether students are paying attention to the details of a text.

Next, Kristina's students read the book *Hurricanes: Earth's Mightiest Storms* by Patricia Lauber (1996). Kristina uses this book to supplement information learned from the science textbook. She arranges the reading according to the abilities and needs of her students. She often has students alternate between reading the text silently, whisper-reading in pairs, and discussing what they have read in small groups or as a whole class. In either case, once students have completed reading, they refer back to the anticipation guide. This time, their objective is to write down the page number from the text that provided them with the information to correctly answer each question. Although this step can be done individually, Kristina often has students work in groups or pairs.

By modifying the anticipation guide and paying close attention to students' responses before, during, and after the reading, Kristina was able to assess students' prior knowledge as well as gauge their learning through their reading of *Hurricanes: Earth's Mightiest Storms*, a key text in the unit. At the end of the unit, Kristina gave students a summative test (see Figure 12.2), referred to as a "Select-a-Test." We use this label because, unlike traditional tests, this assessment provides students with choices. They can choose questions on varied levels—from the knowledge level (with more text-based questions) to the evaluation level, which requires deeper processing—adding up to 100 points. They even have options for completing bonus questions. In short, this test focuses on what students have learned without assuming that all students learned a narrow set of facts. Kristina assesses and honors what students have learned without penalizing them for failing to remember discrete facts. We anticipate that, in some instances, teachers would want to assess students' knowledge of specific information. This assessment format can be adapted such that a set of questions that all students must answer precedes the "selection" part of the test. For instance, all students answer a set of questions that comprises 50% of the test and then select from a menu of questions for the other 50%.

For Kristina, assessment is a continuous process that provides her and the students with information on what they have learned throughout the unit. Assessment is varied, with both formal (such as the end-of-unit test) and informal (activities and assignments such as the anticipation guide) forms. Assessment is also flexible. Tools such as the anticipation guide provide Kristina with a way of assessing students' prior knowledge individually or in small or large groups, depending on the needs of the class.

MULTIPLE PERSPECTIVES, MULTIPLE SOURCES: SIXTH-GRADE UNIT ON THE COLD WAR

In developing a unit on the Cold War, Tomas, a sixth-grade social studies teacher, makes a variety of decisions, not the least of which concerns assessment. Tomas teaches diverse students and values independent research projects as a way to address individual needs, abilities, and interests. However, in laying the groundwork for an independent research project, Tomas must ensure that students possess a certain level of understanding to prepare them for success. Tomas acknowledges that the students' needs are diverse, so his choice of assessment devices takes a variety of forms.

Tomas's choice of activities allows students to use a range of texts to search for information, elicits their own thinking and writing skills, and allows for both student and teacher assessment of student learning. For instance, Tomas recognizes that the textbook is a key source of information that is available to all students. However, he also has learned that students need support in their reading of the text. The textbook guide shown in Figure 12.3 is an excellent tool that Tomas uses to motivate students to read the text but also to assess student learning of key concepts. Just as the anticipation

Name: _____

Date: _____

HURRICANES: EARTH'S MIGHTIEST STORMS FINAL TEST

Directions: Select any combination of the questions below to equal 100 points. You may do 10 extra points for a bonus. Check beside the questions you do and put all your answers on notebook paper with the number and points beside each answer.

Knowledge (5 points each)

_____ 1. When did the Monster Storm occur?

_____ 2. Where did Hurricane Andrew hit?

_____ 3. What are two other names for a hurricane?

Comprehension (10 points each)

_____ 4. Summarize the main idea or facts found in the book.

_____ 5. Explain why scientists started naming hurricanes.

_____ 6. Explain why the eye is calm.

Application (15 points each)

_____ 7. Select at least five key words from your book. Show you know what the words mean.

_____ 8. Illustrate what a town might look like after a hurricane.

_____ 9. Write five questions you would ask a survivor if you could do an interview.

Analysis (20 points each)

_____ 10. Survey 10 people on whether or not they liked learning about hurricanes. Make a bar graph to show your information.

_____ 11. Compare and contrast a hurricane to a tornado. Make a Venn diagram.

Synthesis (25 points each)

_____ 12. Compose a poem about hurricanes.

_____ 13. Design a series of drawings or diagrams to show facts about hurricanes.

Evaluation (30 points each)

_____ 14. Determine the five most important facts you learned about hurricanes. Order them from the most important to the least important. Explain why you picked the most important fact over the others.

_____ 15. Rate this book from 1 to 10. Explain with at least three specific reasons why you gave it that rating.

FIGURE 12.2. Select-a-test for hurricane unit.

Part I: Read pp. 282–283 of your social studies textbook. Number from 1 to 3 on a sheet of notebook paper. List in order of importance three ideas on *The Cold War* that you consider most important. Be prepared to explain your personal reasons for selecting these ideas. Discuss your thinking with your group members.

Part II: Now that we have discussed our ideas, select *one* and write one to two paragraphs describing details on the importance of that *one* idea. Remember to use a combination of what the text (online or other text source) says and what you feel and think about the idea.

Part III. Now, in your preassigned groups, share what you have written with your peers. Jot down three new things you have learned from your group members.

Part IV: On a scale of 1–3 rate your personal understanding of *The Cold War* below.
        1—I could explain this to someone else.
        2—I understand this, but I could not explain this to someone else.
        3—I do not yet understand this.

FIGURE 12.3. Personal Comprehension Text Guide.

guide helped Kristina assess students' prior knowledge of hurricanes in the science unit on weather, so too does the textbook guide help Tomas assess his students' level of understanding. We refer to this guide as the "Personal Comprehension Text Guide" because it asks students to analyze their personal choices regarding what they perceive to be the most significant ideas or concepts in a selection of text. We associate this task with Rosenblatt's (1978) notion of "aesthetic reading" as personal response and reflection and "efferent reading" as attention to facts, details, and information. As teachers, we want to encourage the balanced blending of "reader-based" and "text-based" information, and this is one of the goals of the Personal Comprehension Text Guide.

Often, visual aids can help both students and teachers assess understanding. Figure 12.4 is just one of a variety of graphic organizers that Tomas uses to help students assess comprehension of a topic. He typically provides this simple graphic organizer to students as they watch a video about the Cold War, but he adds that it can be used with a variety of texts. Tomas wants his students to have a firm grasp of the causes of the Cold War and their possible effects, and the graphic organizer allows him to see clearly what students have and have not learned. Also, he finds graphics such as this one provide a visual map for students to see such relationships (such as cause and effect) in a way that a traditional question-and-answer format does not accomplish.

As we have seen, teacher-created guides and information organizers are relatively easy to create and allow for quick student and teacher assessment. Like Kristina, Tomas found that teacher-created guides better fit his goals and the needs of students. He created guides to foster engagement in upcoming text readings or interactive class discussions, as with the cause-and-effect graphic organizer for the Cold War shown in Figure 12.4. Students activate prior knowledge about the causes of the war, and then after accessing information, they return to the statements and reevaluate them. There are opportunities for individual and group work. This particular assessment can provide opportunities for the teacher to compare students' knowledge before and after instruction. In the example displayed in Figure 12.5, Tomas learned that this student (as well as others whose work is not displayed here) had little knowledge of World War II. Prior

Use the information from the video to complete the following cause-and-effect graphic organizer. Be prepared to share your information.

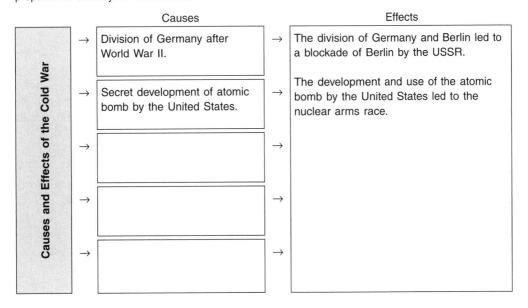

FIGURE 12.4. Cause-and-effect graphic organizer for Cold War unit.

I. Anticipation Guide: Indicate A (agree) or D (disagree) in the first blank before each statement. Leave the second blank empty for now.

D A Stalin was leader of the Soviet Union during and after World War II.

A A The Soviet Union endured great loss of life and property during the war.

A D The economy of the United States was in poor condition after World War II.
   The economy of the U.S. was strong after World War II.

D A Germany was been divided among the allied powers.

II. Read the information from "Iron Curtain: 1945–1947" found at *www.cnn.com/SPECIALS/ cold.war/episodes/02/*. Discuss your findings with your teammates.

III. Now use the second blank space before each statement in Part I to agree or disagree.

IV. For each "disagree" statement, rewrite it to make it accurate.

V. Use the textbook to read information, using the page numbers listed on the board.

VI. On the back of this sheet, write a paragraph summarizing important information about the beginnings of the Cold War that a sixth grader should definitely know. Be ready to share your creation.

FIGURE 12.5. Cold War unit anticipation guide.

to using an assessment strategy like the cause-and-effect graphic organizer, Tomas often failed to see these gaps in knowledge until the summative World War II test. In addition to alerting Tomas to students' needs, the graphic organizer also spurred many students to ask questions concerning key events and figures.

Questioning remains one of the most widely used strategies of informal assessment by teachers (Nessel, 1987). In both formal (tests) and informal (discussions and question-and-answer sessions) assessment formats, questioning helps teachers ascertain what students know. Tomas finds that questions are an effective means of examining levels of understanding and judging readiness for future learning. Document-based questioning (DBQ; Stovel, 1987) is often used in high school social studies classes and especially in advanced placement classes. As one way to prepare his students for the demands that they are likely to meet in the later grades, Tomas has his sixth-grade students use DBQ techniques. For example, as part of the Cold War unit, Tomas shows video clips of pertinent speeches from the era to help students hear and see for themselves key historical moments. Websites such as the History Channel website (*www.historychannel.com*) and the CNN website (*www.cnn.com*) provide video clips that can be used in classrooms. In the example displayed in Figure 12.6, Tomas asks stu-

---

1. Carefully read the document-based question. Consider what you already know about the topic.
2. Carefully read the document. Underline key words or phrases that address the question. Make brief notes in the margin if you wish.
3. Answer the question.

QUESTION: How are these remarks about Communism ironic?

> • "Gentlemen, comrades, do not be concerned about all you hear about Glasnost and Perestroika and democracy in the coming years. They are primarily for outward consumption. There will be no significant internal changes in the Soviet Union, other than for cosmetic purposes. Our purpose is to disarm the Americans and let them fall asleep. We want to accomplish three things:
>
>> One, we want the Americans to withdraw conventional forces from Europe.
>>
>> Two, we want them to withdraw nuclear forces from Europe.
>>
>> Three, we want the Americans to stop proceeding with the Strategic Defense Initiative."
>>
>> —Mikhail Gorbachev, before the fall of Communism
>
> • "In an ironic sense, Karl Marx was right. We are witnessing today a great revolutionary crisis—a crisis where the demands of the economic order are colliding directly with those of the political order. But the crisis is happening not in the free, non-Marxist West, but in the home of Marxism–Leninism, the Soviet Union. . . . [Communism will be] left on the ash heap of history."
>
>> —Ronald Reagan

• "Freedom is the recognition that no single person, no single authority or government has a monopoly on the truth, but that every individual life is infinitely precious, that every one of us put in this world has been put there for a reason and has something to offer. It's so hard for government planners, no matter how sophisticated, to ever substitute for millions of individuals working night and day to make their dreams come true."

—Ronald Reagan

• "Democracy is the worst form of government except for all those others that have been tried."

—Winston Churchill

FIGURE 12.6. Document-based questions (DBQ) from Cold War unit.

dents to look for irony in the remarks of Mikhail Gorbachev and Ronald Reagan. (Prior to this unit, Tomas had used political cartoons and historical vignettes as a way to teach students about irony.)

Tomas uses these assignments to both assess student learning and to lay a foundation for the summative project of the Cold War unit: "The Suitcase Project." This research format provides Tomas and his students with flexible options for researching more than 30 countries and their development through the Cold War. Students gather information in a student-created file folder or "suitcase." Students receive instruction on gathering research from different sources, including print, hypertext (Internet), and video, and they use a scoring rubric to self-assess and guide the development of their work (Figure 12.7). Tomas distributes and discusses the rubric early in the project so that students know what is expected of them. The rubric serves multiple purposes of assessment, establishing guidelines, and communicating expectations. Students prepare and submit descriptions, summaries, and illustrations focusing on elements such as landforms, maps, attractions, climate, and historical facts pertinent to their chosen country.

In addition to as the teacher-developed rubric, Tomas provides students with opportunities for self- and peer assessment. In this case, he included a reflective type of self-assessment at the end of the Cold War unit (Figure 12.8). These open-ended questions are intended to help students internalize key points learned during "The Suitcase Project" but also to provide Tomas with useful information for reviewing and grading the final project.

LISTEN, THINK, DRAW, AND WRITE: AN EIGHTH-GRADE UNIT ON SLAVERY

Brenda draws on a diverse range of literature in her eighth-grade social studies class, including a variety of fictional and informational texts. She finds that when used in conjunction with the textbook, these texts act as a magnifying glass that provides humanizing details frequently missing from traditional textbooks. It is her belief that middle-grade students prefer literary works with subject matter to which they can relate. It is during adolescence that schools place greater emphasis on reading to learn rather than learning to read, and it is also during these later school years that students face greater demands from informational and narrative texts. The textual landscape is varied. Narrative text has a more familiar structure—a beginning, middle, and end and usually a fairly clear sense of problem and solution with which students are familiar. Conversely, textbook formats include more complex organizational patterns. These can be arranged by topic, theme, cause and effect, historically, or in another sequential format. Important information can be communicated through text or visually in pictures, diagrams, or charts.

Multiethnic literature can help middle-grade students develop an appreciation for different backgrounds, although research suggests that students may resist as well as embrace new cultures and ideas (Beach, 1997). Brenda believes that literature offers the opportunity for students to remove themselves from an egocentric perspective and identify with characters' thoughts and feelings, confusion and frustration, fears and hopes. Her objective is for students to empathize with others and to understand how others live and see America. Multiethnic literature also allows her to introduce differ-

Name _____

Country _____

Assessed Areas	5	3	1	My assess-ment	Average of peer assess-ments	Teacher assess-ment
File Folder	Is vividly decorated to represent sites contained in my project; handle with nametag; contents organized.	Is somewhat decorated to represent sites contained in my project; handle with nametag; contents show some organization.	Is minimally decorated to represent sites contained in my project; may have nametag and attempt at organization.			
*Attraction/ Person #1	Summary of attraction or person from my country; illustrated.	Attempt at an organized summary; may be illustrated.	Minimal attempt at summary; may or may not be illustrated.			
*Attraction/ Person #2	Summary of attraction or person from my country; illustrated.	Attempt at an organized summary; may be illustrated.	Minimal attempt at summary; may or may not be illustrated.			
*Attraction/ Person #3	Summary of attraction or person from my country; illustrated.	Attempt at an organized summary; may be illustrated.	Minimal attempt at summary; may or may not be illustrated.			
Climate	Detailed summary of climate in my own words.	Summary of climate in my own words.	Little information given.			
Historical Facts List	20 facts about my assigned country in an illustrated list.	20-fact list included.	An attempt at a 20-fact list is included.			
Landforms	Detailed description of country's landform is included.	Summary of major landforms is included.	An attempt at a summary of landforms is included.			
Physical Map	Detailed colored and hand-drawn map with major physical geographical features is included.	Colored and hand-drawn physical map is included.	A copy of a map is included.			
Political Map	Detailed colored and hand-drawn map with major political features is included.	Colored and hand-drawn political map is included.	A copy of a map is included.			
List of Resources	A minimum of two books and two Internet sources; written correctly in MLA format.	A minimum of two books and two Internet sources; An attempt at MLA format is made.	An attempt to use at least a book and Internet source is made.			

FIGURE 12.7. "Suitcase Project" rubric.

SELF-REFLECTION ON THE SUITCASE PROJECT

1. What was my favorite part of this project?
2. What was my least favorite part of this project?
3. What was the most challenging part of this project?
4. What will I most definitely remember from this project?
5. What will I be sure to do differently next time?
6. If I had to give a piece of advice for the next sixth grader doing this project, what would it be?

FIGURE 12.8. "Suitcase Project" self-assessment.

ing cultural models (Beach, 1995) that are important to understanding the historical and social contexts that are a part of the social studies curricula, and, when possible, to clear up misconceptions that students may have about different cultures or cultural traditions. Brenda says that such diverse texts allow her to spot student resistance to discussing issues such as race, gender, and culture; the use of carefully selected texts can motivate and trigger discussion and further inquiry. Brenda uses these texts and related discussions to challenge stereotypes and push against such resistance.

During a unit on the American Civil War and slavery, students in Brenda's classroom typically listen to portions of Julius Lester's (1998) *To Be a Slave*—accounts of former slaves and their experiences as they travel to America on a slave ship, during their life on plantations, and during and after the process of emancipation. Brenda reads these accounts to the students, and, in her experience, they listen attentively ("The room is absolutely silent"). Brenda asks students to put themselves in the place of the slaves and respond to their thoughts and feelings by illustrating their reactions to being captured. Figure 12.9 shows two "read-aloud assessments," expressive drawings by students demonstrating their understanding of the degradation, cramped quarters, and inhumane treatment of the captives.

In addition to helping Brenda see and assess students' ability to connect to the subject of slavery, these drawings also serve as a springboard for writing about the topic. Students write descriptions of their drawings (as in Figure 12.9), but also use writing for their own self-assessment at the end of the unit (Figure 12.10).

This layering of assessment helps Brenda track student progress throughout the unit: the degree to which students did or did not understand the conditions surrounding slave capture, transportation, and auctioning. At the end of this unit on the Civil War, students in Brenda's class are given an essay in which they are asked to write about their

FIGURE 12.9. "Read-aloud assessments": Student illustrations of slavery conditions.

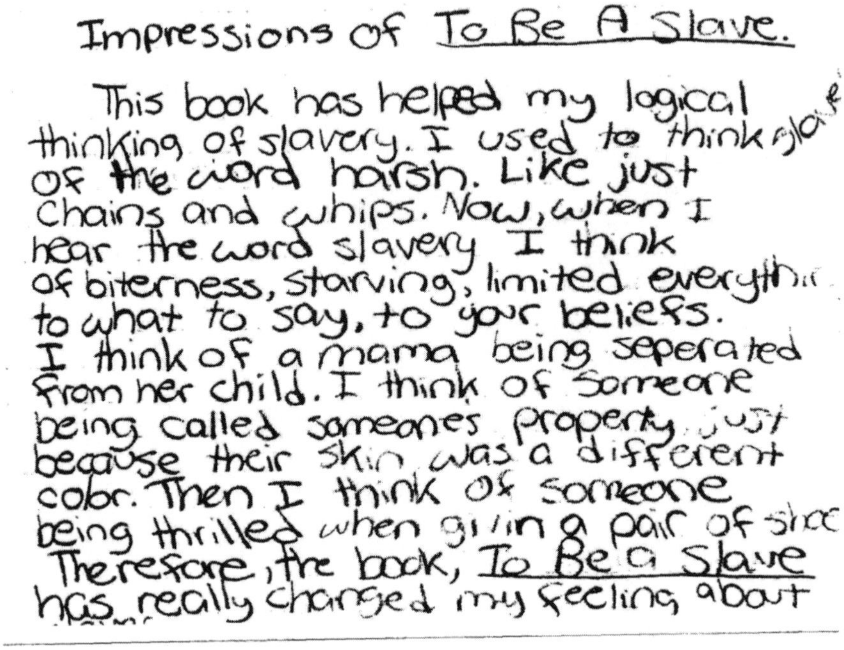

Impressions of To Be A Slave.

This book has helped my logical thinking of slavery. I used to think of the word harsh. Like just chains and whips. Now, when I hear the word slavery I think of biterness, starving, limited everythi to what to say, to your beliefs. I think of a mama being seperated from her child. I think of someone being called someones property just because their skin was a different color. Then I think of someone being thrilled when gi/ing a pair of shoe Therefore, the book, To Be a Slave has really changed my feeling about

FIGURE 12.10. Student writing extension about slavery.

impressions of Julius Lester's *To Be a Slave* and how it has affected their learning in this unit. To assess students' essays, the teacher uses a checklist that addresses the quality of topic sentences, supporting details, and reaction to the narratives (Figure 12.11).

After the essays are written, students work in cooperative discussion groups to share their impressions. Each person in the group evaluates his or her participation in the discussion as well as the degree of participation of other members of the group. The form used for this peer assessment is shown in Figure 12.12.

Brenda views this collection of assessment tools as a way to help students deal with the challenging texts they encounter in her social studies class. The essay evalua-

SOCIAL STUDIES: *TO BE A SLAVE*

Skill Assessed	Excellent (3)	Acceptable (2)	Unacceptable (1)
1. Topic sentence on essay topic			
2. Supporting detail from narratives (1)			
3. Supporting details from narratives (2)			
4. Supporting details from narratives (3)			
5. Student gave their reaction to narrative			

FIGURE 12.11. Teacher assessment form.

SOCIAL STUDIES: *TO BE A SLAVE*

Name: _____   Group Member Assessed: _____

Peer Observation: Yes (1)   No (0)

1. Group member read his or her essay.

2. Essay/discussion contained specific examples from the narratives.

3. Essay/discussion showed group member's impression of the narratives.

4. Group member was cooperative during discussion.

FIGURE 12.12. Peer assessment form.

tion forms provide students with meaningful feedback on their writing and also serve as an engaging platform for learning by involving them in cooperative learning and assessment. Over time, students begin to take ownership of the assessment process, and they use it to monitor their learning and refine their writing skills.

PRINCIPLES OF EFFECTIVE ASSESSMENT

When we reflect on the assessment practices of these exemplary intermediate- and middle-grade teachers, we find many similarities in the underlying goals and the types of assessments used by each teacher. Predictably, we also find that their practices are highly consistent with existing research and theory on effective literacy assessment practices. A synthesis of what we have learned from these teachers' actions and what we have learned from reviewing the professional literature (Johnston, 2005a; Lipson & Wixson, 2003; Valencia & Pearson, 1987) leads us to the following principles of effective literacy assessment:

- Assessment is a continuous process, not just a once-a-year event.
- Assessment must be varied and must include both formal and informal techniques, with a greater emphasis on the latter, more authentic, sources of information.
- Assessment must be flexible and take place in many forms and in many contexts; performance changes when the social structure changes (Johnston & Rogers, 2001).
- Assessment must effectively capture both the scope and objectives of the assignments.
- Assessment is not just for teachers; we need to include the viewpoints of both teachers and students.
- Assessment must be based on students' reading and response to multiple sources, including all of the texts that students read and evaluative prompts that go beyond end-of-chapter questions.
- To help teachers focus on diverse learners, assessment should both be based on instruction and should also inform instruction. That is, assessment should allow

students to display their knowledge in multiple formats (e.g., discussion, illustration, written response), and it should also lead teachers to incorporate students' preferred or strong learning modes into routine instructional activities.

CONCLUSION

In these vignettes we see a clear relationship between good assessment and good instruction. Indeed, they are often reciprocal and interactive processes of learning: Good instruction includes ongoing and effective assessment, and good assessment, in turn, flows from active and engaging teaching. Tools such as the anticipation guide, scoring rubrics, and self- and peer assessment strategies increase student engagement in learning and also help students participate more fully in the assessment process. Effective teachers such as Kristina, Tomas, and Brenda treat assessment not merely as something that happens *to* students but as an active process in which students are engaged. We believe that microlevel assessment often offers greater opportunities for this kind of involvement. It is necessary that teachers help develop in students what Johnston (2005b, p. 685) refers to as a "literate disposition of reciprocity." That is, they must be willing to engage in learning and evaluation as a joint venture in which the perspectives of others are considered, questions are asked, and risks are taken (Carr & Claxton, 2002; Cobb, 2005).

ACKNOWLEDGMENTS

A special thanks to teachers Kay Sehorn and Stephanie Neigel of Charlotte Mecklenburg Schools, North Carolina, and to the fourth-grade teachers at New Salem Elementary School in Union County for their contributions to this chapter.

REFERENCES

Allington, R. (2002). What I've learned about effective reading instruction. *Phi Delta Kappan, 6,* 740–747.

Allington, R. (2005). *What really matters for struggling readers: Designing research-based programs* (2nd ed.). Boston: Allyn & Bacon.

Alvermann, D. E. (Ed.). (2002). *Adolescents and literacies in a digital world.* New York: Peter Lang.

Alvermann, D., & Hagood, M. (2000). Critical media literacy: Research, theory and practice in "New Times." *Journal of Education Research, 93*(3), 193–205.

Beach, R. (1995). Constructing cultural models through response to literature. *English Journal, 84*(6), 87–94.

Beach, R. (1997). Students' resistance to engagement with multicultural literature. In T. Rogers & A. Soter (Eds.), *Reading across cultures* (pp. 64–73). New York: Teachers College Press.

Blanton, W. E., Wood, K. D., & Taylor, D. B. (in press). Rethinking middle school reading: A basic reading approach. *Reading Psychology.*

Boyd-Batstone, P. (2004). Focused anecdotal records assessment: A tool for standards-based assessment. *The Reading Teacher, 58*(3), 230–239.

Carr, M., & Claxton, G. (2002). Tracting the development of learning dispositions. *Assessment in Education, 9*(1), 9–37.

Chappula, S. (2005). Is formative assessment losing its meaning? Commentary. *Education Week.* Available at *www.edweek.org/articles/2005/08/10.*

Cobb, C. (2005). Effective instruction begins with purposeful assessments. In S. J. Barrentine & S. M. Stokes (Eds.), *Reading assessment: Principles and practices for elementary teachers* (2nd ed., pp. 20–22). Newark, DE: International Reading Association.

Johnson, D., & Kress, G. (2003). Globalization, literacy and society: Redesigning pedagogy and assessment. *Assessment in Education, 10*(1), 5–14.

Johnston, P. H. (2005a). Assessment conversations. In S. J. Barrentine & S. M. Stokes (Eds.), *Reading assessment* (pp. 74–76). Newark, DE: International Reading Association.

Johnston, P. H. (2005b). Literacy assessment and the future. *The Reading Teacher, 58*(7), 684–686.

Johnston, P. H., & Costello, P. (2005). Principles for literacy assessment. *Reading Research Quarterly, 40*(2), 256–267.

Johnston, P. H., & Rogers, R. (2001). Early literacy assessment. In S. B. Neuman & D. K. Dickerson (Eds.), *Handbook of early literacy research* (pp. 377–389). New York: Guilford Press.

Lauber, P. (1996). *Hurricanes: Earth's mightiest storms.* New York: Scholastic Press.

Lester, J. (1998). *To be a slave.* New York: Dial Books.

Lipson, M., & Wixson, K. (2003). Assessment and instruction of reading and writing difficulty: An interactive approach (3rd ed.). New York: Longman.

Luke, A., & Elkins, J. (1998). Reinventing literacy in "New Times." *Journal of Adolescent and Adult Literacy, 42*(1), 4–7.

Luria, A. L. (1985). *Cognitive development: Its cultural and historical foundations.* Cambridge, MA: Harvard University Press.

National Reading Panel Report. (2000). *Teaching children to read: An evidence-based assessment of the scientific research literature on reading and its implications for reading instruction* (NIH Publication No. 00–4754). Washington, DC: U.S. Department of Health and Human Services.

Nessel, D. (1987). Reading comprehension: Asking the right questions. *Phi Delta Kappan, 68*(6), 442–445.

Pressley, M. (2000). What should comprehension instruction be the instruction of? In M. Kamil, P. B. Mosenthal, P. D. Pearson, & R. Barr (Eds.), *Handbook of reading research* (Vol. 3, pp. 545–562). Mahwah, NJ: Erlbaum.

Pressley, M. (2002) *Reading instruction that works: The case for balanced teaching* (2nd ed.). New York: Guilford Press.

Rosenblatt, L. (1978). *The reader, the text, the poem: The transactional theory of the literacy work.* Carbondale, IL: Southern Illinois University Press.

Stovel, J. E. (1987). Document-based questions (DBQ) and testing for critical thinking. *Social Science Record, 24*(1), 11–12.

Valencia, S., & Pearson, P. D. (1987). Reading assessment: Time for a change. *The Reading Teacher, 40,* 726–733.

Valencia, S., & Wixson, K. (2000). Policy-oriented research on literacy standards and assessment. In M. L. Kamil, P. B. Mosenthal, P. D. Pearson, & R. Barr (Eds.), *Handbook of reading research* (Vol. 3, pp. 909–935). Mahwah, NJ: Erlbaum.

Vygotsky, L. S. (1978). *Mind in society.* Cambridge, MA: Harvard University Press.

Wilkinson, I. A. G., & Reninger, K. B. (2005, April). *What the approaches look like: A conceptual framework for discussions.* Paper presented at the annual meeting of the American Educational Research Association, Montreal, Quebec, Canada.

CHAPTER 13

Assessing Student Writing

Karen Bromley

Struggling writers often . . .

- Avoid writing.
- Don't write much.
- Think they have nothing to say.
- Write illegibly.
- Fail to express their ideas clearly.
- Lack focus and organization.
- Wander away from the topic.
- Don't enjoy writing or sharing it with others.
- Don't use appropriate capitalization, spelling, or punctuation.

In other words, many struggling writers are not engaged in the act of writing. They find it difficult and are sometimes uncooperative when it is time to write. They learn how to write as little possible in order to get by, and they receive lower grades as a result. Often struggling writers are English language learners (ELLs) or students with learning disabilities. Strong writers on the other hand, often are fluent and write easily. They plan before they write and persevere until they have finished a piece. They produce work that has voice and style. They write clearly and usually legibly, using appropriate mechanics. They enjoy writing and are confident in what they have to say.

Whether students struggle with writing or are strong writers, there are certain factors that promote learning (Goldenberg, 2005). All students benefit from clear instruction, well-designed tasks, group practice, guidance and feedback, and independent practice. For bilingual students, however, the clarity of instruction is even more important, and Goldenberg cautions that teachers "need to build redundancies into instruction and the classroom routine so kids are not constantly so busy trying to figure what they are supposed to do operationally that they can't think about the content of their learning" (p. 8).

How can good classroom assessment practices help struggling writers figure out what they need to do to become strong writers? This chapter begins with a discussion of reasons for assessment and self-assessment and then describes approaches three teachers take in assessing student writing, including examples and descriptions of useful assessment tools.

WHY ASSESS WRITING?

I begin with a simple fact, aptly stated by Shepard (2000): "We have strong evidence that high-quality classroom assessments improve learning tremendously, possibly more effectively than any other teaching intervention" (p. 7). Writing assessment and evaluation not only promote learning; they demonstrate progress and achievement, drive good instruction, facilitate grading, and provide accountability for students, parents, and administrators. Equally important, self-assessment in writing builds metacognitive skills that lead to independence.

The word *assess* derives from the Latin *assidere*, which means "to sit beside." For the teacher of writing, this derivation seems particularly relevant because it situates teachers and students together in the collaborative analysis of written work. For effective writing teachers, assessment means collecting and interpreting information with students so that both can better understand and improve the writing process and product. The word *evaluate* also comes from the Latin, *valere*, which means to judge the "strength or worth" of something. As have authors of other chapters in this volume, I draw a distinction between formative and summative measures. *Formative assessment* is ongoing; it occurs periodically in order to inform learning and teaching. Formative assessment can be collaborative, involving peers and teachers, and often results in a *summative evaluation* which can be a grade and/or written comments at the conclusion of a written assignment, unit, or marking period. Typically, teachers make the summative evaluation, but students may also make their own final decision or make one with a teacher.

Self-Assessment First

Thinking about our own writing practices and knowledge of the writing process and product is a good place to begin. Reflection and self-assessment lead to metacognition, which is knowledge about, and regulation of, cognitive ability. Metacognitive ability in writing involves awareness and monitoring that can result in changes in writing beliefs and practices to better support struggling writers and propel strong writers forward. Here are some places to begin to think about self-assessment.

Those who excel as writing teachers often are writers themselves. Many teachers keep a personal journal and from this experience as a writer they are in a good position to help their students become better writers. When teachers write reports, letters, newsletters, and memos, they know and use the recursive steps in the writing process that include planning, drafting, self-checking, revising, editing, sharing, and publishing the finished product. These teachers often post charts in their classrooms as guides for students to use in the writing process (see Figures 13.1 and 13.2). Good writing teachers know that writing well in different genres means reading in different genres. These

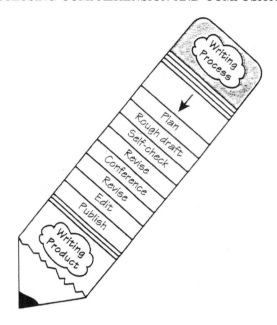

FIGURE 13.1. A wall chart showing that both process and product are important in writing.

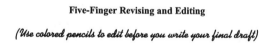

Five-Finger Revising and Editing

(Use colored pencils to edit before you write your final draft)

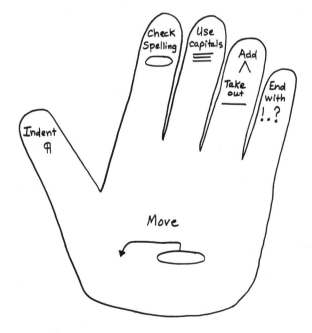

FIGURE 13.2. A wall chart to help students with revising and editing.

teachers study the craft of writing and read books with a writer's eye as they notice an author's style and voice and share this information with their students. They know that there are different forms of writing: *expository*—writing to explain, inform, make clear, or describe a process; *persuasive*—to convince or persuade someone to change an opinion or to influence an action; *descriptive*—to develop an image by using precise sensory words; and *narrative*—to tell a story or give an account of a fictional or nonfictional event. These teachers also know that good writing often includes all four forms, but that many students need explicit instruction in each form individually.

Questions about Writing Assessment

As well as being writers, understanding the writing process, and knowing its forms, answering particular questions can help teachers self-assess in a more focused way to develop better writing assessments. In my work, I have found questions such as those that follow to be especially helpful.

Do I Know My Writing Curriculum, Student Needs, and Resources?

Most states have writing standards and mandated writing tests. Many school districts have developed curriculum maps that identify the writing skills to be taught at each grade level so that students will learn to write and do well on tests. Common planning time and team meetings with colleagues provide opportunities to examine and discuss students' writing needs, share resources, and create schoolwide assessment tools to improve writing. For example, a team of fourth-grade teachers examined their state writing test and identified writing skills they believe are necessary for students to write clearly and do well on the test (see Figure 13.3). From this list, the teachers planned writing instruction across the curriculum and developed a common rubric to use with students (see Figure 13.4).

A *rubric* is a set of criteria for a given piece of student work that describes the quality of the work. It usually contains the critical elements of a piece and descriptions of how each element can be achieved. By cooperatively creating this rubric, these teachers talked about the goals of their writing curriculum, began to use the same writing language with students, and felt ownership of, and commitment to, using the rubric.

- Identifying key words/phrases
- Using graphic organizers
- Grammar
- Seeing connections
- Proofreading
- Editing
- Planning
- Letter writing

- Including beginning, middle, and ending
- Using details to support
- Comparing and contrasting
- Cross-referencing
- Using prior knowledge
- Writing according to directions
- Mechanics

FIGURE 13.3. Fourth-grade teachers examined the state test to determine skills they needed to teach.

Name _____

Date _____

	4	3	2	1
CONTENT	Fulfills all or most requirements • • •	Fulfills some requirements • • •	Fulfills few requirements • • •	Fulfills no requirements • • •
IDEAS	Develops ideas fully through: • details • examples • reasons • explanations	Provides some • details • examples • reasons • explanations	Provides few • details • examples • reasons • explanations	Does not use • details • examples • reasons • explanations
FOCUS	• Clear focus, easily read, fluent • Logical organization	• Generally focuses • Acceptable organization	• Limited focus • Weakness in organization	• Does not maintain clear focus • Lacks a plan of organization
SENTENCE STRUCTURE	• Varied sentence structure • Vivid language (vocab)	• Some sentence variety • Appropriate language (vocab)	• Simple sentences • Occasionally uses inappropriate or incorrect language	• Lack of sentence structure • Frequently uses inappropriate or incorrect language
MECHANICS	• Makes few or no errors in spelling, grammar, and punctuation • Takes risks with sophisticated vocabulary	• Makes minor errors in spelling, grammar, and punctuation that DO NOT interfere with communication	• Makes errors in spelling, grammar, and punctuation that interfere with communication	• Makes errors in spelling, grammar, and punctuation that seriously interfere with communication

FIGURE 13.4. A common writing rubric created by a team of fourth-grade teachers. Reprinted by permission of Melani A. Williamson.

As noted by Spandel (2004), rubrics are important because they "make expectations public and visible" (p. 218). Writing rubrics come in a variety of shapes and sizes. Some rubrics look like the one presented in Figure 13.5, which teachers use when scoring one section in the New York State English Language Arts Test. Checklists are sometimes called rubrics, but checklists only provide a list of criteria without descriptions of quality. No matter how well developed or bare-boned rubrics are, when students and teachers use them, students know the criteria on which their work will be judged and can use the rubric as a guide as they write. Thus rubrics are one concrete way to support and assess struggling writers and ELLs.

There are many generic rubrics for all types of writing (Areglado & Dill, 1997; Fiderer, 1999). However, many teachers find that existing rubrics are best used as springboards for creating their own, because generic rubrics often lack the special characteristics that comprise a unique piece. As noted by DeVries (2004), "The best rubrics are those designed by teachers for their own classrooms because they know the developmental stage of their students and what standards the state requires at each grade level" (p. 280). As well, published rubrics don't involve students in the assessment process.

What Is the Writing Environment in My Classroom?

Creating inviting spaces and a context for writing is critical for writing development (Laidlaw, 2005). Calling students "writers," "authors," or "editors" subtly influences, in a positive way, their view of themselves and how, as well as what, they write. Using tools such as the *Writer Self-Perception Scale* (Bottomly, Henk, & Melnick, 1998; described in greater detail by Gambrell and Ridgeway in Chapter 4), a self-assessment for writing and spelling (Fountas & Pinnell, 2001), or your own attitude or interest survey can help you understand how students perceive themselves, what their interests are, what they are proud of in their writing, what they do well, what conventions they believe they use, and what progress they have made.

Writing flourishes when students have choices, when they write for real purposes, and when they share their work orally. In the case of students who are bilingual, choice may involve more than topic, audience, or genre; it may also involve which language to use to best display their knowledge in writing; as well, students who are bilingual may improve their writing if they are given a chance to share their work-in-progress with a peer who speaks the same first language (Rubin & Carlan, 2005).

As noted by Ruetzel and Morrow (this volume, Chapter 3), a classroom that supports and encourages student writers has a variety of tools available, including dictionaries, thesauruses, paper, envelopes, pens, pencils, markers (thick and thin), white-out, staplers, glue sticks, and scissors. When computers, spell checkers, or AlphaSmarts, for example, are available, posting a schedule or sign-up sheet allows all students an equal opportunity to create and produce writing digitally as they develop keyboarding skills and technology know-how. A classroom that supports writing also builds in plenty of time each day for writing across the curriculum.

Web-based bookmarks can support literacy instruction and provide structure and content for students with special needs (Forbes, 2004). Creating a list of favorite bookmarks provides visual clues for struggling students that aid them in writing. For exam-

SCORING RUBRIC FOR NEW YORK STATE ELEMENTARY ENGLISH LANGUAGE ARTS ASSESSMENT

Task 3: Reading and Writing for Information and Understanding and for Critical Analysis and Evaluation in an Informational Text

Dimensions	Descriptors			
	4 Accomplished	3 Proficient	2 Developing	1 Beginning
Reading Comprehension				
Understanding	Includes a broad range of critical information that explains how and why each animal in each category disguises itself. Elaborates on and thoroughly explains information from the text.	Includes critical information that explains how and/or why each animal in each category disguises itself with some elaboration and explanation.	Presents some information with some explanation. May contain limited factual errors and/or misinterpretations.	Presents information with limited or no explanation. May contain factual errors and/or misinterpretations. May be missing critical information.
Analysis	Goes beyond the factual information presented in the text to interpret and analyze.	Some evidence of interpretation and analysis.		
Writing Effectiveness				
Idea Development	Develops and elaborates ideas clearly and fully using many supportive and relevant details from the text. Draws meaningful connections between ideas.	Develops ideas clearly with some supporting details from the text.	Ideas are stated simply. Few supporting details from the text are referenced. May wander from the topic or task.	Develops ideas in fragmentary manner. Does not use supporting details from the text and/or includes random information and personal details unrelated to the topic. May be off-topic or task completely.
Organization	Writing has a distinctive organizing shape and structure. Ideas are presented in a clear order and logical sequence with transitions made through the use of paragraphing, introductions, and/or conclusions.	Ideas are presented in a clear order and logical sequence. Writing is easy to understand and follow.	Ideas are presented in some sequence, but overall coherence is tentative. Response may require several rereadings to understand what is written.	Ideas are presented with little or no organizational pattern. Difficult to follow.
Language Use	Uses lively and descriptive language that goes beyond what was stated in the text. Engages the reader, has a sense of audience and a distinguishing sense of voice. Varied sentence length and structure.	Uses language and vocabulary from the text. Writes to an appropriate audience. Some sense of voice and sentence variety.	Word choices are simple, as are sentences, with little attention paid to audience.	Vague or unclear language (hard to understand).
Conventions	Writing is generally free of errors in spelling, punctuation, and grammar.	Limited errors in spelling, punctuation, and grammar, but the meaning of the writing is communicated.	Numerous errors in spelling, punctuation, and grammar, but the meaning of the writing is distinguishable.	Mechanics interfere with the reader's ability to understand the response.

FIGURE 13.5. The New York State writing rubric includes content and mechanics.

ple, by bookmarking a dictionary website such as *www.dictionary.com*, students can search a word, click on a button next to the word, and hear the audio pronunciation of the word. An audio component decreases frustration for those who can't spell, and it can expand students' writing vocabularies when they hear a word pronounced, read it and its meaning, and find synonyms.

Modeling the writing process for students, encouraging shared writing, and conferring with students during writing workshop help to establish an atmosphere in which good writing flourishes. When teachers use an overhead projector and colored pens to model the revising process, using their own writing or a volunteer's from the class, they can help students develop an understanding of specific revision strategies, and they can also develop a respectful and risk-free writing atmosphere in the classroom.

Do I Teach Goal Setting and Engage Students in Self-Assessment?

When students think about what they want to learn or need to improve on as writers and then set their own goals, they become active learners with a purpose. For example, Sean, a fifth grader in an after-school program, wrote: "I would like to improve putting more details in my essays. I also think I should print a little bit neater. I only write neat in cursive." Ryan, his tutor, also noted that Sean needed to revisit and revise his written work. Ryan noted that Sean had a lot to say, but often what he knew didn't appear in his writing.

Sean's goals and Ryan's observations helped Ryan plan lessons that included the use of graphic organizers (Bromley, DeVitis, & Modlo, 1999). Sean learned to use a "Central Idea Organizer," a "Comparison Organizer," and a "What Happened Organizer" to help him brainstorm and organize main ideas and supporting details. In assessing a report he had written on pollution, Sean used a "Y-Pie" assessment map (see Figure 13.6) to identify what was positive, what he needed to change, and how he could improve. The Y-Pie feedback sheet could also be used to assess a media presentation or project, and a peer or the teacher could use it as well.

Rubrics and checklists can also help students improve their handwriting (Ediger, 2002). Ryan showed Sean how to use a fine-point felt-tip pen to practice printing the Zaner–Bloser model alphabet his school uses. Using the square-tipped pen was a novelty for him and focused his attention on legibility. Ryan introduced Sean to two checklists, a writing checklist and a handwriting self-assessment that he could use independently to assess and revise his work (see Figures 13.7 and 13.8). At the conclusion of the after-school program, Sean looked at his collected work, saw the progress he had made, and evaluated himself according to the goals he had set.

Is Assessment Collaborative?

Do students and teachers co-construct checklists and rubrics? When students and teachers work together to generate rubrics, students become active participants in assessment, which often improves the quality of their writing. Rubrics allow students to reflect on any gaps in their knowledge or missing elements and explore ways to improve (Skillings & Ferrell, 2000). For example, before beginning most writing,

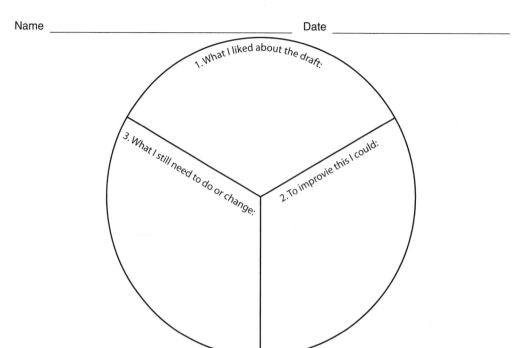

FIGURE 13.6. A "Y-Pie" assessment organizer helps students self-assess. Reprinted by permission of Terry Cooper.

My Writing Checklist _____ (name)
Title of my writing _____

____ I preplanned.
____ I considered my audience.
____ I organized my work.
____ I used paragraphs.
____ I used details.
____ I used words that describe.
____ I used powerful language.
____ I began with an interesting introduction.
____ I ended with a strong conclusion.
____ I proofread my work.
____ I chose an interesting title.
____ I used correct spelling.
____ I used correct punctuation and capitals.
____ I got feedback from a buddy.
____ I revised and edited.
____ I composed neatly.
Next time I would _____
_____
_____

FIGURE 13.7. This checklist for writing can be used with a variety of forms of writing.

MY HANDWRITING

	Yes	No
Are all my letters straight?		
Do they all sit on the line?		
Do tall letters fill the whole space?		
Do short letters fill half the space?		
Are my letters evenly spaced?		
Are there spaces between words?		
Is my paper neat?		

FIGURE 13.8. Ryan made this checklist for Sean, a fifth grader, who wanted to improve his printing.

Melani, a fourth-grade teacher, brainstorms with students to produce a list of attributes that characterize a good finished product. After Melani's read-aloud of *Bud, Not Buddy* by Christopher Paul Curtis (1999), the class had many unanswered questions. She saw this questioning atmosphere as an opportunity to engage students in narrative writing, so she asked them to write another chapter to the story and make a cover page with a picture to represent something from their chapter. The task required writing from another person's perspective, creativity, critical thinking, the use of quotation marks, and so forth, and the project built a context and safe space for writers, who would later read and listen to each other's work. Before writing, Melani and the class analyzed Curtis's style and made a list of things they noticed about his writing and things they thought would make a good chapter:

- Put in some of Bud's sayings, such as "Woop, Zoop, Sloop" and "He can kiss my wrists."
- Invent your own "Rules and Things," like Bud's.
- Use "I" and imagine how Bud would think and react.
- Use correct paragraph form.
- Use quotation marks when someone talks.
- Write neatly so others can read it (use cursive or printing, but don't mix them).
- Write only on one side of the paper.

Next, Melani generated a checklist and duplicated it for students to use as they wrote. Students used the writing process (see Figure 13.1) that was posted on a chart in the classroom. After writing their chapters, students did a "self-check" and revision before first conferring with a friend and then with Melani. Last, students did a second revision and edited before forming small groups for reading their chapters to each other. The chapters were also enjoyed by the fourth-grade students next door, as a way to interest other students in reading Curtis's work.

In the same way, a fifth-grade teacher, Dodie, worked with her students to create a checklist, called the "Biography Self-Assessment Form" (see Figure 13.9), for students to use as they wrote a biography. There were several characteristics she believed were

BIOGRAPHY SELF-ASSESSMENT FORM

Name _____ Date _____

Assignment _____

Writing Partner _____

	Author	Partner	Teacher
I wrote to the assigned topic.			
I have 4–5 complete paragraphs including:			
Introduction			
Character traits			
Interesting facts/events			
Conclusion			
I included detailed supporting material.			
My writing engages the reader.			
I presented my ideas in the correct order.			
I used a variety of sentences.			
I used descriptive language.			
I used complete sentences.			
My spelling is correct.			
I used correct punctuation, capitalization, and margins.			
I have at least 2 references listed.			
I have read and edited my work.			
My writing partner has read and edited my work.			
My teacher has read and edited my work.			

Comments:

FIGURE 13.9. Dodie created this self-assessment form with her fifth graders for their biography writing. Reprinted by permission of Dodie Ainslie.

necessary for a good biography, so she and the class brainstormed a list. Dodie wanted students to use at least two sources, write four to five complete paragraphs, and include character traits, interesting facts, and events. She added the requirement that each student should work with a writing partner to provide feedback before she read the piece and the student revised it. When using this assessment, struggling writers could be paired with strong writers who could give relevant feedback. Ryan, Melani, and Dodie make students active participants in the writing process and guide them to independence through collaboration and self-assessment.

Do I Focus on the Positive and Give Specific Praise and Suggestions?

Constructive responses to students have a positive impact on writing and can make a huge difference in what they write and how they feel about themselves as writers. For example, the statement, "Good job, you're a good writer," implies the possibility of not being a good writer. In contrast, the kind of positive assessment that spurs students to success might be something like the following: "The dialogue you have used to open this draft really got my attention. How did you learn to do that?" (Johnston, 2004, p. 685).

Assessment feedback should be positive, specific, and helpful. Effective teachers first read for, and respond to, the message and content of a piece. An easy acronym to use in assessing a piece of writing, or any other project or performance, for that matter, is PQS, where *P* means "praise," *Q* means "question," and *S* means "suggestion." Ryan used it when he commented on Sean's first draft of the report on pollution:

- *P*—"This is clear! You do a good job of using evidence to show how the Susquehanna River gets more polluted during storms than during good weather."
- *Q*—"What do you mean by 'a few bigger storm sewers'? Can you be specific?"
- *S*—"You need to tell how your proposal will help Binghamton and the people living along the river. Use a colored pencil to make a new paragraph when you start a new idea."

Notice that Ryan's main focus was on content, and his secondary comments relate to mechanics. This kind of constructive feedback helps students because it provides concrete ideas that are framed in a positive way. Struggling writers, including ELLs and students with literacy difficulties, need this kind of affirmation to grow as writers.

Further, the type of feedback teachers give takes on special signficance when working with students who are acquiring English as a second language. Using both languages before one becomes dominant is a part of the developmental process for learning to speak and write a second language (Rubin & Carlan, 2005). Teachers need to encourage bilingual students to view their bilingualism as a strength and to use it as a resource in their writing. Toward this end, it is helpful for teachers to acknowledge with praise when students who are becoming bilingual use words or sounds from one language as they write in the other language.

What Collections of Student Work Do We Keep? How Do These Inform My Instruction?

A portfolio is a collection of student work gathered over time (Cooper & Kiger, 2005). Writing portfolios are an important record of writing development and instruction. Dating each piece of work allows teachers and students to document growth. Often teachers have students attach a self-assessment to each piece that goes into the portfolio (see Figure 13.10). When a piece of writing is accompanied by a self-assessment, students can acknowledge what they do well and establish new writing goals for them-

PORTFOLIO PIECE SELF-ASSESSMENT

Name _____

Title of Work _____

Date of Piece _____

I chose this piece because _____

_____

I think it's strong because _____

_____

I need to improve on _____

_____

FIGURE 13.10. A form to accompany each piece of writing that goes into a writing portfolio.

selves. Examining work in portfolios also allows teachers to provide needed instruction in specific areas. When a portfolio contains evidence of planning, drafting, revision, and finished products, not just final pieces, teachers and students can see progress and identify areas of strength and need by looking for patterns in individual work as well as across a class of students.

For example, when Melani examined student portfolios midyear, she noted that Diyar and several other students' pieces were often brief and lacked descriptive language. From this assessment, Melani planned lessons for these students on developing sensory images with powerful language, for example, adjectives, adverbs, metaphors, and similes. She also could see that several students had problems comparing and contrasting ideas and organizing their work, so she knew they needed instruction in the use of Venn diagrams, T-charts, and other types of graphic organizers to support their writing. Melani made time to sit with students individually to examine their self-assessment and the writing in their portfolios as she talked with them about what they do well and areas they need to develop.

CONCLUSION

There is a widely held belief that "writing instruction has improved dramatically over the last 25 years" (Lenski & Johns, 2000, p. 1). Much of this improvement can be attributed to better writing assessments that inform more effective writing instruction. In this chapter, I emphasized some key ideas that I believe will lead to better assessment and, as a consequence, better instruction. I conclude with a list of a few more ideas that are likely to support students in their development as accomplished writers:

- The goal of all types of writing assessment should be to make students better writers; a secondary goal should be accountability to administrators and parents.
- Not all writing requires formal assessment; effective teachers assess some writ-

ing informally with personal written comments or a symbol, such as a star or happy face, to show that the task is complete.

- Reading and self-correction should be encouraged before a peer or teacher conference; students often see places where they can "fix" their own work just by reviewing it.
- Asking students to create personal assessments of their own writing several times during the year engages them in reflecting on their progress and setting new goals.
- Collecting assessment data on student writing isn't enough unless you reflect on it and act; assessments should determine instruction, and vice versa.
- Writing assessment should be ongoing; periodic assessments (that can be spontaneous) yield important information that keeps teachers and students on track.
- Working toward student independence in writing and assessment is a way to transform struggling writers into strong writers.

ACKNOWLEDGMENTS

I extend special thanks to Dodie Ainslie, sixth-grade teacher at African Road Middle School, and Melani Williamson, fourth-grade teacher at Glenwood Elementary School, both in Vestal, New York, for generously sharing their teaching ideas.

REFERENCES

Areglado, N., & Dill, M. (1997). *Let's write: A practical guide to teaching writing in the early grades.* New York: Scholastic.

Bottomly, D., Henk, W., & Melnick, S. (1998). Assessing children's views about themselves as writers using the Writer Self-Perception Scale. *The Reading Teacher, 51*(4), 287–295.

Bromley, K., DeVitis, L., & Modlo, M. (1999). *50 graphic organizers for reading, writing, and more.* New York: Scholastic.

Cooper, J. D., & Kiger, N. D. (2005). *Literacy assessment: Helping teachers plan instruction* (2nd ed.). Boston: Houghton-Mifflin.

DeVries, B. A. (2004). *Literacy assessment and intervention for the elementary classroom.* Scottsdale, AZ: Holcomb Hathaway.

Fiderer, A. (1999). *40 rubrics and checklists to assess reading and writing.* New York: Scholastic.

Forbes, L. S. (2004). Using Web-based bookmarks in K–8 settings: Linking the Internet to instruction. *The Reading Teacher, 58*(2), 148–153.

Fountas, I. C., & Pinnell, G. S. (2001). *Guided readers and writers grades 3–6: Teaching comprehension, genre, and content literacy.* Portsmouth, NH: Heinemann.

Goldenberg, C. (2005). An interview with Claude Goldenberg. *Reading Today, 23*(1), 8–9.

Johnston, P. H. (2004). *Choice words: How our language affects children's learning.* Portland, ME: Stenhouse.

Laidlaw, L. (2005). *Reinventing curriculum: A complex perspective on literacy and writing.* Mahwah, NJ: Erlbaum.

Lenski, S. D., & Johns, J. L. (2000). *Improving writing: Resources, strategies, assessments.* Dubuque, IA: Kendall Hunt.

Rubin, R., & Carlan, R. G. (2005). Using writing to understand bilingual children's literacy development. *The Reading Teacher, 58*(8), 728–741.

Shepard, L. (2000). The role of assessment in the learning culture. *Educational Researcher, 29*(7), 4–14.

Skillings, M. J., & Ferrell, R. (2000). Student-generated rubrics: Bringing students into the assessment process. *The Reading Teacher, 53*(6), 452–455.

Spandel, V. (2004). *Creating young writers: Using the six traits to enrich writing process in primary classrooms.* New York: Pearson.

CHILDREN'S BOOK

Curtis, C. P. (1999). *Bud, not Buddy.* New York: Delacourte.

PART IV

Broadening the Context

LOOKING ACROSS ASSESSMENTS, CLASSROOMS, AND SCHOOLS

CHAPTER 14

A Classroom Portfolio System

ASSESSMENT *IS* INSTRUCTION

Susan Mandel Glazer

In Judy Finchler's children's book *Testing Miss Malarkey* (2000), teachers, students, and even parents are preparing for THE TEST. Moms and Dads are giving their children pop quizzes instead of reading bedtime stories. The grown-ups tell the children not to worry, but they act strangely distraught. Miss Malarkey bites her nails for the first time. The principal has made himself personally responsible for making sure that all of the pencils are sharpened "perfectly." The gym teacher is teaching stress-reducing yoga instead of sports. And the cafeteria staff is serving "brain food" for lunch. At the PTA meeting, a man dubbed the Svengali of tests, comes to talk to the parents about THE TEST. He made the test sound so important that the parents' conception of the instrument became exaggerated. An animated drawing illustrates one parent frantically asking, "My son is gifted. . . . Will this test hinder his Ivy League chances? Will the grade point average be reflected in the scores? How will the test affect real estate prices?" And the morning of the test, there were more sick teachers than kids, including the principal, waiting for the nurse. "I hope he [the principal] didn't throw up in the hall," remarked one of the children. My colleagues and I laughed when reading this book. But we also realized that the alarm felt by all in this whimsically written story was truly tragic. Sadly, the fictional story reflects society's obsession with school performance as determined by standardized tests.

SOME BACKGROUND ABOUT ASSESSMENT

Our nation is test crazy. We assess constantly and measure almost everything. We begin at birth by measuring our infants for length, weight, blood type, and other attributes. These measurements are compared to growth patterns of other infants in order to determine if our baby is near to normal. As our children grow, their developmental patterns are compared to other children as well. We even go so far as to determine toddlers' IQs prior to entering preschool. If intelligent "enough," these children get pushed into academically oriented preschool programs, because some people believe that this kind of a program will help them get a head start in preparation for acceptance into an Ivy League university. "We do this," says Alan Farstrup, executive director of the International Reading Association (personal communication, June 3, 1996), "because we believe that the solution to all our problems is to give more tests." We believe this, despite evidence of no relationship between high-stakes testing and student achievement (Amrein & Berliner, 2002; Sacks, 1999).

Unfortunately, test scores have guided the public to form inappropriate perceptions of our nation's schools. Teachers are expected merely to get the students to perform well on the tests, collect the students' work, use formalized equations, graphs, or scales to determine level of achievement, and then submit a score to the persons or agents outside of the classrooms who have directed them to do so. Because the testing tools are selected by outsiders who do not know the children to whom they are administered, the materials are cold, impersonal activities that provide performance results that are generally unrelated to students' daily activities. They are vehicles that teachers are required to use, rather than vehicles that promote both students' and teachers' reflections on performances and transactions in classrooms. Student performances on these tests are consequential because in many cases, they are used to determine school funding and appropriation decisions, and they often determine school promotions and placements. These measurement tools provide the main source of accountability data (usually considered teacher performance) to public stakeholders (Murphy, 1997). The results of such testing are used in school districts and state or provincial education departments to rank and compare schools and children at all levels (Meier, 1994). Students take these tests for the purposes of large-scale educational and program evaluation, not for the purpose of supporting classroom instruction and improving their own learning (Taylor & Watson, 1997). When students' scores do not satisfy the community, the public usually blames the teachers. This focus of blame is due, in my opinion, to the public's lack of knowledge concerning how tests are made, used, and administered. For the most part, the public does not know that the assessment tools, the decisions about the information collected through the testing procedures, and the way the test results are evaluated are all determined by outside authorities. In 1996 Regie Routman asserted that as a consequence of societal beliefs about the importance of testing and test scores, "bashing our public schools is a national pastime" (p. 3). A decade later, most would agree that this statement remains an apt description.

WHY, THEN, ARE THESE TESTS STILL FLOURISHING?

Standardized tests still flourish because 70% of the parent population in the United States believes that promoting students to the next grade should be based on performance on a traditional (i.e., multiple-choice) test (Johnson & Immerwahr, 1994). New York City Mayor Michael Bloomberg, to bolster his 2006 political campaign, used the issue of student achievement based on testing to facilitate the abolishment of social promotion in grades 3, 5, and 7. One only has to look at *Tests in Print-V* (Burros Institute of

Mental Measurements, 1999) to learn that the numbers of tests available for use in classrooms increases by 300–400 every 5 years. This steady escalation occurs simply because many believe that there is nothing "truer" than a score. Even those of us who believe that tests are unfair evaluation tools choose *not* to find ways to stop those who mandate the use of them.

CHANGE, HOWEVER, HAS OCCURRED

As is evident in chapters throughout this text, in spite of all of these obstacles, there are communities in which great strides have been made to update alternatives to standardized tests. Changes are based on the knowledge that tests ought to complement today's instructional procedures. In such communities, testing processes are shifting from determining factual knowledge to inquiring about children's learning, reflective abilities, and engagement. Some testing processes also prompt inquiry into teaching strategies, teachers' knowledge, and teachers as learners. Many classrooms in schools worldwide have moved from teacher-centered to student-centered management systems. In these classrooms, determining successes daily, rather than periodically for report-card purposes, has become part of classroom curriculum. Portfolios and classroom rubrics, designed by students and teachers together, guide both to make decisions about strengths and needs. Portfolios provide a management system in which data are organized to inform teachers and their students about what students know and what they need to learn. Rubrics provide a way to evaluate or judge the artifacts within the portfolio. Together, these tools provide a viable alternative to traditional testing that also facilitates negotiable discussions between and among teachers and their students. These discussions, too, become part of the evidence base for understanding children's literacy learning, and the collected evidence, joined with teachers' professional observations and intuitions, develop into narratives educators use to draw conclusions about children's growth and learning. Although some may believe that teachers' observations and intuitions concerning students' needs are not as valid as "solid data" from tests, one only need listen to a teacher's story about a child's life to understand what the youngster is all about. Teachers are experts who know far more about the children they interact with than do test makers. Teachers who are skillful collectors and users of classroom-based evidence organize what they know around principles of teaching and learning and the value systems important in the communities in which their children grow (Braun & Mislevy, 2005).

DEVELOPING A PORTFOLIO TO MAXIMIZE STUDENTS' INDEPENDENT LEARNING

The portfolio system described in this chapter was developed over a period of 25 years and is still changing. It is a means for managing learning and has become a vehicle of inquiry. The data in each child's folder permit participants to seek information about each child's learning needs as well as about the teaching practices that are likely to be most beneficial in meeting those needs. One has only to open these, glance at a product or a collection of products, and use appropriate self-monitoring tools to determine what has been accomplished and what activities need to come next.

The first portfolios used in 1979 in our Center for Reading and Writing at Rider University in New Jersey were very different from those that we use today. We began by asking youngsters, ages 6–16, to collect everything they had produced and put it into their folder. The materials were reviewed once weekly, first in small groups of six children. The purpose was to see what each child had accomplished. These collections became cumbersome because there were no constraints placed on the arrangement of the materials. The approach was one of, "Put them in there and we'll decide what to do with them later." Reviewing the data in the portfolio functioned as an alternative grading system, but we determined that this method was not productive or efficient. The teachers were able to use materials and tests scores and make intuitive judgments about children's growth and needs, but children who needed to find out about their progress had no systematic way to determine what they knew or needed to learn.

Our focus shifted to one that is grounded in a student-centered approach to portfolios that permits youngsters to make decisions about their strengths and needs. As Gambrell and Ridgeway (Chapter 4, this volume) explain, making choices increases student engagement. In our center, this research comes alive as we consistently observe that making decisions provides the empowerment that lures students to want to make more decisions about their learning processes. Becoming empowered permits them to say, with confidence, "I know this," and also say, just as confidently, "This is what I need to learn."

From my years of experience with portfolios, I've found that teachers who are about to use them for the first time are concerned with how to organize the materials that go into them, children's role in using them, and how to use the portfolio when report cards are mandatory. Our system at the Center for Reading and Writing is a deliberate attempt to address each of these concerns. We began with a folder that had four different pieces of colored construction paper enclosed. Students gathered products and sorted them by subject matter behind the designated piece of colored paper. Math products were filed behind the red construction paper, reading and literature behind blue, spelling in back of yellow, and writing behind orange. After several years, these accumulations of papers became unwieldy. Many children at all grade levels would say, "Which one is this color for? I can't find my blue one! This one goes in two places." The teachers realized that the questions were caused by an inefficient management system. We recognized that a more functional approach for guiding students to organize and categorize their products was needed in order to guide them to self-monitor their own learning. Several discussions led the teachers to conclude that there needed to be a portfolio (or folder) just for reading and the language arts. Others might also be created for different content area subjects (e.g., math, science). But putting all of the materials together was befuddling for children's organizational schemes. After 11 years of organizing and reorganizing portfolios, our system emerged in the form of criteria developed by our staff (Figure 14.1).

Our portfolios now are made from two 9" × 11" pocket folders bound together using plastic ringers. One is made for each youngster and one for the teacher. The front of each includes the child's name, the teacher's name, and the time period in which it is being used. These folders might be considered a briefcase for organizing, managing, and categorizing products resulting from children's efforts. They consist of four sections labeled (1) comprehension, (2) composition, (3) word study, and (4) independence. The contents of each section include ongoing work in each of the four categories (see Figure 14.2).

	Check Here
The portfolio guides children to organize materials independently.	☐
The management system promotes an understanding of the purposes for learning to read, write, and understand the study of words.	☐
Students are assisted in learning to define the purposes of their work by the way materials are arranged in the portfolio.	☐
Students are able to identify the skill and category in which their work fits because of the portfolio's organization.	☐
The portfolio acts as an "outline" for guiding children to review their daily activities and progress.	☐
Routine activities are easily accessible so that students can begin, carry out, and complete the activities independently.	☐
Students' self-monitoring tools for assessing products coordinate with routine and other literacy activities promoting independent instruction.	☐
Portfolios are easy to handle, retrieve, store, and refer to for information about strengths and needs.	☐

FIGURE 14.1. Portfolio elements necessary for effective use.

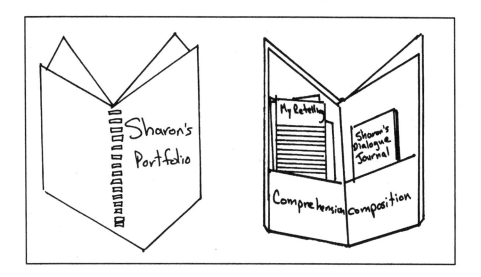

FIGURE 14.2. The portfolio. Reprinted from Glazer (1998). Copyright 1998 by Christopher-Gordon. Reprinted by permission.

Comprehension

The first section of our portfolios, originally named *reading,* was renamed *comprehension.* The decision to change the name was based on the realization that anything one reads, sees, views, hears, touches, or tastes must be understood. The section, therefore, includes evidence that students know how to make meaning of text, and that they are metacognitively aware of their behaviors they use. Teachers agree that there must be evidence that students can (1) recall information immediately after reading, (2) make connections between information they've gleaned from current school experiences and information or ideas already in memory, and (3) express and connect feelings and opinions about things they read based on prior experiences (going beyond the text and reflecting).

Work samples include, among others, a reader response journal in which children recall, respond to, and reflect on literature they are reading. There is also a content journal in which youngsters write about things they recall from content-area activities. We have identified several strategies for guiding children to self-monitor their work using these vehicles in their daily routines. I have chosen two to elaborate on here: oral (tape-recorded and transcribed) and written retellings and oral and written responses to reading literature. My descriptions focus on the self-monitoring aspects of the strategy because a major purpose of our portfolios is to guide students to develop self-assessment skills and independence by self-monitoring their products.

Retellings have been validated as an effective strategy for examining students' reading comprehension (Morrow, 1988). Retellings guide students to develop (1) short-term memory skills to help them recall what was read immediately after reading, (2) oral fluency, and (3) word recognition skills for both reading and writing. Retellings are used primarily to guide learners to determine what they know and what they still need to learn. Students are able to determine their needs and observe their growth by reviewing those retellings carried out, past and present.

In Figure 14.3, I present an example of one student's attempt at a written retelling. Kevin retold everything he remembered about the story *The Three Wishes: An Old Story*

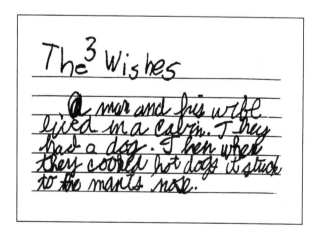

FIGURE 14.3. Kevin's retelling of *The Three Wishes.* Reprinted from Glazer (1998). Copyright 1998 by Christopher-Gordon. Reprinted by permission.

(Zemach, 1986) immediately after he read it. The 8-year-old began to retell in writing, erased, tried again, erased until the paper was illegible, tried a third time, then put that incomplete attempt in the comprehension section of his folder as well. He knew that he was supposed to save all of his attempts so that he could determine what he could do and where he needed guidance. Kevin finally wrote a summary, not a retelling, which was his fourth attempt. His teacher's observations of his four attempts, collected in the comprehension section of the portfolio, guided her to conclude that handwriting was probably the deterrent hampering his ability to demonstrate recall immediately after reading.

"Kevin," commented his teacher, "I was not fair." "What do you mean?" responded the puzzled child. "Well," she continued, "I asked you to retell the story you read in writing, and I saw that you had a difficult time starting." "Yeah, I did," Kevin remarked. "I remember a lot of things, but I can't write them all down so easy." Kevin was asked to take out his four attempts from the comprehension section and place them on the table. As he fumbled, his teacher, although tempted, stopped herself from taking them out for him. As he looked at her, he commented, "My hands don't work as fast as my mind. That's why I started so many times. See, I finally got it right" (holding up the fourth sheet).

Kevin selected the story *Tikki Tikki Tembo* (Mosel, 1999) as his next story reading. When his teacher saw him take the book from his basket of materials, she moved to his table, bent down next to him, and said, "Hurray for you, Kevin. You selected another book you can read." "Yeah," he responded. "I used the fist-full-of-words trick to pick it. I read one page and only put two fingers up. That means that the book was not too hard." "What's the fist rule?" asked the teacher, guiding Kevin to review this self-monitoring strategy. "Well, you put your hand up, and then you turn to a page in the book. When you read it and miss a word, you put a finger down. If you put five fingers down, you try another page. You try this on five pages, and if you miss five words on each page you put five fingers down. Then you know the book is too hard." As Kevin described the strategy, he turned to the independence section of his portfolio and pulled out a written description of the fist-full-of-words rule that also included an illustration. "See, here it is if I forget it." "Now let's see how well you can retell what you remember," said his teacher. She handed the child a recorder with the play button ready to be pushed. "Go to the listening center and retell the story onto the tape as if you were telling it to a friend who had not read it," she said. The teacher's intuition, based on observations of Kevin's many attempts at writing the story, proved to be a correct assessment. Kevin could retell, almost exactly, what the author had written when he told it orally (see Figure 14.4). His ability to write by hand was his hindrance.

Kevin's teacher transcribed his retelling of *Tikki Tikki Tembo* that evening and brought it into school the next day for Kevin to read. He was astounded when he saw the amount of text he had produced. Because being able to use words orally does not ensure the ability to recognize those words when reading, the teacher suggested that they read it together chorally. This approach provided Kevin with the support he might have needed for word identification. As he read, the teacher softened her voice until she no longer read aloud with him, once she realized that he could read it on his own. His smile indicated his self-satisfaction. After reading his retelling, he remarked, "Gosh, I remembered a lot," a comment that led the teacher to the retelling checklist self-monitoring activity (Figure 14.5). "You're right, Kevin. You *did* remember a lot.

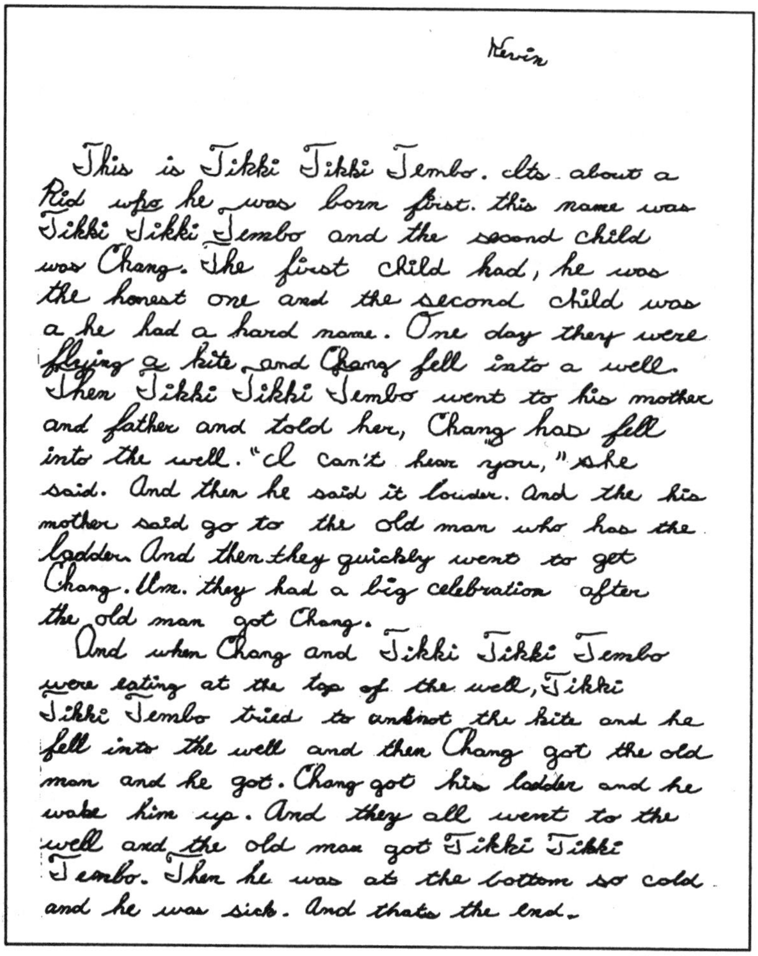

Kevin

This is Tikki Tikki Tembo. Its about a Kid who he was born first. this name was Tikki Tikki Tembo and the second child was Chang. The first child had, he was the honest one and the second child was a he had a hard name. One day they were flying a kite and Chang fell into a well. Then Tikki Tikki Tembo went to his mother and father and told her, Chang has fell into the well. "I can't hear you," she said. And then he said it louder. And the his mother said go to the old man who has the ladder. And then they quickly went to get Chang. Um, they had a big celebration after the old man got Chang.

And when Chang and Tikki Tikki Tembo were eating at the top of the well, Tikki Tikki Tembo tried to unknot the kite and he fell into the well and then Chang got the old man and he got. Chang got his ladder and he woke him up. And they all went to the well and the old man got Tikki Tikki Tembo. Then he was at the bottom so cold and he was sick. And thats the end.

FIGURE 14.4. Kevin's transcribed retelling of *Tikki Tikki Tembo*. Reprinted from Glazer (1998). Copyright 1998 by Christopher-Gordon. Reprinted by permission.

And you now know that you remember the most when you retell orally." "Yep," he confirmed. "I can talk it fast, but writing is ttttttooooooooooo slow." Next the teacher explained, "This retelling checklist will show you what you remembered, Kevin. Watch." She took a bookmark and placed it under the first category of "Setting" and read the first entry: "I began my retelling with an introduction." Kevin's face indicated that he was not quite sure what he was supposed to do. The teacher did not turn the statement into a question, for she knew that doing so might confuse him. She reread the statement and said, "Read the introduction to your retelling, Kevin." The child moved to the transcription and read aloud, "This is Tikki Tikki Tembo." He paused and then said, "I don't have one." "What do you mean, you don't have one?" asked the teacher. "Well, an introduction is a beginning—you know, like once upon a time. I don't have that." "So you just discovered that you did not include an introduction." "Uh-huh," said Kevin sheepishly. "That's terrific," continued the teacher. Kevin's sheepish expres-

STUDENT'S COMPOSITION AND RETELLING CHECKLIST

NAME _Kevin Jourdain_ DATE _7/2_

NAME OF COMPOSITION OR BOOK _Tikki Tikki Tembo_

AUTHOR _Arlene Mosel_

	YES	NO
SETTING:		
I began my composition/ retelling with an INTRODUCTION		✓
I told WHEN the story happened	✓	
I told WHERE the story happened	✓	
CHARACTERS:		
I told about the main character	✓	
I told about the other characters	✓	
PROBLEM:		
I told about the story problem or goal	✓	
EPISODES:		
I included episodes	✓	
SOLUTION:		
I told how the problem was solved or the goal was met	✓	
I told how the story ended	✓	
THEME:		
My story has a theme	✓	

When I compose/ retell on my own, I include: _When, where, main and other characters, problem, episodes, solution, theme_

The next time I compose/ retell, I need to remember to include these things: _Introduction_

FIGURE 14.5. Kevin's retelling checklist. Reprinted from Glazer (1998). Copyright 1998 by Christopher-Gordon. Reprinted by permission.

sion disappeared. "But I forgot it," he said, with some dismay. "You self-monitored your own work, Kevin. You checked it yourself. That's terrific. You know that you did not include an introduction. So what will you check, yes or no?" Kevin looked at the teacher who kept a neutral face. When he realized that it was up to him to make the decision, he checked "No." "Hurray for you, Kevin," said his teacher. You know that you did not include an introduction." And this is how the rest of the session continued. When Kevin reached the bottom of the sheet and read, "When I retell on my own, I include," he had no difficulty completing the sentence. Then he concluded, "All I have to do is to look at the checks and then I know what to write."

After two or three 5- to 7-minute sessions with each child, about half of this teacher's class was able to use the self-monitoring sheet independently. One youngster made a brilliant discovery. He came to me one day and said, "Dr. Glazer, I just cheated, but don't tell my teacher." "I'd love to know what you did, if you want to share it,"

I replied. "Well," continued 7-year-old Gary, "If you put the retelling sheet by the computer, you can write a story all in one piece." "How do you know that?" I asked, assuming that the child knew exactly the correct reason for his actions. "Well, I began my story with an introduction, and just like that, you know that you should write 'once upon a time,' and there's the introduction." "And then," I continued. "And then you go to the next one," Gary said. "I told where the story happened, and I wrote it happened in the swimming pool. So I wrote 'Once upon a time it happened in a swimming pool.' " Gary continued to read his story, moving back and forth with his finger, pointing to the statement on the retelling check sheet and the line or sentence in his story.

Kevin's four tries at writing his retelling were placed behind his oral transcription, which was followed by the retelling checklist. These were stapled together and positioned in the comprehension section of Kevin's portfolio. When he was asked why it went in this section, he responded, "Because it is reading stuff, and it's what I remembered." "You're right. Good readers tell what they read right after they read so they can remember it for a long time." "And," Kevin replied, "I did it best when I talked it into the tape recorder." "You sure did," responded the teacher. "You know that retelling orally is the best way for you to show how much you remember. Good for you!"

Composition

The assessment of composition has been a source of consternation for educators for years. Much of the alarm stems from the fact that defining writing has been controversial. When assessment goes beyond sentence construction and mechanics to include quality of ideas, organization, tone, and audience awareness, teachers often become anxious. This response is expected, because determining how well a person writes is often a subjective endeavor. Expectations and experiences of the teachers who guide children are different and therefore their guidelines for determining the products that reflect growth are also different.

Since the 1970s, however, writing instruction and assessment have reflected the notion that writing, like oral language, is developmental (Clay, 1975, Glazer & Searfoss, 1988; Glazer & Brown, 1993). Vygotsky noted, "as the child gains proficiency, task demands are raised until the child is functioning independently and the teacher functions as a supportive observer" (1962, p. 101). In other words, no amount of direct instruction can hasten the process. However, we know that environment, social interactions, modeling, and instruction facilitate growth (Glazer & Brown, 1993). Mechanics, spelling, punctuation, and handwriting, once the primary focus of writing instruction, are left until the end of a writing project. Students in classrooms from kindergarten through graduate school are writing and rewriting text and discussing these activities. Instruction focuses on guiding processes rather than the products themselves.

Portfolios are well suited to the self-assessment of the processes that produce written products, and they were initially used in classrooms for this purpose. A systematic portfolio that helps to determine growth in writing, however, has been challenging to create. With teachers, I have developed more than 20 tools that students are able to use to self-monitor their own writing. They range from tools that determine how the mechanical aspects of writing are used (spelling, punctuation, handwriting, when appropriate) to guides that assist students to understand the effectiveness of their writing. Space permits me to share only one of these: the About My Writing sheet.

Children need to know about their writing. They learn to write by knowing how they construct their text—and, therefore, how to change it. Seven-year-old Samantha wrote stories, lots of stories. Her sentences were all subject–verb–object constructions, typical of young or new writers. Pointing this pattern out to her may have made her cognizant of how she constructed the text, but providing her with a tool to discover this in her own writing was more effective. Samantha and her teacher sat down next to each other with a copy of her story (Figure 14.6), and the "About My Writing" self-monitoring sheet (Figure 14.7). As is the routine, the child knew to place the index card under the first sentence. "I am writing fiction," she read, and quickly said "No," as she wrote it in the appropriate column on the chart. After several sentences, the teacher left her to complete the self-monitoring of her writing independently. Following lunch, Samantha came to her teacher with her revised paper (Figure 14.8) and remarked enthusiastically, "Mrs. Shapiro, I just wrote the longest sentence in the whole world!" "Wow, I'd love to see it if you want to share it with me." "Sure," responded Samantha, as she proudly placed the paper on her teacher's lap. "See, it has 46 words!" The child did, indeed, write one very long sentence. Although it is only a series of simple sentences connected with the conjunction *and*, the construction was deliberate. Samantha was able to use her original piece of writing and with the guidance of the self-monitoring tool was able to alter sentence constructions intentionally.

Word Study

Word study is just that, the study of words. How words are created, their derivations, roots, and origins, and how language has changed through the centuries are all part of the fascination that makes learning about our language inviting. Spelling is also part of the study of words. For many children, American English spellings appear unique and are often frustrating. The word *enough*, for example, is often spelled ENUFF by children, and logically so. The double *f* at the end of the word, rather than the *gh*, makes sense from a sound–symbol point of view. (See Templeton, Bear, and Madura, Chapter

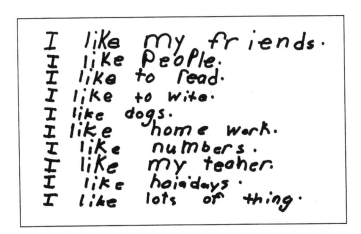

FIGURE 14.6. Samantha's first draft. Reprinted from Glazer (1998). Copyright 1998 by Christopher-Gordon. Reprinted by permission.

About My Writing

	Comments
I am writing fiction.	No
I am writing nonfiction.	Yes
I get ideas for writing from_____ _____.	Books
I am writing a story.	No
I use pictures to help tell about my writing.	No
I am writing an autobiography.	Yes
I begin sentences the same way.	Yes
I begin sentences differently.	No
I write "and" a lot in my compositions.	No
I write short sentences.	yes
I write long sentences.	No
I use different words when I write.	No
I write best by hand.	No
I write best with a computer.	Yes
I write best when I dictate to someone.	Yes

Name: __Samantha__ Date: __1-20__

FIGURE 14.7. "About My Writing" checklist. Reprinted from Glazer (1998). Copyright 1998 by Christopher-Gordon. Reprinted by permission.

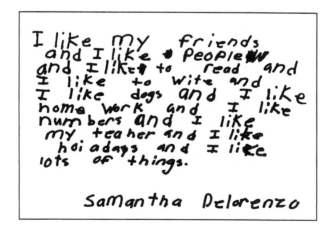

FIGURE 14.8. Samantha's revised writing. Reprinted from Glazer (1998). Copyright 1998 by Christopher-Gordon. Reprinted by permission.

8, this volume, for a more detailed discussion of the patterns in English spelling.) To help teachers and students examine and understand spelling needs, I developed a spelling trend assessment that is categorized in our portfolios in the section titled "word study." Our work with one student, Teresa, provides a window into this particular assessment tool.

Eleven-year-old Teresa was directed to read through her science report to find misspelled words. She found one, looked up at her teacher for a nod of approval, and then circled the word. "You were able to discover that you misspelled the word, Teresa," her teacher noted. The child hung her head sheepishly, indicating that she was either embarrassed or even fearful of consequences. "Teresa, it is really wonderful that you are able to find your spelling mistakes," commented her teacher. "That means you are a good detective of your writing." The child's surprised look at the compliment for discovering an error reminded us that we need to consistently and explicitly commend students for their use of self-checking and error-detection activities.

I encourage teachers to guide children to notice their spellings only after they have completed, and are satisfied with, the contents of their writing. After they've written several drafts, they are asked to read the first line of their composition and circle all of the words that they believe are misspelled. Then they are guided to write each of those words in the first column of the "My Spelling" sheet (Figure 14.9). They are then directed to read the rest of their writing and circle words they believe are misspelled and write these in the first column of the spelling sheet, as well. The second column is the "first try" one. Youngsters are asked to try and write and then try again. If that doesn't work, they are guided to get the correct spelling from a friend, the dictionary, or their teacher. The important part of this self-monitoring tool is for them to notice the differences between their spellings and the correct version. This exercise helps teachers identify the degree of knowledge children have regarding the spellings of the English language. It also helps us determine how much students know about how our language works. Jason noticed that he confuses *ir* and *ur*. "That's logical," commented his teacher. "They sound exactly the same, even though they are spelled differently." The teacher then took this as an opportunity to teach the *ir–ur–er* spelling rule, which informs children that all three endings sound the same. It was a relevant lesson for Jason because in order to share his story, the words needed to be spelled correctly.

Independence

A regular routine of recording one's own progress is rarely carried out in many classrooms. This is unfortunate, because self-assessment is a review process that provides youngsters with a special confidence that may not be achieved when teachers determine progress. Youngsters experience power in discovering what they know; there is even more command of self-capabilities when youngsters are able to determine what they need to learn (or what they don't know). We have developed a daily progress report form at our center that is used by both teachers and their students for making decisions about where instruction is needed (Figure 14.10). After 20 or so minutes of teacher guidance, children are able to determine their own strengths and needs using their portfolio data, and they record their findings on the progress report form.

My Spelling

My Spelling	Try Again	Real Spelling	What's Different?
english	English	English	I used a small e and made it a capital.
wrot	wrot	wrote	I switched the o and r. I forgot the silent e
interisting	interisting	interesting	I wrote is for es. also wrote is instead of e
writting	writing	writing	I forgot the double consonant rule.
soker	soker	soccer	I messed up alot.
hir	her	her	I mix up ir and er a lot of times.

My name: _____Jason_____   Date: __October 13, 2015__

These spelling words came from my __dialog journal__

FIGURE 14.9. "My Spelling" sheet.

Progress Report Form

Your Name: _Dorothy Kim_ Today's Date: _6/28/04_

Your Teacher's Name: _Laura_ Your Age: _9_

What I Can Do	What I Need	My Teacher's Job
• We can add more details • reread • work together to figure out the main idea • look for details they can help put the story in order • look for connecting words	– add a endings – introduction to get the reader excited – a middle – include a lot of details	– help us learn how to include introduction, middle, and ending

FIGURE 14.10. Progress report form.

We begin self-assessment activities at the completion of a lesson, at the end of a specific time segment, at the end of the morning, afternoon, or the day. In this example, 9-year-old Jonathan was able to review his activities all at once. After he worked on a story that he had been writing, he was able to complete his progress report form for that activity independently. The amount of work reviewed depends upon the student's ability to handle one or more of the events experienced during the school day. Jonathan sat with his teacher in a 10-minute conference for a first review. His teacher took out her portfolio and turned to the section labeled *Composition*. Jonathan followed and did the same without need for verbal directions. "Jonathan," said his teacher, "You did a lot today." "Yeah," replied the child, "I sure did!" "Take out the story that you're writing." Jonathan immediately searched the section of his folder labeled *composition* and pulled out his story. "This is your second draft," his teacher commented. "Yep," replied Jonathan, nodding his head affirmatively. He also took out the "Student's Composition and Retelling Checklist" which he had used earlier to determine what he had included in the story and what he still needed in order to finish it. "So," began the teacher, "what did you learn about your story writing?" "Um," he began, pointing to the first item on his progress report form, "I write with a lot of details." "How do you know that?" his teacher asked. "Well, on this sheet (*pointing to the composition checklist*) it told me that I had a lot of episodes and that means I had a lot of details." "Good for you," remarked his teacher. "You are able to use the story composition checklist to discover what you can do. All right, now, what do you need to add to your story?" "That's easy," remarked the youngster. "I need to add an ending." "How do you know that?" asked his teacher. "Here," pointing to the composition checklist. "I saw 'I told how the story ended,' and didn't do it, so I didn't check it and that's how I found out." "And then you wrote 'add an ending' here" (*pointing to the first item under the "What I Need" section of the progress report form*). "Yep," responded the child, and the discussion continued.

The young man completed his progress report form self-assessment sheet and filed it in the appropriate place in the Independence section of his portfolio. "It goes here," he commented, "because I wrote it myself, and it's about what I did today."

The type of activity we used with Jonathan is important becomes it helps students develop self-assessment routines as they complete each task. But we also want students to reflect more generally so that they gain an overall understanding of themselves as readers. I illustrate this point with an example from Morgan, age 11, who is considered by all of the people in his life to be a fine reader. He is achieving as expected and in some areas of language arts, even better than most sixth graders. The responses on his "Good Reader" sheet (Figure 14.11), the first piece of data in our children's portfolios, indicate that he understands something about the reading process. He knows, for example, that in order to clarify ideas, he must read the material at least more than once. He also knows that he must be able to recognize and understand the meanings of words in order to comprehend successfully. Rereading helps not only to recognize words but also to guide readers to see if there is more than one meaning to a specific word (or phrase) in the sentence. Still his response concerning his ability to read was ambiguous. He said, "I am an OK reader but I do not comprehend very well." Although this is not the case, the youngster diminished his reading competence. We found that 93% of 1,500 youngsters ages 6–17 we served in the center "sat on a fence" when asked to identify their abilities as readers. Responses include:

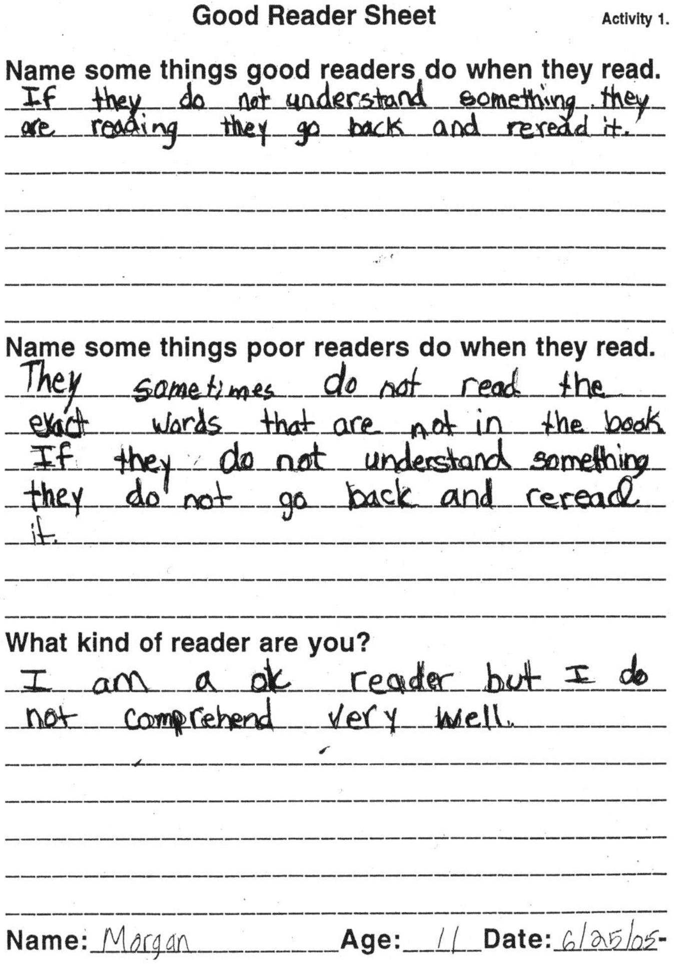

Good Reader Sheet   Activity 1.

Name some things good readers do when they read.

If they do not understand something they are reading they go back and reread it.

_____

_____

_____

_____

_____

Name some things poor readers do when they read.

They sometimes do not read the exact words that are not in the book If they do not understand something they do not go back and reread it.

_____

_____

What kind of reader are you?

I am a ok reader but I do not comprehend very well.

_____

_____

_____

_____

_____

Name: Morgan _____ **Age:** 11 **Date:** 6/25/05

FIGURE 14.11. "Good Reader" sheet.

- "I'm not good, just a little good." (age 6)
- "I'm a reader that makes mistakes and don't know how to say the words right." (age 9)
- "I think that I'm half way in between a good reader and a poor reader because I think about the vocabulary words and make sure I understand what the character is feeling and thinking. But I also don't ask about the book, and I don't understand the book, but I still keep reading. I also don't learn anything from some books that I read." (age 11)

Important to children's successes is their perceptions of themselves as readers and writers. We know that personal expectations can affect their performance. Students need to have knowledge about themselves as writers. We use several strategies, such as the one shown above, to assist children in discovering what they will share about themselves and their literacy skills. Morgan's statement, "I think I am pretty good but I can do better," could indicate that he may not be sure of his writing ability, but more than likely, he's hedging his bet. In a follow-up discussion to this response, Morgan's teacher asked, "Tell me, Morgan, what about your reading could be better?" The child paused for a moment and responded, "I don't know." "Then," his teacher asked, "why did you say you could do better?" Morgan shrugged his shoulders, indicating that he probably does not know or is cautious about sharing his reasons.

The new classroom environment may have caused him to "size up" the situation before sharing his ideas about his writing. Being modest, that is, not admitting to gold-star status, is influenced by our U.S. (and other) culture, which guides us to think of sharing assets as immodest or disrespectful. This 11-year-old, in his new school setting, was probably intuitively aware of this unwritten rule and the fact that to contradict a teacher's opinion concerning his ability could hurt his classroom standing. His second sentence, "The most problem I have is that I repeat words over too many times" informs us that this child has had this aspect of his writing pointed out to him many times.

A REVIEW OF OUR CLASSROOM PORTFOLIOS

The portfolio described in these pages serves as a management tool that guides children to know what to do when they come to class. They are able to secure their materials, get to work, and continue without guidance from their teachers. The folders are organized so that youngsters are able to categorize their work with understanding, which also enhances learning and the recall of information. The portfolio is also a productive tool for illustrating growth over time. Children are able to compare their first contributions in the routine activities daily, weekly, or monthly. Monitoring growth using the many self-assessment sheets allows each to discuss strengths and needs. For the teachers in our center, portfolios provide a guiding document that helps children identify what they know and what they need to learn. Each child manages his or her own portfolio, organizes it, uses it independently, and keeps it with his or her materials all the time. What better way to convince children that it's *their* work and *their* actions that facilitate learning.

REFERENCES

Amrein, A. L., & Berliner, D. C. (2002). *The impact of high-stakes tests on student academic performance: An analysis of NAEP results in states with high-stakes tests and ACT, SAT, and AP test results in states with high school graduation exams.* Tempe, Arizona State University, Education Policy Studies Laboratory. Available at *www.greatlakescenter.org/research.html.*

Braun, J. I., & Mislevy, R. (2005). Intuitive test theory. *Phi Delta Kappan, 86,* 489–497.

Burros Institute of Mental Measurements. (1999). *Tests in print V: An index to tests, test reviews and the literature on specific tests.* Lincoln: University of Nebraska Press.

Clay, M. (1975). *What did I write?* Auckland, New Zealand: Heinemann.

Glazer, S. M. (1998). *Assessment IS instruction: Reading, writing, spelling and phonics for all learners.* Norwood, MA: Christopher-Gordon.

Glazer, S. M., & Brown, C. S. (Eds.). (1993). *Portfolios and beyond: Collaborative assessment in reading and writing*. Norwood, MA: Christopher-Gordon.

Glazer, S. M., & Searfoss, L. W. (1988). *Reading diagnosis and instruction: A C.A.L.M. approach*. Englewood Cliffs, NJ: Prentice-Hall.

Johnson, J., & Immerwahr, J. (1994). *First things first: What Americans expect from public schools*. New York: Public Agenda.

Meier, T. (1994). Why standardized tests are bad. In B. Bigelow, L. Christensen, S. Karp, B. Miner, & B. Peterson (Eds.), *Rethinking our classrooms: Teaching for equity and social justice* (pp. 171–175). Milwaukee, WI: Rethinking Schools.

Morrow, L. M. (1988). Retelling stories as a diagnostic tool. In S. M. Glazer, L. W. Searfoss, & L. M. Gentile (Eds.), *Reexamining reading diagnosis: New trends and procedures* (pp. 128–149). Newark, DE: International Reading Association.

Murphy, S. (1997). Literacy assessment and the politics of identity. *Reading and Writing Quarterly, 13*, 261–278.

Routman, R. (1996). *Literacy at the crossroads: Critical talk about reading, writing, and other teaching dilemmas*. Portsmouth, NH: Heinemann.

Sacks, P. (1999). *Standardized minds: The high price of America's testing culture and what we can do to change it*. Cambridge, MA: Perseus Books.

Taylor, K., & Watson, S. (1997). Co-opting standardized tests in the service of learning. *Phi Delta Kappan, 79*, 66–70.

Vygotsky, L. S. (1962). *Thought and language*. Cambridge, MA: MIT Press.

CHILDREN'S BOOKS

Finchler, J. (2000). *Testing Miss Malarkey*. New York: Walker.

Mosel, A. (1999). *Tikki Tikki Tembo*. New York: Scholastic.

Zemach, M. (1986). *The three wishes: An old story*. New York: Farrar, Straus, & Giroux.

CHAPTER 15

Formative Uses of Assessment

CASES FROM THE PRIMARY GRADES

Camille L. Z. Blachowicz
Roberta Buhle
Sharon Frost
Ann Bates

Aquick review of educational journals will reveal numerous references to "formative assessment," the type of assessment that teachers and other educators can use to make instructional and curricular decisions for their students. The main goal of formative assessment is to inform teachers of the active knowledge, skills, and strategies that their students have under their control and to point to instruction that will move them along the path to learning.

Although teachers are subject to more and more assessment requirements (Bates, 2005), the process by which this assessment leads to instructional decision making is still relatively unexamined. Black and Wiliam (1998), in a perceptive and timely article, refer to this transition from assessment to instruction as the "black box" of assessment—the hidden process by which teachers make sense of assessment in their own instructional contexts. In this chapter we share what we learned about this process as we worked together on Literacy Partners, a staff development project to build instructional and leadership capacity in low-performing urban schools.

ASSESSMENT AS THE FOUNDATION FOR STAFF DEVELOPMENT

For many reasons, we chose to make assessment the key to the staff development that takes place in Literacy Partners. First, assessment focuses the work on student progress, which binds the teachers and the staff developers together in a common cause. Secondly, instructionally focused assessment develops habits of close observation and highlights the critical elements of literacy development and instruction. This focus relates all staff development efforts to a framework for instruction. And, finally, the examination of student outcomes is essential to evaluating the progress of a school-improvement project (Blachowicz, Obrochta, & Fogelberg, 2005).

Accordingly, we have looked closely at how teachers use assessment to make instructional decisions in their classrooms. Further, we have examined the ways in which we, as teacher educators, can play a part in developing school leaders' capability for assessment-informed instruction. Lastly, as reflective practitioners ourselves, we have examined these processes to further develop our own work.

In this chapter we share what we learned by first describing the instrument we used with primary teachers to develop an initial framework for assessment-informed instruction. This instrument is the Illinois Snapshot of Early Literacy, a standardized test designed to make the transition between assessment and instruction as seamless as possible. Then we present three cases of its use: (1) assessment as a formative tool for examining classroom instruction, (2) assessment as a formative focus for the professional development of literacy leaders, and (3) assessment as a formative tool for teacher reflection. We conclude with overall observations about using assessment to inform instruction in primary-grade settings.

THE ILLINOIS SNAPSHOT OF EARLY LITERACY

The *Illinois Snapshot of Early Literacy* (ISEL-K/1) (Barr et al., 2002) was developed to assess key beginning literacy skills of primary students in order for teachers to plan meaningful classroom instruction. The ISEL-K/1 is unique for several reasons. First, it is a standardized literacy assessment that has many of the characteristics of informal assessment. That is, it provides qualitative information pertinent to instructional planning; it can be administered in a brief period of time (5–20 minutes) without extensive training by classroom teachers; and significant insights can be gained from the ISEL-K/1 results that facilitate planning and implementation of differentiated instruction.

Second, unlike many standardized assessments that focus on a single aspect of reading development, such as phonemic awareness, letter sound recognition, or fluency, the array of snapshots included in the ISEL-K/1 provides a comprehensive overview of a child's competencies in a variety of vital literacy skills needed for success in reading. The term *snapshot* is used for each subtest to suggest a pattern of reading behaviors, in the same way a photograph captures a picture of person *at a moment in time*. The ISEL-K/1 snapshots assess the following skills:

- Alphabet recognition
- Story listening
- Phonemic awareness
- One-to-one matching
- Letter sounds
- Spelling

- Word recognition
- Passage accuracy and comprehension

Third, the ISEL-K/1 was designed *with* teachers: Master teachers and reading specialists across the state of Illinois were interviewed as the first step in the design process. Then artifacts and assessments from their classrooms, schools, and districts were collected and used as the basis for the design of the snapshots. Finally, each snapshot assessment was subjected to over a year of field testing in a variety of classrooms across the state. To the extent possible, the snapshots were holistic in nature and replicated the types of activities teachers might use in more informal assessment—listening and responding to a story, naming alphabet letters, using developmental spelling, and reading and responding to small books. (The complete assessment and manuals can be downloaded from the Illinois State Board of Education website, *www.isbe.net*, or from the Reading Center website at National-Louis University, *www2.nl.edu/reading_center*.

CASE 1: ASSESSMENT AS A FORMATIVE TOOL FOR EXAMINING CLASSROOM INSTRUCTION

Systems literature sometimes uses the term *silo communication* to describe an organization in which people or groups do not communicate with other people or groups within their system. There is a tendency to operate as though each department or person is a separate entity, and each unit frequently makes decisions that do not take other aspects of the organization into consideration.

Even more complex is the lack of communication that sometimes occurs *within* a person's, or a group's, thinking; that is, the tendency not to use or connect one known body of information with another. It is as though the individual or group has two separate "silos" of related knowledge that do not inform each other. This metaphor may describe teachers' thinking when they make instructional decisions with apparently little regard for available assessment data. Our work suggests that it takes more than just presentation of data to impact teacher thinking. Rather, teachers may need coaching and facilitation to learn how to study their data and to engage in the kind of problem solving and root analysis of progress that helps to build bridges between students' assessment data and teachers' knowledge of how to deliver their curriculum (Bernhardt, 2004). This approach requires sensitive leadership approaches that include discussions to clarify, encourage, reflect, and negotiate these two bodies of information (Glickman, 2002).

In this first case, we describe our experience working through this process with kindergarten teachers in two districts. One was a very large, high-performing district where the ISEL-K/1 was administered to a carefully randomized group of incoming kindergarten students. The scores were intended to inform a district kindergarten teacher committee that had been chosen to develop and implement a year-long pilot of a new literacy curriculum for their grade level. The district's literacy director presented and facilitated a discussion of the ISEL-K/1 results (Figure 15.1). Teachers on the committee did not seem surprised by the students' above-average scores and agreed that the data seemed to fairly represent the majority of their students, although they all also

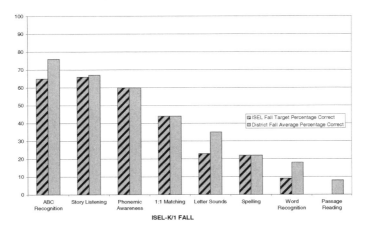

FIGURE 15.1. Fall kindergarten ISEL-K/1 average percentage correct: District 1.

agreed that each school had at least one group of students that did not score as well as the others.

Immediately following an extensive and rich discussion of the test results, the kindergarten teachers began to develop their plans for alphabet recognition and letter sound knowledge activities they would include in their pilot curriculum. Meredith, an experienced teacher known for high end-of-year literacy outcomes of her kindergarten students, described a whole-group, letter-of-the-week curriculum that included extensive work in letter recognition for all students. She suggested more complex activities, such as emergent writing, but she did not propose beginning these until later in the semester. Several people on the committee agreed with Meredith's suggestion, and no alternative plan was discussed. It was as though Meredith's (and the group's) knowledge about, and discussion of, the district's high fall alphabet recognition and letter sound knowledge on the ISEL-K/1 was situated in one silo of their thinking, and their extensive internal menus of literacy activities and rich literacy curriculum knowledge were situated in another silo, and neither silo communicated with, or informed, the other.

This was perplexing for several reasons. First, Meredith and her group had seen and discussed the ISEL-K/1 information that clearly suggested that extensive whole-group activities in letter recognition were not necessary for many incoming students. Second, those same alphabet recognition scores, combined with the letter sound knowledge and phonemic awareness scores, suggested that many beginning kindergarten students in this district could respond positively to earlier opportunities to write. Furthermore, during previous in-service meetings, the group discussed and advocated writing as an excellent way to teach *multiple* literacy skills, including such as letter sound knowledge, phonemic awareness, and concept of word. Our observations led us to pose two questions: (1) Why were these teachers not combining their knowledge of effective instruction with the data they had? (2) How might literacy support staffs and building administrators help well-informed teachers such as Meredith and her colleagues build bridges between assessment and instruction, two key areas of related knowledge?

In this case, the literacy director chose to prompt the kindergarten teachers with questions such as these:

"Do any of these ISEL-K/1 scores suggest a different kind of literacy opportunity for your students at the beginning of the year?"

"Is there something you could do sooner in the year, given this assessment information?"

"What does the district average in alphabet recognition tell you about your students?"

As teachers responded to these questions, an important issue surfaced. Teachers explained that many other parts of their kindergarten curricula were tied to a letter-of-the-week routine, including activities in social science, math, and even free-choice options in the students' play areas. Clearly, changing the letter-of-the-week curriculum could have a domino effect, impacting other aspects of a well-established and successful curriculum.

Acknowledging and respecting how difficult this would be, the literacy coach asked whether the teachers could add a small writing activity at the beginning of the year to see how students responded. Teachers agreed and later reported that they were impressed with the sophistication of the students' early writing attempts. Over time, the teachers cut back on their whole-group letter sound instruction and used the extra time to give *all* students earlier opportunities to write, while providing intensive letter instruction only to those students whose ISEL-K/1 scores indicated the need. In this case, the literacy director had negotiated respectfully and sensitively to construct a bridge between the district's ISEL-K/1 scores and the kindergarten teachers' instructional expertise.

In a second district, a literacy coach worked with a single kindergarten teacher to reflect on literacy growth of the students in her class, comparing beginning-of-the-year (Figure 15.2) and end-of-year (Figure 15.3) ISEL-K/1 average scores. The coach and teacher hoped to use the information to inform decisions about the following year's curriculum and instruction.

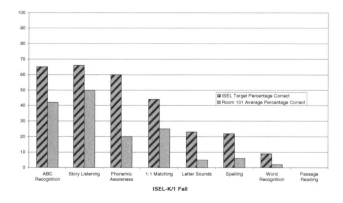

FIGURE 15.2. Fall kindergarten ISEL-K/1 average percentage correct: District 2.

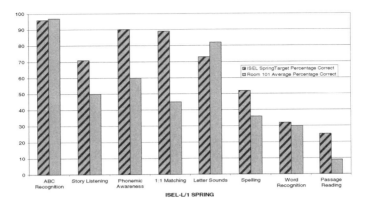

FIGURE 15.3. Spring kindergarten ISEL-K/1 average percentage correct: District 2.

Here, the school's literacy coach first prompted the teacher to compare the two charts and to acknowledge that these students had achieved the target scores in three of the snapshots—alphabet recognition, letter sound knowledge, and word recognition—even exceeding the target score in alphabet recognition and letter sound knowledge. Through an additional set of questions, the literacy coach helped the teacher to see that the snapshots in which growth was the greatest were all measures of individual item knowledge. The areas in which students had not begun to "catch up" to the target were snapshots in which they had to orchestrate multiple items and perform more complex tasks, such as spelling, matching words in a sentence, and trying to read a simple book.

Unlike the teachers in the first example, this teacher had only recently been provided with rich, capacity-building professional development. As a result, to assist the teacher in making effective use of the assessment data, the coach needed to do more than ask probing questions. There was a need to explain the difference between item knowledge (alphabet recognition) and complex forms of literacy knowledge such as passage reading and spelling. As in the earlier example, the coach's goal was still to build bridges, but this time between the teacher's knowledge of the ISEL-K/1 assessment scores and her increasing knowledge of how literacy develops. The coach concluded with a productive offer: "Let me show you how the kind of instruction that helps children acquire these more complex forms of literacy knowledge might look. We can use a big book or a chart story to talk about it."

We speculate that teachers in each of these two very different school districts had two silos of knowledge—one for their curriculum and instructional plans and one for their assessment data. Fortunately both districts provided an instructional leader who helped teachers to begin a conversation that could help them build bridges between their two "silos." We learned that, even when assessments such as the ISEL-K/1 use a format and routine that are closely tied to classroom practice, simply encouraging or telling teachers to use assessment data to inform instruction is unlikely to result in meaningful change in instructional practices—unless such pronouncements are accompanied by the facilitation needed to help teachers begin the process.

CASE 2: ASSESSMENT AS A FORMATIVE FOCUS FOR THE PROFESSIONAL DEVELOPMENT OF LITERACY LEADERS

The 10 schools in the Literacy Partners project had something in common: Their students were failing to make expected progress in reading. They had tried a variety of solutions, including test-preparation workbooks, computer software programs focused on individualized practice in phonics, and extended school days for students determined to be at risk. Unfortunately, these efforts had not achieve the desired results. While our schools were frantically applying Band-Aids, the core issue was being ignored: how to analyze and modify the curriculum.

The Literacy Partners project attempted to make the process of curriculum analysis and modification a bit easier by enrolling lead literacy teachers and core classroom teachers (grade-level representatives from each school) in the same professional development class, Teaching Beginning Reading, which was located within the district. The idea was to have classroom teachers and lead literacy teachers hear the same message at the same time and to accompany this message with instructional strategy trials, sharing, and feedback.

Organizing Staff Development Content and Process

To develop a shared vocabulary and knowledge base, the classroom teachers and lead literacy teachers received instruction in theoretical frameworks and instructional strategies to support children in developing the essential elements of literacy. The ISEL-K/1 was the portal to begin the conversation about curriculum. All of the children in kindergarten through second grade had been assessed using the ISEL-K/1 and the school lead literacy teachers, who attended a separate monthly session on leadership and coaching, had examined their students' ISEL-K/1 scores to identify the needed changes for their school's literacy curriculum. To emphasize the connection between assessment and instruction right from the start, a grid of instructional strategies related to the assessment categories of the ISEL-K/1 provided the organizational framework for the content of the professional development course (see Figure 15.4).

The class met once a month, a schedule that was intended to give classroom teachers and lead literacy teachers adequate time to practice and become proficient in using the focal strategy that was introduced in each class meeting. Each session began with a presentation of the theoretical framework for a focal strategy. The strategies included read-aloud, shared reading, word and picture sorts, language experience approach, interactive writing, journal writing, poem of the week, and independent and guided reading—all with an emphasis on integration and practice in multiple areas. Class participants were encouraged to ask questions and make connections to their own experiences. Then they were introduced to ways to use the strategy to support children in developing proficiency in areas assessed on the ISEL-K/1.

Following each class meeting, lead literacy teachers and core classroom teachers were expected to try the focal strategy with their students and bring related feedback and artifacts to the next meeting. We called these "strategy trials," and the lead teachers assumed the role of strategy coach.

	Letter recognition	Letter sounds	Phonemic awareness	One-to-one matching	Spelling	Sight words	Passage reading	Vocabulary and comprehension	Fluency
Read-aloud								X	X
Shared reading	X	X	X	X		X		X	X
Word and picture sorts	X	X	X						
Language experience approach	X	X	X	X	X	X	X		
Interactive writing	X	X	X	X	X	X		X	
Poem of the week	X	X	X	X	X	X		X	X
Guided reading		X		X		X	X	X	X
Journal writing	X	X	X	X	X				
Independent reading				X		X	X	X	X

FIGURE 15.4. Strategy grid.

Sweeney (2003) recommends that lead literacy teachers follow three steps in helping teachers implement a new instructional strategy: (1) provide observation with feedback, (2) conduct demonstration lessons, and (3) utilize co-teaching. Consistent with this model, the core classroom teacher taught the first lesson using the strategy while the lead literacy teacher observed. Although teachers are often uncomfortable being observed, the goal of this observation was not evaluative but rather as a basis for discussion and feedback.

After the lesson, the classroom teacher and the literacy leader scheduled a debriefing conference. The tone of the conference was more collaborative than evaluative. The classroom teacher took the lead and discussed his or her perceptions of the lesson. The classroom teacher and the literacy lead teacher problem-solved any challenges that the classroom teacher encountered, and they planned the next lesson together. The literacy lead teacher then taught the second lesson as a demonstration lesson. This lesson was also followed with a debriefing conference.

In the next phase the literacy lead teacher and the core classroom teacher co-planned and co-taught a lesson. When the teacher and the literacy lead teacher were satisfied with the strategy implementation, plans were made to demonstrate the strategy for other classroom teachers. Lead literacy teachers used two ways to demonstrate strategies for other teachers. One way was to invite the other classroom teachers into the core teacher's classroom to observe as he or she taught his or her own students. The other way was to have the core classroom teacher visit other classrooms and teach the lesson to the students in that class. Often, both approaches were used over the course of the month.

After following each of these steps, the core classroom teachers and the literacy lead teacher were comfortable and experienced with the focal strategy. As well, some of the other teachers in the school had been introduced to the strategy. The literacy lead teacher and the core classroom teachers then planned a professional development workshop for all of the other teachers in the school. The teachers in the school reported that these workshops were especially helpful because they were aware that the recommended strategies had been implemented in their school with their students. This addressed the commonly heard concern that "this [approach] will never work in *our* school with *our* students."

At the next class meeting, the lead literacy teachers and core classroom teachers shared their experiences implementing the strategy. Teachers often brought children's literature, artifacts, and samples of children's work. They shared management tips and attempted to problem-solve the challenges and pitfalls that were encountered in implementing the strategy. As each discussion ended, the course instructors reminded the teachers that using this strategy would support the curriculum changes needed to help their students become more proficient readers.

Problem Solving

Though our process helped core classroom teachers learn new instructional strategies and lead literacy teachers learn ways to help implement new instruction, learning a strategy in isolation isn't very likely to have a lasting or measurable impact on the literacy curriculum. Lead literacy teachers quickly learned that some classroom teachers were viewing the professional development workshops as "the strategy of the month." They were willing to have the literacy lead teacher come in and do some demonstration lessons. They would even teach a couple of lessons for the literacy lead teacher to observe. However, they would soon return to their regular instructional routines.

Lead literacy teachers, in their separate coaching meetings, engaged in several tasks to prepare to support teachers in making meaningful changes to their school's curriculum. Each lead literacy teacher completed the "whole-school reading audit" (Ogle, 2002), which provided a general overview of the school's literacy program. This process helped them to objectively identify the strengths and needs of their school's literacy program. Many of the lead literacy teachers were surprised that their perceptions of their school's literacy program were very different from what they actually found taking place in the school.

Next, they took a closer look at what was happening in the classrooms. The lead literacy teachers each selected one student to shadow during the reading/language arts block (2 hours of instruction). The purpose was to find out how much instructional time was being devoted to the essential elements of reading and writing and how much time the student was spending on connected reading and writing.

Finally, the lead literacy teachers completed a critical examination of their school's reading textbooks. In many classrooms the reading textbook *was* the reading curriculum. The lead literacy teachers highlighted lessons that supported the students' areas of needed and developed supplemental lessons as needed. They analyzed textbook selections to determine the level of difficulty. They ordered their series' accompanying "leveled books" to provide instructional level texts for all students. In some cases, the "below-level" books were still too difficult for students, and additional, easier "little books" were ordered.

At this point, the lead literacy teachers had amassed comprehensive and pertinent information about their school's literacy program and teachers' instructional practices, including:

- ISEL-K/1 scores for students in grades K–2
- Suggested instructional groupings based on the ISEL-K/1 scores
- The whole-school reading audit
- Observations from shadowing the student
- The reading textbook examination

The lead literacy teachers met with the core classroom teachers and school administrators to discuss the information. Based on the discussion, the literacy team made plans to implement the needed changes in the literacy curriculum, and they did so as they worked with teachers during grade-level meetings.

One example of curricular change that occurred in most classrooms was the daily read-aloud. The whole-school audit revealed that a daily read-aloud was taking place routinely in kindergarten classrooms, but less so in first- and second-grade classrooms. As children progressed through the grades, teachers apparently believed that it was more important to devote time to pencil-and-paper tasks, and they deemphasized reading aloud.

The lead literacy teachers encouraged daily read-alouds by modeling the practice in classrooms. Their demonstration lessons showed teachers that reading aloud was an effective way to teach vocabulary and comprehension skills. The lead literacy teachers also collected and circulated books that made good read-alouds. One literacy lead teacher volunteered to do special read-alouds on days in which the class was not scheduled for any special classes, such as physical education or music. With the observed increase in daily read-alouds across almost all K–2 classrooms, the lead literacy teachers and classroom teachers looked forward to improved ISEL-K/1 scores on the story-listening snapshot.

The curricular change that presented the greatest challenge was guided reading. The ISEL-K/1 scores in most classrooms showed that children were reading at a range of abilities. However, most teachers taught reading to the entire class at the same time, using grade-level texts. Teachers were reluctant to teach reading in small groups. They expressed concern about management issues. Lead literacy teachers attempted to support this change by helping teachers set up learning centers and modeling guided-reading lessons. They also established book rooms with leveled books for teachers to use with small groups. Some lead literacy teachers even developed extension activities to accompany the books.

Guided reading did become part of the daily routine in the classrooms of the core teachers, and some of the other teachers are making steady progress toward implementing guided reading with all students. We credit the ISEL-K/1 and its evidence of students' individual and varied learning needs for helping teachers reach the conclusion that they could no longer justify whole-class reading instruction.

CASE 3: ASSESSMENT AS A FORMATIVE TOOL FOR TEACHER REFLECTION

In addition to helping teachers and lead literacy teachers analyze instruction and curriculum and plan and execute staff development, the ISEL-K/1 also proved to be a tool to stimulate teacher reflection and gave us a basis for looking at the ways in which teachers develop and integrate their philosophies of assessment and instruction. This aspect of the project also provided qualitative data for us as teacher educators to reflect on our own learning and work.

Because of federal initiatives, kindergarten has been one level at which teacher perceptions and attitudes have undergone substantial scrutiny. For this reason we interviewed kindergarten teachers, using the issue of assessment to focus our discussion. The inclusion of teacher voices through interpretive research acknowledges the role they play in the success or failure of reform efforts for accountability. Their perspective is often absent in discussions around new initiatives, especially those related to school reform. Yet implementation lies squarely with the classroom teacher, whose belief in a program is essential to its success. Abelmann and Elmore (1999) found that when external policy was not aligned with teachers' expectations for achievement, teachers essentially ignored the policy and followed the internal, or school, accountability system. Similarly, Price (2001) found that teachers view assessment in a contextual framework: what they learned was determined by their own beliefs and experiences.

The case study of Sandy (a pseudonym), one of several constructed from teacher interviews during ISEL-K/1 trials, illustrates the value of listening to teachers as they reflect on their beliefs and classroom practices regarding assessment.

Sandy is a master kindergarten teacher who, when she entered the ISEL-K/1 project, had already been assessing her students regularly using materials of her own design. For Sandy, the ISEL-K/1, with its sponsorship by the Illinois State Board of Education, represented new and welcome attention to early literacy. She saw this as hopeful: Those in decision-making roles were finally acknowledging the importance of her life's work. Sandy's reflections indicated a desire to use ISEL-K/1 data to better inform her instruction, and to advocate for perspective on kindergarten curriculum to those in positions of power.

Sandy thrived on discussing educational issues; armed with data to support her positions, she was eager to confront those in decision-making roles. "Let me get on my soapbox," she would say and laugh as she launched into a diatribe. Sandy entered the ISEL-K/1 project with confidence and curiosity. She expected her students to perform well on the literacy assessment, and she wondered what a new instrument could offer that she herself had not already devised. She was eager to put her own work as a classroom teacher against what a team of university researchers had designed.

Sandy taught full-day kindergarten at Elm School (pseudonym) on the north side of a large, urban school district. Poverty levels in the school were steadily declining as more students were being accepted from the surrounding neighborhood. Sandy has taught for 18 years, 16 of those at Elm and 8 of them in kindergarten. Dedicated to teaching in an urban school, Sandy was proud of her unofficial position as an instructional leader in her building, one who had the "ear" of the principal, and was thus able to facilitate changes in programs and staffing. It was assessment that had helped cast Sandy in this role; the informal kindergarten-screening instrument she developed prior to the introduction of the ISEL-K/1 was used by other teachers at Elm, and she had used those data to advocate for her view of the kindergarten curriculum to her principal.

Accountability, the idea that schools or teachers are responsible for learning outcomes and should be evaluated based on students' test scores, was not new to Sandy when she joined the ISEL-K/1 project. It was with pride that she described Elm School as "one of the best testing schools in the city." It had been that way for as long as she could remember. "When I first started working here, I said to myself, 'This is a test-driven school.' It's been that way forever, not just since this big accountability thing has been going on." Sandy had initiated kindergarten assessment voluntarily; no testing, formal or otherwise, was required in kindergarten, as it was in the other grades. According to Sandy, expectations for kindergarten achievement were high at Elm School. But it was not the state or even the city that imposed the pressure to perform. "The leadership in our school buys into it—it's the principal, really." Further discussion would reveal Sandy to be an equal partner in this pressure.

Connecting New Assessments with Prior Work

The literacy assessment Sandy had devised prior to the ISEL-K/1 project included tasks such as letter name recognition and letter sound knowledge and was administered at the beginning of each quarter. Her purpose was to identify students at risk for underachievement and to provide classroom interventions to meet those students' needs. Sandy found that the ISEL-K/1 was similar to and exceeded what she had been using in her own design, covering skills she had not assessed before, such as listening comprehension, passage reading, and developmental spelling at the beginning of the year—a skill she had previously assessed at midyear. In addition, the ISEL-K/1 results were consistent with what Sandy saw in her students' daily performance in literacy activities. This informal evidence of the test's reliability and correlation to classroom performance caused her to question her previous, quarterly assessment schedule. "I'm rethinking that now—it's too cumbersome."

Sandy's previous assessment had early intervention as a primary goal. In seeking to identify those students at risk for underachievement, she had not been accustomed to looking closely at those students who were already reading. The ISEL-K/1 provided information not only about students who were likely to struggle, but also about those who were meeting or exceeding grade-level expectations. In Snapshot 8, for example, the student reads aloud from a set of leveled books that includes second-grade text. The outcomes led Sandy to exclaim, "My readers! That's where the surprise came—my gosh, they can read!"

The length of the test and the time to administer it were not a problem for Sandy, because much of it was similar to what she had done before on her own. To manage all of this testing at the beginning of the year, when kindergarten students lack independence in the classroom, Sandy used her associate teacher and a parent volunteer to monitor students at learning centers while she worked with individual students. She considered it time well spent: "It's one of the things I need. You believe in it so you make it happen."

The fact that the ISEL-K/1 came with the imprimatur of the Illinois State Board of Education worked in its favor as far as Sandy was concerned. She believed teachers would take it more seriously than they did mandates from within their own system, which tended to be abandoned as quickly as they were implemented. In addition, she saw the ISEL-K/1 as evidence that policy makers were beginning to value "what we do down here."

Uses of Assessment Data

Perhaps because she was voluntarily using performance-based assessment to test her students periodically, Sandy viewed the instrument and the data as tools for her own use rather than to meet external accountability demands. This attitude seemed to characterize her approach to the ISEL-K/1 data as well. She found it useful for planning her instruction, evaluating her effectiveness as a teacher, and demonstrating to those in decision-making roles the need for more attention to the issues around early literacy instruction.

The fall ISEL-K/1 data provided Sandy with a more detailed profile of her class, enabling her to teach accordingly: "It influences what I teach . . . you can see a general picture and you tweak your teaching." In addition, it prompted her to enlist parents to help at home:

> "I'll call parents of kids who are struggling and I'll say, 'Let's work as a team and practice letter recognition!' This [ISEL-K/1] is a tremendous tool for working with parents. Some are in denial as to how far behind their children are. At report card time I can say 'I know what your kid knows in this area.' I could do a better job of convincing them because of this assessment."

She also found it useful for grouping students and tracking the progress of her 33 full-day kindergarten students. "When there's a group that needs a certain skill, we can track it. With all the bodies, you sometimes lose track of this stuff. This way I know what's going on."

Sandy considered certain subtests, such as developmental spelling, particularly useful as tools for self-evaluation. She saw this particular subtest as representing the convergence of several isolated skills into one meaningful task that was practiced and honed in an authentic literacy activity: connected writing. Her students made significant progress on this subtest from fall to spring, particularly compared to other groups in the norming sample. "This shows they're really getting it. It's an example of the pieces coming together. It shows that I'm making progress; I'm doing my job as an educator."

Assessment and Change

Sandy, experienced in using assessment data to inform her instruction, was less eager to support immediate curricular or methodological changes in response to ISEL-K/1 data. Because there can be marked differences from one group of children to another, what one group shows may not be relevant to the next. "I see this as a snapshot of this year's group compared to last year's," she remarked when looking at graphed data from two kindergarten classes. "That's the clay you have to work with. I would need a few years of data to make judgments about my curriculum." Thus, Sandy illustrates the difference between using the data to make immediate instructional decisions at the student or classroom level and using it to change the focus of a school's curriculum.

She also saw the data as another opportunity to enlighten others, particularly administrators, about the nature of an effective kindergarten literacy program.

"Let's say you had a principal who was not so big on Writer's Workshop. . . . It's not the most structured setting in the world. But it [developmental spelling] is an example of the pieces coming together. My theory is that writing leads; writing helps kids learn to read. This would help me explain that and show that what I'm doing is worthwhile."

According to Sandy, these data provide rich opportunities to capture the attention of administrators and to lobby for change.

"I'll take the assessments and walk into an office and say, 'Look! You want these kids reading? I can't do it by myself.' The developmental spelling test is a big PR piece. You can show what's going on."

Confrontations such as this have reaped results for Sandy: An extra part-time teacher was hired to help with small-group instruction in kindergarten classrooms at Elm.

Assessment and Advocacy

For Sandy, appropriate use of the ISEL-K/1 data by policy makers and stakeholders would result in more funding for smaller classes and reading specialists to help kindergarten teachers meet the needs of at-risk students. She persisted in her desire to use assessment data to push for policy changes, including help that would allow teachers to administer the ISEL-K/1 themselves.

"Maybe this is a tool to say, 'This [ISEL-K/1] is important and we need to make this happen.' Whether they give me a sub so I can spend a day on the ISEL-K/1— something has to come of this. A task force needs to see that kids are struggling."

Although the time needed to administer the ISEL-K/1 was not a problem for Sandy— she was accustomed to doing some individual assessment with her students and believed it to be important—it was a concern for other teachers interviewed for this study. The menu approach to the ISEL-K/1 suggested in the teacher's guide directs teachers to administer only those snapshots that are most useful at the beginning and end of kindergarten and first grade, or at any point in the school year, substantially reducing the amount of time spent testing. Although Sandy valued the ISEL-K/1's potential to provide progress-monitoring data through the use of pre- and postscores on all of the snapshots, she eventually realized that she needed less front-loading of assessment "to get started at the beginning of the year."

Learning from Sandy

Sandy was not concerned that ISEL-K/1 data would be used to impose unwanted changes in the way that kindergarten was conceptualized or taught at Elm, even though her colleagues in other grades have experienced such changes as a result of local and state testing. Rather, the ISEL-K/1 represents what Sandy believes kindergarteners should know and be able to do in literacy; it supported her need to establish clear instructional goals for her students. She saw the ISEL-K/1 as a tool for teachers to use, and one that is within their control: to guide instruction and monitor student progress,

But Sandy expected more from the ISEL-K/1; she recognized its potential to influence policy in her school and beyond. With its sponsorship by the Illinois State Board of Education, she saw it as a vehicle for change, an instrument that could inform the thinking of those in decision-making positions. The test content set forth clear expectations for literacy achievement in kindergarten and first grade; as such, the resulting data would shed light upon the needs presented by at-risk students and schools to meet these benchmarks: mainly class size and assistance in the form of qualified professionals who could provide consistent support in the classroom. She had been successful using assessment data to achieve these goals in a limited way at her own school. The ISEL-K/1 would make it possible to take these issues to a larger, more public arena.

Sandy's reflections helped us see that experienced teachers could recognize the value of new assessments when they dovetailed with existing practice. They also were able to gain some new ideas for instruction, but they didn't instigate change unless the changes were also confirmed by instructional observations. Lastly, she reminded us of the positive uses of assessment for advocacy for teachers, students, and schools.

A FINAL WORD

Early literacy assessment has always provided a rich fund of information related to student potential and progress. In this chapter we have made a case for multiple formative uses of assessment. We have provided cases from primary classrooms describing how teachers use assessment to make instructional decisions in their classrooms. Further, we described a case detailing the ways in which we, as teacher educators, can play a part in developing this capability in school leaders. Lastly, as reflective practitioners ourselves, we shared cases of teachers using assessment as a lens through which to view their own beliefs about assessment, teaching, and learning. We believe these thoughtful reflections on curriculum, instruction, and teacher learning are essential for the growth of a reflective and formative pedagogy that affects instruction and student growth. As Black and Wiliam note:

> Standards can be raised only by changes put into direct effect by teachers and students in classrooms. There is a body of firm evidence that formative assessment is an essential part of classroom work and can raise standards of achievement. (1998, p. 148)

ACKNOWLEDGMENT

The research for this chapter was supported in part by the Chicago Community Trust.

REFERENCES

Abelmann, C., & Elmore, R. (1999). *When accountability knocks, will anyone answer?* (Corisortium for Policy Research in Education, Research Report Series RR-42). Philadelphia: University of Pennsylvania.

Barr, R., Blachowicz, C. L. Z., Buhle, R., Chaney, J., Ivy, C., & Suarez-Silva, G. (2002). *Illinois snapshots of early literacy*. Springfield, IL: Illinois State Board of Education. Retrieved January 1, 2004, from *www.isbe.net/curriculum/isel/ISEL.html*.

Bates, A. (2005). *Kindergarten in the age of accountability: Listen to teachers about literacy assessment*. Unpublished doctoral dissertation. National Louis University, Evanston, IL.

Bernhardt, V. L. (2004). *Data analysis for continuous school improvement*. Larchmont, NY: Eye on Education.

Blachowicz, C. L. Z., Obrochta, C., & Fogelberg, E. (2005). Literacy coaching for change. *Educational Leadership, 62*, 55–58.

Black, P., & Wiliam, D. (1998). Inside the black box: Raising standards through classroom assessment. *Phi Delta Kappan, 80*(2), 139–148.

Glickman, C. D. (2002). *Leadership for learning*. Alexandria, VA: Association for Supervision and Curriculum Development.

Ogle, D. (2002). *Coming together as readers*. Arlington Heights, IL: Skylight Professional Development.

Price, N. (2001). *Policy in action: The influence of mandated early reading assessment on teachers' thinking and practice*. Unpublished doctoral dissertation, University of Washington, Seattle.

CHAPTER 16

Authentic Assessment of Authentic Student Work in Urban Classrooms

Kathryn Glasswell
William H. Teale

ASSESSMENT FOR LEARNING

Two principles of assessment underpin the work we discuss in this chapter: Assessment is part of a "system" for teaching and learning, and students are best served when teachers engage in authentic assessment practices. Our first principle means that we view assessment as an integral part of what we teach (curriculum) and how we teach it (pedagogy) rather than as a process that is conducted in addition to—and apart from—instruction. In other words, assessment is one means of understanding what happens in classrooms as teachers teach and children learn.

Thinking about assessment in this way prompts consideration of key questions that assessment may answer for teachers. One common question teachers ask regarding assessment in the classroom is, "How well are my students doing?" This question is useful in many respects. For example, reporting on the literacy progress, or developmental "level," of a classroom of learners is informative to parents and the community at large about how the group is doing (typically in comparison to a norming group at that grade or age level). In addition, assessing the literacy proficiency of the class overall helps a teacher get a general sense of whether the curriculum is promoting student progress as well as or better than would be expected, or if there are major shortcomings in the pattern of student literacy achievement. But the question "How well are my students doing?" also has its limitations. Thinking of assessment only in this way tends to locate the reasons for progress—or lack of it—within the student. In other words, if Sonia is not doing well, it is because of something she doesn't know or can't do. In essence, when we ask only about how well students are doing, we end up separating assessment from teaching and learning.

Following the principle that assessment is part of a "system" for teaching and learning suggests that instead of asking only about the learner, a more useful assessment question is, "How effectively is my teaching promoting student learning?" This question allows us to connect assessment explicitly to considerations about what has already been taught, what the student learned, and how this information may guide further instructional decision making. Framing our thinking about assessment in this way means that teachers can still gather information about individual students at a given point in time, but that they also use assessment as a tool to stimulate their own reflection and to help them plan their teaching.

The second, and complementary, principle we use to help define the role of assessment in the classroom is that it should focus on student work done within authentic reading and writing activities. Our approach to this issue is informed by the work of other scholars who have defined authentic literacy assessments as those that reflect reading and writing practices of the real world (e.g., Valencia, Hiebert, & Afflerbach, 1994; Wiggins, 1990). It is the case that in many classrooms the literacy activities children complete are decontextualized and narrowly focused exercises designed to teach a particular skill or strategy; but elementary-school teachers have shown that it is possible to create authentic contexts for literacy in school settings—contexts that involve children in reading and writing that are designed to help accomplish real-life goals, similar to what ethnographic, cognitive, and historical studies (e.g., Heath, 1980; Teale, 1986; Venezky, 1991) have shown are the functions of reading and writing in literate societies. When we gather assessment data from contexts that stress authentic literacy rather than from contexts that primarily use worksheets, skill-and-drill computer exercises, or writing in response to a prompt for an assignment that has only the teacher-as-examiner for an audience, chances are better that we will get a more accurate picture of children's literacy strengths and needs. This picture of what students do while engaged in authentic practices enables the design of instruction that helps children develop the knowledge and strategies that will serve them not only on test day but also throughout their lives.

TEACHING, LEARNING, AND ASSESSING IN URBAN CONTEXTS: IN2BOOKS

In this chapter we discuss the application of the two underlying principles of assessment in the context of a specific program—In2Books (I2B)—that was designed to foster reading, writing, and thinking abilities in children's grades 2–5. We examine how teachers in two large urban school districts—District of Columbia Public Schools (DCPS) and Chicago Public Schools (CPS)—worked with us and other teacher educators to develop and implement an assessment/instruction system that enabled them to "teach to" district/state literacy standards in the context of authentic literacy instruction.

It has been thoroughly documented that, overall, children educated in urban schools do not read and write as well as their suburban or rural counterparts (*nces.ed.gov/nationsreportcard/reading/*; *nces.ed.gov/nationsreportcard/writing/*). Moreover, this differential achievement pattern has existed for many years. Numerous studies have provided insights into why urban students experience disproportionate difficulty in reading and writing: funding inequities, poverty, high student and teacher mobility, a home–school "disconnect," lack of adequate teacher preparation, and institutionalized racism, among others, have all been described as playing a role. (See, e.g., Clark's 2002 research review, or information from the International Reading Association's [2005] Urban Education Initiatives [*www.reading.org/resources/issues/focus_urban.html*], or portrayals such as those developed by Kozol, 1991, 2005.) However, despite these, and other sometimes seemingly intractable structural or societal barriers, several studies describing success in improving elementary-school literacy achievement among urban and high-poverty children have appeared in recent years (see, e.g., Au, 2001, 2005; Au, Hirata, & Raphael, 2005; Taylor, Pearson, Peterson, Clark, & Walpole, 2000; Taylor, Pearson, Peterson, & Rodriguez, 2003, 2005). In a similar vein to these initiatives is the implementation of the In2Books program and the evaluation of it that we have been conducting.

The I2B program is a sophisticated response to the complex problem of student underachievement often encountered in urban schools. The program itself involves a classroom-based framework of authentic literacy activity for teachers and children, a year-long series of professional development sessions focused on effective literacy practices, the use of high-quality assessment practices to support teaching and learning, and the development of support materials for use by teachers and school-based literacy leaders. The evaluation includes a study that has examined achievement patterns: An analysis of over 2,000 DCPS grades 2–4 students in In2Books classrooms on the nationally normed, standardized Scholastic Aptitude Test–9 (SAT-9) reading test and a group of approximately 8,500 students in comparison classrooms showed that the I2B students significantly outperformed comparison students, indicating that what occurred in the In2Books classrooms contributed to these urban students' literacy skills more than the regular curriculum did (Teale & Gambrell, 2007).

Another part of the initiative—the part we discuss in the remainder of this chapter—involved applying in practice the principles of assessment just discussed. We worked closely with teachers involved in implementing the authentic practices of I2B classrooms to explore what it would take to develop an assessment tool that would provide them with useful information—information they could apply on an ongoing basis to indicate appropriate "next instructional steps" for the children in their classes. The intent was that the tool would make explicit the links among assessment, teaching, and learning, and that it could be integrated meaningfully and readily into the authentic instructional contexts for reading, writing, and thinking that are part of the I2B classroom program.

I2B: Promoting Reading, Writing, and Thinking in the Context of a Pen Pal Program

The overall approach of the classroom program for I2B provides frequent and multiple opportunities for students to read real books and to participate in a set of authentic and cognitively challenging literacy tasks: discussing with others their thoughts, feelings, and interpretations of the books; reading and studying letters from their pen pals; and then writing, revising, and sending their own letters to the pen pals.

During the 2004–2005 school year, I2B was used in DCPS and CPS with nearly 5,000 children and their 230-plus teachers in grades 2–5. The program works like this:

Across the course of the school year, students receive five carefully selected, grade-level books in different genres: fiction, social studies, biography, folktales, and science. The books are the students' to keep. For each of the five cycles during the year, teachers receive, in addition to these books, related read-aloud books and a curriculum guide designed to help them plan reading and writing activities for a unit around the books/genre.

The authentic context for literacy activity is extended into writing as students are matched with adult pen pals recruited from leading businesses, nonprofit organizations, and government agencies in the area. The pen pals read the same books and use a rich website environment (Pen Pal Place®, *www.penpals.in2books.org/*) to learn how to write effective letters to students about the books, thereby helping the adults to act as mentors to the children. Their letters are intended to be a way to establish a personal relationship with the students, but, more specifically, in the letters the pen pals are guided to discuss the books in ways that contribute to the students' literacy growth.

In the classroom during each cycle, students and teachers study that cycle's genre, focusing especially on the I2B book (for each cycle at each grade level, up to three books at varying difficulty levels are available for students) and engaging in various discussion, comprehension, vocabulary, and writing activities shown by research to be effective (details on activities can be found in the five I2B genre guides archived at In2Books Teacher Place®, *www.teacher.in2books.org/*). In class, on an appointed delivery day, each student receives the letter from his or her pen pal. This is always a time of great excitement for the children. They read and reread their letters, and then, over a number of days, engage in the culminating activity for each cycle—writing letters about the books in response to the pen pal letters they received. The letter writing is completed instructionally through a writing process approach (e.g., Fletcher & Portalupi, 2001).

The letters written by students are scanned and sent electronically via I2B to the adult pen pals. Over the course of the year, meaningful, contextualized, and cumulative written conversations take place between the adult and child pen pals as they enjoy each other's company and read, think, and write together around the books. Our challenges in assessment were to understand what this culminating, authentic activity of writing a letter to one's pen pal could tell us about each child's developing skills as a reader, thinker, and writer, and how to obtain information that would inform a teacher about how to further scaffold the learning of all of the children in the class.

Assessment for I2B

Like other work in authentic literacy assessment (e.g., Valencia & Pearson, 1987; Wolf & Gearhart, 1994), the assessment tool and procedures we developed for use in conjunction with the students' authentic literacy activities placed value on more than just the product (in this case, the letter the student wrote). Our approach to assessment also valued children's thinking as readers and writers, that is, their processes and strategies. Our reason for this slant was not merely philosophical; we believe such an orientation is critical if assessment information is to inform teaching and learning rather than merely act as an end unto itself. In other words, teachers come to see the point of such assessment as focusing on what needs to be learned in order for students to engage successfully in authentic literacy tasks. With these principles in mind, we set out to design a rubric for I2B that teachers could use productively with their students in the natural course of instruction to assess the letters the students wrote.

The Design Process

During the 2003–2004 and 2004–2005 school years, the vast majority of I2B classrooms were located in DCPS, so we used that context for initial development of the rubric. Our first design consideration was related to the goals for teaching and learning in DCPS classrooms. To establish a reference point for judging student performance and tracking student growth over time, we looked to the DCPS learning standards for grades 2–5. Unlike writing assessment tools, such as 6+1 Trait® Writing (Bellamy, 2005), that have been developed independent of any specific state standards, we wanted an assessment tool that related directly to the learning goals to which teachers were expected to teach.

Our reasons for linking the assessment directly to district literacy standards also went beyond providing a reference point for teachers to judge student performance. We drew on recent research on the standards-based change process in schools (e.g., Au, 2001, 2005; Au et al., 2005) that indicates that a focus on standards allows not only individual teachers but also the whole school to articulate goals for student learning—a process that links curriculum, pedagogy, and assessment. Furthermore, the standards-based change studies demonstrated the importance of instructional coherence across grade levels in raising students' literacy achievement. Therefore, one of our major aims in developing an assessment tool was ensuring that it could provide information that would be useful both within and across grade levels. We wanted teachers using the tool to be able to obtain detailed information about each student's performance and simultaneously gain insight into next-steps teaching that would be most likely to benefit each student.

In addition, because we designed a common assessment tool across four grade levels, it was possible to see how what has been taught/learned at one grade level is related to what teachers at subsequent or previous grade levels may need to teach. We wanted the tool to make transparent the expectations at each level and provide a context for meaningful schoolwide discussion of children's progress toward common goals.

The I2B Rubric:
Authentic Assessment of Authentic Student Work

Assessing performance in the context of authentic student work meant assessing skills that were at the core of students' engagement in the complex social acts of reading, discussing, and thinking, as well as writing, about a book. The culminating task of each cycle is the letter the children write to their adult pen pals. This letter is central to the authentic literacy activity. It provides a focus and a means of expression for developing readers and writers. The letter is representative of the orchestration of the complex set of actions required to accomplish the literacy goals of the program and of the cognitively challenging authentic student work that many scholars see as essential to improving educational outcomes in urban contexts.

Designing an appropriate rubric to help teachers understand what children had learned and what they might yet need to learn required thoughtful consideration of which aspects of the complex sets of actions should be assessed when children communicate in writing with a responsive other. We needed to make judgments about which aspects were integral to success in the authentic activity. Considering all of these factors and the written letter as the task, we identified seven dimensions of literacy skills/thinking processes that we saw as central to the teaching and learning activities in the I2B classrooms and that also were related to key learning areas in DCPS learning standards. These dimensions were: Comprehension, Thinking about the Book, Connecting to the Pen Pal, Organization, Sentences, Word Choice/Vocabulary, and Mechanics. These dimensions of performance comprised the frame of an analytic rubric, which permitted the complex task to be viewed as comprising a number of related competencies. It was important to us that the complexity of the task was made visible at all levels, and, therefore, using the DCPS grade-level standards as a guide and working closely with hundreds of student letters, we turned our attention to developing a descriptive scale, or continuum, for each dimension to represent student performance within and across the four grade levels.

For each of the dimensions of the letter-writing activity, a 6-point scale of developmental descriptors, referenced to the learning standards, was developed. The analytic rubric, displayed in Figure 16.1, provides opportunities to identify both similarities and differences in children in terms of what each can already do and what he or she still needs to learn to do.

This rubric met design goals and our specific desire to ensure that it be useful to teachers. It could be used to assess children's performance on the letter-writing task on the seven dimensions and reveal which aspects of the complex task the students had mastered and which required further instruction. For classroom teachers, the rubric has an important pragmatic feature related not just to gaining information for individual students but also for organizing instruction for the whole class or small groups. Previous research had led us to expect that student performance on the various dimensions of complex tasks varies (Brown, Glasswell, & Harland, 2004; Glasswell, Parr, & Aikman, 2001). In other words, within a particular classroom some students would show strengths in areas where others showed needs. A different kind of rubric—for example, a holistic rubric, a grading chart, or a rating scale for overall letter quality—would have masked differences that are important to identify in order to teach to individual needs or group students with similar performance patterns. The benefit of the I2B rubric, when used with a classroom of learners, is that it allows the teacher to see exactly where to apply her instructional force with an individual and which children with similar profiles might benefit from being grouped for instruction.

The Rubric in Use:
Applying Theory and Instrument in the Classroom

In order to illustrate teachers' classroom applications of the tool, we examine two aspects of rubric use that proved to be especially productive. One is a close look at the letters of individual I2B children. Teachers found such analyses helpful for what they indicated about current achievement as well as next steps in instruction that would enable children not merely to create a better product/letter, but to become more accomplished literate beings who could perform complex, authentic literacy activities suc-

In2Books Rubric: Reading, Writing, and Thinking about Books with a Pen Pal

Communication of Ideas About the Book

SCORE	1	2	3	4	5	6
COMPREHENSION	Not clear to reader if student read the book.	Details show student read the book but not clear if main ideas are understood.	Moves beyond merely reporting details to identifying and explaining main idea(s) of the book.	Begins to link main idea(s) to saying something about the book theme and/or genre.	Some deeper understanding evident. Main idea(s) and theme(s) are elaborated and linked to details. May reflect on genre.	Letter is a well developed, thoughtful discussion of main ideas, themes, and significant details. Shows deeper reflection about genre(s) and reading in general.
THINKING ABOUT THE BOOK	Makes no connections to the book.	Makes one type of personal relation to book (e.g., notes similar/different, expresses opinion/evaluation, describes learning).	Makes more than one type of simple connection (text-to-self, text-to-text, text-to-world).	Makes connection(s) (t-s, t-t, t-w) related to main idea(s) and/or to theme(s) of the book.	Makes connection(s) (t-s, t-t, t-w) to main ideas/themes that have some detail and are elaborated.	Letter shows comprehensive understanding of wide and deep connections (t-s, t-t, t-w) to main ideas and related themes.
CONNECTING WITH PEN PAL	The only reference to pen pal is in the salutation.	Acknowledges pen pal (e.g., asks or responds to personal questions, offers personal information, expresses thanks, etc.).	Communicates directly with pen pal about the book (e.g., general book-related/reading-related questions/comments/responses).	Communicates with pen pal about the book by including two or more questions/comments/responses related to main ideas and/or theme.	Parts of the letter show detailed and thoughtful communication about the book main ideas and/or related themes.	Whole letter represents a personal dialogue around the book and its themes. May acknowledge a fellow reader relationship that extends beyond individual book.

Use of Language and Organizational Features

SCORE	1	2	3	4	5	6
ORGANIZATION	Stream of consciousness writing. Overall, the letter feels disorganized.	Writing makes sense and shows one or two clusters of ideas (e.g., two or more related sentences placed together).	Some (two or more) paragraph-like groupings of ideas are evident. Overall letter structure (opening, main body, closing) is emerging.	Paragraphs are used to organize. Mainly include sentences on the same topic. An overall letter structure is obvious.	Paragraphs contain relevant information focused on paragraph topic but may remain limited. Attempts at links between paragraphs evident. Letter is structured from beginning to end.	Paragraphs are detailed and well developed. Transitions between paragraphs make language flow naturally. Whole text is effectively structured.
SENTENCES	Uses simple and/or compound sentences with similar patterns. Overall, letter feels repetitive.	Uses mainly simple and compound sentences. Some variety in length and beginnings.	Simple and compound sentences mainly correct. Attempts at complex sentences may not be accurate.	Simple and compound sentences mainly correct. Has some (two or more) successful complex sentences.	Many examples of correct simple, compound, and complex sentences. Use of different sentence structures adds variety to the letter.	Uses simple, compound, and complex sentences with few errors. May vary or repeat sentence structures to maintain reader interest or for effect.
WORD CHOICE/VOCABULARY	Words used do not demonstrate familiarity with book.	Includes several (three or more) words, phrases, or names from book.	Uses book vocabulary to identify and explain something about book ideas.	Uses book vocabulary and other words/phrases related to the book's main idea(s)/theme(s)/genre.	Expands beyond book vocabulary to discuss abstract ideas/themes/genre relating to the book.	Extensive vocabulary indicates control of book and related thematic and genre vocabulary. Word choices build deeper understanding of the writer's thinking.
MECHANICS	Frequent mistakes in simple spelling, sentence punctuation and grammar distract reader's attention throughout letter.	Problems with simple spelling, simple punctuation, and correct grammar are noticeable.	Simple spelling, simple sentence punctuation, and grammar mainly correct.	Mainly correct. Contains several (three or more) attempts at more complex spelling and complex punctuation.	Few errors in grammar, complex spelling patterns, and complex punctuation.	No significant errors indicate writer exhibits extensive control of more complex spelling patterns, complex punctuation, and grammar.

FIGURE 16.1. In2Books rubric. Copyright 2005 by In2Books, Inc. Reprinted by permission.

cessfully in their lives. The other application was the examination of rubric–score patterns for the entire classroom of children. Teachers indicated that such an approach helped them think about what was needed for whole- class instruction as well as small-group work and one-on-one conferences.

Looking Closely at Individual Children

We selected the letters of Ronnie (grade 2), Michael (grade 4), and Chantelle (grade 4) to show how their work presents "snapshots" of developing writers at various points on the continuum. Teachers found such comparisons extremely helpful for conceptualizing development in writing as a gradual, long-term movement toward more sophisticated understandings and performances. Individuals' letters also helped teachers anchor performances for children at different grade levels. We'll begin with Ronnie.

Ronnie

Ronnie, a second grader, read *The Rainy Day Grump* (Eaton, 1998), a short narrative about young African American siblings, Rosie and Clay. Rosie wants Clay to play "dress-up"; however, he is grumpy because he wants to play ball but can't because of the rain. Figure 16.2 depicts Ronnie's first book-related letter to his pen pal, written not too long into the school year. Ronnie seems to be very much enjoying sharing things about his life with pen pal Maria. There is no doubt that he is engaged in an authentic literacy task. His letter is filled with information relating to what he likes and dislikes and what he has been doing. However, he devotes little of his letter to discussing the book he and Maria are reading; and when we examine the letter using the rubric, we see that there are many ways to tailor instruction to move Ronnie along the continuum so that he engages in more challenging intellectual work. Table 16.1 summarizes the rubric-based analysis of Ronnie's letter and where we see him on the continuum of skill development for this complex literacy task.

As a beginning grade 2 writer near the start of his I2B experiences, Ronnie demonstrates that he is quite capable of writing a friendly letter to his pen pal but has yet to understand how to communicate effectively about the book. His understanding of this complex authentic task is emerging and needs to be further scaffolded by his teacher. The information gained from using the assessment tool indicates to his teacher that Ronnie's greatest needs are instruction that gets him thinking about, and connecting to, the book's main ideas and details. She can plan to involve Ronnie in more complex discussions about the book and show him how to invite his pen pal to engage in conversation about his ideas as he learns to make statements and ask his pen pal questions that relate to bigger ideas. When Ronnie's teacher uses assessment information in this way, she is, in essence, making assessment part of a system for teaching and learning in an authentic context. She takes advantage of the meaningful literacy activity in which she already engages him as a context for developing specific skills that assessment has shown Ronnie needs to develop if he is to become a more expert reader, writer, and thinker.

Next, we focus on the letters of two fourth-grade children to give a sense of the range of writing development that exists in virtually any classroom and to illustrate the importance of linking assessment to teaching and learning via differentiated instruc-

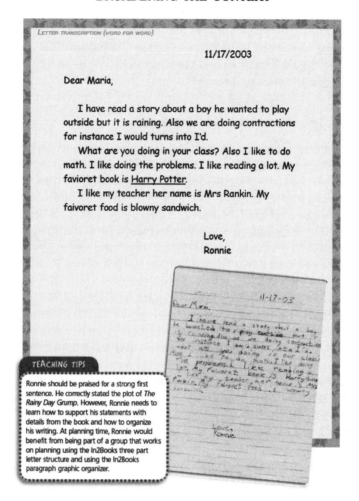

FIGURE 16.2. Ronnie's letter.

tion. Some fourth graders excel in reading and writing whereas others struggle long and hard. Michael's and Chantelle's letters differ in sophistication and illustrate the importance of using an assessment tool that has the capacity to provide information about children's actual developmental levels (rather than information telling the teacher where the children are not). The important point is to acknowledge existing levels of skill while building development toward the high expectations maintained for all learners.

Michael

Michael is a grade 4 writer who has just read *Kids Communicate* (Rossi, 2002) and writes to his pen pal Sandra about it. *Kids Communicate* is a social studies informational book that describes the development of ways of communicating from preliterate ages to inventions such as the printing press, telegraph, movies, and radio, to present-day communication in the "Information Age." Issues about finding and evaluating information are raised; and the story of how one 12-year-old boy, Hunter Scott, used information and communication technologies to make a difference in the world is related. Figure 16.3 shows the letter that Michael wrote about this book; this was his second pen pal letter of the school year.

Like many of the letters from the program, Michael's is lively and interesting. Unlike Ronnie, though, Michael has clearly engaged with this book, and his letter shows some good thinking. Many teachers might believe that Michael deserves a good grade for a piece like this. They would see Michael's letter as a more than an acceptable example of fourth-grade writing. We agree with them, but we'd also offer more. Table 16.2 summarizes the description of Michael's developing skills and the next instructional steps indicated by the rubric that we see as important for him.

The rubric analysis confirms the initial impression that Michael is doing well for a fourth-grade writer. Examining this placement profile on the continuum of development we laid out for this reading, writing, and thinking task informs Michael's teacher about where to go next with him, as he learns more about engaging in this complex literacy task. Michael could be coached on making thematic connections to the texts he reads or asked to discuss the significance of the book's ideas in a broader context, so that when engaging with his pen pal, his discussions become richer and more deeply rooted in understandings about books and lived experiences. Through discussions of themes and broader connections in this authentic context, Michael will be guided as he comes to understand more about how to reflect deeply on what he reads. He'll also learn how engaging with others in conversations can help to develop his thinking. Like Ronnie's, the profile of Michael that emerges from the assessment provides his teacher with the information she needs to pull him forward along the continuum to more com-

TABLE 16.1. Analysis of Ronnie's Letter

Characteristics	Placement on rubric	Annotations
Comprehension	1	Ronnie says so little about the book that we are not really sure that he read it. Ronnie's discussion with Maria would benefit from a focus on the book they are reading.
Thinking	1	Ronnie makes no connections to the book.
Pen pal	1	Apart from the salutation, Ronnie makes no attempt to engage Maria directly in discussion about the book.
Organization	1	Overall, this letter feels disorganized. Ronnie seems to write things down as they occur to him and does not structure his letter from beginning to end.
Sentences	2	Ronnie uses mainly simple sentences. He does attempt one compound sentence, but it is unsuccessful because it is part of a long run-on sentence.
Words	1	The words Ronnie uses do not demonstrate familiarity with the book. He does not name characters or use words that indicate he know details from the story.
Mechanics	1	Ronnie's frequent mistakes in simple spelling and simple punctuation distract the reader's attention throughout this letter.

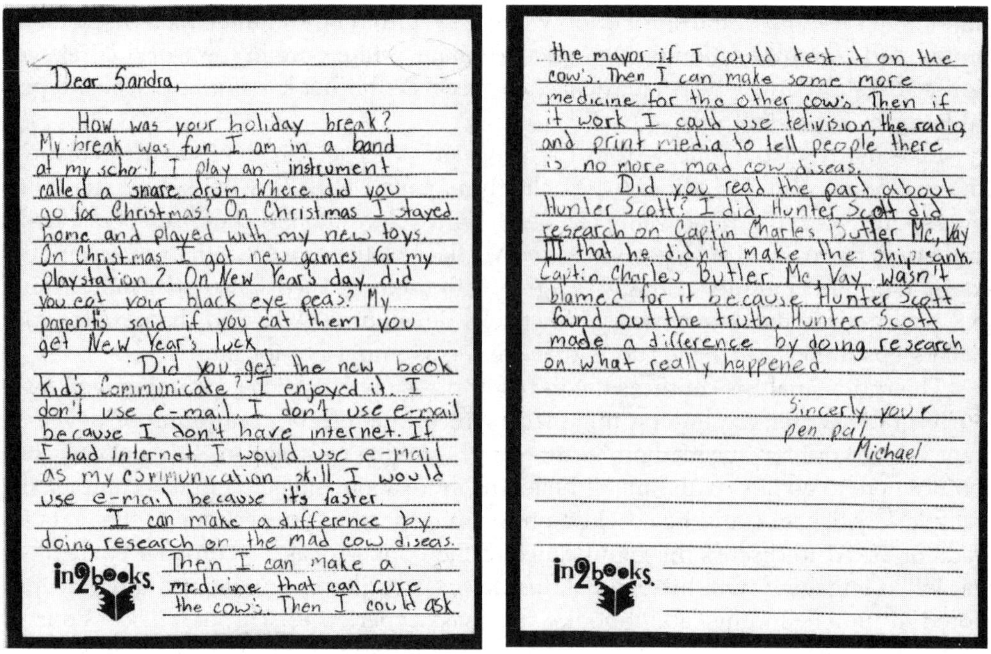

FIGURE 16.3. Michael's letter.

plex understandings. This path is charted by using what he already knows and can do in order to plan teaching that scaffolds his reading, thinking, and writing and thus "ups the ante" so that he moves closer to the goals for accomplished readers and writers who engage with others in literate activities.

Chantelle

Chantelle is also a fourth grader in the I2B program, and she wrote to her pen pal about the same book as Michael (*Kids Communicate*). Chantelle's letter to Anita is friendly, open, and even charming in many respects (see Figure 16.4). She clearly knows that her task as a letter-writer is to talk with Anita about the book, and most of her letter focuses on details in the book and her connection to it. Table 16.3 contains our analysis of Chantelle's letter based on the rubric. What is most obvious when looking at this analysis of Chantelle's reading, writing, and thinking skills is that she has several aspects of this complex communication task in hand. She seems to understand much about writing a letter. She can organize her letter effectively; her sentences are well structured; and her control of the mechanics of spelling, punctuation, and grammar is good. Most striking, however, is that even though Chantelle is adept with the aforementioned surface features of writing the letter, she is not showing that she knows how to engage with her pen pal in a way that challenges both of them to consider any of the complex issues related to the book. Her deep features scores (comprehension, thinking about the book, connecting with the pen pal) are lower, indicating that, as a reader and a writer, she would benefit greatly from instruction and coaching in the challenging work of thinking more deeply, connecting to, and communicating ideas about the book. This authentic context for literacy instruction can provide opportunities for the teacher to guide Chantelle's development in ways that deepen her cognitive engagement in literacy activities. With support in targeted areas, Chantelle will learn to read and think in new and deeper ways, and she will learn that literacy is as much about thinking as it is about mastering the codes of written language.

These snapshots of Ronnie, Michael, and Chantelle show three writers who have clearly different skill levels for engaging in this complex communicative task. The assessment tool we designed with teachers provided them with information not just about each child's level of development, but it also allowed us to demonstrate how teachers can use this information to work at the cutting edge of their children's future

TABLE 16.2. Analysis of Michael's Letter

Characteristics	Placement on rubric	Annotations
Comprehension	4	Michael is beginning to link main ideas and details in his letter by talking about how he can make a difference using the media to communicate. He also demonstrates this point by discussing Hunter Scott's research, which made a difference.
Thinking	4	Michael makes a number of simple, unelaborated text-to-self connections (e.g., "I don't use email/Internet"). He also makes one elaborated connection to the text by developing a scenario about what he could do about mad cow disease.
Pen pal	3	Michael talks to his pen pal, and this is good enough to place him at a 3 on the scale. He asks two direct questions about the book ("Did you get the new book? Did you read the part about Hunter Scott?") and makes a statement about it ("I did" [read it]), but he does not indicate a desire to ask the pen pal challenging and thought-provoking questions about main ideas.
Organization	3	Though Michael develops the paragraphs well, there is no obvious and complete letter structure. As far as his whole text structuring is concerned, he has a beginning and a middle but no end other than "sincerely."
Sentences	4	Michael does a good job of controlling his individual sentences. Nearly all simple and compound sentences are correct (one run-on is present, p. 2 of the letter). Most complex sentences are also correct. Although he includes different types of sentences, the initial part of the letter is a little "choppy" and the middle section, with the repetition of "then," is cumbersome, indicating that Michael shows some control of sentence structure but is not yet using structures to add variety (which would be a 5 on the continuum)
Words	4	Michael uses words and phrases related to the topic of the book. He includes the title of the book, words related to main ideas (e.g., "making a difference"), and other words for communication modes (e.g., "email, Internet, tv, radio, print, media").
Mechanics	4	Mechanics are mainly correct, and Michael's grammar is good. Most spelling is correct. This letter contains more than three examples of correct spelling of polysyllabic words (*communicate, medicine, research, instrument*). Two apostrophes of possession are present; one, correct (New Year's) and one, incorrect (cow's).

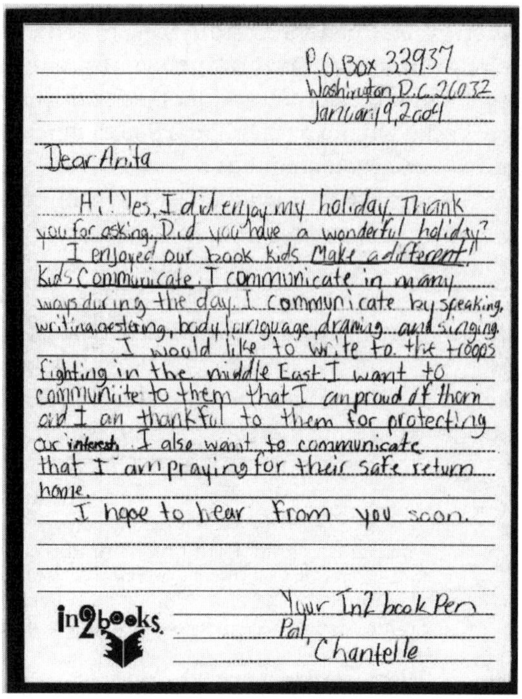

P.O. Box 33937
Washington D.C. 20032
January 9, 2004

Dear Anita

Hi! Yes, I did enjoy my holiday. Thank you for asking. Did you have a wonderful holiday?
I enjoyed our book Kids Make a difference! Kids Communicate. I communicate in many ways during the day. I communicate by speaking, writing, gesturing, body language, drawing and singing.
I would like to write to the troops fighting in the middle East. I want to communiite to them that I am proud of them and I am thankful to them for protecting our interest. I also want to communicate that I am praying for their safe return home.
I hope to hear from you soon.

Your In2 book Pen Pal,
Chantelle

in2books.

FIGURE 16.4. Chantelle's letter.

TABLE 16.3. Analysis of Chantelle's Letter

Characteristics	Placement on rubric	Annotations
Comprehension	2	Chantelle gives a number of details about modes of communication that show she read the book. We note that she does not talk about main ideas or themes of making a difference or critical consumption of information.
Thinking	2	Chantelle makes one fairly lengthy and detailed text-to-world connection to troops in the Middle East.
Pen pal	2	She shares personal information.
Organization	3	Chantelle uses paragraphs to organize her letter. An overall letter structure is obvious.
Sentences	4	All Chantelle's sentences are correct. She uses two complex sentences correctly.
Words	2	Chantelle uses some words from the book to explain the concept of communication (e.g., "I can communicate by speaking, writing . . . ").
Mechanics	3	Chantelle has control of grammar, simple spelling, and simple punctuation. They are "mainly correct."

competencies. Through engaging in the authentic literacy activities that form the basis of the I2B program, teachers use the information from the assessment to promote the specific support needed in relation to each child's profile of strengths and needs. The teachers with whom we worked in our professional development sessions saw this as a powerful feature of the assessment tool and as something that gave them more leverage in their provision of needs-based instruction in real and meaningful contexts.

Looking at Whole-Class Patterns from Rubric Analyses

In addition to the insights gained from deep analyses of individual children in their classes, a number of teachers found it helpful to plot the rubric scores of all the children in their class for each cycle. Looking closely at the scores, the teachers searched for patterns in the performances of children. One way they examined the scores of the whole class was to study the pattern on each of the seven dimensions to discern particular dimensions of the task that would benefit from more attention in a whole-class focus. Through such a global whole-class analysis, teachers understood better how to target whole-class instruction in ways that were likely to benefit many children. The second way they examined whole-class scores was to look for patterns that were common to several children in the class. The identification of such patterns across children (rather than within particular dimensions) led to productive groupings for small-group instruction, in which children of similar needs could receive targeted instruction around the cluster of dimensions that were identified as in need of scaffolding to promote more sophisticated understandings. These patterns of scores helped them think about instructional needs in ways that complemented what they had learned from the assessment of individual children.

As an example, Ms. Yount conducted ongoing analyses of the rubric data for her 22 fourth-grade students (9 girls, 13 boys; mixed ethnicities; three special education students; one English language learner [ELL]) across the first four cycles of book reading/ pen pal letter writing for the year. During each cycle she charted the children's scores, looking especially at patterns across the two rubric groupings of deep features (comprehension, thinking about the book, connection with the pen pal) and surface features (organization, sentences, word choice/vocabulary, mechanics).

From her analysis of cycle 1 letters, for example, she found that for most of her students, control of the deep features was more difficult than control of organization, sentences, vocabulary, and mechanics. Overall, she noticed that most students in the class were at 2 or 3 on the continuum for comprehension, thinking, and connecting. Moreover, as she looked more closely, she found:

> "Although students made it clear in their letters that they read the book and they touched on the main ideas, they were weak in supporting their ideas with details from the book. . . . I also found that . . . many of their connections were superficial connections rather than meaningful connections."

Accordingly, she planned "whole-class (writing) mini-lessons on using details to support their ideas about books," geared her read-alouds to lessons about character traits and supporting details, and provided a variety of instruction focused on making connections that were meaningful (I thought I understood how Justin felt because. . . . ") rather than superficial ("I have blond hair, too"). She also commented:

"I identified six students who were at 2 on both comprehension and thinking and did additional work with them in guided reading and in reader's workshop conferences."

In these and other ways, Ms. Yount exemplified the process envisioned for productive use of the assessment tool: She used the data both to indicate next teaching steps for whole-class instruction and to suggest directions for differentiating instruction according to individual needs.

The Rubric in Use: What We've Learned

We began this chapter by discussing two underlying principles of our work: Assessment is part of a "system" for teaching and learning, and students are best served when teachers engage in authentic assessment practices. Assessing to identify next steps in teaching in order to provide challenging and developmentally appropriate literacy instruction for each child is a complex task. We spent 2 years working with teachers and applying these principles in order to develop an assessment tool and integrally related instructional implications that would be both useful and usable in classrooms. That effort has taught us a number of lessons.

One significant lesson that became clear is that simply selecting a rubric—no matter how "good" the rubric—putting it in teachers' hands, and expecting them to use it productively in their classrooms is *not* a process that creates high-quality reading and writing instruction. The I2B rubric grew out the goals and methods of the literacy program that we were attempting to establish in elementary-school classrooms: children engaged in authentic, challenging work that involved reading, rereading, studying, and discussing different genres of high-quality children's literature, and then participating in "written conversations" with adult pen pals about that literature. Thus, there was a tight theoretical and practical connection between the assessment and the instruction.

Related, and equally important, was the insight that many classroom teachers and even literacy specialists have been taught to operate on the premise that obtaining a score from a rubric is the end purpose of using it rather than a beginning point for differentiating instruction. Many teachers did not typically see assessment in the terms that we outlined above—as a way of understanding the impact that teaching has on student learning and a means to fine-tune instruction to make it more effective. Integrating teaching, learning, and assessment sounds almost easy, but what became clear in the course of this project is that gathering assessment information and knowing how to use it to inform and improve instruction are not at all the same undertaking. As we worked with groups of teachers in Washington, DC, and Chicago, we learned to adjust our materials production and to focus on ongoing professional development in order to incorporate an explicit emphasis on linking the assessment information gained through the use of the rubric to organizational and instructional responses in classrooms. For example, part of each of the five professional development sessions throughout the school year was devoted to activities and discussion of assessment as part of a system of teaching and learning. In these sessions teachers spent time with us assessing student letters, discussing strengths and needs, and identifying instructional priorities for both a class and for individual children.

We especially wanted teachers who were using the rubric in their classrooms to see how it could help them identify students who were not performing at expected standards for their grade level and, in turn, help them move these students forward. So, for example, when we examined Chantelle's letter (Figure 16.4) and her profile (Table 16.3), the teachers could see that Chantelle is in need of significant instructional intervention if she is to move closer to meeting the grade-level standards. As can be seen from examination of Figure 16.5, the expectation for grade 4 writers is that they perform in the 3/4/5 band of scores, and Chantelle's profile on a number of dimensions (particularly deep features) clusters around 2. Although Chantelle writes a perfectly charming and friendly letter, she is not showing that she can engage in the complex and cognitively challenging work needed to comprehend, think deeply about texts, and use writing to express and explore her understandings. With this information in hand, the teacher can plan a series of authentic reading-response activities or targeted read-aloud activities (highlighted in the professional development sessions and the I2B Genre Guides) to foster Chantelle's skills related to comprehension of main ideas, significant details, and the themes of the book. Further, if the teacher identified other students with similar score profiles, she could organize targeted, effective, small-group instruction.

Most of the teachers with whom we worked in Washington, DC, and Chicago indicated that engaging in this kind of approach to assessment was not something that came naturally to them, nor was it part of their other professional development experiences. So it was clear that the real goal of the overall initiative was to enable teachers to employ, productively and confidently, an ongoing assessment–instruction cycle in their classrooms.

Another lesson we learned related to our decision to encourage teachers to take a long-term view of writing and reading development. This decision was manifested in the use of a single rubric across four grade levels rather than a separate rubric for each grade. It turned out that this approach created significant difficulty for many teachers, but that it was important to work through the challenge. The difficulty came about because the rubric stimulates the question "What does this performance mean for this child, right here, right now?" As a result, teachers at grades 2 and 3, especially, had trouble understanding whether or not the rubric told them if a child was doing well. The issue typically played itself out like this:

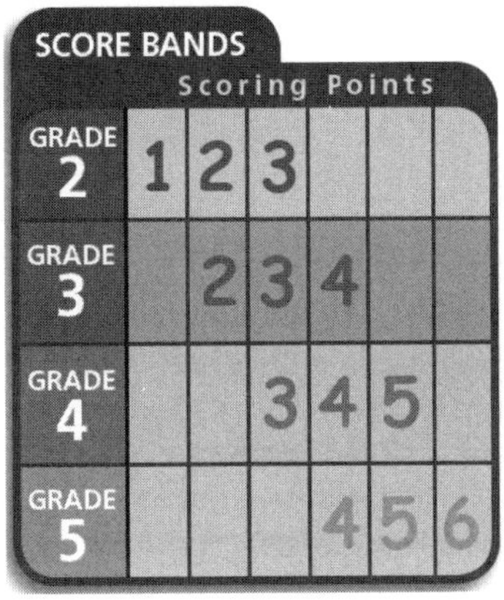

FIGURE 16.5. Rubric grade-level score bands.

Cassandra, a second-grade teacher, is in a professional development session focused on rubric use. She reads and scores the letter that her student, Marcus, had written about the cycle 2 book *I Am Rosa Parks* (Parks, 1997). Then she looks at the 6-point scale and the seven scores given by trained rubric scorers, most of which were at least 2 points lower than what she had assigned. "But," said Cassandra, "this is a good letter for a second grader, and they only gave him 2s and a couple 3s!"

Marcus had indeed written a good letter. Cassandra reacted to a pattern of scores putting him at "only . . . 2s" (out of a possible 6) even though his letter was better than most of the other students in her class. This "it's-not-fair" reaction was typical of many, many teachers who wanted to recognize students' "good" work and who were used to assessing students vis-à-vis others at their grade level rather than taking a long-term view of ultimate reading, writing, and thinking standards. These common misunderstandings provided a useful learning opportunity for us as researchers and professional developers, as well as for the teachers themselves. To help clarify everyone's thinking, we developed the chart shown in Figure 16.5 to encourage careful consideration about what might be expected of different children at different grade levels. It required protracted discussions of the score bands chart (Figure 16.5) and a true paradigm shift for many of the teachers to get comfortable with an approach to assessment based on a multigrade-level trajectory wherein reading, writing, and thinking are seen as developmental. Over time, participants came to understand the value of the long-term perspective for teaching and learning embodied in the I2B rubric, but we want to stress how important and challenging an issue this was for everyone to work through.

We focused the I2B implementation in urban schools, operating with materials specially selected to relate to diverse children, on the premise that children from less economically and educationally advantaged circumstances could especially benefit from a mentoring relationship with an adult. However, our work on integrating assessment into a system for teaching and learning is applicable in the range of elementary school settings across the country. Taking such a perspective especially helps teachers recognize students who underachieve as needing additional support to help them meet the same standards as other children in the class. We do not advocate a different, less challenging curriculum for students who struggle. We do not suggest isolated skills practice. Rather, we maintain our focus on authentic and challenging work, hold rigorous, high standards for all our children, and contend that authentic assessment can help us understand how to vary the level of support that we give to ensure their success.

REFERENCES

Au, K. H. (2001). Elementary programs in the context of the standards movement. In S. B. Wepner, D. S. Strickland, & J. T. Feeley (Eds.), *Administration and supervision of reading programs* (2nd ed., pp. 42–58). New York: Teachers College Press.

Au, K. H. (2005). *Multicultural issues and literacy achievement*. Mahwah, NJ: Erlbaum.

Au, K. H., Hirata, S. Y., & Raphael, T. E. (2005). Improving literacy achievement through standards. *California Reader, 39*(1), 5–10.

Bellamy, P. (Ed.). (2005). *Seeing with new eyes: Using the 6 + 1 Trait® writing model* (6th ed.). Portland, OR: NW Regional Educational Laboratory.

Brown, G. T., Glasswell, K., & Harland, D. (2004). Establishing reliability and validity of a national assessment tool for writing. *Assessing Writing, 40*, 105–121.

Clark, R. (2002). Building student achievement: In school and out-of-school factors. *NCREL Policy Issues, 13* [Online]. Retrieved June 27, 2005, from *http://www.ncrel.org/policy/pubs/html/pivol13/dec2002c.htm*.

Fletcher, R., & Portalupi, J. (2001). *Writing workshop: The essential guide*. Portsmouth, NH: Heinemann.

Glasswell, K., Parr, J. M., & Aikman, M. (2001). *Development of the asTTle writing assessment rubrics: Report to the New Zealand Ministry of Education*. Auckland: University of Auckland, Uniservices.

Heath, S. B. (1980). The functions and uses of literacy. *Journal of Communication, 30*, 123–133.

International Reading Association. (2005). *Focus on urban education initiatives: IRA programs and resources* [Online]. Retrieved December 27, 2005, from *www.reading.org/resources/issues/focus_urban.html*.

Kozol, J. (1991). *Savage inequalities: Children in America's schools*. New York: Crown.

Kozol, J. (2005). *The shame of the nation: The restoration of apartheid schooling in America*. New York: Crown.

Taylor, B. M., Pearson, P. D., Peterson, D. P., Clark, K., & Walpole, S. (2000). Effective schools and accomplished teachers: Lessons about primary-grade reading instruction in low-income schools. *Elementary School Journal, 101*, 121–165.

Taylor, B. M., Pearson, P. D., Peterson, D. P., & Rodriguez, M. C. (2003). Reading growth in high-poverty classrooms: The influence of teacher practices that encourage cognitive engagement in literacy learning. *Elementary School Journal, 104*, 3–28.

Taylor, B. M., Pearson, P. D., Peterson, D. P., & Rodriguez, M. C. (2005). The CIERA school change framework: An evidenced-based approach to professional development and school reading improvement. *Reading Research Quarterly, 40*, 40–69.

Teale, W. H. (1986). Home background and young children's literacy development. In W. H. Teale & E. Sulzby (Eds.), *Emergent literacy: Writing and reading* (pp. 173–206). Norwood, NJ: Ablex.

Teale, W. H., & Gambrell, L. (2007). Raising urban students' literacy achievement by engaging in authentic, challenging work. *The Reading Teacher, 60*.

Valencia, S. W., Hiebert, E. H., & Afflerbach, P. P. (1994). Realizing the possibilities of performance assessment: Current trends and future issues. In S. W. Valencia, E. H. Hiebert, & P. P. Afflerbach (Eds.), *Authentic reading assignment: Practices and possibilities* (pp. 286–300). Newark, DE: International Reading Association.

Valencia, S. W., & Pearson, P. D. (1987). Reading assessment: Time for a change. *The Reading Teacher, 40*, 726–733.

Venezky, R. L. (1991). The development of literacy in the industrialized nations of the West. In R. Barr, M. L. Kamil, P. B. Mosenthal, & P. D. Pearson (Eds.), *Handbook of reading research* (Vol. 2, pp. 46–67). New York: Longman.

Wiggins, G. (1990). The case for authentic assessment. *Practical Assessment, Research and Evaluation, 2*(2) [Online]. Retrieved September 8, 2005, from *www.PAREonline.net/getvn.asp?v=2&n=2*.

Wolf, S. A., & Gearhart, M. (1994). Writing what you read: Narrative assessment as a learning event. *Language Arts, 71*, 425–444.

CHILDREN'S BOOKS

Eaton, D. (1998). *The rainy day grump*. Photographs by D. Handelman. Brookfield, CT: Millbrook.

Parks, P. (1997). *I am Rosa Parks*. Illustrated by W. Clay. New York: Puffin.

Rossi, A. (2002). *Kids communicate*. Washington, DC: National Geographic.

CHAPTER 17

Putting the CIA System to Work

LINKING CURRICULUM, INSTRUCTION, AND ASSESSMENT TO IMPROVE STUDENT ACHIEVEMENT

Douglas Fisher
Diane Lapp
Nancy Frey
James Flood
Kelly Moore

Have you noticed that when the question of how to improve student achievement is posed, educators and administrators become instantly engaged? This response may occur because of increased state and national accountability and performance pressures that are creating the need to explore new ways to improve educational outcomes, especially for students who live in poverty. Although extremely interested, teachers remain isolated and often do not have adequate opportunities for structured conversations with their peers about teaching and learning issues that may affect student achievement (Schmoker, 1999). In this chapter we posit that this professional isolation must be changed if effective supports for student growth are to become shared realities among colleagues. We also believe that meaningful student gains will not be realized until such exchanges occur. We begin with a description of three initiatives that are designed to create a context for shared dialogue, and as such, a solution to issues of teacher isolation and student underperformance. These initiatives include standards-based curriculum, systems for reviewing student performance, and focusing on quality instruction. Then we provide examples of how such a system of collaboration works in one school district.

STANDARDS-BASED CURRICULUM

Creating national and state grade-level content and related performance standards is seen by many as a way to raise student achievement (Tucker & Codding, 2002). A national focus on standards is believed to ensure that all children at a particular grade are exposed to the same content, regardless of the school they attend or the teacher they are assigned. This focus is an attempt to secure access to the same curriculum for students attending underperforming schools as well as those at higher-achieving schools (Bracey, 1999; Creemers & Reezigt, 1996; Tschannen-Moran, Hoy, & Hoy, 1998; Datnow, Borman, Stringfield, Overman, & Castellano, 2003).

Standards-based educational reform advocates suggest that both content and performance standards be developed. Content standards provide general descriptions of what students should know across subject areas, including language arts, mathematics, science, social studies, and the arts, and performance standards provide the criteria for how well students must perform to demonstrate that they have obtained the skills and knowledge described by the content standard (i.e., how well students must read, write, or calculate).

Four steps provide the format for creating a standards-based curriculum. First, the standards must be identified. This identification typically occurs as state department of education personnel, with input from teachers and advocates, decide what every child should learn. Second, a curriculum to accomplish the identified standards at each grade level is developed. It is common for this step also to occur at the state level. Third, specific courses of study and instructional strategies are designed or developed. It is at this point that individual schools and teachers become involved. Teachers decide on the day-to-day content of the classes and the instructional methods they prefer. They also choose instructional materials, often from a state-approved list. Finally, measures are designed to assess student performance as compared with the standards. Standards-aligned assessments are used to determine student success and to hold schools accountable for these results. Unfortunately, the results from these particular types of assessment are often not available in time to make instructional decisions or changes during the school year. Thus, however valid such assessments might be, they are not especially useful to teachers who wish to use assessment data as they plan day-to-day instruction.

REVIEWING STUDENT PERFORMANCE

In response to the lag time between assessing student performance and getting the data into teachers' hands that is characteristic of large-scale, state-supported standards-aligned system, groups of teachers have begun to meet and discuss samples of students' routine work. Langer, Colton, and Goff (2003) describe a system in which groups of teachers volunteer to meet to collaboratively examine their students' performance and products. Similarly, Schmoker (1999) suggests that teachers set goals, collect data to analyze those goals, and meet in groups to discuss the findings. A sample goal might read:

The percentage of my students who will be at or above the proficient standard in reading comprehension will increase from 36% at the end of the 2005–2006 school year to 54% at the end of the 2006–2007 school year, as reported on the California Standards Tests.

The teacher who wrote this goal would need to provide a great deal of reading comprehension instruction and have a way of measuring his or her students' achievement along the way to ensure that the goal was met. This teacher would also likely want to meet with other teachers who were focused on reading comprehension to discuss instructional strategies designed to meet the goal.

The difficulty is that if teachers work individually to establish goals and review student work, they may establish different goals for their classes, and whole-school conversations will be difficult. Further, there is no guarantee that the goals and lessons will be standards-aligned or that teachers have ways of collecting assessment data that is linked to the content standards that are linked to the state test. On the other hand, if there is a process or a routine, it encourages teachers to work in small groups, and there is likely to be more coherence in the goals between classrooms. It is also more likely that the goals created by teachers will be aligned with state-level standards to which teachers and students are held accountable.

FOCUSING ON QUALITY INSTRUCTION

One of the very positive outcomes of the focus on working with groups of teachers to review student work has been conversations about "what works" in teaching and learning. Those who observe and study such group trends note that groups of teachers are meeting to discuss their craft as well as their successes and challenges in teaching diverse learners. As Murnane, Sharkey, and Boudett (2005) discovered from their study of 10 schools attempting to meet accountability demands, teachers and schools need a process for engaging in conversations around teaching and learning. One such process for discussing teaching and learning are inquiry groups or teacher study groups (e.g., Clark, 2001; Cramer, Hurst, & Wilson, 1996)

In their review of teacher study groups, Lefever-Davis, Wilson, Moore, Kent, and Hopkins (2003) noted that group conversations result in change possibly because teachers are responsible for their own learning and because isolation is reduced. One of their examples focuses on a new teacher who wanted to implement an instructional strategy called concept circles. As this person noted, "I learned so much from our discussions [in the teacher study group] and the examples the other teachers shared that I wasn't afraid to try concept circles in my classroom. Now we use them frequently, and more of my struggling students understand the sounds and letters connection" (p. 783).

There is no shortage of instructional strategies for groups of teachers to discuss, but the concern about the link between standards, assessment, and instruction remains. Further, as Lefever-Davis et al. (2003) note, teacher study groups "are formed on a voluntary basis, with teachers selecting the topics for study and determining their own plan of action for implementation" (p. 782). Although there are certainly positive aspects to self-selected professional development, we believe that schools should also have systems of improvement and empowerment that are a common feature of the overall operation of the system.

LINKING CURRICULUM, INSTRUCTION, AND ASSESSMENT

To realize the potential of these three initiatives—standards-based reform, systematic review of student performance, and conversations about instruction—a concerted, schoolwide initiative needs to be developed. Each of these initiatives assumes that there is a link between assessment and instruction; that is, that assessment data guide the instruction that students receive (Frey & Fisher, 2005; Johns, Lenski, & Elish-Piper, 2002; Lapp, Flood, Brock, & Fisher, 2006; Valencia & Buly, 2004). When assessment and instruction are seen as linked, they have the potential to help teachers to meet the needs of students and ensure that all children reach high standards (Fisher, Lapp, & Flood, 2005). Next we explore the components of a system we developed, and then we consider an example from an urban school that has begun to implement such a system.

CONSENSUS SCORING AND PEER PLANNING

One system for assessment and instruction includes five steps: (1) develop pacing guides, (2) develop common assessment, (3) select instructional materials and methods, (4) administer assessments and conduct an item analysis, and (5) review findings and revise plans. We describe each of these steps in the sections that follow.

Step 1: Develop Pacing Guides

Given that state content and performance standards exist, our first step focuses on teacher-developed pacing guides. Pacing guides give teachers an opportunity to develop timelines for teaching the standards and to agree on a sequence of skill development. Regardless of the sequence, focusing on a pacing guide requires that all teachers attend to the standards. The conversations among teachers during this step focus on the articulation of the standards and how to best teach them.

Step 2: Develop Common Assessments

As part of the process, teachers develop standards-aligned benchmark assessments that allow them to gauge their students' progress toward the standards. As we have already noted, state assessments are usually too late to guide day-to-day instructional guidance. In addition, writing standards-aligned assessment items provides teachers with a structured approach to return to the standards and discuss with their colleagues the ways in which standards could be assessed. The conversations teachers have during this step focus on the ways in which standards are assessed and how to design valid and reliable measures of student performance.

Step 3: Select Instructional Materials and Methods

Although many components of this system require schoolwide support and commitment, the selection of instructional materials and methods is still left to the teacher. Of course, teachers must comply with their state and district guidelines. But within these parameters, teachers make choices based on their individual styles and students' needs. Importantly, teachers share their materials and methods with one another during conversations about teaching and learning. The conversations teachers have during this step focus on a range of instructional innovations, lesson plans, teaching ideas, and curriculum units.

Step 4: Administer Assessments and Conduct an Item Analysis

At a specific time as determined on the pacing guide, every student in the grade or course participates in the same benchmark assessment. The assessment data are aggregated for the grade or course (e.g., third-grade or seventh-grade math), and an item analysis is conducted. This means that teachers analyze each question and identify the percentage of students who has selected each choice. The data are disaggregated to identify achievement trends for targeted groups of students. For example, schools may need to focus on English language learners, students with disabilities, a particular ethnic group or gender, or students who live in poverty. The conversations teachers have during this step focus on student performance and students who have not yet met the standards.

Step 5: Review Findings and Revise Plans

Although groups of teachers are meeting and talking about teaching and learning throughout this process, specific time needs to be set aside to ensure that teachers have an opportunity to discuss the assessment results. Teachers may want to reteach their students if large groups have failed to meet the standards, or they may need to meet with individuals or small groups to address particular needs. Alternatively, teachers may decide to revise the assessments or change the pacing guides as a result of their discussions. The conversations teachers have during this step focus on reflection and next steps.

IMPROVING ACHIEVEMENT THROUGH CONSENSUS SCORING AND PEER PLANNING: AN EXAMPLE

Despite increased achievement in reading comprehension and literary analysis and response, a group of fifth-grade teachers at a large urban school in San Diego expressed frustration with the lack of change in their students' writing achievement. Although their students were able to identify content to be shared, their presentation strategies and conventions were not at grade level. During the teachers' first planning meeting of the year, they discussed the instructional steps they should undertake, identified related content standards, and developed a pacing guide to enable their students to reach proficiency for these two California language arts standards. They decided that during the first 6 weeks of the school year, they would focus on specific aspects of grammar, punctuation, capitalization, writing organization and focus, and research skills in all content areas. Because they used the state standards framework to guide their planning, they did not have to "make up" their focus.

Their next step was to create a common assessment. The team decided to write a 12-item assessment with sample questions from each of their focus areas. Figure 17.1 contains a copy of this assessment. The questions on the assessment were modeled after the state assessment of released items provided on the Department of Education website. The teachers also used a checklist to improve the reliability and validity of the assessment (see Figure 17.2).

During their regularly scheduled grade-level meetings, teachers discussed the materials they were using, the methods they liked and didn't like, and their successes and challenges. As one of the teachers said during a meeting, "I'm not sure how to get them to understand this punctuation. They get the periods, but the more complex punctuation seems to confuse them." This conversation turned to ways that each of the other fifth-grade teachers focused on punctuation—from focused time during shared readings to homework assignments that provided repeated practice.

Approximately 6 weeks into the school year, every fifth grader was given the common assessment. The students' achievement is summarized, by standard, in Figure 17.3.

During the next grade-level meeting, the teachers congratulated themselves on the success they'd had with some of the standards, particularly the grammar. They also focused their conversation on the areas in which students were still performing below grade level. At first, they were concerned that the vast majority of their students could not name an independent clause (question 7) or correctly identify conjunctions (question 8). As they talked about test results, they decided that these areas would not be their priority. Instead, they believed that it was more important to focus on punctuation and capitalization, because these skills would also transfer into students' writing and reading, whereas identifying an independent clause was "just something that they test."

Their conversation led to a discussion about revising the pacing guide and the decision to maintain a focus on grammar, punctuation, and capitalization. They shared a number of ideas with one another and wanted to know which students performed best on these tasks and which students performed poorly. Each teacher was given the performance record for his or her class as well as disaggregated data on English language learners and students with disabilities—two of the significant subpopulations at risk at the school. These data provided teachers with an opportunity to evaluate their own performance against the group's performance and to consider their instructional plans accordingly. As one of the teachers said as the meeting ended, "My students didn't do very well on the research and technology section. I probably brought down the whole school score. If any of your students did really well, I'd like to talk with you about what you did. E-mail me and let me know."

Although fifth graders are not assessed on their actual writing performance, these teachers understand that the skills related to writing must be put into practice in authentic writing situations. The content of a writing piece is of utmost importance to these teachers, who realize that reading and writing fluency develops throughout one's lifetime. As such, they require that every student participates in a schoolwide writing

Directions: Read the words in the box very carefully. Look at the part that is underlined. If the underlined part is correct, mark answer D, *Correct as written*. If the underlined part is *not* correct, read all the answer choices carefully. Find the answer that shows the *best* way to write the underlined part and mark that answer. There is only one correct answer for each item.

Sample A | The sun <u>rised</u> over the mountains. |

    A. raised
    B. rose
    C. rosed
    D. Correct as written

Sample B | <u>She and I</u> are going to the park. |

    A. She and me
    B. Her and I
    C. Me and her
    D. Correct as written

GRAMMAR

Directions: Look at the way words are used. Find the underlined part. If the underlined part is correct, mark answer D, *Correct as written*. If the underlined part is *not* correct, mark the correct answer.

1. | He walked up the stairs <u>most quick</u>. |

    A. more quick
    B. quick
    C. quickly
    D. Correct as written

2. | <u>Her scoring and their passing</u> won the soccer game. |

    A. She scoring and them passing
    B. Her scoring and they passing
    C. Her scoring and them passing
    D. Correct as written

PUNCTUATION

Directions: Look at the punctuation in each sentence. Find the underlined part. If the underlined part is correct, mark answer D, *Correct as written*. If the underlined part is *not* correct, find and mark the correct answer.

3. | Maria liked many <u>colors, such as: red</u>, purple, yellow, and pink. |

    A. colors, such as; red
    B. colors: such as red,
    C. colors, such as red,
    D. Correct as written

4. | The fifth graders' favorite song was <u>Stars and Stripes</u>. |

    A. "Stars and Stripes."
    B. Stars and Stripes."
    C. "Stars and Stripes.
    D. Correct as written

CAPITALIZATION

Directions: Read each sentence. Find the underlined part. Look at the capitals in each word. If the underlined part is correct, mark answer D, *Correct as written*. If the underlined part is *not* correct, find and mark the correct answer.

5. | We went to see <u>Dr. Segal, one other doctor, and a Dentist</u>. |

    A. Dr. Segal, one other doctor, and a dentist.
    B. Dr. Segal, one other Doctor, and a dentist.
    C. Dr. Segal, one other Doctor and a Dentist.
    D. Correct as written

FIGURE 17.1. Assessment created by a group of teachers, modeled on items provided by the Development of Education website.

6. | Her favorite movie was <u>The Lord of the Rings</u>. |

    A. The Lord of the rings
    B. the lord of the rings
    C. The Lord Of The Rings
    D. Correct as written

PART 2

Directions: Read each question and the answer choices carefully. Find the correct answer and mark it.

7. | An example of an independent clause is: |

    A. After Mary won the race
    B. Juan almost won the race
    C. When the race started
    D. Since the runners were late

8. | Which answer choice below lists two conjunctions? |

    A. to, or
    B. and, to
    C. and, but
    D. so, on

ORGANIZATION AND FOCUS

Directions: Read the paragraph in the box. Then read each question and the answers carefully. Choose the *best* answer and mark it. Use the paragraph to answer questions 9–10.

Firemen and Your Safety

Although you may have a smoke detector in your home, firemen can help make sure your house is a safe place to live. Firemen can make sure your home has escape routes in case a fire occurs. Firemen can check for gas leaks in the kitchen. Firemen can install rope ladders in case you need to climb out of a high window.

9. | What is the purpose of this paragraph? |

    A. to tell us many of the things firemen can do for us and our safety
    B. to explain how firemen look for escapes in your house
    C. to tell us about the training firemen receive
    D. to tell how firemen check for gas leaks

10. | Which is the best topic sentence for this paragraph? |

    A. Firemen can install rope ladders in case you need to climb out of a high window.
    B. Firemen can make sure your home has escape routes in case a fire occurs.
    C. Although you may have a smoke detector in your home, firemen can help make sure your house is a safe place to live.
    D. Firemen can check for gas leaks in the kitchen.

RESEARCH: AND TECHNOLOGY

Directions: Read each question carefully. Find the correct answer and mark it.

11. | The title page of a book gives all but one of the following. Which one does it <u>not</u> give? |

    A. the name(s) of the author(s)
    B. where the publisher's offices are
    C. the name of the publisher
    D. the copyright date

12. | Which one is <u>not</u> true for the index of a book? |

    A. It may list many pages for the same word or entry.
    B. It is found at the beginning of the book.
    C. It lists entries (words, etc.) in alphabetical order.
    D. It gives page, section, or chapter numbers for entries.

STOP
END OF ASSESSMENT

FIGURE 17.1. *(continued)*

All Items

☐ Is this the most appropriate type of item to use for the intended learning outcomes?

☐ Does each item or task require students to demonstrate the performance described in the specific learning outcome it measures (relevance)?

☐ Does each item present a clear and definite task to be performed (clarity)?

☐ Is each item or task presented in simple, readable language and free from excessive verbiage (conciseness)?

☐ Does each item provide an appropriate challenge (ideal difficulty)?

☐ Does each item have an answer that would be agreed upon by experts (correctness)?

☐ Is there a clear basis for awarding partial credit on items or tasks with multiple points (scoring rubric)?

☐ Is each item or task free from technical errors and irrelevant clues (technical soundness)?

☐ Is each test item free from cultural bias?

☐ Have the items been set aside for a time before reviewing them (or reviewed by a colleague)?

Short-Answer Items

☐ Can the items be answered with a number, symbol, word, or brief phrase?

☐ Has textbook language been avoided?

☐ Have the items been stated so that only one response is correct?

☐ Are the answer blanks equal in length (for fill-in responses)?

☐ Are the answer blanks (preferably one per item) at the end of the items, preferably after a question?

☐ Are the items free of clues (such as *a* or *an*)?

☐ Has the degree of precision been indicated for numerical answers?

☐ Have the units been indicated when numerical answers are expressed in units?

Binary (True–False) and Multiple-Binary Items

☐ Can each statement be clearly judged true or false with only one concept per statement?

☐ Have specific determiners (e.g., *usually, always*) been avoided?

☐ Have trivial statements been avoided?

☐ Have negative statements (especially double negatives) been avoided?

☐ Does a superficial analysis suggest a wrong answer?

☐ Are opinion statements attributed to some source?

☐ Are the true and false items approximately equal in length?

☐ Is there approximately an equal number of true and false items?

☐ Has a detectable pattern of answers (e.g., T, F, T, F) been avoided?

Matching Items

☐ Is the material for the two lists homogeneous?

☐ Is the list of responses longer or shorter than the list of premises?

☐ Are the responses brief and on the right-hand side?

☐ Have the responses been placed in alphabetical or numerical order?

☐ Do the directions indicate the basis for matching?

☐ Do the directions indicate how many times each response may be used?

☐ Are all of the matching items on the same page?

FIGURE 17.2. Checklist for creating common assessments. Adapted from Linn and Gronlund (2000). Copyright 2000 by Pearson Education. Adapted by permission.

Multiple-Choice Items

☐ Does each item stem present a meaningful problem?

☐ Is there too much information in the stem?

☐ Are the item stems free of irrelevant material?

☐ Are the item stems stated in positive terms (if possible)?

☐ If used, has negative wording been given special emphasis (e.g., capitalized)?

☐ Are the distractors brief and free of unnecessary words?

☐ Are the distractors similar in length and form to the answer?

☐ Is there only one correct or clearly best answer?

☐ Are the distractors based on specific misconceptions?

☐ Are the items free of clues that point to the answer?

☐ Are the distractors and answer presented in sensible (e.g., alphabetical, numerical) order?

☐ Have *all of the above* been avoided and *none of the above* used judiciously?

☐ If a stimulus is used, is it necessary for answering the item?

☐ If a stimulus is used, does it require use of skills sought to be assessed?

Essay Items

☐ Are the questions designed to measure higher-level learning outcomes?

☐ Does each question clearly indicate the response expected (including extensiveness)?

☐ Are students aware of the basis on which their answers will be evaluated?

☐ Are appropriate time limits provided for responding to the questions?

☐ Are students aware of the time limits and/or point values for each question?

☐ Are all students required to respond to the same questions?

Performance Items

☐ Does the item focus on learning outcomes that require complex cognitive skills and student performances?

☐ Does the task represent both the content and skills that are central to learning outcomes?

☐ Does the item minimize dependence on skills that are irrelevant to the intended purpose of the assessment task?

☐ Does the task provide the necessary scaffolding for students to be able to understand the task and achieve the task?

☐ Do the directions clearly describe the task?

☐ Are students aware of the basis (expectations) on which their performances will be evaluated in terms of scoring rubrics?

For the Assessment as a Whole

☐ Are the items of the same type grouped together on the test (or within sections; sets)?

☐ Are the items arranged from easy to more difficult within sections or the test as a whole?

☐ Are items numbered in sequence, indicating so if the test continues on subsequent pages?

☐ Are all answer spaces clearly indicated, and is each answer space related to its corresponding item?

☐ Are the correct answers distributed in such a way that there is no detectable pattern?

☐ Is the test material well spaced, legible, and free of typos?

☐ Are there directions for each section of the test and the test as a whole?

☐ Are the directions clear and concise?

FIGURE 17.2. (*continued*)

Item Analysis: Answer Distribution by Standard							
Grade 5: All Students			Percent of students who selected each answer choice1				
Question Number	Strand/Standard	Total Students	A	B	C	D	Blank
1	Conventions 1.2	214	9.81%	4.21%	83.64%	1.87%	0.47%
2	Conventions 1.2	214	7.94%	7.01%	11.68%	71.96%	1.40%
3	Conventions 1.3	214	9.81%	14.49%	47.20%	28.04%	0.47%
4	Conventions 1.3	214	69.16%	2.80%	5.14%	21.96%	0.93%
5	Conventions 1.4	214	34.11%	6.07%	39.25%	18.69%	1.87%
6	Conventions 1.4	214	4.21%%	2.80%	22.90%	69.16%	0.93%
7	Conventions 1.1	214	27.10%	28.04%	25.70%	8.41%	10.75%
8	Conventions 1.1	214	20.09%	17.29%	34.11%	21.50%	7.01%
9	Strategies 1.0	214	79.91%	10.75%	5.14%	3.74%	0.47%
10	Strategies 1.2a	214	9.81%%	21.50%	62.62%	4.67%	1.40%
11	Strategies 1.3	214	21.96%	42.52%	10.75%	22.43%	2.34%
12	Strategies 1.3	214	22.90%	31.31%	32.24%	12.15%	1.40%

1 Shaded cells indicate correct answers.

Strand-Standard	**Standard Description**
Conventions 1.1	Identify and correctly use prepositional phrases, appositives, and independent and dependent clauses; use transitions and conjunctions to correct ideas.
Conventions 1.2	Identify and correctly use verbs that are often misused (e.g., *lie/lay, sit/set, rise/raise*), modifiers, and pronouns.
Conventions 1.3	Use a colon to separate hours and minutes and to introduce a list; use quotation marks around the exact words of a speaker and titles of poems, songs, short stories, and so forth.
Conventions 1.4	Use correct capitalization.
Strategies 1.0	Students write clear, coherent, and focused essays. The writing exhibits the students' awareness of the audience and purpose. Essays contain formal introductions, supporting evidence, and conclusions. Students progress through the stages of the writing process as needed.
Strategies 1.2a	Create multiple-paragraph expository compositions: Establish a topic, important ideas, or events in sequence or chronological order.
Strategies 1.3	Use organizational features of printed text (e.g., citations, end notes, bibliographic references) to locate relevant information.

FIGURE 17.3. Item analysis: Answer distribution by standard.

prompt each time they give a common assessment. The fifth-grade writing prompt that coincided with the multiple-choice test in Figure 17.1 focused on the summer reading book, *Tales of a Fourth Grade Nothing* (Blume, 1972). As a group, the fifth-grade teachers scored the papers using the state 4-point rubric (see *www.cde.ca.gov/ta/tg/sr/documents/cst47teacher.pdf*). As they read each paper, they noted areas of general concern. During their conversation about this group of papers, the teachers noted the students' success with conventions and mechanics. Once they noted that the majority of papers had a logical flow and sequence, they focused on content and message conveyance.

After the papers were all scored, they were separated into piles by the scores. From the pile of "1" papers ("1" = "worst") an example was randomly selected. They all read this paper and discussed the type of instruction the student would need to move to the next level in his or her writing. Figure 17.4 contains the randomly selected "2" paper.

The discussion about this paper focused on the need to help the writer move from the factual focus on the connections between the book and the child's life to a focus on the significant *events* from the text, the author's way of conveying (telling) the story, and on additional formats for sharing the information.

The teachers planned to encourage the writing development of this child, and others with similar strengths, by modeling how to reread, edit, and expand their responses. They suggested that first the writer should think about the potential reader

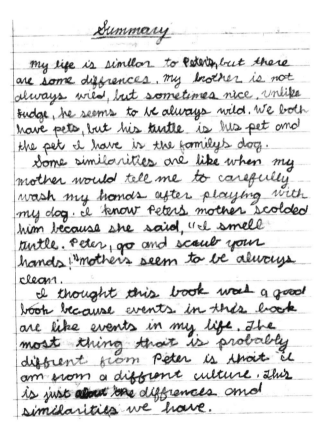

FIGURE 17.4. Randomly selected "2" paper.

and what he or she would need to be told in order to better understand the personal comparison being drawn between the book and the author of the response. Once the writer identified the intent, the teachers further modeled how to separate relevant and irrelevant information and make expansions that would include additional examples and conversation designed to support the comparison while holding the reader's attention. When the comparison was well established, the teachers planned to use this authentic piece of writing to again model how to return to the text to focus on character and setting details and then to help the child move from report to diary writing. They planned to accomplish this shift by modeling how to write diary entries that shared their reflections throughout the story, their feelings while reading various sections of the book, language and elements of style that held their attention, and details about characters that made them come to life. Each entry would be used as a focus to talk about the writing style, tone, and language, as well as the content. The teachers also focused on word choice for this paper and discussed ways to help the student increase her use of descriptive language and sensory details (e.g., Flood, Lapp, & Fisher, 2004). Because of this shared dialogue, writing instruction was scaffolded according to each student's writing development as related to the standards.

LESSONS LEARNED FROM CONSENSUS SCORING AND PEER PLANNING

First, we learned that consensus scoring works. As we noted earlier in this chapter, the fifth-grade scores on writing conventions and strategies had not changed for 2 years. As teachers met, discussed, and reviewed student performance on a systematic basis, scores changed. The students whose teachers used consensus scoring and peer planning outperformed their historical control groups, and the results were statistically significant.

Second, we learned that although consensus scoring is intended as an assessment strategy and a way to impact student achievement, it also serves as a foundation and context for professional development. This process provides teachers with opportunities to review content and performance standards in meaningful ways and for authentic reasons. They learn to design pacing guides and assessment tools, and these skills transfer to other aspects of their professional life. They also have conversations about teaching and learning and share their instructional ideas and successes with their colleagues.

Third, we learned that when engaged in consensus scoring, teachers tend to set high expectations for students and then to design instruction that will enable students to meet the expectations. Importantly, these heightened expectations extend to traditionally underperforming groups of students who may have been excluded from discussions in the past. In our experience, consensus scoring and collaborative planning focus attention on groups of students who are not yet performing well, as groups of teachers attempt to improve the achievement of all students.

Our final lesson concerns assessments in general. We know that assessments are the link between teaching and learning. We have had the opportunity to work alongside a group of teachers who used assessments to guide their instruction and their professional conversations. Rather than complaining about the "assessment demands" or the lost instructional time devoted to assessments, teachers who use the assessment data to inform their instruction realize that *information is power*. In the end, this may be the most important lesson of all in changing the context for teaching and learning.

REFERENCES

Bracey, G. W. (1999). Research: Poverty and achievement. *Phi Delta Kappan, 81*(4), 330–331.

Clark, C. (2001). *Talking shop: Authentic conversations and teacher learning.* New York: Teachers College Press.

Cramer, G., Hurst, B., & Wilson, C. (1996). *Teacher study groups for professional development.* Bloomington, IN: Phi Delta Kappa Educational Foundation.

Creemers, B., & Reezigt, G. (1996). School level conditions affecting the effectiveness of instruction. *School Effectiveness and School Improvement, 7,* 197–228.

Datnow, A., Borman, G. D., Stringfield, S., Overman, L. T., & Castellano, M. (2003). Comprehensive school reform in culturally and linguistically diverse contexts: Implementation and outcomes from a four-year study. *Educational Evaluation and Policy Analysis, 25,* 143–170.

Fisher, D., Lapp, D., & Flood, J. (2005). Consensus scoring and peer planning: Meeting literacy accountability demands one school at a time. *The Reading Teacher, 58,* 656–666.

Flood, J., Lapp, D., & Fisher, D. (Eds.). (2004). *Teaching writing: Strategies for developing the 6 + 1 traits.* San Diego: Academic Professional Development.

Frey, N., & Fisher, D. (2005). *Language arts workshop: Purposeful reading and writing instruction.* Upper Saddle River, NJ: Merrill Prentice-Hall.

Johns, J. L., Lenski, S. D., & Elish-Piper, L. (2002). *Teaching beginning readers: Linking assessment and instruction.* Dubuque, IA: Kendall Hunt.

Langer, G. M., Colton, A. B., & Goff, L. S. (2003). *Collaborative analysis of student work: Improving teaching and learning.* Alexandria, VA: Association for Supervision and Curriculum Development.

Lapp, D., Flood, J., Brock, C., & Fisher, D. (2006). *Teaching reading to every child* (4th ed.). Mahwah, NJ: Erlbaum.

Lefever-Davis, S., Wilson, C., Moore, E., Kent, A., & Hopkins, S. (2003). Teacher study groups: A strategic approach to promoting students' literacy development. *The Reading Teacher, 56,* 782–784.

Linn, R. L., & Gronlund, N. E. (2000). *Measurement and assessment in teaching* (8th ed.). Upper Saddle River, NJ: Merrill Prentice-Hall.

Murnane, R. J., Sharkey, N. S., & Boudett, K. P. (2005). Using student-assessment results to improve instruction: Lessons from a workshop. *Journal of Education for Students Placed at Risk, 10,* 269–280.

Schmoker, M. (1999). *Results: The key to continuous school improvement.* Alexandria, VA: Association for Supervision and Curriculum Development.

Tschannen-Moran, M., Hoy, A., & Hoy, W. (1998). Teacher efficacy: Its meaning and measure. *Review of Educational Research, 68,* 202–248.

Tucker, M. S., & Codding, J. S. (2002). *Standards for our schools: How to set them, measure them, and reach them.* San Francisco: Jossey-Bass.

Valencia, S. W., & Buly, M. R. (2004). Behind test scores: What struggling readers really need. *The Reading Teacher, 57,* 520–531.

CHILDREN'S BOOK

Blume, J. (1972). *Tales of a fourth grade nothing.* New York: Dell.

CHAPTER 18

Developing an Individualized Education Plan

WHAT COUNTS AS EVIDENCE?

Rachel L. McCormack
P. David Pearson
Jeanne R. Paratore

This chapter is different from the others in this text in that its particular focus is on children who are identified as having special learning needs and on the efforts of teachers and other educators to assess and support those learning needs. It is based on work we did over the course of 2 years in an elementary school in which classroom teachers and other learning specialists allowed us to examine their special education referral process. The result was not one, but rather, two studies. In this chapter we have merged the two in order to emphasize the interconnections between them. The first part of the chapter describes the first investigation, in which we set out to discover the types of evidence used in the decision making for students with special learning needs. We were particularly interested in the ways in which the professionals and parents worked together to make decisions of consequence for students.

Though unintended, we had reason to believe that our first research study had taken on the character of an intervention, prompting changes in the views of the teachers and administrator in the school and, more importantly, in the practices they used to make these consequential decisions. So we decided to check in 2 years later with new questions: What happened after we left the site? What changes, if any, resulted from our close scrutiny of the school's special education referral process? While collecting data for the first study, our goals were neither to engage the elementary school in a self-assessment of their special education referral process nor to encourage change in that process. The second part of the chapter describes how, as a result of our inquiry, both occurred.

THE BEGINNING OF OUR INVESTIGATION

Over the past few decades, concurrent with the national movement toward inclusion of special education students in regular education (U.S. Department of Education Public Law 92-142, 1974) and similar authorizing legislative efforts at the state level (e.g., Massachusetts, Public Law 766), the use of a referral conference as the primary site for deciding upon entry into special programs has grown rapidly. These meetings, which include key decision makers (e.g., parents, teachers, specialist, and school administration), are ostensibly structured to ensure that all relevant data—including scores on tests, reports of classroom performance and behavior, informal classroom assessments, and reports on out-of-school behavior from parents—are taken into account in the decision-making process.

Because referral conferences are designed to play a pivotal role in these consequential decisions for individual children and their families, they provide an important context in which to study the uses to which various sorts of assessment are put. These data can range from scores on standardized tests at one end of the "formality" continuum to anecdotal reports and narrative observations by teachers and parents at the other end of the continuum.

Mehan (1991, 1993) argues that formal evaluation plays a powerful and potentially dehumanizing role in this ubiquitous and highly politicized classification process. He characterizes formal evaluation tools as "officially sanctioned props," which, he says, often employ technical terms that silence the voices and observations of others. Because "speakers and hearers do not share the same conventions of a common register," a dichotomy develops between the quasi-scientific discourse of school psychologists and other evaluation specialists and the more informal and conventional discourse of parents and classroom teachers (Mehan, 1993, p. 253).

What happens, we wondered, in schools where there is a commitment to using authentic, curriculum-relevant, classroom-based assessment to monitor student growth? What roles do different assessment tools play in the process by which students become classified as learning disabled? In these contexts, are the roles of the "officially sanctioned props" diminished? Or do formal testing measures wield the same or even more weight during the referral process? In addition, we wondered if classroom-based assessment tools—those that are curriculum relevant and grounded in firsthand observations—might change the discourse of the referral process by painting a more complex and qualitative portrait of the child than can be accomplished with the "paint by numbers" approach to norm-referenced and standardized assessments.

To learn more about these questions, we found a school that had made a commitment to classroom-based assessment, at least for its regular education program, and was willing to submit its special education referral process to the sort of close and detailed examination necessary to achieve an understanding of the role of different assessment tools.

The Hoyt School and Its Referral Process

Hoyt Elementary School is located in a middle-income district, with a predominantly European American school population of 650 K–5 students. At the time of our investigation, approximately 17% of the students at Hoyt Elementary had individualized education plans (IEPs) and received special education services. The process for referring students for special education services involved three steps and three types of meetings.

Step 1: Teacher Assistance Team

The purpose of the teacher assistance team (TAT) meeting was to gather a team of professionals to discuss the academic performance of students with whom the classroom teachers had concerns and to make recommendations for interventions. The team was led by one of the reading specialists and consisted of the current classroom teacher, the classroom teacher from the previous year, the school psychologist, and one or more special education teachers who agreed to serve on the TAT on a rotating basis. Classroom teachers almost always initiated this stage of the process. The evidence the teacher used to present a case included classroom-based assessment such as running records (Clay, 1993), writing samples, and teacher-designed assessments. At times, anecdotal evidence from the parents was included, although the parents were not usually invited. The purpose of including the student's teacher from the previous year was to provide additional anecdotal evidence of the student's performance during the prior year. After hearing and examining the evidence provided by the classroom teachers, the TAT offered suggestions for interventions, and, in many cases at the Hoyt School, the reading specialists agreed to provide temporary in-class or pull–put assistance to the child in order to give more support to the teacher and the student. Typically, the classroom teacher agreed to implement the interventions the TAT suggested for approximately 6 weeks. Then the teacher could either continue the interventions and halt the process at that stage, or, if the student's performance was still a concern, schedule a step 2 meeting.

Step 2: Initial Referral

The purpose of the step 2 meeting was to discuss further the academic performance of a student if teachers, parents, or other professionals continued to have concerns about his or her academic progress. Either a professional or a parent could initiate this step of the process. The school psychologist chaired the meeting and other participants included the parents, school principal, reading specialist, classroom teacher, and all the special education professionals who represented the areas of concern: speech/language/occupational therapy, moderate special needs. The step 2 meeting typically ended with agreement among the participants that more information about the student's abilities and performance was needed. This information was obtained through a battery of testing, including intelligence tests and reading and writing standardized tests. Parents gave permission at this meeting for the tests to be administered, and the special education professionals, who would administer the tests, had 45 school days to complete the testing and write the report.

Step 3: Evaluation Results and Discussion

The purpose of the step 3 meeting was to formally present the reports of the results of the standardized tests and to make recommendations for special education services, if needed. The step 3 meeting also included many participants: the parents, the school principal, the school psychologist, the classroom teacher, the reading specialist who chaired the TAT, and all the special education professionals who administered the standardized tests to the student. At this meeting, everyone had a chance to contribute to the end product: a recommendation for special education services and the drafting of an IEP, further testing, or no recommendation for additional services by the special education professionals.

The Inquiry

Circumstances worked in our favor during our investigation. As it turned out, at the time of our visit to the school, there were five students who were at various stages of the special education referral process; we were thus allowed a naturally occurring opportunity to examine this process at different stages. We looked closely at their cases to better understand the role of formal and informal evidence at these different stages. We interviewed the parents and all the professionals involved in each case before and after each meeting, and we audiotaped the meetings themselves in order to document the process as carefully as possible. In addition, we collected and reviewed classroom assessments and artifacts, as well as test results and reports when they were available. We paid particular attention to the artifacts that were brought to the table at each meeting and the ways in which they were used to support the decisions in the various stages. IEPs were forwarded to us as they were written. As we reviewed the documents, we asked the following questions:

> What assessments took precedence at each of the stages?
> How important was the parent's anecdotal evidence?
> How important was the teacher's anecdotal evidence?
> What was the nature of the talk and how did the professionals use their positions to make their points?
> When were the parents the most vocal and the least marginalized?
> Whose voices were privileged?
> Whose voices were silenced?

The Children

We were presented with the academic lives of five children, each with distinct learning experiences and profiles. We learned about Katherine, a second grader, at a combination of step 1 and step 2, as the parents had requested a meeting and wanted everyone present. The classroom teacher and the parents were concerned about the organization of Katherine's written work. The writing was "wobbly," and the ideas were often not cohesive and organized. In her oral language she often had difficulty recalling words, and this transferred to her writing. Her language was imprecise. The classroom teacher used writing samples from her daily work to illustrate her concerns. In addition, the reading specialist had taken running records and provided some anecdotal evidence. They concluded that her reading was fluent for a second grader, but her ability to retell was limited. Although Katherine's mother was initially reluctant to approve a formal evaluation process, protesting that her daughter was "quiet and shy," the team convinced her to proceed to the testing stage. Katherine was scheduled to be tested by the special education teachers in speech/language and motor skills.

Next, we learned about the complex case of Jake, a fourth grader. His case was undergoing a step 3 review of the tests that had been given. Jake had undergone psychological tests and a battery of tests for learning disabilities. Although the special education professionals agreed that Jake might benefit from their services, they attributed his problems primarily to "behavior difficulties." His classroom teacher disagreed. She believed his needs were far more complex, and that Jake needed an "aggressive" IEP. She presented numerous classroom-based assessments and anecdotal evidence to challenge and rebut the decisions made by the special education professionals. In the end, Jake was given an IEP that included 3 hours per week of special services.

The case of Taylor, a second grader, was discussed at a step 2 meeting. Taylor's teacher had already completed the step 1 process because of her concerns about Taylor's oral and written language abilities. The teacher explained that Taylor's undeveloped oral language ("uses wrong tenses in conversation") transferred to her writing, and she shared work samples that illustrated Taylor's "messy writing." She also reported that Taylor's phonics skills were not progressing. The reading specialist, who had recently included Taylor in a "benchmark group" (Benchmark Word Detective Program, Gaskins, 2004) as a result of the step 1 meeting, reported that she was making progress, but not enough. In this small group she did intensive word study, including spelling, phonics, and vocabulary development. After listening to the parent, classroom teacher, and reading specialist, the special education professionals concluded that, despite a fair amount of support, Taylor's "written output [was] not reflecting a lot of growth." They noted that her "organization [was] very poor, especially spatially and sequentially," and that there was evidence of "left/right confusion." After listening to the informal assessments of the special education professionals, the parents agreed to have Taylor tested in the areas of motor skills, speech and language, learning disabilities, and intelligence.

Second grader Brendan's lengthy step 2 meeting involved a discussion of his performance in all aspects of the curriculum. Brendan's first-grade teacher had recommended retention at the end of first grade (partly because he was the youngest in the class and had made the "cutoff date" for kindergarten eligibility by 1 day), but his mother had not agreed to retention. Perhaps as a result, many of the comments about his performance, including his mother's, related to his young age and perceived immaturity. The professionals, in lieu of testing, tried to convince Brendan's mother to retain him at the end of second grade; Brendan's mother, however, remained firmly opposed to retention. The team agreed to test Brendan in the areas of intelligence and learning disabilities.

At kindergartener Aaron's step 3 meeting, the team reviewed a battery of early literacy testing, speech and language screening, and motor skills assessments. The results confirmed his parents' and classroom teacher's hunches about his strengths and weaknesses. Participants discussed Aaron's "delay" in recognizing alphabet letters and his articulation and speech difficulties. In particular, his fine motor skills prompted a lengthy discussion. The team decided to place Aaron on an IEP and to provide speech and language support and occupational therapy.

What We Learned

As we reviewed the cases of all five students—Katherine, Jake, Taylor, Brendan, and Aaron—we found that they yielded four interesting similarities in terms of the role and efficacy of the evidence used in the decision-making process. We describe these similarities as follows.

1. *Classroom-based and anecdotal assessments were used to get the conversation started.* Day-to-day performance evidence served to alert the classroom teachers that something was awry, or at least in need of closer investigation. In the case of second grader Katherine, the process was in an early stage, and no formal assessments had been administered, giving us an ideal opportunity to examine the role of work samples, portfolios, and other forms of assessment. Her classroom teacher's anecdotal reports of her oral language repertoire convinced the members of the team that more formal tests were in order. In the case of Aaron, the kindergartner with language and motor difficulties, his teacher's detailed observations of his daily performance in regular kindergarten activities (i.e., cutting, pasting, learning letters, handling books) were compelling enough to convince the team that a closer look was warranted. Fourth grader Jake's classroom teacher used numerous work samples and her own observation journals to persuade others to take a closer look at his abilities as a learner. In the earliest stages of the referral process, the team appeared to place a good deal of trust in curriculum-related work and relied on classroom-based work samples, observations, and anecdotal records to make decisions about children's learning needs.

2. *Formal assessments were used to verify and substantiate earlier impressions and to officially admit students to the special education system.* In two of the five cases, formal test data were presented at the final stages we observed. In Brendan's case, the classroom teacher was almost relieved when formal tests revealed that he had learning disabilities, because it meant that her original hunch was more "reliable." In Jake's case, however, the classroom teacher did not have as much trust in the formal testing protocol as Brendan's teacher did. Although Jake's formal test scores largely confirmed her own careful observations and documentation, she believed that the test scores were, in fact, less accurate, and that they overestimated Jake's performance. She attributed the differences to the contexts for formal and classroom assessments:

> " . . . in our school building, the testing is done in a small, enclosed space, usually quiet, and we are teaching in open classrooms. So, how the kid functions in my room is going to be different from how that kid functions one-on-one with you. . . . I think that frequently when they are tested one-on-one, they come out as better. They test higher than they function in the classroom . . . so I'm frustrated looking at their test scores."

3. *The decision to refer a child was motivated by the teacher's belief that some children need a safety net to protect them from uneven support at home or at school as they progress from grade to grade.* As we reviewed each of the cases, we noted that in every instance, the children were already receiving some sort of additional or specialized instructional

support. At times it was in the course of classroom instruction—a form of differentia-tion skillfully integrated within the classroom teacher's ongoing instructional routines. At other times, although not formally identified, the child already received extra ser-vices from a special education teacher. Despite the fact that for the present, each of the teachers believed that the student was receiving appropriate instructional support, they each also believe that it was important to formally identify the children as eligible for special education services. They perceived the formal classification to be a shield against teachers who might be less attentive to the child's individual needs or less effective in their teaching practices, as well as parents who might be less knowledge-able about how and when to advocate for their children. As noted by the special educa-tion teacher participating in Jake's team meeting, the label itself would increase the likelihood of special attention:

> "Well, I think what will be different for him is that he will almost have a safety net—
> 'Well, this kid is a SPED kid, and he does need such and such,' and I think it's more
> protection for Jake. . . . Sadly, usually your best advocate is your father or your
> mother."

4. *Parental insights were politely received and even politely commented upon following the meeting, but they seldom carried the day.* The extent to which testing varied as a result of the information gathered from the parents was unclear. The evidence seemed to sug-gest that a standard battery of formal tests was administered in just about every case. In Aaron's case, for example, his mother provided extensive information during the step 2 conference, describing the types of activities she and Aaron did at home. The in-formation was received warmly and enthusiastically, particularly by the occupational therapist, although there was no point at which a particular example or comment was linked to a similar observation or event in the classroom or school setting. It was unclear how Aaron's mother's information influenced the decision about which tests to administer.

Katherine's mother and Brendan's mother played similar roles during the discus-sions of their children. They used their insights and anecdotes mostly in the service of presenting a different, more human, and more positive account than was being pre-sented by evidence from the professional staff. When talking about Katherine, her mother said:

> "Well, it's funny, because when I had the first meeting I left that meeting shocked. I
> thought we were talking about two different children. Katherine comes home every-
> day. She's very happy! She does her homework. She loves to read. I know she's com-
> prehending because she can TELL everything she read. . . . "

Despite the apparent disconnect between her own observations and those of the teachers and specialists, Katherine's mother agreed to the battery of tests recom-mended by the team. Her insights as a mother had little or no influence on the deci-sions of the professionals who worked with Katherine. What struck us in relation to this finding was not so much that parents' comments and insights were not binding, but rather that they often seemed to be treated entirely as an "aside," not irrelevant, but also not especially pertinent to the decision-making process.

The Bottom Line

Having examined all the data, our bottom-line conclusion was that even in a setting in which many other forms of data were available to help construct a rich portrait of a child's literacy, when it came to the classification process, the Hoyt Elementary School consistently painted by the numbers—that is, the final, formal classification and description of the child was drawn from the results of formal tests. However, we did see two very important roles for less formal evidence. First, either directly or indirectly, it served as the catalyst for getting the classroom teacher to think about starting the referral process in the first place, and the teacher effectively used this evidence to convince the team that the process should go forward. Second, when all the hubbub of the case reviews died down and the teachers got back to the business of translating the IEP into daily practice, the formal test data faded into the background and the informal assessments and observations served as the basis for the classroom remedial plan.

It is almost as though the formal and informal assessment systems traveled down two separate and independent tracks. The formal assessment system was used to measure and document—it ensured that the school was in compliance with federal or state legislative requirements. The informal system, though, had little to do with the students' permanent record files. It formed the basis for the instruction prior to the special education identification process, and later, it formed the basis for day-to-day instructional decisions.

And, this brings us to the last point: Why, if instructional life was essentially unchanged for these children, should or would these teachers, who cared deeply about these children, bother to go through such a time-consuming, tension-producing, and awkward process? The answer, captured in the comments of the teachers, is that they are concerned about guaranteeing children's access to resources. In the case of classroom teachers, in particular, it is access to resources that they are not sure they, or any other classroom teacher on his or her own, can provide. They want to make sure that kids "get the support they need," that they get "the help they are entitled to," and that they "have a safety net."

TWO YEARS LATER

Soon after we completed our initial investigation, we shared our data with the Hoyt Elementary School faculty and administration who were involved in the case meetings on the days we visited. These data included the report we wrote, and, more importantly, the artifacts used to generate our report. That meant that case review transcripts and artifacts used during the meetings were made accessible to the team participants, and they were encouraged to review them.

Frankly, we did not anticipate that the data would have any sort of impact on the participants or on the referral process used at the Hoyt School. We shared the data because we viewed it as our ethical responsibility to do so, consistent with modern practices regarding the rights of participants in research. However, it became clear, through numerous follow-up conversations with Sam, the building principal, that things were happening in the school. So we undertook an effort to document how the process of reviewing the data from the initial investigation influenced the referral process at the Hoyt School. We chose to focus on the principal because as team leader, he had the responsibility to facilitate the discussion and maintain the integrity of the referral conference. We wanted to understand his reactions as he read the transcripts and the actions he had taken as a result of his reading.

A New Role for Classroom Assessment

It appeared that our original investigation prompted the principal, and consequently the other members of the team, to elevate the importance of the role of classroom-based assessment, including portfolios, anecdotal observations, and work samples. The classroom data had always been considered during step 1 meetings, when the TAT first met to troubleshoot problems occurring in the classroom. These data were critical in painting an initial portrait of the student, and they were crucial in getting the process moving. Although classroom-based evidence was privileged at this point of the process, it must be remembered that there were usually no standardized, formal data to compete with them.

Recall that we found that the voice of the classroom teacher and the privilege accorded to classroom-based evidence diminished after step 1 of the process; this was not the case when we investigated 2 years later. Sam reported that the anecdotal evidence, work samples, and other classroom-based assessments accompanied the students during every step of the referral process. In addition, they were used to confirm or even challenge the findings from the formal, standardized assessments. Classroom teachers, who, by their own admission, felt silenced during the final stages when the results of the standardized tests were shared and interpreted, were now routinely invited (by the principal) to contribute during every stage of the process:

> "we've given the prereferral documentation—information that is not standardized testing—more weight, more credence in the whole process. . . . Even when we're going to the meeting to [discuss] test results, I'll always ask the classroom teacher just how things are going. I don't think I did that prior to the study."

Changing the Discourse of the Referral Meeting: Clarity, Equity, and Accessible Language

The initial investigation also prompted reflection on the labels and terminology used by various team members. During one interview, Sam became aware that different members of the team used distinctly different labels to describe the same steps in the referral process. In an attempt to clarify, he developed a chart that reflected a redefinition and a relabeling of the process itself. He explained:

> "I think the thing I remembered the most in the interview was when David sat down with me, and he was shocked at the different terminology we used to identify the same thing. . . . He was puzzled. . . . So, I think that one of the best things that came out of that is that we cleaned up that process by creating a flow chart of the three processes that we use . . . so that we are all walking the same walk and talking the same talk."

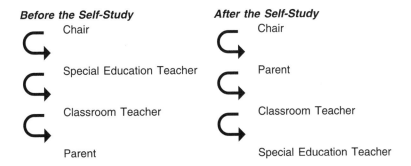

FIGURE 18.1. Positioning of discourse of the referral meeting.

Sam also noted the types of interview questions we asked parents and other partic-ipants. He was particularly struck by a question that prompted parents to describe what they would like to see happen during the meeting, and he responded by altering the "position" of parents during the referral meeting conversations. Prior to and during our original investigation, the meeting protocol for the final review was as follows: First, Sam introduced the parents to other members of the team. Next, the special edu-cation teachers took turns reporting and interpreting the standardized tests results. Next, the classroom teacher was given an opportunity to speak. Finally, the parents were given the floor.

Sam explained that he changed the positioning by making the parents "first among equals"; by first offering the floor to the parents, followed by the classroom teacher, then closing with the standardized test results of the special education teachers (see Figure 18.1). This new format seemed to suggest that the parents' and classroom teacher's understanding of the child was fundamental to understanding the formal test results. The individuals—parents and classroom teachers—who were most likely to provide informal, narrative, and observational accounts of the students were asked to initiate the conversations, before the litany of standardized scores could set a more for-mal and ponderous tone that might marginalize the narrative registers of the parents and classroom teachers.

Our inquiry also prompted Sam to revise the ways in which he facilitated the dis-cussions of the team meetings. This was especially evident when we examined his actions on behalf of the parents. Sam explained that it was the reading of the transcripts that made him aware that different types of language and terminology served to either invite or encourage parents to join the conversation, or alternatively, to silence parents in the conversation. The language, especially the technical and quantitative regis-ter insinuated by the formal reports from the standardized assessments, sometimes marginalized parents in the conversations about their children.

> "I was floored. I read them over and put them away and then I read them over
> again. . . . I really looked at the discourse and the dialogue that take place in our
> team meetings—and by transcribing them and seeing them in print—it gave me an
> opportunity to go over them. I think even though we tried to come at it from a

layperson's perspective, some of the vocabulary and dialogue that took place in those meetings . . . if I were a parent, I wouldn't have a clue what people were talking about."

In addition to his concern about the use of particular language forms, Sam was troubled by the nature of the interactions among the professionals. He discovered that team members frequently interrupted each other during the meetings, and they lacked clarity about each other's roles and responsibilities. This perception caused him to reflect on his strengths and weaknesses as a team leader, to ask himself, "What can I do as the team facilitator to ensure that it doesn't happen in the future?"

LINGERING QUESTIONS

Sam believed that he and the faculty at Hoyt School had made significant changes to the special education referral process. We were somewhat satisfied that our initial investigation took on a life of its own and helped the professionals at the Hoyt School examine, and we believe, improve, their evaluation process. However, an interesting—and rather disappointing—realization was this: Even in the stages when the classroom assessments were vital to the process, not much was offered beyond an occasional running record and writing sample. A "portfolio" was often just a collection of student writing with no rubrics or other criteria attached. Anecdotal evidence was the most prevalent form of assessment, so it was not surprising that it did not hold much weight in the decision-making process.

As we ponder our lingering questions, we return to our original one: In this time of high-stakes testing and high accountability, what are the rules for collecting the type of evidence that counts in making consequential decisions? Our observations here were consistent with those of Mehan (1991, 1993): The formal tests did, indeed, seem to dehumanize the evaluation process and reduce it to a numbers-driven transaction. However, the informal measures—those that can guard against the tendency to be misinformed by the very measures that are intended to inform—were themselves often inadequate in a number of ways. Even in this context in which teachers clearly valued authentic, curriculum-relevant measures, classroom-based collections of evidence were disappointingly thin, especially so in comparison to the lengthy and diverse battery of standardized tests used to develop each child's learning profile. The "portfolio" evidence they provided typically contained one or more running records, some weekly spelling tests, and samples of daily writing that usually included journal entries unaccompanied by any type of rubric or criteria for scoring. So, it seems, the question that remains yet unanswered is how we might work with teachers, specialists, and administrators to change not only the ways we position authentic and curriculum-relevant evidence, but also, how child-study teams might systematically and consistently collect evidence that will lead to a rich and vibrant (and complex) characterization of the full range of the child's literacy abilities.

But here's the encouraging part—the one that supports our belief that teachers are in the business of helping kids; that teachers use their own professional expertise (joined with pretty good intuition) about what kids need and do whatever they can to provide help for them. The teachers at the Hoyt School, although they were slowly finding their voices in the referral conference meetings, were confident about their voices in the classrooms. They used their expertise and classroom-based assessments—however slim—to plan instruction. They didn't need standardized tests to tell them what they already knew. They didn't even need to an IEP to help them plan for those students about whom they had the most concerns. They were already doing it.

REFERENCES

Clay, M. (1993). *An observation survey of early literacy achievement.* Portsmouth, NH: Heinemann.

Gaskins, I. (2004). Word detectives. *Educational Leadership, 61,* 70–73.

Mehan, H. (1991). The school's work of sorting students. In D. Boden & D. H. Zimmerman (Eds.), *Talk and social structure: Studies in ethnomethodology and conversation analysis* (pp. 71–90). Berkeley: University of California Press.

Mehan, H. (1993). Beneath the skin and behind the ears: A case study in the politics of representation. In S. Chailkin & J. Lave (Eds.), *Understanding practice: Perspectives on activity and context* (pp. 241–268). New York: Cambridge University Press.

CHAPTER 19

Classroom Assessment and Standards-Based Change

Kathryn Au
Taffy Raphael

MariAnne George and her third graders are in the midst of a book club unit in which they are reading, writing, and talking about texts that involve family stories. MariAnne tells the students that they will be identifying an important family artifact that has been passed down from at least their grandparents' generation. She wants students to work with their parents to learn the story behind the artifact and its importance to their family. Students will have the opportunity to share the artifact and tell their family stories in class. As MariAnne explains the details of this assignment, she notices that Arun is waving his hand, eagerly asking to be called on to share something with the class. When MariAnne calls on him, Arun enthusiastically points toward a list of "I can" statements that describe end-of-year goals in different areas of literacy. "Look, Ms. George!" Arun cries out. "I know why we're doing this! Look! It's 'I can retell a story in my own words!' "

What is it that Arun was suggesting and why was he so excited? Arun and the other students in MariAnne's classroom had a clear understanding of the connections between their assignments and the goals their teacher had established for their learning. MariAnne was using a system of classroom assessment and instruction tied to standards. She aligned her curriculum to the Michigan state standards and, more importantly, worked to make her goals, instructional activities, and lessons transparent to her students. She helped the students understand what they were learning, why they were learning it, and how different areas of learning were related to one another. Her assessments did not start as a set of tests. Rather, they started with clearly articulated goals and a commitment to build on students' prior knowledge. MariAnne used assessment to address the questions: "What do I need to teach? To whom do I need to teach it? What approaches will I use to teach what is needed?"

In this chapter we discuss the critical role of teacher-developed classroom assessments in improving students' literacy achievement. Our work is guided by a social constructivist or sociocultural perspective (Au, 1998) and is based on the assumption that teachers must construct their own understandings of standards-based education while working within schools as professional learning communities (DuFour, 2004). MariAnne George was one of the teacher researchers whose work convinced us that the power of classroom assessment needed to be taken beyond the level of the individual teacher to whole schools. In the rest of this chapter, we present examples from schools in the Standards Network of Hawaii (SNOH) and the Chicago-based Partnership READ (Reading Essentials and Assessment Development). We describe our work with teachers in two districts—one district is a state (Hawaii) and the other a city (Chicago). These "sister" projects share the purpose of improving students' literacy achievement, especially in high-poverty schools, by providing teachers with professional development that enables them to create a coherent literacy curriculum that revolves around classroom assessment.

Across the United States, teachers and schools are striving to improve students' achievement in the context of rising standards for literacy. In many states, beginning in the 1990s, the push for academic rigor resulted in demanding new standards and challenging tests for reading and writing based on these standards. However, tests were often implemented before teachers had the opportunity to participate in systematic, long-term professional development efforts (Darling-Hammond, 2003). Such efforts are especially needed when teachers must provide instruction in reading comprehension and other forms of higher-level thinking, as opposed to lower-level skills that can be taught through traditional, rote methods.

PRINCIPLES FOR STANDARDS-BASED SCHOOL IMPROVEMENT

Our approach, the standards-based change (SBC) process (Au, 2006), seeks to address the need for long-term professional development. The SBC process is guided by four principles:

- Standards should be met through an emphasis on higher-level thinking.
- Teachers should be encouraged to take ownership of school improvement efforts.
- Curriculum coherence should cross grade levels.
- Schoolwide participation should be encouraged to improve student performance levels.

The first principle derives from the fact that globalization and the dominance of the knowledge and service economy are fueling rising standards (Friedman, 2000). Increasingly, the economic well-being of developed nations depends on their workers' ability to out-think workers in other parts of the world. In the case of literacy, this focus on higher-level thinking causes us to emphasize reading comprehension and the writing process.

The second principle derives from our experience in which teacher buy-in is often the main obstacle to the implementation of standards-based education. Why? Because teachers tend to see standards as imposed from the outside, rather than as a professional choice they have made for themselves. In our professional development work, we ask teachers to engage in substantive discussions about literacy assessment and instruction and build their professional background so that they can make informed decisions while developing their own curricula. Teachers' ownership grows as they take control of their school's curriculum improvement efforts.

The third principle derives from the fact that achievement is best improved through a coherent curriculum in which instructional goals and teaching are coordinated across the grades (Newmann, Smith, Allensworth, & Bryk, 2001). We use the metaphor of a staircase curriculum, in which kindergarten teachers move students to the first step, first-grade teachers to the next step, and so on, up the grades, as shown in Figure 19.1.

The fourth guiding principle is that professional development aimed at raising literacy achievement must involve a schoolwide effort and cannot be confined to just a handful of teachers (Au, 2005). Students—struggling learners, in particular—usually require several years of consistent, high-quality literacy instruction to become strong readers and writers. To provide this continuity in quality instruction across the grades, all the teachers in a school must collaborate to form a professional learning community (DuFour, 2004), engaging in an ongoing conversation about what everyone is doing to improve student achievement through standards.

In our work with schools in Hawaii and Chicago on long-term professional development in the context of rising standards, we have found that classroom assessment plays a central role. We turn now to a description of the components of our SBC process. This description helps set the stage for discussing three lessons we have learned about how classroom assessment can be used both to foster teachers' growth as effective literacy educators and to promote students' literacy achievement.

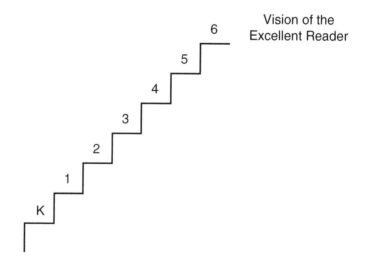

FIGURE 19.1. Staircase curriculum.

THE SBC PROCESS

The SBC process (Au, 2006; Au, Hirata, & Raphael, 2004) is designed to help teachers develop and implement assessments in a purposeful manner that improves student learning. The SBC process moves through four broad phases that help teachers decide what they need to teach and to whom. Teachers (1) set goals for student learning, (2) create an assessment system for collecting evidence of student performance, (3) analyze the evidence, and (4) develop instructional improvements on the basis of assessment results. When we work with teachers, we break these four phases down further into nine steps, which we call the "to-do list." Figure 19.2 shows the phases, and the to-do-list steps associated with each phase appear in the ovals. The following description assumes that the school has decided to focus on reading, the subject area most often addressed first. Many elementary schools in Hawaii have also used the SBC process to develop staircase curricula in writing and mathematics.

Setting Goals for Learning

Goal setting involves articulating the school's philosophy about teaching, learning, and literacy; establishing the vision of the excellent reader who graduates from the school; and determining what each grade level will contribute to move students toward the vision of the excellent reader.

School Philosophy

To create their school philosophy, teachers work in small groups, by grade levels or departments, to arrive at two key beliefs each about teaching, learning, and literacy. Each small group records its beliefs on chart paper and then shares its beliefs with the whole school. Figure 19.3 illustrates the working drafts prepared by teachers at Drake

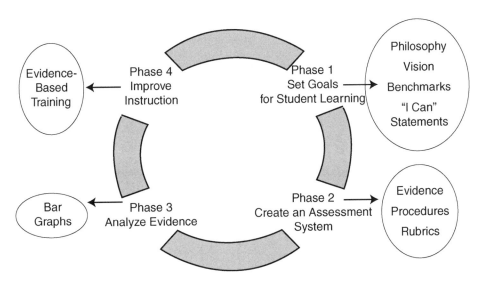

FIGURE 19.2. Standards-based change process phases and steps in the to-do list.

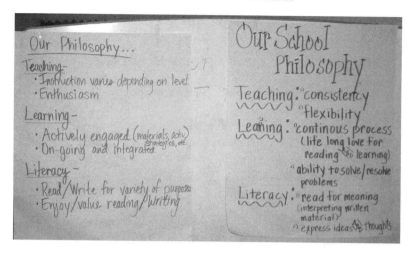

FIGURE 19.3. Drake's working draft from session 1.

Elementary School during their first schoolwide philosophy discussion. The leader or facilitator of the meeting highlights common beliefs that cut across the small groups and appear to be held by most of the faculty. A discussion of philosophy helps make shared beliefs explicit and provides a firm foundation for bringing the school together and moving forward through the next steps on the to-do list.

Vision of the Excellent Reader

The next step in goal setting requires teachers to create a vision statement describing the excellent reader who graduates from the school. The vision of the excellent reader provides a common goal toward which all grade levels and departments in the school can direct their efforts in the teaching of reading. The vision of the excellent reader has a specific academic focus and differs from the general school vision statement many schools have developed while engaged in strategic planning or accreditation. Grade levels or departments each draft a vision statement of the excellent reader who graduates from the school. Figure 19.4 illustrates the initial draft generated by a group of teachers from Drake, following their discussion of the school philosophy. A draft such as this one is usually refined by a committee, then brought back to the whole school for final approval. Here is the vision statement developed by a middle school in Hawaii, based on drafts from the school's different departments:

> The successful reader who leaves Wheeler Middle School will be able to read with a clear purpose, engage in an ongoing process of questioning to understand big concepts and generalizations, and continue to apply and make connections.

Grade-Level or Department Benchmarks

Once the vision of the excellent reader is in place, teachers have a common point of reference and are ready to develop grade-level or department benchmarks. For elementary schools, we define grade-level benchmarks as high but achievable end-of-year out-

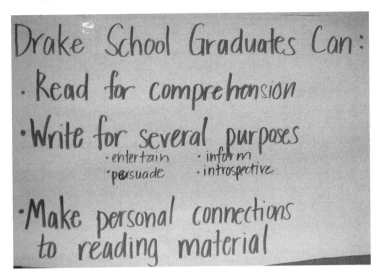

FIGURE 19.4. Drake's draft vision statement.

comes for the hypothetical "average" student. For secondary schools, benchmarks are end-of-course outcomes. In Hawaii, we ask teachers to develop a total of five to seven grade-level benchmarks, with one or two benchmarks in each of the following areas: attitudes, comprehension, and strategies and skills. Here are examples of typical reading benchmarks for the primary and upper grades developed by teachers at schools in Hawaii.

Attitudes
- Children will enjoy reading every day. (kindergarten)
- Students will have favorite authors and topics for voluntary reading. (grade 5)

Comprehension
- Children will identify the problem and solution in the story. (grade 1)
- Students will construct the theme for the story and give reasons for their idea. (grade 4)

Strategies and skills
- Children will read a grade-level text aloud with 90% accuracy. (grade 2)
- Students will monitor their comprehension and seek clarification when necessary. (grade 6)

In Chicago, teachers develop benchmarks guided by the four areas in the Chicago Reading Initiative: fluency, comprehension, word knowledge, and writing. Some schools have chosen a single focus area to serve as their "jumping-off point"—the area they will use as they learn the SBC process. Other schools chose to start with benchmarks across all four areas of the Chicago Reading Initiative. The actual number of benchmarks, or the number of areas framing the benchmarks, is less important than the quality of thinking and reflection on the goals being set and the fact that teachers are working with a common vision.

We find it works best if teachers first brainstorm benchmarks on their own, without initially referring to sources such as state standards or basal reader scope and sequence charts. The reason is that when teachers begin with such documents, they tend to select items without much thought or discussion. In our experience, teachers who fail to construct their own benchmarks may never move beyond a superficial understanding of benchmarks and standards. In contrast, teachers who construct their own benchmarks have to think deeply about the reading outcomes most important for their students, and they develop a sense of ownership over the benchmarks they construct. Assessments become meaningful to teachers because the benchmarks driving the assessments reflect important goals for student learning that teachers established for themselves, not just abstract targets imposed by the state or district.

Of course, alignment with relevant state and district standards is an important next step in public schools. We ask teachers to check the benchmarks they construct to make sure that they (1) cover all the necessary content and (2) are at an appropriate level of rigor. The process of alignment proceeds smoothly in both Hawaii and Chicago because teachers rarely omit important outcomes and usually need to make only minor adjustments, if any, to the benchmarks they draft. In Hawaii, we let teachers know that the state standards describe the floor, or the lowest level of performance to be expected of students, but should not be seen as setting a ceiling or imposing limits on expectations for student achievement. At some Hawaii schools that have worked with the SBC process for 3 years or more, teachers routinely work with benchmarks and rubrics more demanding than those presented in state documents.

"I Can" Statements

In efforts to boost achievement, it is not enough for teachers to set goals. As implied in the example from MariAnne George's classroom, students must be actively involved as well. They must know what they are learning, why they are learning it, and when and how what they are learning can be applied, as Paris, Lipson, and Wixson (1983) described in unpacking the concept of metacognition. Metacognitive knowledge within the SBC process is represented through making literacy learning goals visible to students by rephrasing the benchmarks as student-friendly, "I can," statements (cf. Cleland, 1999). This process of rewording is usually more important in the primary grades than in higher grades. Teachers may work with colleagues to develop the wording of "I can" statements, or they may develop the "I can" statements through discussions with students. The following "I can" statements are based on the Hawaii primary-grade benchmarks presented earlier.

- "I can tell about the problem in the story and how it was solved."
- "I can read the words in a story written for second graders."

Large posters displaying "I can" statements are easy to spot in the classrooms of teachers who are successful in improving students' literacy achievement with the SBC process. The posters of "I can" statements serve to remind both the teacher and students of the literacy learning goals set for the year.

Creating an Assessment System

The next steps in the to-do list help teachers create the assessment system that will give them the evidence they need to (1) chart students' progress toward reaching the benchmarks, and (2) identify their instructional needs. These steps include identifying evidence for each benchmark, establishing procedures for collecting the evidence, and developing the tools needed to score the evidence.

Identifying Evidence

To address this item on the to-do list, teachers identify the evidence to be collected to monitor students' progress toward meeting the benchmarks and "I can" statements. We recommend that teachers consider using as evidence the work they typically assign to develop students' proficiency in the targeted benchmark. For example, many teachers have students read novels and write responses that include summaries, personal connections, and interpretations of the author's message. If a benchmark focuses on summarization, these written responses could be used as evidence.

Table 19.1 gives examples of benchmarks with the evidence that teachers might collect. Experienced teachers working with the SBC process seldom rely on tests developed by outsiders, such as the end-of-level tests that accompany packaged reading programs. Because these tests tend to focus on lower-level text-related skills, rather than on comprehension, response, and higher-level thinking, they generally do not match the benchmarks developed by teachers. Also, test results that simply report the number of items correct do not help teachers pinpoint the kind of instruction that will help students advance.

Procedures for Collecting Evidence

Once they have decided on the evidence they want to analyze, teachers within a grade level or department collaborate to develop the procedures they will follow for collecting the evidence. These procedures must be spelled out in detail so that all the teachers in the grade level or department collect their evidence under the same conditions, making it possible to aggregate the evidence across classes. For example, teachers could not aggregate evidence if one teacher allowed her students 20 minutes to read the text and write a response, whereas another teacher in that department allowed her students 40

TABLE 19.1. Benchmarks and Evidence

Benchmark	Evidence
Students have the habit of daily reading.	Book logs for sustained silent reading and home reading
Students comprehend informational text.	File cards with notes for research reports
Students understand the characteristics of different genres.	Completed matrices for biography, historical fiction, fantasy
Students monitor their own comprehension.	Double-entry journals showing questions and reflections on the novel

minutes. Clearly, students in the second classroom have an advantage. In addition to time allowed, other factors that affect students' performance include the degree of scaffolding (e.g., whether students must work independently or can confer with a peer) and the wording of the instructions given to the students (e.g., whether students are told simply to write a summary or to write a summary containing specific story elements, such as the problem and solution).

Rubrics

Once the evidence has been collected, teachers use the same tool—a rubric or a checklist—to score the students' work. Rubrics are the most detailed description of teachers' expectations for students' performance. Effective rubrics contain clear descriptors that identify areas for further instruction rather than simply yielding a score (see Figure 19.5). A strong rubric can be equated to a list of mini-lessons, making it easy for teachers to identify students' needs and design appropriate instruction. In contrast, the rubric shown in Figure 19.6 does not provide the teacher with information about what to teach students in the "still working" category. Notice the difference between the rubrics in Figures 19.5 and 19.6. In Figure 19.5, the descriptors in the "still working" category point to specific needs that lead to instructional decisions. For example, if some students did not make a clear connection to the story, the teacher can create a flexible group to provide these students with lessons on how to make text-to-text, text-to-self, and text-to-world connections.

Name: _____   Teacher: _____

Date: _____   Title of Work: _____

	Criteria				Points
	1	2	3	4	
Understanding	Your response is either totally irrelevant or totally wrong.	You address some aspects of the story.	You address most important aspects of the story.	You address all important aspects of the story.	—
Connecting	You made very little attempt to respond.	You made an attempt to connect to the story, but the connection is not clear.	You relate the information in the passage to your own experiences.	You relate the information in the story to your own experiences and use portions of the text to back up your connections.	—
	Still Working	Still Working	Meets	Exceeds	—

I Can Statement:

FIGURE 19.5. Sample rubric that informs instruction.

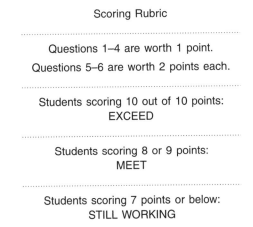

Scoring Rubric

Questions 1–4 are worth 1 point.
Questions 5–6 are worth 2 points each.

Students scoring 10 out of 10 points:
EXCEED

Students scoring 8 or 9 points:
MEET

Students scoring 7 points or below:
STILL WORKING

FIGURE 19.6. Sample rubric that does not inform instruction.

Analyzing the Evidence and Going Public

This phase of work involves analysis of the students' work and sharing the findings with colleagues within and across grade levels. With rubrics in hand, teachers gather to analyze and score students' work. In both Hawaii and Chicago, teachers often score the work of other teachers' students, gaining the chance to see a wider range of student work than that in their own classroom. Teachers learn to follow the rubric closely. In Chicago, the following guidelines have proven useful:

- Don't score a student's work lower than the rubric would suggest because you feel the student "should have done better."
- Don't score a student's work higher than the rubric would suggest because you feel that the student "seems to have really tried."

In the course of analyzing student work, teachers discuss student evidence that proves difficult to score. Often, these discussions lead teachers to tweak or refine their rubrics.

Bar Graphs

Once the evidence has been scored, teachers are in a position to begin the analysis of what these scores mean by first creating bar graphs to show the overall pattern or distribution of the students at the grade level, and then looking at the distribution in light of the areas of the rubric that are still a challenge to students. The bar graphs show the number of students whose evidence has been shown to fall in each of the categories (e.g., as still working, meets, exceeds) at each of three assessment points (pretest, midyear check, posttest). Bar graphs give everyone in the school an overview of students' progress across grades and departments, and the sharing of bar graphs shows that teachers are addressing accountability concerns and closely monitoring student achievement.

Improving Instruction

In addition to identifying students in each of the categories, teachers must go to the next step of analyzing their specific strengths and weaknesses. For example, a group of third-grade teachers in Hawaii were working with a benchmark on summarization. By closely examining students' work, they found that students in the "still working" category were familiar with story elements. However, these students had included inaccurate and unimportant information in their summaries. This discovery led teachers to conclude that these students needed help in two areas. First, they had to learn to read carefully and to include in their summaries only information that could be identified as coming from the story. Second, they had to learn how to determine the important information in the story. As a result of their analysis, these teachers pulled these students aside for small-group comprehension lessons focused on reading carefully and determining important information.

Evidence-Based Teaching

This is the last, but certainly not least, of the items on the to-do list. In our view, students' literacy achievement can be expected to rise only when changes to instruction are made in a principled manner, on the basis of assessment results, as illustrated in the example of the third-grade teachers. In the SBC process, evidence-based teaching occurs after teachers have carefully assessed their students' strengths and weaknesses with respect to the benchmarks and rubrics. After the teachers have reviewed the evidence collected to determine students' strengths and weaknesses in reading, they focus on developing specific lessons to address the weaknesses. They may need to provide differentiated, small-group instruction, as in the case of the third-grade teachers, or, as shown in the next example, they may need to teach whole-class lessons.

A group of fifth-grade teachers in Hawaii worked with a benchmark stating that students would be able to comprehend fiction and nonfiction texts. They had students read passages written at the fifth-grade level, then respond to questions requiring short or extended written responses, modeled after those in the state reading test. These teachers learned from pretest evidence that students could respond to short-answer questions about details in the text. However, they had difficulty with open-ended questions requiring that they make an inference and present evidence for their inference. Some of the students could state inferences, whereas others could not, indicating that the teachers needed to provide small-group mini-lessons to those students who needed to learn to how to make and state an inference. Almost all students failed to present evidence for their interpretations, and the teachers decided that they should conduct whole-class mini-lessons in this area, for example, to teach students how to include brief quotations or cite a particular paragraph in the text as evidence.

At most schools with a firm commitment to the SBC process and a professional learning community solidly established, teachers require about a year to experiment and become familiar with the nine items on the to-do list. Following initial implementation, the teachers and school establish a regular, three-times-per-year schedule of collecting evidence (elsewhere, we describe the levels of professional development that schools move through as they work with the SBC process over a period of years; Au, 2005). Most schools in Hawaii establish a 2-week window for each of these evidence collection periods (e.g., first 2 weeks in September, first 2 weeks in January, and last 2 weeks in May) when all the teachers gather evidence on their students' performance. Teachers at many schools are accustomed to collecting pre- and posttest results. The SBC process includes a midyear check to allow teachers time to make any necessary adjustments to instruction before the high-stakes, large-scale testing that occurs in the spring in many districts. Some schools in the SBC process collect evidence on a quarterly basis, but many schools do not, because the results for the first and second quarters tend to be quite similar.

Lessons about Classroom Assessment

As you have learned, assessment is a critical element in the success of the SBC process. At the same time, it continues to present a considerable challenge at the school level. In the past, many teachers tended to see their role in assessment as that of administering tests developed by outsiders. In standards-based education in general, and the SBC process in particular, the teacher's role in assessment is seen very differently. We now understand that, if assessment and instruction are to work in tandem, classroom teachers must be the ones to design and coordinate both.

In our work in schools, we find that many teachers are still struggling to come to terms with current views of assessment. The SBC process and to-do list offer teachers the chance to learn about the theory and research underlying current views of assessment and gain hands-on experience by developing classroom assessments and analyzing students' performance. Here are three lessons that this work has taught us about assessment.

First Lesson: Benchmarks as the Starting Point

One of the most common misconceptions about assessment is that it is largely a matter of choosing the right technique or test. Teachers unfamiliar with the SBC process often ask us questions of the form, "Which is better, X or Y?" where X and Y are, for example, running records (Clay, 1993), the Qualitative Reading Inventory (Leslie & Caldwell, 2001), the Stieglitz Informal Reading Inventory (Stieglitz, 2002), the Developmental Reading Assessment (Beaver & Carter, 2002), or any number of other approaches or programs.

The first lesson to be derived from the SBC process is that sound literacy assessment, contributing to effective instruction, does not begin with a test or technique. Instead, it begins with teachers having clarity about the literacy outcomes they would like students to achieve. Teachers can make good decisions about *how* to assess only after they have established *what* to assess. In other words, classroom assessment begins with teachers having clear benchmarks or end-of-year targets for student performance. In the SBC process, every item in the to-do list is actually leading toward assessment. However, we do not begin by having teachers think about the assessment technique. Instead, we have teachers gain clarity about what they want students to achieve through a focus on the vision of the excellent reader, grade level or department benchmarks, and "I can" statements.

In our view, assessment techniques or packages, such as the running record or informal reading inventories, cannot be judged as good or bad in and of themselves.

The "which is better" question cannot be answered until we know the benchmarks, because an appropriate assessment is one that provides accurate information about students' progress with respect to a particular benchmark. Sound assessments must be matched to benchmarks, which in turn are aligned with state or district standards.

Once teachers know their benchmarks, they may either develop their own assessments to monitor students' progress toward meeting the benchmarks, or they may choose an available approach that serves this purpose. In schools following the SBC process, teachers generally use classroom assessments they have developed themselves, although they sometimes use a combination of their own assessments and measures developed by others. For example, at several elementary schools in Hawaii, the primary teachers use their own assessments to assess students' reading comprehension and running records to assess students' word identification.

At a school in Chicago, as a result of their first whole-school "reporting out"—when grade levels present their assessment results to the whole school—teachers realized they had very different conceptions of fluency at different grade levels. Some thought of it in terms of accuracy and were using commercial assessments to test accuracy, whereas others thought in terms of speed and were using formulas related to speed. Even those who had combined speed and accuracy were concerned that they had not connected the fluency assessment to comprehension. The literacy coordinator helped teachers create study groups where they read articles and a book about fluency (Rasinski, 2003), then put together ideas from their readings, sample tests, and their own experiences. Together, they created their school's fluency assessments that ensured coherence across the grades and maintained a focus on fluency for improving comprehension.

Second Lesson: Teachers as Decision Makers

The second lesson we have learned about assessment has to do with the importance of teachers acting as decision makers and taking ownership for assessment. In our work in schools with the SBC process, we have found that teachers must assume responsibility for assessment because the process of improving students' literacy achievement depends on a close connection between assessment and instruction. If teachers see themselves as responsible for instruction but someone else as responsible for assessment, the necessary connection between the two is lost. When teachers develop their own classroom assessments, they are in a much better position to understand the evidence: how the results were obtained, what the results indicate about the strengths and weaknesses in students' performance, and the implications for instruction.

Initially, teachers may be reluctant to develop their own classroom assessments, in part, because they lack confidence in their own professional knowledge and judgment. In a few schools in Hawaii, teachers decided to continue using the results of the end-of-level tests that came with their basal reading programs, rather than attempting to develop their own classroom assessments. These teachers discovered that these results did not provide good evidence for their benchmarks because many of the test items focused on lower-level skills, such as the sequence of events, rather than on higher-level thinking with text, such as making connections or critical evaluation. After a year or two, these teachers concluded that they needed to devise their own comprehension tasks matched to their benchmarks. A school new to the SBC process in Chicago had a similar experience. Following their first whole-school reporting, teachers began to question the information they were able to get from the basal reading tests and to analyze whether their comprehension assessments formed a coherent sequence from kindergarten to grade 8.

Because state standards tend to be stated in general terms, they may be subject to a range of interpretations. If a major goal is to raise test scores, teachers must make sure that the way they operationally define standards and benchmarks in classroom assessments is similar to the way that standards are operationally defined in the state test. This is a vital step given the pressures on many schools to raise test scores. In Hawaii, Illinois, and other states, teachers receive ample information about how standards are tested through printed guides and websites that include sample test items. These are valuable resources that should inform teachers' decision making.

For example, a group of fifth-grade teachers in Hawaii conducted writers' workshops in which students often had several weeks to complete assignments ranging from memoirs to essays to research reports. However, when they developed classroom assessments, the teachers decided to use as evidence writing that students would complete on an assigned topic within a 2-hour period, because this was the format used on the state writing test. These teachers continued to teach the process approach to writing (e.g., Graves, 1983), but they also believed that students should have experience with timed writing as preparation for the state test. Under pressure to show good test results, these teachers made a sensible and realistic decision. In Chicago, several Partnership READ schools chose to use question–answer relationships (QARs; Raphael & Au, 2005) as a way into test preparation. School staff met together to analyze the types of QARs in released state test items. They then analyzed each QAR in terms of the comprehension strategy or strategies that would enable a reader to answer the question accurately. They used this information to design their instructional activities prior to testing, so that they could help students become more strategic by taking the mystery out of questioning and making explicit the relationship between strategies they had learned and the types of questions they would encounter on the state test. Rather than simply engaging in test practice, these teachers provided students with instruction in analytic thinking and strategy use—knowledge that would help them in authentic reading situations as well as on the state test.

In schools successful at improving literacy achievement, we see that teachers have come to the point where they feel comfortable making decisions about assessment and have assumed ownership of the assessment process. Systematic, ongoing literacy assessment is time consuming and demanding; teachers who feel ownership have the motivation and commitment to continue collecting and analyzing assessment evidence year after year. Improving instruction based on assessment has become a habit for these teachers, and literacy achievement rises as a result of the informed instruction they provide to their students.

Third Lesson: Regular Reporting of Results

The third lesson we have learned about classroom assessment has to do with the importance of reporting results regularly. As mentioned earlier, in schools successful in using the SBC process to improve student achievement, teachers collect evidence three times per year (pretest, midyear check, and posttest) to monitor students' progress toward meeting grade-level or department benchmarks. Teachers then report their results at whole-school meetings held three times per year to correspond with the evidence collection periods. Teachers gain a great deal from the time spent meeting with their grade-level or department to prepare their presentation. These meetings are marked by collegiality and rich reflection as the group jointly analyzes assessment evidence and decides upon instructional improvements. Usually the results shared are aggregated across the grade level or department. At a number of schools in Hawaii, teachers have chosen to present student results for their own individual classrooms, demonstrating an acceptance of accountability and openness to sharing their work with others. In one case, first-grade teachers presented bar graphs for their individual classrooms to show that one teacher in their grade level was doing an exceptional job with writing instruction, and that they were all trying to learn from her success.

Interestingly, the accuracy of student results on classroom assessments may be less significant over the long run than the teacher learning and reflection stimulated by these results. For example, in the first year a school is working with the SBC process, teachers often encounter problems with assessment. At one school in Hawaii, the third-grade teachers found that their reading comprehension task had been poorly designed. They wanted to assess students' performance in constructing a theme for the story, but they had neglected to specify that students write about the theme in the directions. Thus many students wrote summaries without discussing this story element. These teachers wanted to revise their procedures for collecting evidence, but they were concerned that once they changed the task, their pretest results would not be aligned with their midyear check and posttest results. The teachers were encouraged to revise their assessment task and simply to explain the reason for the change in their presentation to the whole school, rather than hold to assessments that they knew were not valid.

What benefits are gained from regular, whole-school reporting of results? One of the benefits is that teachers are motivated to be especially thoughtful and thorough in their analysis of results and instructional improvements when they know that their work is going to be shared with an audience of their peers. Another benefit is that teachers have the opportunity to learn from the work of other grade levels and departments. For example, at one school in Hawaii, the third-grade teachers learned from a presentation by the fourth-grade teachers that students were experiencing difficulty reading and comprehending informational text. During a later discussion, the third-grade teachers told the fourth-grade teachers that they were planning to have students read more informational text. The third-grade teachers said that they had been thinking of introducing more informational text anyway and now recognized that they should make this change immediately. In some schools, presentations reveal that different grade levels are aiming at the same benchmark (e.g., "Students know story elements"), and follow-up discussions are required to sort out how benchmarks should be adjusted to build the staircase curriculum and make sure that students are taught new concepts and strategies at each grade level.

A final benefit occurs at the level of the professional learning community. At many schools, teachers and principals have told us that working with the SBC process and sharing results across the whole school have helped to bring the school together. Teachers at some schools have told us that they previously had only a vague idea about what teachers at other grade levels were teaching and were delighted to have specific information.

CONCLUSION

Our work with school change in two very different settings—Hawaii and Chicago—has convinced us of the centrality of classroom assessment in improving literacy achievement. In our experience, the positive effects of classroom assessment are enhanced when all the teachers in a school participate in the entire process described by the four phases in the SBC process. Setting goals for student learning, creating an assessment system for collecting evidence of student performance, analyzing the evidence, and developing instructional improvements on the basis of assessment results. As mentioned earlier, these phases are introduced to teachers as a nine-step to-do list.

A dramatic example of the benefits of whole-school sharing of assessment results occurred at an elementary school in Hawaii where the faculty decided to use the SBC process to improve their writing curriculum. During the first two meetings, it became apparent that teachers in the lower grades were focusing their writing instruction on mechanics, whereas teachers in the upper grades were emphasizing the writing process and the author's craft. The teachers in the lower grades were surprised to learn of the high expectations for composition held by the upper-grade teachers, and they saw assessment evidence showing that most students could meet these expectations. After a year, the teachers in the lower grades had raised their expectations and changed their instruction to include the writing process and author's craft, in addition to the skills they had taught all along. Over the next 3 years, student results on the state writing test showed substantial improvement. Such improvements in achievement become possible when teachers come together as a professional learning community, informed by assessment results, and build a staircase or coherent curriculum with an emphasis on higher-level thinking.

REFERENCES

Au, K. H. (1998). Social constructivism and the school literacy learning of students of diverse cultural backgrounds. *Journal of Literacy Research, 30,* 297–319.

Au, K. H. (2005). Negotiating the slippery slope: School change and literacy achievement. *Journal of Literacy Research, 37*(3), 267–286.

Au, K. H. (2006). *Multicultural issues and literacy achievement.* Mahwah, NJ: Erlbaum.

Au, K. H., Hirata, S. J., & Raphael, T. E. (2004, December). *Improving achievement through standards.* Paper presented at the National Reading Conference, San Antonio, TX.

Beaver, J., & Carter, M. (2002). *Developmental reading assessment.* Upper Saddle River, NJ: Celebration Press.

Clay, M. M. (1993). *An observation survey of early literacy achievement.* Portsmouth, NH: Heinemann.

Cleland, J. V. (1999). We Can charts: Building blocks for student-led conferences. *The Reading Teacher, 52*(6), 588–595.

Darling-Hammond, L. (2003, February 16). Standards and assessments: Where we are and what we need. *Teachers College Record.* Retrieved October 3, 2006, from *www.tcrecord.org.*

DuFour, R. (2004). What is a "professional learning community"? *Educational Leadership, 61*(8), 6–11.

Friedman, T. L. (2000). *The Lexus and the olive tree: Understanding globalization.* New York: Farrar, Straus & Giroux.

Graves, D. (1983). *Writing: Teachers and children at work.* Exeter, NH: Heinemann.

Leslie, L., & Caldwell, J. (2001). *Qualitative Reading Inventory–3.* New York: Longman.

Newmann, F. M., Smith, B., Allensworth, E., & Bryk, A. S. (2001). Instructional program coherence: What it is and why it should guide school improvement policy. *Educational Evaluation and Policy Analysis, 23*(4), 297–321.

Paris, S. G., Lipson, M. Y., & Wixson, K. K. (1983). Becoming a strategic reader. *Contemporary Educational Psychology, 8,* 293–316.

Raphael, T. E., & Au, K. H. (2005). QAR: Enhancing comprehension and test-taking across grades and content areas. *The Reading Teacher, 59*(3), 206–221.

Rasinski, T. V. (2003). *The fluent reader: Oral reading strategies for building word recognition, fluency, and comprehension.* New York: Scholastic.

Stieglitz, E. L. (2002). *The Stieglitz Informal Reading Inventory: Assessing reading behaviors from emergent to advanced levels.* Boston: Allyn & Bacon.

Index

f following a page number indicates a figure; *t* following a page number indicates a table.

Accountability in assessment, No Child Left Behind (NCLB) and, 3
Action, inquiry-oriented assessment and, 10–11
Adolescent Motivation to Read Profile (AMR), 57–58, 57*f*, 58*f*
Alliteration, preschool assessment and, 71
Alphabetic principle
    preschool assessment and, 72–74, 73*f*
    spelling development and, 114
    word recognition and, 86, 87*t*
AMR (Adolescent Motivation to Read Profile), 57–58, 57*f*, 58*f*
Anticipation guide, 196–198, 197*f*
Assessment planning, 77–78
Assessment tools
    alphabet knowledge and, 70
    classroom environment and, 44–47
    literacy motivation and, 53–58, 54*f*, 55*f*, 56*f*, 57*f*
    vocabulary assessment and, 138
    word recognition assessment and, 90*t*
Authentic assessment
    In2Books (I2B) program, 263–278, 268*f*, 270*f*, 271*t*, 272*f*, 273*t*, 274*f*, 274*t*, 276*f*
    overview, 262–263
Automatic phase of reading development, 87*t*

B

Background knowledge, 198, 200, 200*f*
Backward mapping
    connecting testing to standards using, 27–28, 28*f*

examples of, 23–27, 24*f*, 25*f*, 26*f*, 30–31
    inquiry-oriented assessment and, 12
    overview, 22–27, 24*f*, 25*f*, 26*f*, 31
    teaching students about, 28–30
Benchmark assessments
    overview, 284
    standards-based change and, 310–312, 313–314, 313*t*, 317–318
Blending skills, 71–72
Book knowledge, 74–76, 75*f*
Book talk
    meaning making and, 156–167, 158*f*, 160*f*, 162*f*, 164*f*–165*f*, 166*f*, 168*f*, 169*f*, 170*f*
    overview, 155–156, 167, 171

C

Checklists
    assessment of strategic reading and, 180–184, 181*f*
    for creating common assessments, 288*f*–289*f*
    standards-based change and, 314
    strategic reading and, 189–190, 190*f*
    writing skills and, 217, 218*f*, 219*f*
Classroom assessments. *see also* Teacher-guided classroom assessment
    classroom environment and, 44–47
    consequences of, 5–6
    goal of, 8
    inquiry-oriented assessment and, 7–11, 11–16, 13*t*
    overview, 4, 229

Classroom assessments *(continued)*
  referral process for special education and,
    299, 302
  shifts in, 4–7
  standards-based change and, 306–307, 309–
    320, 309*f*, 310*f*, 311*f*, 313*t*, 314*f*, 315*f*, 321
  strategic reading and, 179, 179–191, 181*f*,
    190*f*, 191–192
Classroom assessments, teacher-guided. *see
    also* Classroom assessments
  inquiry-oriented assessment and, 7–11, 15–
    16, 17*f*–18*f*
  interaction and action elements of, 10–11
  overview, 4–7
  standards-based change and, 309–320, 309*f*,
    310*f*, 311*f*, 313*t*, 314*f*, 315*f*
Classroom environment. *see also* Literacy-rich
    classroom environments
  overview, 33, 47
  portfolio system and, 229, 244
  print-rich classrooms, 34, 35–39, 37*f*, 38*f*, 39*f*
  training in using print-rich classrooms
    and, 40–44, 40*f*, 42*f*, 43*f*
  writing skills and, 215, 217
Classroom environment, literacy-rich. *see also*
    Classroom environment
  overview, 47
  preparing, 35–39, 37*f*, 38*f*, 39*f*
  print-rich classrooms, 34
  theory and research regarding, 34–35
Classroom Literacy Environmental Profile
    (CLEP), 45–46
Classroom, print-rich. *see also* Classroom en-
    vironment
  overview, 34, 47
  preparing, 35–39, 37*f*, 38*f*, 39*f*
  teaching students to use, 40–44, 40*f*, 42*f*,
    43*f*
Cognitive development, 66
Collaboration
  examples of, 284–292, 286*f*–287*f*, 288*f*–289*f*,
    290*f*, 291*f*
  instruction and, 282–283
  linking curriculum, instruction and assess-
    ment, 283
  overview, 280
  reviewing student performance, 281–282
Collaborative assessment, 217, 219–220, 220*f*
Common assessments
  consensus scoring and peer planning and,
    283–284, 292–293
  examples of, 284–292, 286*f*–287*f*, 288*f*–289*f*,
    290*f*, 291*f*

instruction and, 282–283
linking curriculum, instruction and assessment, 283
overview, 280
referral process for special education and,
  302–304
reviewing student performance, 281–
  282
Communication, professional
  consensus scoring and peer planning and,
    283–284, 292–293
  examples of, 284–292, 286*f*–287*f*, 288*f*–289*f*,
    290*f*, 291*f*
  instruction and, 282–283
  linking curriculum, instruction and assess-
    ment, 283
  overview, 280
  referral process for special education and,
    302–304
  reviewing student performance, 281–282
Comprehension assessment
  alphabet knowledge and, 68–70, 69*f*
  language and literacy development and,
    67–68
  overview, 14, 22–23
  phonological and phonemic awareness,
    70–72
  portfolio system and, 232–236, 232*f*, 234*f*,
    235*f*
  writing skills and, 216*f*
Comprehension, reading, 88
Comprehensive assessment model, 65–67
Consensus scoring
  examples of, 284–292, 286*f*–287*f*, 288*f*–289*f*,
    290*f*, 291*f*
  overview, 283–284, 292–293
Consequential validity of classroom assessments, 5–6
Consolidated alphabetic phase of reading development, 87*t*
Content-area centers. *see also* Classroom environment
  preparing, 39, 39*f*
  teaching students to use, 40–44, 40*f*, 42*f*,
    43*f*
Cooperative learning, 146–150, 147*f*, 148*f*,
  149*f*, 150*f*
Curriculum standards
  assessments and, 283–284
  linking curriculum, instruction and assess-
    ment, 283
  overview, 27–28, 28*f*, 281
  reviewing student performance, 281–282

D

Data-driven decision making, 5
DBQ. *see* Document-based questioning (DBQ)
Decision making
    standards-based change and, 318–319
    word recognition assessment and, 88
Descriptive writing, 213
Development. *see also* Language development
    fluency, 102–103
    oral reading fluency, 102–103
    spelling knowledge, 114–116
    strategic reading, 177–178
    word recognition, 86–88, 87t
    writing skills, 236
Development, language. *see also* Development
    alphabet knowledge and, 68–70, 69f
    comprehensive assessments and, 67–68
    concepts about print, books and words,
        74–76, 75f
    oral comprehension and vocabulary, 76–77
    phonics and the alphabetic principle and,
        72–74, 73f
    phonological and phonemic awareness,
        70–72
    preschool assessment and, 66, 77–81, 80f,
        81–82, 81f
Developmental assessment, 66
Diagnosis, 10, 91–93, 92t
DIBELS
    alphabet knowledge and, 70
    inquiry-oriented assessment and, 13–14,
        13t
    Reading First initiative and, 5
    word recognition assessment and, 89, 90t,
        94
Discipline, 9–10
Document-based questioning (DBQ), 202,
        202f
Dramatic play
    classroom environment and, 35
    concepts about print, books and words
        and, 74–75
Drawings by children, 167, 168f
Dynamic assessment, 10
Dynamic Indicators of Basic Early Literacy
        Skills (DIBELS)
    alphabet knowledge and, 70
    inquiry-oriented assessment and, 13–14,
        13t
    Reading First initiative and, 5
    word recognition assessment and, 89, 90t,
        94

E

Early Language and Literacy Classroom Ob-
        servation (ELLCO), 44–45
Early Literacy Knowledge Assessment
        (ELKA), 77
Engagement
    intrinsic motivation and, 50
    portfolio system and, 230
    in self-assessment, 217
    struggling writers and, 210
    vocabulary assessment and, 143–146, 144f,
        145f–146f
English language learners (ELLs)
    vocabulary assessment and, 139
    word recognition assessment and, 96–97
    writing instruction and, 210
Environment, classroom. *see also* Literacy-rich
        classroom environments
    overview, 33, 47
    portfolio system and, 229, 244
    print-rich classrooms, 34, 35–39, 37f, 38f, 39f
    training in using print-rich classrooms
        and, 40–44, 40f, 42f, 43f
    writing skills and, 215, 217
Environment, literacy-rich. *see also* Classroom
        environment
    overview, 47
    preparing, 35–39, 37f, 38f, 39f
    print-rich classrooms, 34
    theory and research regarding, 34–35
Envisionment-building theory, 156–158, 159
Evidence-based teaching, 316–317
Explicit instruction, 141–143, 142f–143f
Expository writing, 213
Expressive One-Word Picture Vocabulary
        Test—Revised, 76
Expressive oral reading, 102–103
External assessments
    inquiry-oriented assessment and, 11–13
    overview, 4–7

F

Finger point reading, 75
Flexibility, assessing the understanding of in-
        formational text and, 196–198, 197f
Fluency. *see also* Fluency assessment
    development of, 102–103
    ineffective instruction in, 103
    oral reading, 110–111
    overview, 101–102

Fluency assessment. *see also* Fluency
    conducting, 107–108
    determining reading levels and, 109
    determining the need of students for, 108–
        109
    inquiry-oriented assessment and, 13–15,
        13*t*
    overview, 22–23, 101, 104–107, 105*t*, 106*f*
    repeated readings and, 109–110, 110*f*
Fluency Oriented Reading Instruction (FORI),
    109
Formative assessment
    Illinois Snapshot of Early Literacy (ISEL-K/
        1), 247–248
    instruction and, 248–251, 249*f*, 250*f*, 251*f*
    overview, 195, 211, 246, 260
    professional development and, 246–247,
        252–255, 253*f*
    teacher reflection and, 255–260
    writing skills, 211
Fully alphabetic phase of reading develop-
    ment, 87*t*

G

Gender, literacy motivation and, 52
Get It Got It Go! assessment, 71
Goal setting
    reviewing student performance, 281–282
    standards-based change and, 309–312, 309*f*,
        310*f*, 311*f*
    writing skills and, 217
Grading of tests, 5
Graphic organizers
    assessing the understanding of informa-
        tional text and, 200–202, 201*f*
    writing skills and, 217, 218*f*
Guided practice, teaching backward mapping
    and, 30

H

Head Start, preschool assessment and, 66
History instruction, 188–191, 190*f*

I

Illinois Snapshot of Early Literacy (ISEL-K/1)
    instruction and, 248–251, 249*f*, 250*f*, 251*f*
    overview, 247–248

professional development and, 252–255,
    253*f*
teacher reflection and, 255–260
In2Books (I2B) program, 263–278, 268*f*, 270*f*,
    271*t*, 272*f*, 273*t*, 274*f*, 274*t*, 276*f*
Independent learning, portfolio system and,
    229–244, 231*f*, 232*f*, 234*f*, 235*f*, 237*f*, 238*f*,
    240*f*, 241*f*, 243*f*
Individualized education plan
    overview, 294–295
    referral process, 295–305
Informational text, assessing the understand-
    ing of
    effective practices in, 207–208
    flexibility and, 196–198, 197*f*
    literature study and, 203, 205–207, 205*f*,
        206*f*, 207*f*
    multiple sources, 198–203, 199*f*, 200*f*, 201*f*,
        202*f*, 204*f*
    overview, 195–196, 208
Inquiry, 8–9
Inquiry-oriented assessment
    discipline element of, 9–10
    external assessments and, 11–13
    inquiry element of, 8–9
    interaction and action elements of, 10–11
    overview, 7–11
    in practice, 11–16, 13*t*, 17*f*–18*f*
    teacher-guided classroom assessment and,
        15–16, 17*f*–18*f*
Instruction. *see also* Teaching
    assessment of strategic reading and, 192
    explicit, 141–143, 142*f*–143*f*
    fluency and, 102–103
    Illinois Snapshot of Early Literacy (ISEL-K/1)
        and, 248–251, 249*f*, 250*f*, 251*f*
    In2Books (I2B) program, 263–278, 268*f*,
        270*f*, 271*t*, 272*f*, 273*t*, 274*f*, 274*t*, 276*f*
    learning disabilities and, 95–96
    linking curriculum, instruction and assess-
        ment, 283
    literacy motivation and, 51
    in oral reading, 103
    oral reading fluency and, 110–111
    professional dialogs and, 282–283
    referral process for special education and,
        301
    selection of materials and methods, 284
    spelling development and, 115
    standards-based change and, 316–317
    vocabulary, 136–137
    vocabulary assessment and, 137–140
    writing skills, 236

Instructional planning
  formative assessment and, 252–255, 253*f*, 255–260
  preschool assessment and, 81
  professional development and, 252–255, 253*f*
  word recognition assessment and, 88–89
Integration in vocabulary instruction, 137
Interaction, 10–11
Interest, 52–53
Internal assessments, 4–7
Intrinsic motivation, 50. *see also* Motivation, literacy
ISEL-K/1 (*Illinois Snapshot of Early Literacy*)
  instruction and, 248–251, 249*f*, 250*f*, 251*f*
  overview, 247–248
  professional development and, 252–255, 253*f*
  teacher reflection and, 255–260

K

Knowledge, disciplinary, 9–10

L

Language development. *see also* Development
  alphabet knowledge and, 68–70, 69*f*
  comprehensive assessments and, 67–68
  concepts about print, books and words, 74–76, 75*f*
  oral comprehension and vocabulary, 76–77
  phonics and the alphabetic principle and, 72–74, 73*f*
  phonological and phonemic awareness, 70–72
  preschool assessment and, 66, 77–81, 80*f*, 81–82, 81*f*
Learning disabilities, 95–96
Learning to Read and Spell: The Child's Knowledge of Words (Henderson, 1981), 113
Letter recognition, 86, 87*t*
Literacy center, classroom, 37–38, 38*f*
Literacy development. *see also* Development
  alphabet knowledge and, 68–70, 69*f*
  comprehensive assessments and, 67–68
  concepts about print, books and words, 74–76, 75*f*
  oral comprehension and vocabulary, 76–77
  phonics and the alphabetic principle and, 72–74, 73*f*

phonological and phonemic awareness, 70–72
  preschool assessment and, 66, 77–81, 80*f*, 81–82, 81*f*
Literacy motivation
  assessment of, 51–58, 54*f*, 55*f*, 56*f*, 57*f*
  decline in over time, 51–52
  overview, 50, 58–59
  reasons to assess, 51
Literacy Partners project. *see* Professional development
Literacy-rich classroom environments. *see also* Classroom environment
  overview, 47
  preparing, 35–39, 37*f*, 38*f*, 39*f*
  print-rich classrooms, 34
  theory and research regarding, 34–35
Literature study
  assessing the understanding of informational text and, 203, 205–207, 205*f*, 206*f*, 207*f*
  meaning making and, 156–167, 158*f*, 160*f*, 162*f*, 164*f*–165*f*, 166*f*, 168*f*, 169*f*, 170*f*
  overview, 155–156, 167, 171

M

Mandated assessments, 13–15, 13*t*
Math tests
  backward mapping and, 23–24, 24*f*
  overview, 23
Matthew effect, 86
Me and My Reading Survey (MMRS), 53–54, 54*f*
Meaning making
  book talk and, 156–167, 158*f*, 160*f*, 162*f*, 164*f*–165*f*, 166*f*, 168*f*, 169*f*, 170*f*
  overview, 167, 171
Meaning principle, 114–115
Meaningful use in vocabulary knowledge
  overview, 137
  vocabulary assessment and, 146–150, 147*f*, 148*f*, 149*f*, 150*f*
Metacognition
  self-assessments and, 140
  vocabulary assessment and, 150
  writing skills, 211
MMRS. *see* Me and My Reading Survey (MMRS)
Modeling
  of strategic reading, 177–178
  teaching backward mapping and, 30
  writing skills and, 217

Motivation, literacy
    assessment of, 51–58, 54f, 55f, 56f, 57f
    decline in over time, 51–52
    overview, 50, 58–59
    reasons to assess, 51
Motivation to Read Profile (MRP), 54–56, 55f

N

Narrative writing, 213
National Assessment of Educational Progress
    (NAEP) Oral Reading Fluency Scale,
    106–107, 106f
National Council on Education Standards
    and Testing (NCEST), 4
National testing, 28–30
No Child Left Behind (NCLB)
    accountability in assessment and, 3
    curriculum standards and, 27
    formative assessment, 195
    preschool assessment and, 66
    strategic reading and, 179
    testing and, 21

O

Observation Survey of Early Literacy
    Achievement
    alphabet knowledge and, 70
    concepts about print, books and words
        and, 75–76
Observational assessments
    assessing the understanding of informa-
        tional text and, 197
    preschool assessment and, 77–81, 80f, 81f
Oddity task, 71
Onset, 70
Oral "1 minute read" assessment, 13
Oral comprehension, 76–77
Oral reading assessment, 101
Oral reading fluency
    development of, 102–103
    ineffective instruction in, 103
    overview, 110–111
Oral Reading Fluency Scale, 106–107, 106f
Oral Recitation Lesson, 109

P

Pacing guides
    examples of, 285
    overview, 283, 284

PALS (Phonological Awareness Literacy Sur-
    vey), 5, 116
PALS-Pre-K (Phonological Awareness Liter-
    acy Survey-Pre-K)
    alphabet knowledge and, 70
    overview, 71
Partial alphabetic phase of reading develop-
    ment, 87t
PAT (Phonological Awareness Test), 71
Peabody Picture Vocabulary Test—Revised,
    76
Peer planning
    examples of, 284–292, 286f–287f, 288f–289f,
        290f, 291f
    overview, 283–284, 292–293
Pen pal program, In2Books (I2B) program,
    263–278, 268f, 270f, 271t, 272f, 273t, 274f,
    274t, 276f
Personal Comprehension Text Guide, 198,
    200, 200f
Persuasive writing, 213
Phases of reading development, 87t
Phonemic awareness
    preschool assessment and, 70–72
    word recognition and, 86, 87t
Phonics, preschool assessment and, 72–74, 73f
Phonological Awareness Literacy Survey
    (PALS), 5, 116
Phonological Awareness Literacy Survey-Pre-
    K (PALS-Pre-K)
    alphabet knowledge and, 70
    overview, 71
Phonological awareness, preschool assess-
    ment and, 70–72
Phonological Awareness Test (PAT), 71
Planning, instructional
    formative assessment and, 252–255, 253f,
        255–260
    preschool assessment and, 81
    professional development and, 252–255,
        253f
    word recognition assessment and, 88–89
Play, dramatic
    classroom environment and, 35
    concepts about print, books and words
        and, 74–75
Portfolio system
    independent learning and, 229–244, 231f,
        232f, 234f, 235f, 237f, 238f, 240f, 241f, 243f
    overview, 227, 229, 229–230, 231f, 244
    writing skills and, 221–222, 222f
PQS acronym, 221
Praise, writing skills, 221

Pre-CTOPPP. *see* Preschool Comprehensive Test of Phonological and Print Processing (Pre-CTOPPP)
Prealphabetic phase of reading development, 87*t*
Preschool assessments
  alphabet knowledge and, 68–70, 69*f*
  concepts about print, books and words, 74–76, 75*f*
  effective practices in, 77–81, 80*f*, 81*f*
  language and literacy development and, 67–68
  meaning making and, 159
  oral comprehension and vocabulary, 76–77
  overview, 65, 81–82
  phonics and the alphabetic principle and, 72–74, 73*f*
  phonological and phonemic awareness, 70–72
  role of, 65–67
Preschool Comprehensive Test of Phonological and Print Processing (Pre-CTOPPP), 71
Print concepts
  preschool assessment and, 74–76, 75*f*
  word recognition and, 86, 87*t*
Print-rich classroom. *see also* Classroom environment
  overview, 34, 47
  preparing, 35–39, 37*f*, 38*f*, 39*f*
  teaching students to use, 40–44, 40*f*, 42*f*, 43*f*
Prior knowledge, 198, 200, 200*f*
Professional development
  assessment of strategic reading and, 192
  formative assessment and, 246–247, 252–255, 253*f*
  Illinois Snapshot of Early Literacy (ISEL-K/1), 247–248
  instruction and, 248–251, 249*f*, 250*f*, 251*f*
  standards-based change and, 308
Professional dialogs
  consensus scoring and peer planning and, 283–284, 292–293
  examples of, 284–292, 286*f*–287*f*, 288*f*–289*f*, 290*f*, 291*f*
  instruction and, 282–283
  linking curriculum, instruction and assessment, 283
  overview, 280
  referral process for special education and, 302–304
  reviewing student performance, 281–282

Progress monitoring
  classroom assessments and, 5
  word recognition assessment and, 93–94, 93*f*
Prosodic reading, 106–107, 106*f*

Q

QARs. *see* Question–answer relationships (QARs)
Qualitative Spelling Inventory
  examples of, 117–128, 118*f*, 119*f*, 120*f*, 121*f*, 122*f*, 124*f*, 125*f*, 126*f*, 127*f*
  overview, 116–117
Question–answer relationships (QARs)
  standards-based change and, 319
  strategic reading and, 186–187
Questioning, 202–203, 202*f*

R

Read-aloud assessments, 205, 205*f*
Reading assessment, 178–179
Reading development, phases of, 87*t*
Reading First initiative
  accountability in assessment and, 3
  classroom assessments and, 5
Reading levels, 109
Reading rates, 104–106, 105*t*
Reading, strategic
  assessment of, 179–191, 181*f*, 190*f*, 191–192
  examples of, 179–191, 181*f*, 190*f*
  knowledge regarding, 178–179
  overview, 177–178, 191–192
Reading tests
  backward mapping and, 25–26, 25*f*
  overview, 22
Record keeping
  book talk and, 167, 169*f*, 170*f*
  preschool assessment and, 79
  writing portfolios as, 221–222, 222*f*
Reflection, 255–260
Repeated readings, 109–110, 110*f*
Repetition in vocabulary instruction, 137
Response-to-intervention model, 95–96
Responsive instruction, 81
Retelling, story
  portfolio system and, 232–236, 232*f*, 234*f*, 235*f*
  preschool assessment and, 76–77

Rhyming words
   concepts about print, books and words
     and, 75
   preschool assessment and, 70–71
Rime, 70
Round robin reading, 103
Rubric
   In2Books (I2B) program, 266–278, 268f,
     270f, 271t, 272f, 273t, 274f, 274t, 276f
   independent learning and, 229
   standards-based change and, 314, 314f,
     315f
   writing skills and, 213–215, 214f, 216f

S

Scaffolding
   fluency and, 102
   inquiry-oriented assessment and, 10
   strategic reading and, 186–187
Schoolwide assessment teams (SWAT teams),
   6
Science tests, 22–23
Scoring of tests, 5
Screening, 89–91, 90f, 90t
Segmenting of words, 71–72
Self-assessments, student. see also Portfolio
   system
   independent learning and, 239, 242–244,
     243f
   inquiry-oriented assessment and, 14–15
   overview, 4
   vocabulary assessment and, 140, 143–144,
     144f–145f, 148f
   writing skills, 55–56, 56f, 211–213, 212f,
     215, 217, 219–220, 220f, 223
Self-perception of students, 55–56, 56f
Silo communication, 248
Social construction of knowledge, 163
Social studies tests
   backward mapping and, 26–27, 26f
   overview, 23
Socioeconomic status, 105–106
Special education services
   external assessments and, 4
   referral process, 294–295, 295–305
Spelling development, 114–116
Spelling knowledge
   development of, 114–116
   examples of assessing, 117–128, 118f, 119f,
     120f, 121f, 122f, 124f, 125f, 126f, 127f

   overview, 113–114
   portfolio system and, 239, 240f
   qualitative spelling inventory and, 116–
     117
Staff development. see Professional development
Standards-based change
   classroom assessments and, 306–307
   overview, 307–308, 308f, 321
   process of, 309–320, 309f, 310f, 311f, 313t,
     314f, 315f
Standards-based curriculum
   assessments and, 283–284
   linking curriculum, instruction and assess-
     ment, 283
   overview, 27–28, 28f, 281
   reviewing student performance, 281–282
Standards-based testing. see also Testing,
   high-stakes
   backward mapping and, 27–28, 28f
   In2Books (I2B) program and, 266
   overview, 21–22
State assessments
   overview, 4
   teaching backward mapping and, 28–30
Strategic reading
   assessment of, 179–191, 181f, 190f, 191–
     192
   examples of, 179–191, 181f, 190f
   knowledge regarding, 178–179
   overview, 177–178, 191–192
Student self-assessments. see also Portfolio
   system
   independent learning and, 239, 242–244,
     243f
   inquiry-oriented assessment and, 14–15
   overview, 4
   vocabulary assessment and, 140, 143–144,
     144f–145f, 148f
   writing skills, 55–56, 56f, 211–213, 212f,
     215, 217, 219–220, 220f, 223
Summative evaluation, 211

T

Teacher assistance team, 296
Teacher-guided classroom assessment. see also
   Classroom assessments
   inquiry-oriented assessment and, 7–11, 15–
     16, 17f–18f
   interaction and action elements of, 10–11

overview, 4–7
standards-based change and, 309–320, 309f, 310f, 311f, 313t, 314f, 315f
Teachers
classroom assessments and, 5–7
interaction and action elements of inquiry-oriented assessment and, 10–11
referral process for special education and, 304–305
standards-based change and, 308
Teaching. *see also* Instruction
regarding backward mapping, 28–30
regarding the use of print-rich classrooms, 40–44, 40f, 42f, 43f
standards-based change and, 316–317
Teaching to the assessments, 5–6
Test of Language Development: Primary (TOLD), 76
Test preparation, time spent on, 4
Test-taking skills
connecting testing to standards and, 27
curriculum standards and, 23–27, 24f, 25f, 26f
Testing. *see also* Testing, high-stakes; Testing, standardized; Testing, standards-based
overview, 21–22
preschool assessment and, 77
vocabulary assessment and, 135–136, 144
Testing, high-stakes
accountability in assessment and, 3
backward mapping and, 27–28, 28–30, 28f
inquiry-oriented assessment and, 11–13
overview, 21–22, 227–229
strategic reading and, 179
word recognition assessment and, 88
Testing, standardized
overview, 4, 227–229
preschool assessment and, 66, 77
teaching backward mapping and, 28–30
word recognition assessment and, 88
Testing, standards-based. *see also* Testing, high-stakes
backward mapping and, 27–28, 28f
In2Books (I2B) program and, 266
overview, 21–22
TEX-IN3, 46–47
Texas Primary Reading Inventory (TPRI), 5
Textbook guide, 198, 200f
"The First Year" film, 9
Think-alouds, 190–191
TOLD, 76
TPRI, 5

U

Urban students
In2Books (I2B) program, 263–278, 268f, 270f, 271t, 272f, 273t, 274f, 274t, 276f
overview, 263–264

V

Verbal efficiency theory, 88
Visual images, meaning making and, 167, 168f
Vocabulary assessment. *see also* Vocabulary knowledge
applications, 141–150, 142f–143f, 144f, 145f–146f, 147f, 148f, 149f, 151f
effective practices in, 137–140
overview, 22–23, 135–136, 150, 152
preschool assessment and, 76–77
Vocabulary knowledge. *see also* Vocabulary assessment
instruction and, 136–137
vocabulary assessment and, 137–140

W

Whole-class analysis, In2Books (I2B) program and, 275–276
Whole-class instruction, 41
Woodcock Reading Mastery Tests—Revised (WRMT-R), 74
Word concepts, 74–76, 75f
Word knowledge. *see also* Vocabulary assessment
instruction and, 136–137
vocabulary assessment and, 137–140
Word recognition
assessment of, 88–95, 90f, 90t, 92f, 93f
development of, 86–88, 87t
English language learners (ELLs) and, 96–97
fluency and, 101–102
learning disabilities and, 95–96
oral reading assessment and, 104–106, 105t
overview, 85–86, 97
Word study, portfolio system and, 237, 239, 240f
Wordsmith strategy in vocabulary assessment, 146–150, 147f, 148f, 149f, 150f
Writer Self-Perception Scale (WSPS), 55–56, 56f, 215

Writing concepts, preschool assessment and, 74–76, 75*f*
Writings by children, assessment of
  overview, 210–211, 222–223
  portfolio system and, 236–237, 237*f*, 238*f*
  professional dialogs regarding, 285, 291
  reasons to assess, 211–222, 212*f*, 214*f*, 216*f*, 218*f*, 219*f*, 220*f*, 222*f*
Writings by children, meaning making and, 163, 166, 166*f*

WRMT-R (Woodcock Reading Mastery Test-Revised), 74
WSPS (Writer Self-Perception Scale), 55–56, 56*f*, 215

Z

Zone of proximal development, 10